In *The Cambridge Companion to the Victorian Novel*, a series of specially commissioned essays examine the work of Charles Dickens, the Brontës, George Eliot, and other canonical writers, as well as that of such writers as Olive Schreiner, Wilkie Collins, and H. Rider Haggard, whose work has recently attracted new attention from scholars and students. The collection combines the literary study of the novel as a form with analysis of the material aspects of its readership and production, and a series of thematic and contextual perspectives that examine Victorian fiction in the light of social and cultural concerns relevant both to the period itself and to the direction of current literary and cultural studies. Contributors engage with topics such as industrial culture, religion and science and the broader issues of the politics of gender, sexuality and race. The *Companion* includes a chronology and a comprehensive guide to further reading.

Deirdre David is Professor of English at Temple University in Philadelphia. She is the author of *Fictions of Resolution in Three Victorian Novels* (1982), *Intellectual Women and Victorian Patriarchy* (1987) and *Rule Britannia: Women, Empire, and Victorian Writing* (1996).

THE CAMBRIDGE
COMPANION TO

THE VICTORIAN
NOVEL

CAMBRIDGE COMPANIONS TO LITERATURE

The Cambridge Companion to Greek Tragedy
edited by P. E. Easterling

The Cambridge Companion to Virgil
edited by Charles Martindale

The Cambridge Companion to Old English Literature
edited by Malcolm Godden and Michael Lapidge

The Cambridge Companion to Dante
edited by Rachel Jacoff

The Cambridge Chaucer Companion
edited by Piero Boitani and Jill Mann

The Cambridge Companion to Medieval English Theatre
edited by Richard Beadle

The Cambridge Companion to Renaissance Humanism
edited by Jill Kraye

The Cambridge Companion to English Renaissance Drama
edited by A. R. Braunmuller and Michael Hattaway

The Cambridge Companion to Shakespeare Studies
edited by Stanley Wells

The Cambridge Companion to Shakespeare on Film
edited by Russell Jackson

The Cambridge Companion to Ben Jonson
edited by Richard Harp and Stanley Stewart

The Cambridge Companion to English Poetry, Donne to Marvell
edited by Thomas N. Corns

The Cambridge Companion to Milton
edited by Dennis Danielson

The Cambridge Companion to English Restoration Theatre
edited by Deborah C. Payne Fisk

The Cambridge Companion to English Literature, 1500–1600
edited by Arthur F. Kinney

The Cambridge Companion to English Literature, 1650–1740
edited by Steven N. Zwicker

The Cambridge Companion to British Romanticism
edited by Stuart Curran

The Cambridge Companion to the Eighteenth-Century Novel
edited by John Richetti

The Cambridge Companion to Samuel Johnson
edited by Greg Clingham

The Cambridge Companion to Jane Austen
edited by Edward Copeland and Juliet McMaster

The Cambridge Companion to Oscar Wilde
edited by Peter Raby

The Cambridge Companion to Thomas Hardy
edited by Dale Kramer

The Cambridge Companion to George Bernard Shaw
edited by Christopher Innes

The Cambridge Companion to Joseph Conrad
edited by J. H. Stape

The Cambridge Companion to James Joyce
edited by Derek Attridge

The Cambridge Companion to T. S. Eliot
edited by A. David Moody

The Cambridge Companion to Ezra Pound
edited by Ira B. Nadel

The Cambridge Companion to Modernism
edited by Michael Levenson

The Cambridge Companion to Virginia Woolf
edited by Sue Roe and Susan Sellers

The Cambridge Companion to Henry David Thoreau
edited by Joel Myerson

The Cambridge Companion to Walt Whitman
edited by Ezra Greenspan

The Cambridge Companion to Mark Twain
edited by Forrest G. Robinson

The Cambridge Companion to American Realism and Naturalism
edited by Donald Pizer

The Cambridge Companion to Edith Wharton
edited by Millicent Bell

The Cambridge Companion to Ernest Hemingway
edited by Scott Donaldson

The Cambridge Companion to William Faulkner
edited by Philip M. Weinstein

The Cambridge Companion to Eugene O'Neill
edited by Michael Manheim

The Cambridge Companion to Tennessee Williams
edited by Matthew C. Roudané

The Cambridge Companion to Arthur Miller
edited by Christopher Bigsby

The Cambridge Companion to American Women Playwrights
edited by Brenda Murphy

The Cambridge Companion to Modern British Women Playwrights
edited by Elaine Aston and Janelle Reinelt

The Cambridge Companion to the French Novel: from 1800 to the Present
edited by Timothy Unwin

The Cambridge Companion to the Classic Russian Novel
edited by Malcolm V. Jones and Robin Feuer Miller

The Cambridge Companion to Chekhov
edited by Vera Gottlieb and Paul Allain

The Cambridge Companion to Ibsen
edited by James McFarlane

The Cambridge Companion to Brecht
edited by Peter Thomason and Glendyr Sacks

The Cambridge Companion to Beckett
edited by John Pilling

The Cambridge Companion to Victorian Poetry
edited by Joseph Bristow

The Cambridge Companion to the Victorian Novel
edited by Deirdre David

CAMBRIDGE COMPANIONS TO CULTURE

The Cambridge Companion to Modern German Culture
edited by Eva Kolinsky and Wilfried van der Will

The Cambridge Companion to Modern Russian Culture
edited by Nicholas Rzhevsky

The Cambridge Companion to Modern Spanish Culture
edited by David T. Gies

THE CAMBRIDGE
COMPANION TO
THE VICTORIAN
NOVEL

EDITED BY

DEIRDRE DAVID

CAMBRIDGE
UNIVERSITY PRESS

PUBLISHED BY THE PRESS SYNDICATE OF THE UNIVERSITY OF CAMBRIDGE
The Pitt Building, Trumpington Street, Cambridge CB2 1RP, United Kingdom

CAMBRIDGE UNIVERSITY PRESS
The Edinburgh Building, Cambridge CB2 2RU, UK   www.cup.cam.ac.uk
40 West 20th Street, New York, NY 10011–4211, USA   www.cup.org
10 Stamford Road, Oakleigh, Melbourne 3166, Australia
Ruiz de Alarcón 13, 28014 Madrid, Spain

First published 2001

Printed in the United Kingdom at the University Press, Cambridge

Typeset in Baskerville 10/13pt.   System 3b2   [CE]

A catalogue record for this book is available from the British Library

Library of Congress cataloging in publication data
The Cambridge companion to the Victorian novel / edited by Deirdre David.
p.   cm. – (Cambridge companions to literature)
Includes bibliographical references.
ISBN 0 521 64150 0 (hardback) – ISBN 0 521 64619 7 (paperback)
1. English fiction – 19th century – History and criticism.
I. David, Deirdre, 1934–   II. Series
PR871.C17 2001
823'.809–dc21   00-028928

ISBN 0 521 64150 0 hardback
ISBN 0 521 64619 7 paperback

CONTENTS

Notes on contributors   *page* xi
Chronology   xiii

Introduction   1
DEIRDRE DAVID

1   The Victorian novel and its readers   17
    KATE FLINT

2   The business of Victorian publishing   37
    SIMON ELIOT

3   The aesthetics of the Victorian novel: form, subjectivity, ideology   61
    LINDA M. SHIRES

4   Industrial culture and the Victorian novel   77
    JOSEPH W. CHILDERS

5   Gender and the Victorian novel   97
    NANCY ARMSTRONG

6   Sexuality in the Victorian novel   125
    JEFF NUNOKAWA

7   Race and the Victorian novel   149
    PATRICK BRANTLINGER

8   Detection in the Victorian novel   169
    RONALD R. THOMAS

9 Sensation and the fantastic in the Victorian novel   192
   LYN PYKETT

10 Intellectual debate in the Victorian novel: religion, science, and the
   professional   212
   JOHN KUCICH

11 Dickens, Melville, and a tale of two countries   234
   ROBERT WEISBUCH

   Guide to further reading   255
   Index   262

NOTES ON CONTRIBUTORS

NANCY ARMSTRONG is Nancy Duke Lewis Professor of Comparative Literature, English, Modern Culture and Media, and Women's Studies at Brown University. Her publications include *Desire and Domestic Fiction* (1987), *The Imaginary Puritan*, with Leonard Tennenhouse (1991), and *Fiction in the Age of Photography* (1999).

PATRICK BRANTLINGER is former editor of *Victorian Studies*. Among his books are *Rule of Darkness: British Literature and imperialism, 1830–1914* (1988) and *The Reading Lesson: the Threat of Mass Literacy in Nineteenth-Century British Fiction* (1999).

JOSEPH W. CHILDERS teaches English literature at the University of California, Riverside. He is the author of *Novel Possibilities: Fiction and the Formation of Early Victorian Culture* (1995) and is co-editor of *The Columbia Dictionary of Modern Literary and Cultural Criticism* (1995).

SIMON ELIOT is Professor of the History of Publishing and Printing at the University of Reading and Associate Director of the History of the Book Research Centre at London University. He is co-editor of volume VI (1830–1914) of the *Cambridge History of the Book in Britain*, editor of the journal *Publishing History*, and associate editor of the *New Dictionary of National Biography*, responsible for the entries relating to the book trade from the eighteenth to the twentieth century.

KATE FLINT is Reader in Victorian and Modern English Literature at the University of Oxford. She is the author of *The Woman Reader, 1837–1914* (1993) and *The Victorians and the Visual Imagination* (2000), as well as numerous articles on nineteenth- and twentieth-century fiction, painting, and cultural history. Her current research is on the place of the Americas in the Victorian cultural imagination.

JOHN KUCICH is Professor of English at the University of Michigan. He is the author of *Excess and Restraint in the Novels of Charles Dickens* (1981), *Repression in Victorian Fiction* (1987), and *The Power of Lies: Transgression in Victorian Fiction* (1994). He is co-editor of *Victorian Afterlife: Postmodern Culture Rewrites the Nineteenth Century* (2000) and has written numerous essays on Victorian literature and culture.

JEFF NUNOKAWA teaches English literature at Princeton University. He is the author of *The Afterlife of Property: Domestic Securities and Victorian Fiction* (1994) and is completing a book about the social coordinates of the fantasy of manageable desire in the work of Oscar Wilde.

LYN PYKETT is Professor of English at the University of Wales, Aberystwyth. She is the author of *The Improper Feminine: The Women's Sensation Novel and the New Woman Writing* (1992) and *The Sensation Novel from "The Woman in White" to "The Moonstone"* (1994). She has edited Braddon's *The Doctor's Wife* for the Oxford University Press Classics Series (1998) and a collection of critical essays on Wilkie Collins (1998). She is currently completing a book on Charles Dickens.

LINDA M. SHIRES, Professor of English at Syracuse University, is the author of books on British war poetry and narrative theory, as well as many articles on Victorian subjects, and editor of Thomas Hardy's *The Trumpet Major* (1995) for Penguin and *Re-Writing the Victorians: Theory, History and the Politics of Gender* (1992). She is currently writing two books, one on Victorian careers and one on Judaism.

RONALD R. THOMAS is Professor of English at Trinity College, Hartford, where he also serves as Vice President and Chief of Staff. He is the author of *Detective Fiction and the Rise of Forensic Science* (1999) and *Dreams of Authority: Freud and the Fictions of the Unconscious* (1990). He has published numerous articles on the novel, photography, and film and is co-editor of the forthcoming *Nineteenth-Century Geographies: Anglo-American Tactics of Space*.

ROBERT WEISBUCH is President of the Woodrow Wilson National Fellowship Foundation and Professor of English at the University of Michigan. His published books include *Emily Dickinson's Poetry* (1975) and *Atlantic Double-Cross: American Writers and British Influence in the Age of Emerson* (1989). He co-edited *Dickinson and Audience* (1996) and has published essays on Emerson and James and on issues in higher education.

CHRONOLOGY

1801	Union of England and Ireland
1805	Battle of Trafalgar; Lord Nelson dies
1807	Atlantic slave trade outlawed
1812	War with America Charles Dickens born
1815	Napoleon defeated at Waterloo by British and Prussian troops; Congress of Vienna redraws map of Europe Corn Law passed, establishing protective tariff on imported grain
1818	Mary Shelley's *Frankenstein* published Jane Austen's *Northanger Abbey* and *Persuasion* published
1819	Peterloo Riot Stamp Act taxes periodicals Princess (later Queen) Victoria and Mary Ann Evans (George Eliot) born Walter Scott's *Ivanhoe* published
1820	Death of King George III; George IV ascends to the throne
1830	Death of George IV; William IV ascends to the throne
1832	Passage of the First Reform Bill, doubling the electorate Charles Lyell's *Elements of Geology* published

1833   Slavery abolished throughout the British Empire

1834   Poor Law Amendment Act forces able-bodied poor into
        workhouses in order to receive assistance
        Houses of Parliament severely damaged by fire

1836   Factory Act limits children under thirteen to no more than forty-
        eight hours per week in textile mills
        Charles Dickens's *The Pickwick Papers* begins serialization
        (volume publication 1837)

1837   Death of William IV; Victoria ascends to the throne, formally
        beginning the era that bears her name
        Benjamin Disraeli elected to Parliament
        Charles Dickens's *Oliver Twist* begins serialization in *Bentley's
        Miscellany* (volume publication 1838)

1838   Great Western Railway opens

1839   Custody of Infants Act gives woman separated from husband
        right to see and seek custody of children under seven; first legal
        recognition of women as independent entities under the law
        First Chartist petition presented to Parliament
        Thomas Carlyle's *Chartism* published

1840   Queen Victoria marries Prince Albert of Saxe-Coburg-Gotha
        Penny Post established
        Thomas Hardy born

1841   London Library established
        Punch begins publication

1842   Mudie's Circulating Library opens
        Pentonville model prison opens
        London police establish detective department
        Chadwick's *Sanitary Condition of the Labouring Population*
        published

1843   First telegraph line in service
        Factory Act limits women and children under eighteen to a
        twelve-hour work day

Charles Dickens's *Martin Chuzzlewit* begins serialization (volume publication 1844)

1845   Irish potato crop fails; beginning of the Great Famine
Benjamin Disraeli's *Sibyl; or the Two Nations* published
Friedrich Engels's *The Condition of the Working Class in England* published

1846   Charles Dickens's *Dombey and Son* begins serialization (volume publication 1848)

1847   Ten-hour Act limits women and children under eighteen to ten-hour work day in textile mills (maximum of fifty-eight hours per week)
Charlotte Brontë's *Jane Eyre* published
Emily Brontë's *Wuthering Heights* published
William Makepeace Thackeray's *Vanity Fair* begins serial publication (volume publication 1848)

1848   Revolutionary upheaval in France, Vienna, Berlin, Parma, Rome
Cholera epidemic
Queen's College, Oxford, founded to train and examine governesses, opening higher education to women
Karl Marx's *Communist Manifesto* first printed in London
Anne Brontë's *The Tenant of Wildfell Hall* published
Elizabeth Gaskell's *Mary Barton* published

1849   Corn Laws abolished
Henry Mayhew's *London Labour and the London Poor* begins publication in *The Morning Chronicle* (two volumes published 1852; four volumes 1862)
Charles Dickens's *David Copperfield* begins serial publication (volume publication 1850)

1850   Public Libraries Act

1851   The Crystal Palace Exhibition
William Thompson (later Lord Kelvin) publishes first and second laws of thermodynamics
Cambridge University adds degree in natural sciences

1852   New Houses of Parliament open
       Harriet Beecher Stowe's *Uncle Tom's Cabin* published and
       becomes a bestseller in England and America
       Charles Dickens's *Bleak House* serial publication begins (volume
       publication 1853)

1853   Cholera epidemic
       Charlotte Brontë's *Villette* published

1854   Crimean War begins; Earl of Cardigan leads the Charge of the
       Light Brigade at Balaclava that inspires the Tennyson poem of the
       same year
       Construction of London Underground (the first subway) begins
       Elizabeth Gaskell's *North and South* begins serialization (volume
       publication 1855)
       Charles Dickens's *Hard Times* begins serialization in *Household
       Words* (volume publication also 1854)

1855   Stamp Tax abolished, making newspapers more widely
       affordable
       Charles Dickens's *Little Dorrit* begins serial publication (volume
       publication 1857)

1857   Indian Mutiny
       Matrimonial Causes Act makes divorce available without a
       special act of Parliament

1858   Lionel de Rothschild seated in Parliament despite failure to take
       Christian oath; opens door for Jewish civil rights in England
       Property qualification for election to the House of Commons
       abolished

1859   Charles Darwin's *Origin of Species* published
       Wilkie Collins's *The Woman in White* begins serialization in *All
       the Year Round* (volume publication 1860)
       George Eliot's *Adam Bede* published

1860   George Eliot's *Mill on the Floss* published
       John Stuart Mill's *On Liberty* published
       Charles Dickens's *Great Expectations* begins serialization in *All
       the Year Round* (volume publication in 1861)

1861   Prince Albert dies of typhoid
Louis Pasteur publishes germ theory of disease
Duty on paper abolished, making published material widely
affordable
Ellen Price (Mrs. Henry) Wood's *East Lynne* published

1862   Mary Elizabeth Braddon's *Lady Audley's Secret* published
Death of William Makepeace Thackeray

1864   First Contagious Diseases Act passed, mandating registration,
compulsory medical examination, and detainment of prostitutes
in garrison towns
Charles Dickens's *Our Mutual Friend* begins serial publication
(volume publication 1865)

1865   Reform League founded to promote extension of the vote for
working-class men

1866   Women's suffrage petition presented to Parliament by
John Stuart Mill
Last major cholera epidemic
Atlantic telegraph cable completed
George Eliot's *Felix Holt* published

1867   Passage of the Second Reform Bill, further reducing property
qualification for the vote; Mill's amendment to substitute
"person" for "man" defeated

1868   Disraeli, then Gladstone, serve as Prime Minister, beginning a
long-standing rivalry: Benjamin Disraeli (Conservative) becomes
Prime Minister in February, but loses the office to William
Gladstone (Liberal) in December. Gladstone holds post through
1874, but is then succeeded by Disraeli, who holds it until 1880.
Gladstone regains power until 1885, when Liberal Party splits
over Irish Home Rule; he serves a final term from 1892 to 1894
Wilkie Collins's *The Moonstone* serialized in *All the Year Round*
and then published in volume form

1869   Suez Canal opens
Debtors Act abolishes imprisonment for debt

Matthew Arnold's *Culture and Anarchy* published
John Stuart Mill's *On the Subjection of Women* published

1870   Education Act makes elementary education available to all
children in England and Wales
First Married Women's Property Act: women gain right to their
own wages earned after marriage
Home Government Association founded in Ireland
Death of Charles Dickens

1871   Trade unions legalized
Charles Darwin's *Descent of Man* published
George Eliot's *Middlemarch* begins serial publication (volume
publication 1872)
Anthony Trollope's *The Eustace Diamonds* begins serial
publication in *Fortnightly Review* (volume publication 1872)

1872   Voting by secret ballot instituted

1874   Anthony Trollope's *The Way We Live Now* begins serial
publication (volume publication 1875)

1876   George Eliot's *Daniel Deronda* published

1877   Queen Victoria proclaimed Empress of India
Transvaal (Boer) Republic annexed to British Empire
Annie Besant and Charles Bradlaugh tried for publishing
inexpensive book on birth control. They are acquitted of obscenity
charge, but Besant loses custody of her seven-year-old daughter

1878   Zulu War; Second Afghan War
Matrimonial Causes Act allows judicial separation for cruelty
and assault
University of London opens all degrees and prizes to women
Electric lights installed on some streets in London

1879   Charles Stewart Parnell founds Irish National Land League
General public granted unrestricted access to British Museum

1880   Elementary education made compulsory from age seven to ten
Employer's Liability Act makes employers liable for injuries to

workers obeying the orders of superintendents
First South African War
Death of George Eliot

1881   Irish Land Acts provide some land reforms in Ireland
Flogging abolished in the army and navy
Death of Benjamin Disraeli

1882   Married Women's Property Act: women have the right to all their
property earned or acquired before or after marriage
Death of Charles Darwin

1884   Third Reform Bill extends franchise to all male householders
Steam turbine for generation of electricity invented

1885   Criminal Law Amendment Act raises the age of consent for girls
to sixteen and makes sexual acts between males illegal
Wilhelm Gottlieb Daimler invents the internal combustion engine
Khartoum falls after insurrection in Sudan, General Gordon
killed
H. Rider Haggard's *King Solomon's Mines* published

1886   Irish Home Rule bill defeated in the House of Commons
Contagious Diseases Acts repealed
Robert Louis Stevenson's *Dr. Jekyll and Mr. Hyde* published

1887   Queen Victoria's Golden Jubilee

1888   Matchworkers' strike
"Jack the Ripper" murders five women in London

1889   London Dock Strike, the first major success by male unskilled
workers
Cecil Rhodes given Royal Charter for British South Africa
Prevention of Cruelty to Children Act prohibits employment of
children under ten

1891   United States Congress passes the Platt-Simonds Bill (also known
as the Chace Act) ending years of literary "piracy" by affording
British authors copyright protection in America

Thomas Hardy's *Tess of the D'Urbervilles* published
Oscar Wilde's *The Picture of Dorian Gray* published

1892   First automatic telephone switchboard

1893   Irish Home Rule Bill passed by Commons but defeated in the
House of Lords
Miners' strike successfully resists 25 percent paycut
George Gissing's *The Odd Women* published

1895   Oscar Wilde's trial results in his conviction and imprisonment
Max Nordau's *Degeneration* published
Thomas Hardy's *Jude the Obscure* published

1896   Cinema begins at Empire Theatre, London
Both Oxford and Cambridge reject proposals to grant degrees to
women

1897   Queen Victoria's Diamond Jubilee
First volume of Havelock Ellis's *Studies in the Psychology of Sex*
published
Bram Stoker's *Dracula* published

1898   Death of William Gladstone

1899   Boer War
School attendance mandatory to age twelve
Joseph Conrad's *Heart of Darkness* begins serialization in
Blackwood's (volume publication 1902)

1900   British Labour Party founded
Sigmund Freud's *The Interpretation of Dreams* published

1901   Victoria dies; Edward VII ascends to the throne
Rudyard Kipling's *Kim* published

DEIRDRE DAVID

Introduction

> Novels are in the hands of us all; from the Prime Minister down to the last-appointed scullery maid. We have them in our library, our drawing-rooms, our bed-rooms, our kitchens – and in our nurseries.
>
> Anthony Trollope, 1870[1]

Victoria's coronation in 1837 signals the official inception of the literary form that we now designate the Victorian novel, just as her death in 1901 marks its official demise. However, for at least a century before the start of the period in literary history we term "Victorian," the British novel had enjoyed cultural visibility and weathered critical scrutiny, so in a sense there was nothing momentously new about the novel in 1837. But critical discussion generated by the genre's increasing popularity in a profitable marketplace acquired a distinctive intensity as authors and literary intellectuals initiated an almost century-long debate about the moral and aesthetic nature of the novel.[2] The central questions that fueled this debate tended to revisit with some regularity issues of whether novels should retain their racy affiliations with romance, teach uplifting moral lessons, educate curious readers about a rapidly changing society, or aim for a narrative singularity that would provide aesthetic correlation for the domestic realism that ruled the form for most of the period. By the end of the nineteenth century, after decades of cultural rule, novel-reading itself had become identified with those attitudes we now term "Victorian" (primarily to do with sexual repression, stultifying middle-class family life, and cramped vistas for women's lives), then being vigorously rejected. In George Gissing's *The Odd Women* (1893), for example, the feminist character Rhoda Nunn traces the defection from women's causes on the part of a Miss Royston to novel-reading, asking contemptuously, "What is more vulgar than the ideal of novelists?"[3] Soon after, Leslie Stephen included novels in his lofty dismissal of all things Victorian when he announced, "however far the rage for revivalism may be pushed, nobody will ever want to revive the nineteenth century,"[4] and in 1911, H. G. Wells echoed Stephen by wondering whether anyone, a century later, would "consent to live in the houses the Victorians built, travel by their roads or railways, value the furnishings they made to live among, or esteem, except for curious or historical reasons, their prevalent art and the clipped and limited literature that satisfied their souls?"[5]

History has proved Stephen and Wells entirely wrong. A late twentieth-century revival of Victorian domestic style may be found in many upscale stores offering overstuffed chintz sofas, paisley piano shawls, and so-called "Victorian" jewelry and "antique" clothing. It is also certain that Victorian literature has long enjoyed a popular revival that would have astonished Stephen and Wells. In the field of mass entertainment, the novel form of that "clipped and limited" writing became the source of many popular Hollywood films in the 1930s and 1940s (one thinks of W. C. Fields as Wilkins McCawber, Laurence Olivier as Heathcliff, Joan Fontaine as Jane Eyre); and through BBC serializations over the past twenty-five years, millions of viewers have come to possess a familiarity with the foggy London of *Bleak House*, the 1832 provincial politics of *Middlemarch*, and the Yorkshire moors of *Wuthering Heights*, even if they have not read the source of the serializations. Moreover, since the 1960s the Victorian novel has gained increasing visibility in the curricula of Anglo-American schools and universities to the extent that virtually every middle-class eighteen-year-old has read *Great Expectations* (1861), or if not that, has been instructed to do so. Rather, then, than late twentieth-century and early twenty-first-century Anglo-American culture having rejected Victorian literature, it has embraced it, popularized it, enshrined it in an imaginative construction of nineteenth-century life. This collection of essays, as it explains the cultural dominance of the Victorian novel in its own time, also explains, intentionally or not, the appeal of a literature that continues to attract readers entering a new millennium. As we come to understand the ways the Victorian novel participated energetically in the construction of individual and national identity, as we begin to see how it assisted in the making of powerful ideologies of gender, sexuality, and race, and also how it engaged actively in debates about the value of reading, the proper aesthetic rules for fiction, the appropriate integration of changing ideas about religion into the national life, we also come to understand that rather than being a "clipped" or "limited" literary form, the Victorian novel is generous, expansive, and always deeply entertaining. In addition, the essays also provide a critically and theoretically sophisticated elucidation of the debate about the moral and aesthetic nature of the novel that was initiated at the close of the 1820s.

Perhaps the most famous of late-Victorian jibes directed at the novel, part of his forceful intervention in the discussion of realism and elegant form, is that delivered by Henry James. Writing about *The Newcomes*, *The Three Musketeers*, and *War and Peace*, he asks, "What do such large loose baggy monsters, with their queer elements of the accidental and the arbitrary, artistically *mean*?"[6] When considering James's provocative question, one needs first to recall that even as he lamented an absence of unifying aesthetic form, James also passionately advocated – and superbly displayed in his own work – the essential presence of an "air of reality" in the novel. He defined this "air of reality" as "solidity of specification" and declared that it was for him "the supreme virtue of a novel – the merit in which all its other merits . . . helplessly and submissively depend. If it be not there, they are all as nothing, and if these be there, they owe their effect to the success with which the author has produced the illusion of life."[7] In a memorable articulation of the serious responsibility entailed in the task of producing an "illusion of life," George Eliot's narrator in *Adam Bede* (1859) vows "to give a faithful account of men and things as they have mirrored themselves in my mind . . . I feel as much bound to tell you as precisely as I can what that reflection is, as if I were in the witness-box, narrating my experience on oath."[8] In this connection, the artistic dedication to producing such an illusion affirmed by James and Eliot in their non-fictional writings and novels must not be taken, of course, either as an exclusive characterization of the Victorian novel, or as an ambition necessarily shared by all Victorian novelists. Since the early 1970s, Anglo-American literary critics and theorists have analyzed a narrative awareness, a phenomenon that Edward Said has termed a "molestation," an awareness of duplicity, that inevitably accompanies an author's assumption of authority.[9] Such molestation must undercut, say, the narrative ingenuousness of *Adam Bede*. In addition, a number of critics have observed that the fantastic and sensationalistic aspects of Victorian fiction inherited from early nineteenth-century gothic narratives undermine the devotion to formal realism shared by the majority of Victorian novelists and readers. Finally, James's identification of shapelessness in the Victorian novel is not entirely off the mark. If not loose and baggy, many Victorian novels were indeed extraordinarily long. *Bleak House* (1853), for example, runs to sixty-seven chapters and ran for eighteen months in serial form.

In general, the Victorian novel is notably ambitious. Eager to show it knows everything and everyone from probate law to dolls' dressmaking, from cosmopolitan financier to working-class river dredger, its pervasive omniscience has led J. Hillis Miller to speculate that a Victorian reading public dislodged from religious certainty by scientific discovery, found consolation in a novelistic power that both resembled divine omniscience and accepted responsibility for creation.[10] Novels such as Thackeray's *Vanity Fair* (1848), Dickens's *Little Dorrit* (1857), and Eliot's *Middlemarch* (1872) guide us skillfully through the domestic scene, on to the battlefields of Waterloo, across the Alps and down to Venice, through the farms, vicarages, and country houses of Warwickshire, and then to Rome. They take us into Mayfair drawing rooms, the Marshalsea debtors' prison, the studies of an ambitious country doctor and a disappointed clerical intellectual, the minds of an embittered, middle-aged son (Arthur Clennam in *Little Dorrit*) and an intelligent farmer's daughter (Mary Garth in *Middlemarch*). They take us everywhere. Moreover, the cast of characters in each of these three novels is enormous and the challenge posed to Victorian readers in keeping track, say, of George Dobbin, Flora Finching, and Peter Featherstone was considerable, even allowing for such mnemonic devices as the endowing of minor characters with idiosyncratic visual or verbal gestures that is found in Dickens's fiction. Victorian novels demanded a lot from the reader, and delivered a lot in return. And they are often monstrous, if not always in the fashion Henry James had in mind.

By monstrous James meant something imperfect, irregular, de-formed from an ideal shape or pattern. In all likelihood, while we might concur there *is* something large, loose, and baggy about many Victorian novels, we tend to locate the monstrous more in thematic content than in undisciplined form, and many of the following chapters will show that the monstrous is to be discovered in deformities different from those James imagined. Inhumane working conditions disclosed by the social problem fiction of the 1840s are a deformation from ideal bourgeois governance; the domestic cruelty practiced by an unfeeling father in *Dombey and Son* (1848), the rapacious use of a woman's body in *Tess of the d'Urbervilles* (1891), the manipulation by male villains of female frailty as delineated in much sensation fiction – all these are deformations from decent human behavior. A telling instance of how we might read the monstrous somewhat differently from Henry James is to be found in George Eliot's *Daniel Deronda* (1876), fatally flawed for many critics by virtue of its divided, but overlapping, narrative structure. Roughly half the novel recounts the life of a shallow, upper middle-class girl, Gwendolyn Harleth, neurotically fearful of men yet forced to enter the marriage market after a failure of family fortunes, and the other half records the quest for origins and identity of an upper-class Englishman, Daniel Deronda, who by the novel's end discovers he is the son of an Italian Jewish actress and singer. Rather than schizophrenic narrative structure, what appears monstrous to many readers, indeed a deformation from the decent, is the psychological misery inflicted upon Gwendolyn Harleth by her husband. Henleigh Grandcourt is a superbly realized sadist, practiced in a domestic monstrosity instantly recognizable by Victorian and late twentieth-century adult readers alike.

In sum, we may differ from Henry James in defining the monstrous, but we are likely to agree that the Victorian novel lacks a certain economy. This is probably because it is about so many things: provincial politics, ecclesiastical infighting, city squalor, repressed sexuality, making money, losing money, imperial adventure, angels in the house, frightening New Women, scientific challenges to established religious beliefs, the value and function of the aesthetic life in a materialistic society (to name a few). To be sure, the postmodern novel is equally voracious in its thematic appetites, ranging as it does, say, from postcolonial Pakistan in Salman Rushdie's fiction, to the imaginative mingling of actual figures such as Siegfried Sassoon and fictional characters in the World War I novels of Pat Barker, to the confounding of fact and fiction to be found most recently in Michael Cunningham's *The Hours* (1999), a novel that interweaves the related fantasies of Virginia Woolf writing *Mrs. Dalloway*, a Clarissa Vaughan planning a Greenwich Village party, and the California mother of a character part Richard Dalloway and part Septimus Smith reading *Mrs. Dalloway* in the 1950s. What is so particular, then, with the Victorian novel when it comes to thematic scope? Most would agree that the historical time span from 1837 to 1901 has a great deal to do with it.

The population of England grew enormously during the nineteenth century, from 8.9 to 32.5 million.[11] This increase was accompanied by profound alterations in where and how people lived. In great numbers, they left rural areas and agrarian employment for work in the city, mostly in the new northern and midlands centers of industrialization. Rather than walking, riding, or taking coaches, they got from one place to another by railway, and concomitantly with these alterations in habitat and employment, the working class began to lobby for unionization and universal male suffrage, most notably in the latter case through membership in the Chartist movement. Chartism, combined with serious economic depressions in the 1830s and 1840s and middle-class fears that continental revolution might cross the Channel, led to national debate about what Thomas Carlyle termed "The Condition-of-England" question. Making fictional contributions to this debate were novels such as Elizabeth Gaskell's *Mary Barton* (1848) and Dickens's *Hard Times* (1854) that alerted middle-class readers to wretched living and working conditions in the industrial cities. Victorians also witnessed the passing of two tremendously important Parliamentary Reform Bills, the first in 1832 and the second in 1867, and they faced daunting challenges to religious faith with the publication of Darwin's *Origin of Species* in 1859 and Huxley's "On the Physical Basis of Life" in 1868. As Walter Houghton observes, Victorian literature is a virtual catalogue of imaginative responses "to a constant succession of shattering developments."[12]

At the middle of the century, after the demise of Chartism and the establishment of an improved economy, Britain felt herself to have come through: busy factories, bustling shipyards, active financial markets – all this testified to the national rewards of following a Gospel of Work. This wealth and well-being, now fed by the rapidly expanding growth of a profitable empire, was celebrated at the Great Exhibition of 1851. Held at the shimmering Crystal Palace, brought into dazzling existence under the direction of an enthusiastic Prince Albert, it was praised by one of the organizers for having been "carried out by its own private means," for being "self-supporting and independent of taxes and employment of slaves, which great works had exacted in ancient days"; and, most importantly, for having been managed by the queen's husband, a man of "pre-eminent wisdom, of philosophic mind, sagacity, with a power of generalship and great practical ability."[13]

This hymn to royal sagacity coupled with commercial initiative celebrates the alliance between a middle class solidifying its political power and a royal family perceived in the popular imagination as a model of high bourgeois happiness. Unaided by government money, a monument to imperial governance far superior to that of "ancient days" by virtue of its moral devotion to creating "civilized" colonies rather than gutting them of resources, and developed under the paternal direction of Prince Albert, this myth of the Great Exhibition was a grand national booster. The Crystal Palace was extraordinary to behold. A huge glass conservatory designed by a former head gardener at Kew, it was 1,848 feet long, 404 feet broad, and 66 feet high with transepts reaching to 108 feet to accommodate live elm trees.[14] All the girders and columns were identical and this shimmering palace was divided into four areas displaying raw materials, machinery, manufacturing, and fine arts. In a sense, the Great Exhibition provided visual and textual knowledge about how the world worked, in much the same way that the social problem novels of the 1840s provided knowledge about industrialization, Anthony Trollope's Palliser novels provided knowledge about parliamentary politics, and, at the end of the century, the Anglo-Indian novels provided information about running the empire. This is not to reduce Victorian fiction to a kind of information machine, but rather to point to *one* of the ways in which people read novels during the period. Novels allowed you to learn something about things, places, and people, formerly unknown.

By the time of the Great Exhibition in 1851, the novel was firmly established as the literary form of the age, and as the epigraph to this introductory chapter suggests, by 1870 that form had gained such a hegemonic hold over the British reading public that it was to be found virtually everywhere. With the aim of suggesting a small part of the significant transformation in Victorian fiction that occurred during the period from its beginnings to its cultural sovereignty when it was deemed both "clipped" and "baggy," I'd like to put Dickens's *Oliver Twist*, serialized in irregular parts and at uneven intervals in *Bentley's Magazine* from February 1837 to April 1839, alongside Joseph Conrad's *Nostromo*, published as a serial in *T. P.'s Weekly* in 1904. This alignment is not intended to serve as a definitive analysis of the Victorian novel in 1837, nor as a comprehensive assessment of what it had become a few years after the end of Victoria's reign; and neither should it be read as the simple elevation in moral and aesthetic terms of one novel over the other. My intention is to point to historically grounded difference. Sentimentalism, unambiguous narrative voice, and straightforward narrative structure did not end with *Oliver Twist*, and neither did nihilism, narrative complexity, and political interest in a world outside England begin with *Nostromo*. I want to suggest that although sentimental novels were being written in the early twentieth century and narrative experimentation was practiced throughout the Victorian period, the differences between *Oliver Twist* and *Nostromo* usefully frame general transformations in fiction during the period and in a reading public that became larger and more intellectually curious by the end of the century. Moreover, in terms of the critical debate about the moral and aesthetic nature of the novel that was conducted between the publication of these two works, Dickens's novel registers a sincere commitment to fiction as a morally transforming force and a palpable belief that its form emerges naturally from its moral imperatives, whereas Conrad's novel expresses an authorial self-awareness that suggests the painful struggle to create appropriate aesthetic form for a dense and complicated narrative.

When Dickens began *Oliver Twist* he was a newly minted celebrity, the young, confident author of the wildly successful *Pickwick Papers* (1837). Having already spent some eight years of his active working life as a journalist, he sensed that his reading public would eat up a novel dealing with the controversial new Poor Law that had been introduced in 1834, and he was correct. Dickens aimed to shock his audience with the corrupt horror of the workhouse and the perverse allegiance of boy criminals to their monstrous surrogate father, Fagin. He succeeded so well that the Lord Chamberlain's office banned theatrical adaptations on the grounds of the novel's imputed depravity.[15] Defending himself in the 1841 Preface to *Oliver Twist*, Dickens declared he saw "no reason . . . why the dregs of life . . . should not serve the purpose of a moral"; his artistic aim was to draw criminal characters as they "really did exist . . . to show them as they really were," and all of this, he claimed, was in the service of attempting "something which was needed, and which would be a service to society."[16] In notable contrast, the cosmopolitan subject of *Nostromo* is the internecine battles of a fictional South American republic that bears some resemblance to Venezuela. What's more, Conrad's stated motives for writing lack the moral urgency of those of Dickens.

Conrad averred that he had only one task before him in writing novels: "by the power of the written word, to make you hear, to make you feel . . . to make you *see*"; writing is a desperate, perilous enterprise, mandating for the novelist an attempt to "snatch in a moment of courage, from the remorseless rush of time, a passing phase of life . . . The task approached in tenderness and faith is to hold up unquestioningly, without choice and without fear, the rescued fragment before all eyes and in the light of a sincere mood."[17] What we hear in this Preface to *The Nigger of the Narcissus* (1897) is the voice of a novelist almost agonizingly aware of himself *as* novelist, painfully conscious of the virtually impossible task of "rescuing" from experience a fragment that can be placed before the reader's senses, after having been fashioned through the medium of art itself. Writing *Nostromo* became imaginatively dangerous activity, entailing a loss of self in the world imagined, and he likened its demanding labor to "venturing on a distant and toilsome journey into a land full of intrigues and revolutions," a place full of dangerous attractions where one might lose oneself "in the ever-enlarging vistas."[18] When it first appeared in serial form, *Nostromo* was greeted with puzzled dismissal. Readers were both disappointed and indignant since it lacked the simple pleasures of adventurous derring-do associated with Conrad's sea stories, and he recalled that they "wrote many letters complaining of so much space being taken by utterly unreadable stuff."[19]

In terms of transformations in novelistic subject matter and setting that occurred during the Victorian period, it is significant that in 1837 Dickens turns his satiric indignation upon domestic problems, the resolution of which is found also in the domestic sphere (a common trope in his fiction), while in 1904 Conrad's cool gaze is turned upon imperial politics and the forming of a nation from the material interests of Anglo-American capitalism and the idealistic ambition of an Englishman. The world of *Oliver Twist* is the back alleys of criminal London and the secluded pastoralism of its emerging suburbs, that of *Nostromo* bougainvillea-filled patios and the sprawling campo. *Oliver Twist* is peopled by an angelic English boy, assorted low-lifes from the East End, and good-hearted upper middle-class ladies and gentleman with no interest in national politics; *Nostromo* is inhabited by Europeans and South Americans, the formation of their subjectivity explicitly connected with the volatile formation of a nation. These differences point to the enlarged geographical scope of the Victorian novel to which I have earlier referred, to a moving outward from the metropolis to the India of Rudyard Kipling, the South Africa of Olive Schreiner, and the South Sea Islands of Robert Louis Stevenson. To be sure, from the time of Walter Scott, the British novel had left England, whether aboard one of Captain Marryat's adventuring vessels or on horseback with Disraeli and the Crusaders to the East in *Tancred* (1847). In addition, foreign places had long served as a means of characterization or plot advancement (one thinks of the West Indies in *Jane Eyre* [1847] and the somber Brussels of *Villette* [1853], the German gaming tables across which Daniel Deronda first sets eyes on Gwendolyn Harleth, Thackeray's chapters in *Vanity Fair* dealing with Waterloo and its aftermath). But it is only toward the end of the nineteenth century that nations other than Britain become full subjects of representation.

To *Oliver Twist*, Dickens brings his boyhood reading in eighteenth-century picaresque narrative, his intense pleasure in following the adventures of Smollett's Roderick Random and Henry Fielding's Tom Jones. A picaresque boy hero purged of the guile and wit that define such characters, Oliver is immune, however, to the polluted social environment in which he is placed by virtue of his picaresque journey. Next, Dickens's evocation of criminal London and menacing Fagin derives in part from conventions of the gothic, from a fascination with the shrouded, the ghostly, the vampiric – Fagin, feeds, after all, on the extracted wealth purloined by his boys from the wealthy classes. And, lastly, Dickens's novel is intensely melodramatic as it stages, say, Bill Sikes's death by hanging from the chimney pots.[20] The literary inheritance for Conrad is larger than that enjoyed by Dickens, in part because of his own deep reading in French nineteenth-century literature, and, most obviously, because of all that came after *Oliver Twist*: an enlargement of the novel in political subject matter and in the development of psychological realism. The finely calibrated nuances of *Nostromo*'s characters, for instance, owe something to George Eliot's acute explorations of human psychology as disclosed, say, in Dorothea Brooke and Edward Casaubon.

It is notable that the eponymous hero of *Oliver Twist* is an emblematic character, the embodiment of an absolute goodness inherited from a wronged and saintly mother that defeats an absolute evil embodied in his half-brother Monks, whereas the eponymous hero of Conrad's novel is a psychologically complex Italian immigrant to Central America. Oliver is untransmutable by virtue of his birth, Nostromo alters from flamboyant captain of the stevedores to secretive possessor of stolen treasure, and he is but one figure in Conrad's panoramic unfolding of Central American politics. In sum, the characters in *Oliver Twist* lean to the one-dimensional and inspire in the reader uncomplicated release in tears or laughter: Conrad's characters disclose the complex formation of individual subjectivity by social and psychological experience, constructed as they are by ambition, idealism, and in some instances, a nihilistic skepticism that renders them intellectually and politically passive; they prompt in the reader ambivalent responses and permit very little emotional release.

Finally, a narrative directness that matches the straightforward familiarity with which Dickens's narrator addresses the reader, parallels the nature of Oliver's experiences. He is born in the workhouse, travels his unhappy way to familial contentment, and watches his tormenters receive gruesome justice. A coolly ironic narrative voice absorbed in the aesthetic difficulties of creating James's "illusion of reality," together with a narrative intricateness, match the political and psychological complexity of Conrad's novel. Conrad offers no moral alliance with the reader and *Nostromo* moves around in time, confounding all narrative certainty, dislodging the reader from a stable, secure interpretive position from which to get a grip on events. This narrative disallowing of forward movement matches both the intricate interweaving of political events that are the subject of the novel, and also the intricate workings of the minds of individual characters. We can see that Conrad's 1904 text registers an epistemological inquiry into questions of national identity and individual subjectivity that had become increasingly visible in the second half of the Victorian period. Its ambiguous interrogation of a global imperialism weaving across South America is a long way from Dickens's ferocious attack on the workhouse.

The foregoing brief discussion of *Oliver Twist* and *Nostromo* has suggested, in passing, some of the desires that were gratified (or not) by Victorian novels. The chapters that follow explore and explain in great detail the cultural dominance and gratifications of the Victorian novel in its own time. They also prompt us to consider the enduring cultural capital of Victorian fiction at the beginning of the twenty-first century, and in this regard, the different emphases of the chapters are notably relevant for our own historical moment. Discovering how Victorians obtained their novels, what was considered suitable reading for different social classes, and for men and for women, leads us to think about how we obtain our books now, whether assigned in college courses or recommended by reviewers. Learning about the regulation of gender and sexuality in the Victorian novel prompts consideration of whether and how gender roles and sexual practices are less disciplined now than in the Victorian period. The long-standing presence of racism in Anglo-American society is brought home to us as we discover similarities in the Victorian novel to late twentieth-century prejudicial stereotyping. Similarly, one finds a surprising similarity between the nineteenth-century reader's vicarious thrill in consuming sensation fiction and our own taste for horror films and science fiction. The Victorian novel's participation in intellectual debates anticipates the twentieth-century's preoccupations with battles between the sexes, the ravages of war, struggles for social justice, alterations in traditional family structures, and the unpredictability of future technological advancement proceeding at a furious rate. And consideration of how nineteenth-century Anglo-American literary battles took place as if there were no other literature in the world, brings home to us the globalized nature of our late twentieth-century and early twenty-first-century novel reading.

First, Kate Flint and Simon Eliot provide important information and analysis regarding how Victorian readers obtained their novels; and how social class, gender, and religious affiliation influenced individual choices of what might be read. Flint explores the ascension of the novel to cultural dominance in the period and Eliot provides details of the material conditions that led to widespread availability of novels, whether from circulating libraries, through serialization in magazines or in monthly parts, or, in the case of cheaper fiction, from bookstalls. Reading novels in the Victorian period, whether in secrecy if such activity was discouraged or as an act of moral duty was, Flint concludes, a way of "inhabiting other lives, and potentially, changing one's own." And how one got a chance to do that depended upon one's access to the different modes of publication. Eliot tells us, among other things, how much novels actually cost, who could afford them, how much profit was made by publishers, and how libraries as well as publishers got around the astronomical costs of production and distribution.

Aesthetic alterations in the novel prompted, in part, by the material conditions of reading and publication is one of the issues taken up by Linda Shires. Shires examines the relation of aesthetics to hermeneutics and epistemology, and she illuminates changes such as the shift from the mid-Victorian consensus that the novel provided a faithful, realistic depiction of social and psychological processes, to a later impressionism more self-conscious by virtue of its inscriptions of artistic practice. Shires's insistence that we examine the novel and its aesthetic together with Victorian lyric, dramatic monologue, or verse epic revises Victorian critical judgment that literary modes must be kept apart. Shires does not dispute the fact that poetry moved to the cultural margin; she insists we see that Victorian poetry worked in its own aesthetic way and according to its own aesthetic rules.

For Joseph Childers, the bond between industrial culture and the Victorian novel is created by the desire of a reading public analyzed by Flint, and a publishing world described by Eliot, for information about a rapidly changing society. As Childers points out, industrialism and the novel looked to each other for ways of controlling as well as understanding change. Novels and the bluebooks (those records of investigations into conditions in the mines and factories) acted as a kind of sanitary insulation between social classes. Childers concludes by arguing that by the end of the Victorian period industrial culture leaves the fictional stage to be replaced by a desire for information about empire and national identity. If one ideological function of the Victorian novel was to provide knowledge about industrial culture, then another was to construct rules for the management of gender and sexuality. Nancy Armstrong and Jeff Nunokawa explicate these rules.

Armstrong argues that the novel allies itself with the emergent human sciences to refine the rules governing the social and biological reproduction of the respectable classes; in this alliance, the novel performs a containing, constraining, and normalizing function in order to reinforce emerging systems of social classification. Armstrong's chapter indicates how critical and theoretical writing about the Victorian novel situates itself within larger discourses, those, say surrounding Malthus's *Essay on the Principle of Population* (1798) and Darwin's *The Descent of Man, and Selection in Relation to Sex* (1871). Armstrong concludes that our late twentieth-century and early twenty-first-century ideas about gender differences originate in the Victorian novel's discursive alliance with non-fictional writings about reproduction and correct modes of masculine and feminine behavior. Nunokawa argues that Victorian sexual desire is similarly regulated and that social, cultural and political history is felt in the depiction of erotic passion. Through analysis of five case studies taken from Victorian fiction he shows how sexual desire is described and organized, how individual characters express erotic passion and how they are trained to define and discipline it. As we learn, it is disciplined in *The Tenant of Wildfell Hall* (1848), it contaminates the cool dealings of the marketplace in *Vanity Fair*, its homosexual nature survives as heterosexual marriage in *Jane Eyre*, it becomes hidden behind closed doors in *Adam Bede*, and in *Our Mutual Friend* (1865), it depends upon differences in social class in order to be felt at all. It is through the delineation of passion that the forces of history make themselves felt to Victorian readers.

"All is race; there is no other truth": Patrick Brantlinger begins his analysis of the presence of race in the Victorian novel with this quotation from Disraeli's *Tancred*. With reference to such texts as Robert Knox's *The*

Races of Men (1850) and Darwin's *Origin of Species* (1859) and *The Descent of Man* (1871), and works of early cultural anthropology such as Edward Burnett Tylor's *Primitive Culture* (1872), Brantlinger demonstrates how racial stereotypes, as depicted in the Victorian novel, formed an important part of Victorian thinking about national identity. From the Saxon racial stereotypes of Walter Scott's historical romances, through Jewish characters such as Anthony Trollope's Jewish con-men as encountered in *The Eustace Diamonds* (1872) and *The Way We Live Now* (1874), and racially exotic figures in adventure tales such as Rider Haggard's *King Solomon's Mines* (1885), all, indeed, is race. Brantlinger concludes his chapter with a telling instance of the enduring presence of racism in Victorian fiction with reference to Bulwer-Lytton's *The Coming Race* (1871), a science fiction fantasy featuring a people who, although far superior to late-Victorian mankind, are not reluctant to exterminate any creatures (human or otherwise) whom they consider both inferior and inimical to themselves. Racism, Brantlinger concludes, is "likely to remain an influential aspect of human cultures well into the future."

In a wide-ranging review of detection in Victorian fiction, Ronald Thomas observes that almost every Victorian novel has at its heart some crime that must be uncovered, some false identity that must be unmasked, some secret that must be revealed, or some clandestine plot that must be exposed. Tracing the figure of the detective from Dickens to Sherlock Holmes, Thomas claims that the literary detective, in his increasing preoccupation with bringing under surveillance criminal figures, is also engaged in the discipline of potentially anarchic forces unleashed by revolutionary movements, democratic reform, urban growth, national expansion, and imperial engagements. Suspect individuals are identified, monitored, and, if necessary, punished. Thomas also argues that the fundamental concept of character in the Victorian period develops from the classifying procedures of criminology and forensic science.

Lyn Pykett examines the forms of the fantastic that invaded various sub-genres of fiction in the Victorian period. Her primary example is the Gothic, which remained a significant presence in the Victorian novel in the form of ghost stories, the detective story, and a range of late-Victorian degenerationist fantasies and imperial romances, long after the waning of the vogue for Gothic romances. Pykett argues that the prominence of sensation and the fantastic in Victorian novels may be seen as an expression of the personal or political unconscious, and as a confrontation, management, and staging of taboos associated with excess and the irrational. Taken together, these forms of confrontation and management may be seen as a contest between opposing models of reality. The fantastic, Pykett concludes, interrogates conventional concepts of language, time, space, unified character, and the Victorian taste for linear narrative.

John Kucich's discussion of intellectual debate in the Victorian novel concentrates on the issues that occupied Victorian intellectuals, literary and non-literary: religion, science, the social importance of the secular professional. As Kucich observes, the Victorian novel was predominantly a novel of domestic manners, not a novel of ideas: intellectual life was seen primarily as belonging to the public male sphere, and initially, therefore, not an appropriate subject for a form with a predominantly female readership. However, with the "rushing swiftness of its intellectual advance," as G. M. Young terms it,[21] the Victorian age and the Victorian novel opened out from the domestic scene. Through attention to the work of George Eliot, George Meredith, and Thomas Hardy, Kucich argues that the intellectual engagements apparent in their novels were, in fact, broadly shared by other novelists, even if disguised in various ways. Kucich's interest is in the Victorian novel's attempt to establish a semblance of social and moral order in a disjunctive world, and he concludes that the figure of the secular professional provides consolation for the diminishing importance of the clergyman in late-Victorian life.

The concluding chapter in this volume takes the Victorian novel across the Atlantic, initially to show how American novelists engaged in a literary struggle in a post-colonial culture, working to find a place for a literary genre whose literary meaning was uncertain in the new nation. Robert Weisbuch traces a kind of transatlantic fisticuffs, a hurling of charges from the British that because Americans as yet possessed no history, they could possess no literature, and the rejoinder from the Americans that the British possessed too much of both. If the British asked how Americans could write without established structures of class, military organization, diplomatic service, and religious life, then the Americans wondered how the British could write anything with so much clutter in their way. Weisbuch makes the important point that, in part, it is through this jousting that figures such as Poe and Cooper created an American literature, and his chapter explores the crucial question of possibilities for the novel form in a democratic United States. Providing fascinating evidence of how this question dominated the pages of cultural periodicals in the first half of the nineteenth century, Weisbuch concludes that competitive mockery is the keynote of relations between British and American novelists.

Competitive mockery is also, in a sense, a constitutive characteristic of the dismissal of Victorian values and literature that was voiced by Leslie Stephen and H. G. Wells at the beginning of the twentieth century. In concert with Stephen and Wells, in a witty demolition of what he saw as the stifling morality of the period, Lytton Strachey announced in *Eminent Victorians*, "The history of the Victorian Age will never be written: we know too much about it."[22] The chapters that follow do not, of course, constitute a history of the Victorian age but they do provide a comprehensive history of the literary form that is virtually synonymous with it. And the richness of these chapters, I venture to say, leads us to feel, unlike Strachey, that we can never know too much about the Victorian age, nor, indeed, about its defining literary genre, the novel.[23]

NOTES

1 "On English Prose Fiction as a Rational Amusement," in M. L. Parrish, ed., *Anthony Trollope: Four Lectures* (London: Constable, 1938), 108.

2 For an informative review of this debate, see the Introductory Essay by Edwin M. Eigner and George J. Worth to *Victorian Criticism of the Novel* (Cambridge: Cambridge University Press, 1985).

3 George Gissing, *The Odd Women* (1893; London: Virago, 1980), 58.

4 Quoted in Asa Briggs, *Victorian People: A Reassessment of Persons and Themes 1851–67* (Chicago: University of Chicago Press, 1955) 6.

5 Quoted in *ibid.*, 6.

6 Preface to *The Tragic Muse, The Art of the Novel*, ed. R. P. Blackmur (New York: Scribners, 1934), 84.

7 Henry James, "The Art of Fiction," in Eigner and Worth, eds., *Victorian Criticism of the Novel*, 202.

8 George Eliot, *Adam Bede* (1859; New York: Signet, 1961), 174.

9 Edward W. Said, *Beginnings: Intention and Method* (New York: Basic Books, 1975), 9.

10 J. Hillis Miller, *The Form of Victorian Fiction* (Notre Dame: University of Notre Dame Press, 1968), 62–68.

11 Robin Gilmour, *The Novel in the Victorian Age: A Modern Introduction* (London: Edward Arnold, 1986), 2.

12 Walter Houghton, *The Victorian Frame of Mind 1830–1870* (New Haven: Yale University Press, 1957), 67. Houghton's commanding review of the age remains indispensable reading.

13 Briggs, *Victorian People*, 16.

14 "Exhibition of 1851," in Sally Mitchell, ed., *Victorian Britain: An Encyclopedia* (New York: Garland Publishing, 1988), 276–78.

15 Philip Collins, *Dickens and Crime* (Bloomington: Indiana University Press, 1968), 257–65.

16 Charles Dickens, *Oliver Twist* (1838; London: Oxford University Press, 1949), xv.

17 Joseph Conrad, Preface to *The Nigger of the Narcissus* (1897; London: J. M. Dent and Sons, 1950).

18 Author's Note, *Nostromo: A Tale of the Seaboard* (1904; London: J. M. Dent and Sons Ltd., 1947) xviii.

19 Quoted by Richard Curle, Introduction, *ibid.*, vi.

20 For a fascinating reading of villainy, and Fagin as a pederast, see Gary Wills,

"Love in the Lower Depths," *The New York Review of Books*, October 26, 1989.

21 G. M. Young, *Portrait of an Age* (1936; Oxford: Oxford University Press, 1960) 153.

22 Lytton Strachey, *Eminent Victorians* (1918; New York: Capricorn Books, 1963), v.

23 I would like here to acknowledge the assistance of Alicia Gribben as I worked on this *Companion*.

I

KATE FLINT

The Victorian novel and its readers

When the emancipated slave, William Wells Brown, visited England in 1850, he made a short visit to the "far-famed city of Oxford . . . one of the principal seats of learning in the world." Here, he admired the architectural beauties of the university, and, when night fell, walked around the colleges which back onto Christ Church meadow:

> I could here and there see the reflection of light from the window of some student, who was busy at his studies, or throwing away his time over some trashy novel, too many of which find their way into the trunks or carpet-bags of the young men on setting out for college. As I looked upon the walls of these buildings I thought, as the rough stone is taken from the quarry to the finisher, there to be made into an ornament, so was the young mind brought here to be cultivated and developed.[1]

Brown's focus of interest is salutary. Reading provoked a good deal of anxiety during the Victorian period. At the centre of this anxiety about what constituted suitable reading material and ways of reading lay concerns about class, and concerns about gender. In both cases, fiction was regarded as particularly suspect: likely to influence adversely, to stimulate inappropriate ambitions and desires, to corrupt. But in the case of Brown, a man who is painfully aware of the value of education, and of the advantages which privilege bestows, we see someone who is less troubled by the thought that this young man might be learning dangerous lessons from his novel, than someone who cares that he is frittering away his time, wasting those opportunities for learning from which others could gain so much. He seizes the chance to regret how "few of our own race can find a place within their walls," and to emphasize the need, among black people, to turn their attention seriously to self-education.

So much Victorian commentary on reading is written from a dominant social position, one which brings with it an assumption of inbuilt superiority, that it is well to be reminded that debates about the consumption of fiction were not confined to those who held strong views about the material consumed by the working classes, the volumes devoured by women. And yet, the assumption that novels were a particularly influential form of communication meant that their effects, or presumed effects, on these groups of readers were repeatedly put under scrutiny. Examining the contents and tone of reading material became, too, an apparently simple way of practising social investigation. The prevailing assumption – one hard to contradict – was that most people read without much system, "to gratify natural taste," as William Alexander put it, "or an easy curiosity." He went on to draw what was, for him, an easy conclusion: that their reading material must therefore form "a true and reliable index to both their moral and mental habits and condition."[2] Yet even if casual, indiscriminate readers, especially those who consumed only popular fiction in its various forms, were thought of as being particularly vulnerable to having their ideas and actions moulded by texts, they were not the only ones to be affected. As George Eliot wrote in an early letter, men and women are "imitative beings. We cannot, at least those who ever read to any purpose at all . . . help being modified by the ideas that pass through our minds."[3] It was this belief, or rather the fear that, for some people, accompanied it, that lay behind the complete prohibition on fiction reading in some quarters – especially in the early decades of the Victorian period – and the extreme caution with which the genre was approached in others. The distrust was strongest among Dissenters. The journalist, William T. Stead, son of a Congregationalist minister in Yorkshire, looked back on how he was born and brought up in a home where life was "regarded as the vestibule of Eternity, and where everything that tended to waste time, which is life in instalments, was regarded as an evil thing." Theatre and cards were regarded, respectively, as the Devil's chapel and the Devil's prayerbook, and the novel was considered "a kind of Devil's Bible, whose meretricious attractions waged an unholy competition against the reading of God's word."[4] In a few extreme cases, this absolute prohibition endured past the early decades of the century. Thus Edmund Gosse's parents, members of the Plymouth Brethren, refused, in the 1850s, to have fiction of any kind in their house. He learned about missionaries, he tells us in his autobiography, *Father and Son* (1907), but never about pirates. To tell stories was a sin. This prohibition made him hungry for narrative. He recounts how, when a boy, he found sheets from a sensation novel glued to the lid of a trunk in the garret, and the fact that the story came to an abrupt halt "in the middle of one of its most thrilling sentences, wound me up almost to a disorder of wonder and romance."[5] His father and mother "desired to make me truthful; the tendency was to make me positive and sceptical," rejecting, relatively rapidly, their religious teaching (*Father and*

Son, 17). But in general, strict evangelical censorship had softened by the mid-century. As Anthony Trollope recorded in his *Autobiography* (1883), fifty years prior to the time of writing, "The families in which an unrestricted permission was given for the reading of novels were very few, and from many they were altogether banished." However, there is, at the time of writing, "no such embargo." Rather, "Novels are read right and left, above stairs and below, in town houses and in country parsonages, by young countesses and by farmers' daughters, by old lawyers and by young students."[6]

Why did the novel come to be such a dominant literary form in the Victorian period? Who read novels, and what motivated them? And where did they obtain their fiction? These questions are, of course, interlinked. In purely numerical terms, the audience for novels grew enormously during the nineteenth century. In part, this was due to economic factors: the growth of cities, which provided concentrated markets; the development of overseas readerships in the colonies; cheaper production costs when it came to both paper and printing processes; better distribution networks, and the advertising and promotion of books. It is hard to be confident about literacy figures – methods used to measure the ability to read and write are notoriously unreliable. If, in 1840, 67 percent of men and 51 percent of women could sign the marriage register, this tells us nothing about the nature and extent of their engagement of the written word – and nor do the literacy figures from the 1851 census: 69.3 percent for men, 54.8 percent for women. The 1870 Education Act certainly made education easier to obtain, and by 1900 the percentage of literates was 97.2 men, and 96.8 women. On the one hand, there exists, despite the statistics, plenty of discursive evidence throughout the century which laments the faltering quality of the reading, and the tendency for the faculty to decay once someone left school. On the other, a growing number of jobs demanded at least some ability to read, and an increasing number of cheap texts, aimed at those with unsophisticated reading abilities and targeted at their tastes, made printed material attractive: material which reached a still wider audience when, as was frequently the case, it was shared through reading aloud. Fiction was preeminent in this print culture; above all, the stories of crime and violence, and the exaggeratedly impossible romances which so disturbed those who commented on the reading of the working classes.

Among the middle classes, patterns of employment, with the increasing separation of home and working environment, and the rise of commuting, together with the consolidation of the assumption that a male head of a household should be able to provide for the female members of his family, without them having to take paid work, contributed to the establishment of clearly demarcated leisure time and space for both women and men. "A novel's a splendid thing after a hard day's work, a sharp practical tussle with the real world," remarks one of the characters in Mary Braddon's *The Doctor's Wife* (1864).[7] Reading fiction was a way of winding down; a mental space from the complicated business of running a home; a means of filling hours that for otherwise under-employed women were figured as "empty." As "those about to write a novel" were advised in the *Saturday Review* of 1887, the average reader of novels is not a critical person, cares little for art for art's sake, and has no fixed ideas about the duties and responsibilities of an author: "all he asks is that he may be amused and interested without taxing his own brains."[8] Increasingly, a distinction developed between intellectually, psychologically and aesthetically demanding fiction, and that which primarily served the needs of escapism and relaxation. This was a distinction which novelists, as well as critics, wrote about, both within their fiction and outside it: Egremont, in George Gissing's *Thyrza* (1887), sneers: "If one goes on the assumption that the ill word of the mob is equivalent to high praise, one will not, as a rule, be far wrong, in matters of literature";[9] Henry James's "The Figure in the Carpet" mocks both critic and reader who wish to reduce the essence of elusive, suggestive fiction to a nameable quality. When, in 1897, James sent Joseph Conrad a complimentary copy of *The Spoils of Poynton*, the latter, whilst warmly admiring of the style, writes with awkward condescension of how he imagines "with pain the man in the street trying to read it! And my common humanity revolts at the evoked image of his suffering. One could almost see the globular lobes of his brain painfully revolving and crushing, mangling the delicate thing. As to his exasperation it is a thing impossible to imagine and too horrid to contemplate."[10] A rhetorically absolute division between the intellectuals and the masses was emerging during the final decades of Victoria's reign.[11] Nonetheless, despite the desire of certain critics and novelists to distinguish their standards from those of "the man in the street," autobiographies, letters and journals demonstrate eclecticism and unpredictability on the part of readers. Reading serves different needs on different occasions: the important thing to note is that there was an ever-widening and increasingly cheap range of fiction with which to satisfy these varied needs.

Until the end of the century, the majority of Victorians did not purchase their "serious" fiction – the kind of fiction that could be assured reviews in the major weeklies – brand-new when it came out in volume form, but borrowed it from circulating libraries. New fiction was expensive. For most of the period, a novel cost thirty-one shillings and sixpence. Publishers were reluctant to risk their capital on bringing out cheaper original editions:

Richard Bentley's brief and far from extensive experiment in that respect in 1854 foundered when the Crimean War caused a slump in book sales, a reminder of the volatile nature of the market. Chief among the circulating library proprietors was Charles Edward Mudie. Having loaned books in a small way for ten years, he set up his New Oxford Street headquarters in 1852, charged a guinea a year subscription for the right to borrow a volume at a time (as opposed to his competitors' two, although more lavish deals were available from Mudie), and distributed books by van in London, by railway to the provinces, and in tin trunks overseas. This practice of accounting per volume, rather than per title, was the chief factor in maintaining the dominance of the three-decker novel until nearly the end of the century. At the height of his dominance of the borrowing scene, Mudie was taking more than £40,000 a year in subscriptions. When he died, in 1890, his library had about 25,000 subscribers. He entered into deals with the major publishing houses, securing pre-publication orders, and they looked to him for a substantial slice of their sales. Bentley sold 3,864 novels by subscription in 1864, for example, and 1,962 of these were to Mudie. Mudie prided himself on the moral tone of the books he stocked. Whilst his choice of the word "select" to describe his library hinted, too, at a class exclusiveness, the boast in his advertising that to his library "the *best* Works of Fiction are . . . freely admitted" suggests the careful vetting of their quality, a process in which he himself took an active part.

Other circulating libraries, notably (from the early 1860s) W. H. Smith and Son, as well as those run by countless local shops, also prospered. By comparison with Mudie's, W. H. Smith had 15,000 subscribers in 1894: in both cases, these figures very probably represented a substantial decline from the figures of the 1860s. The Ewart Act, which provided for free public libraries in England, was passed in 1850, although the spread of such libraries was initially relatively slow, until the rapid development of the 1890s. Their emphasis tended to fall on usefulness and education – their users were frequently, though not invariably, from the working classes, and a philanthropic attitude towards them prevailed – and although many librarians could see the advantages in fostering a taste for reading in any form, others were very chary about the type of fiction they admitted. Some went so far as to ban modern novels entirely: that of Newcastle upon Tyne feared that if they were to allow them on their shelves, "their library would be flooded with unmitigated trash."[12] No such censoring mechanisms operated among those who stocked railway bookstalls. Whilst bookselling, outside major urban centres, was not a profitable trade during the Victorian period, these particular conjunctions of text and modernity were a major outlet for reprints of contemporary fiction (customarily priced at

6s. or 7s. when brought out by the original publisher, and at 1s. or 2s. when appearing in "railway editions") and for the increasing number of series which produced cheap (and often badly printed and flimsy) reprints of English classics, together with translations and abridgements. The interval before serious novels were reprinted in popular, 6s. form varied considerably, from a year or so, in the case of George Eliot and Trollope, to between three to five years, when it came to Thackeray, and even longer for the perennially financially cautious Dickens. Bookstalls sold even cheaper fiction, too. Agnes Repplier noted, in 1893, how

> The clerks and artisans, shopgirls, dressmakers, and milliners, who pour into London every morning by the early trains, have, each and every one, a choice specimen of penny fiction with which to beguile the short journey, and perhaps the few spare minutes of a busy day. The workingman who slouches up and down the platform, waiting for the moment of departure, is absorbed in some crumpled bit of pink-covered romance. The girl who lounges opposite to us in the carriage, and who would be a very pretty girl in any other conceivable hat, sucks mysterious sticky lozenges, and reads a story called "Mariage à la Mode, or Getting into Society"[13]

The easy availability of popular fiction was one of the factors which, towards the end of the century, put pressure on publishers to change their pricing system. "The three-shilling book is our great want," demanded Matthew Arnold in 1880, not "a cheap literature, hideous and ignoble of aspect, like the tawdry novels which flare in the bookshelves of our railway-stations, and which seem designed, as so much else that is produced for the use of our middle-class seems designed, for people with a low standard of life."[14] The publication of George Moore's *A Mummer's Wife* in 1885 at 6s. inaugurated the appearance of new fiction at affordable prices. By nine years later, both Mudie's and Smith's told publishers that they would pay no more than 4s. a volume. Cheaper libraries multiplied, and sales of first editions to private individuals escalated rapidly.

Not all novels appeared first in volume form: some initially emerged as serials. The self-publishing Dickens brought out most of his fictions in monthly parts, famously creating an urgent demand for each new number. This appeal crossed classes. G. H. Lewes noted of *Pickwick Papers* (1836–37) that "even the common people, both in town and country, are equally intense in their admiration. Frequently, have we seen the butcher-boy, with his tray on his shoulder, reading with the greatest avidity the last 'Pickwick'; the footman (whose fopperies are so inimitably laid bare), the maidservant, the chimney sweep, all classes, in fact, read 'Boz'."[15] In its turn, this expressed the effectiveness of Dickens's maxim that "a story-teller and a story-reader should establish a mutual understanding as soon as possible,"[16] and his own skill in doing just this. Although Trollope occasionally employed it, this practice of bringing out fiction in parts was not widely imitated, and had virtually died out by 1880. But Dickens was symptomatic as a fiction publisher in another way. Editing two magazines – *Household Words* and *All the Year Round* – in which he published not just *Hard Times* (1854), *A Tale of Two Cities* (1859), and *Great Expectations* (1860–61), but works by Elizabeth Gaskell, Wilkie Collins, and others, Dickens facilitated a mode of publication which implicitly encouraged the reading of novels alongside other forms of writing. Thus *Hard Times* could be brought into ready dialogue with pieces on the evils of failing to fence in factory machinery; his novel of the French Revolution with discussions of the Italian Risorgimento in the late 1850s; *Great Expectations* with the debates which surrounded the appearance of Charles Darwin's *Origin of Species* (1859). And his magazines were but two among a large number which brought out novels in part form: the *Cornhill*, *Temple Bar*, *Belgravia*, *Once a Week* and, later in the century, *Blackwood's*, the *Strand*, and *Tit-bits* were among those prepared to pay considerable sums of money, sometimes running into thousands of pounds, for fiction.

These different modes of publication exerted particular pressures on novelists, extending their stories in order to fill three volumes; cutting and compressing in order to meet the space constraints of a magazine column; concocting the regularly spaced moments of suspense which paced serial publication and encouraged the purchase of a subsequent issue; never allowing characters to fade too long from sight. "The writer," as Trollope showed himself to be very aware, "cannot afford to have many pages skipped out of the few which are to meet the reader's eye at the same time."[17] The traces of the original form of production remain, creating hiatuses which structure the reading of the text even once it has been reprinted in a single volume. Thus *The Mill on the Floss* (1860), for example, which is divided into three parts, concludes volume one with the young Tom and Maggie returning from Tom's school at the news of their father's loss of property and physical collapse, ending on the words: "They had entered the thorny wilderness, and the golden gates of their childhood had for ever closed behind them."[18] Volume two terminates with Mr. Tulliver's death, and the brother and sister turning to one another. Maggie speaks: "'Tom, forgive me – let us always love each other,' and they clung and wept together" (*The Mill on the Floss*, 316). With this build-up, it is a an inevitability that the novel as a whole will conclude with Tom and Maggie joined in a way that will dramatize their instinctual need for one another. This need has been determined not just psychologically, but by the work's material structure.

Reading on trains signified modernity, and hence was a convenient trope on which commentators about current trends could seize. Apart from anything else, it was a mode of consumption in which the reader was visible, public, available for scrutiny – and yet frequently withdrawn from contact with anything outside the text, immersed in a private imaginative world, and hence a vulnerable figure onto which to project ideas about quite what the effects of their reading material on them might prove to be. But in general, reading fiction was associated, above all, with the domestic environment. The fact that reading was a common sociable family activity within the middle-class home, members taking it in turn to read aloud from the current volume, set up a demand that nothing should appear in print which was not suitable for every potential listener. "The censorship of prudery," as Thomas Hardy termed it in an angry article of 1890, ensured that realistic depictions of "the relations of the sexes" – "the crash of broken commandments" that formed the necessary accompaniment to the catastrophe of a tragedy – had, right through the century, to be glossed over, if not completely concealed.[19] When this concealment was only partial, as in the case of sensation fiction, or the realist fiction of the 1880s and 1890s by such writers as George Moore (who produced his own polemic against the tyranny of circulating libraries in *Literature At Nurse, Or Circulating Morals*, 1885), or, indeed, of some of Hardy's own later works, such as *Tess of the d'Urbervilles* (1891) and *Jude the Obscure* (1895), concern about the potential corrosive effect on the reader's – especially the young reader's – moral standards was ritualistically trotted out. As Hardy commented in a letter to Edmund Gosse, thanking him for his discriminating review of *Jude* and contrasting it to some of the other responses which the novel had provoked, "one cannot choose one's readers."[20]

Nonetheless, authors entered into various types of dialogue with their readers, attending to their desires in various ways, and, effectively, trying to ensure that their potential purchasers chose *them*. Sometimes this involved acting on the responses of readers in their intimate circle, seeking to please both them, and the wider audience whose reactions they could be seen as anticipating. Thus Patrick Brontë was anxious that his daughter Charlotte's *Villette* (1853) "should end well," as he disliked novels which left a melancholy impression on the mind; and he requested her to make her hero and heroine (like the heroes and heroines in fairy tales) "marry, and live very happily ever after."[21] She was only prepared to compromise up to a point, producing enough uncertainty over Paul Emanuel's fate to "leave sunny imaginations hope,"[22] and thereby drawing a distinction between her own imaginative integrity and the wishes of those who demanded that fiction provided the consolatory, neat happy endings which life fails to deliver. Dickens had originally intended Walter Gay, in *Dombey and Son* (1848) to trail away gradually "into negligence, idleness, dissipation, dishonesty and ruin,"[23] but his close friend Forster, probably with an eye to sales, dissuaded him. Similarly Bulwer Lytton protested against the original conclusion to *Great Expectations* as too downbeat, leading Dickens to substitute one in which the eventual reunion of Pip with Estella is, at the very least, a possibility.

The demand for a happy ending, particularly one which was based on romance, endured throughout the nineteenth century. Ella Hepworth Dixon, writing in the 1890s, shaped her own writing skills to the market, producing short stories, humorous articles, art reviews, and a novel which both participated in the current vogue for "New Woman" fiction and showed quite what its practitioners had to contend with when it came to getting their works published – at least until they found themselves, for a few years, fashionably marketable. In *The Story of a Modern Woman* (1894), Mary, the heroine, proposes a realist novel to her publisher, but he maintains that something in the style of French and Russian writers would only displease the British public, who wanted a ball in the first volume of their three-decker; a picnic and a parting in the second, and an opportune death in the third: best of all would be "a thoroughly breezy book with a wedding at the end."[24] This is not a very dissimilar set of clichés to those against which George Eliot had protested forty years earlier in her 1856 *Westminster Review* article, "Silly Novels by Lady Novelists." In what she characterises as the *"mind-and-millinery* species," "the heroine is usually an heiress, probably a peeress in her own right, with perhaps a vicious baronet, an amiable duke, and an irresistible younger son of a marquis as lovers in the foreground, a clergyman and a poet sighing for her in the middle distance, and a crowd of undefined adorers dimly indicated beyond."[25] Such a heroine is intelligent, witty, eloquent, beautiful, and with an undefinable but surefire capacity of bewitching men.

> For all this, she as often as not marries the wrong person to begin with, and she suffers terribly from the plots and intrigues of the vicious baronet; but even death has a soft place in his heart for such a paragon, and remedies all mistakes for her just at the right moment. The vicious baronet is sure to be killed in a duel, and the tedious husband dies in his bed, requesting his wife, as a particular favour to him, to marry the man she loves best, and having already dispatched a note to the lover informing him of the comfortable arrangement.[26]

Increasingly, Eliot's own novels were structured to refuse her readers the kind of satisfaction promised by the works she attacks here. In *Middle-*

march (1872), she rewrites the scenario she outlined earlier. Casaubon, the tedious husband, shows no post-mortem generosity, but rather does all he can to make it difficult for Dorothea to marry Will after his death. Moreover, when Eliot finally brings the pair together, and Dorothea becomes the wife of this "ardent public man," we are told that "Many who knew her, thought it a pity that so substantive and rare a creature should have been absorbed into the life of another, and be only known in a certain circle as a wife and mother."[27] These "many who knew her" are curiously unspecified. They cannot plausibly be located among the socially conservative characters we have already encountered in provincial Middlemarch. Rather, they belong to a new metropolitan circle – or, we might say, they are ventriloquizing what readers themselves might feel. A romance plot that serves the protagonist's happiness may not, Eliot hints, satisfy the sophisticated reader – or rather, such a reader needs to curb their own desire for fiction to supply the exceptional, and learn, rather, of the importance of the typical, the ordinary, of the power of "unhistoric acts" to contribute to the future shaping of society (*Middlemarch*, 825).

The debates which recurrently circled around romance plots, with their capacity to attract readers and their limitations, show the degree to which both novelists and critics recognized a range of needs among their readers: needs which could be fulfilled by the protean forms of fiction. Romances have a long history of providing escapism, and not just for women, despite the conventional assumption that they formed the genre's primary audience, and that they set into train a particular set of unpragmatic desires. "The best romance," wrote John Ruskin in *Sesame and Lilies* (1865), "becomes dangerous, if, by its excitement, it renders the ordinary course of life uninteresting, and increases the morbid thirst for useless acquaintance with scenes in which we shall never be called upon to act."[28] George Gissing, in *The Odd Women* (1893) has the feminist Rhoda Nunn complain of a woman who had become a married man's mistress that she had been corrupted by reading novels: "Love – love – love; a sickening sameness of vulgarity. What is more vulgar than the ideal of novelists? . . . This Miss Royston – when she rushed off to perdition, ten to one she had in mind some idiot heroine of a book."[29] But against this we can set Beth's husband in Sarah Grand's *The Beth Book* (1897), who sends her off to the library to borrow three-decker novels which she reads aloud to him in an endless succession as he smokes and drinks his whiskies-and-sodas. She becomes unspeakably weary of golden-haired paragons of perfection, determining, when she writes herself, not to "make a pivot of the everlasting love-story, which seems to me to show such a want of balance in an author, such an absence of any true sense of proportion, as if there was nothing else of interest in life but our sexual relations."[30] The stereotype of the woman who gorged herself on romances as though they were boxes of sugar-plums, at first deliciously palatable but increasingly inducing an unhealthy, sickly saturation was a familiar one in advice works which sought to encourage women to take more substantial mental sustenance, or to read something more spiritually or socially improving. It was not a stereotype based on fantasy: reviews of fiction in, say, the *Saturday Review*, the *Spectator*, and the *Athenaeum*, weekly journals which provide invaluable sources for uncovering the plots and themes which were aimed at the middle-class readership, confirm quite how frequently novelists employed the formula of a woman placed in adverse social or emotional conditions, finally having her qualities, her forbearance, her attractiveness rewarded by marriage to a suitably sensitive yet manly husband. Once a particular model worked successfully, imitators could be readily anticipated.[31] Yet the stereotype also served those writers who wanted to challenge broader assumptions about women's tastes: their heroine's dissatisfaction with romance fiction's limitations standing for their wider repudiation of easy pigeonholing of women's roles as well as cultural preferences.

The thought that a novel might lead a woman to become dissatisfied with her mundane domestic duties was one of the accusations most commonly levelled against the sensation fiction which became so popular in the 1860s. Fussily moralistic was the *Christian Remembrancer*, fretting that the genre of writing practiced by Mary Braddon, by Ellen Wood, and Wilkie Collins could, for the woman reader, "open out a picture of life free from all the perhaps irksome checks that confine their own existence."[32] Here and elsewhere, romance – in the sense of heterosexual paradigms of desire and fulfillment, predicated on protestations of love, with sexual promptings alluded to with varying degrees of explicitness – was not the only type of escapism that fiction could offer. Other types of fiction developed which offered very different possibilities for readers to project themselves into a life more exciting than that which they actually inhabited. Throughout the period, there was a strong market for adventure fiction ostensibly aimed at a boys' market (if very often read by girls, as well). The very promotion of such fiction, by publishers such as Blackie's, was itself symptomatic of a commercial exploitation of a presumed diversification of readership. The imperialist exuberance of writers like G. A. Henty, W. H. G. Kingston, and R. M. Ballantyne was related, too, to the late-century fashion for what Patrick Brantlinger has influentially termed the "imperial Gothic," in which adventure stories blend with Gothic elements, and Western rationalism is disrupted by superstitions and the supernatural.[33] Readers are simultaneously offered thrills predicated on dangerous, exotic locations and on far less tangible threats of atavistic degeneration, and yet the *fin-de-siècle* anxieties exploited by writers like Rider Haggard and Bram Stoker are invariably kept in check by their neat plot conclusions.

Nor were readers only offered possibilities for overseas, exotic exploration. The industrial fictions of Elizabeth Gaskell, for example, contain strong internal suggestions that here is a narrator familiar with the northern urban context which it is her task to present to the uninitiated. In *North and South* (1855) she makes a Southerner's learning experience particularly easy by tracing the reactions of Margaret as she comes from a background shaped both by the life of a vicar's daughter in a pastoral village and an acquaintance with fashionable London society, gradually encountering, and becoming more understanding of, the conditions and tensions of northern industrial life. Later in the century, the subject matter of such fiction writers as George Gissing, Arthur Morrison, and – in his earlier work – George Moore not just borrowed from the naturalist premises of French novelists such as Zola, but shared much in common with social investigators such as Charles Booth and George Sims.

A reverse fascination may be seen, although without the didactic underpinning, and certainly without the strict care for verisimilitude, in what one commentator called "the natural craving of the uneducated for exaggerated representations of 'high life'," a craving fed by penny novelettes which fancifully showed lords visiting workshops and mills to pick out a wife, laden with jewels and gold to bestow on the object of their choice, and ladies choosing their maids for their most intimate confidences.[34] But fiction, particularly for those who led lives of relative material comfort, also offered possibilities for identification which lay in similarity rather than difference. Lillian Faithfull acknowledged the pull of wholesome romance to be found in Charlotte M. Yonge's fiction in the mid-century, and also the appeal of ecclesiasticism to a girl in her teens going through a period of religious doubt and difficulty which she regarded with immense seriousness. What rendered them especially effective was the sense that the characters comprised a kind of extended family: "people of like passions, emotions, hopes and fears, and we were as intimate with every detail of their lives described in volume after volume as with the lives of our sisters, cousins and aunts."[35] She – unlike some who looked back queasily at Yonge – does not seem to have been put off by the heavy Christian didacticism and the strongly enforced dose of domesticity.

Novels could certainly provide guidance, wisdom, consolation, patterns to follow which were not necessarily the pernicious ones mocked by Gissing's Rhoda Nunn. Some commentators encouraged precisely this mode of reading, suggesting that one should be continually matching oneself against fictional models: "Am *I* like this or that? Do *I* cultivate this virtue or yield to this propensity?"[36] Fiction itself, however, was frequently the medium for mocking those who took its premises too seriously, a disingenuous way of asserting its status as truth whilst apparently deriding the genre's capacity to absorb the reader into its viewpoints. Thus at the opening of *Miss Marjoribanks* (1866) Margaret Oliphant's heroine, Lucilla, is away at school when she hears the news of her invalid mother's death. "All the way home she revolved the situation in her mind, which was considerably enlightened by novels and popular philosophy" and she constructs an idealized role for herself in which, between bouts of tears, she will sacrifice her own feelings, and "make a cheerful home for her papa."[37] Fiction, as Janice Radway has noted in the context of twentieth-century romantic novels, can encourage forms of identification which are empowering, especially to women: allowing them to feel at the centre of their own lives. Oliphant captures the moment at which this enablement slides over into an equation of the fictional and the real worlds. Others confront the inadequacy of fiction when it comes to providing a model through which to lead one's life more directly. In *Felix Holt* (1866), Eliot shows her heroine, Esther, living away from home at Transome Hall, and despite the ready availability of a library, she "found it impossible to read in these days; her life was a book which she seemed herself to be constructing – trying to make character clear before her, and looking into the ways of destiny."[38] In *Daniel Deronda* (1876), Gwendolen Harleth draws many of her expectations from romances, and – one presumes – sensation fiction. But these prove utterly inadequate when she is confronted by the presence of the mistress, and children, of the man who wishes to marry her: "Gwendolen's uncontrolled reading, though consisting chiefly in what are called pictures of life, had somehow not prepared her for this encounter with reality."[39] These novels anticipate a readership sophisticated enough to recognize, and enjoy, the slippage between fictional conventions and their own lives. At the same time, they tacitly suggest a major reason why fiction and life can blur into one another: both are concerned with making sense of experience through the formulation of narratives, themselves containing patterns, or presumed patterns, of cause and effect.

The desire for reading material which reinforces moral norms was most frequently noted in fiction written for the working classes. An article of 1866 in *Macmillan's Magazine* on "Penny Novels" – those which appeared in such popular publications as the *London Journal* and the *Family Herald* – remarked that whereas fifteen or so years earlier, an enormous amount of anxiety was being stirred up by the fact that "our lower classes were being entertained with tales of seduction, adultery, forgery, and murder," now a "strong moral tone" pervades the writing: one which exactly replicates the sentiments expressed in the answers to correspondents to be found elsewhere in the magazine. It would appear that the "heart of the *plebs* in this country is not to be reached but in gushes of moral wisdom."[40] But twenty years later, the sanctimoniousness at one time found in "love-and-murder concoctions" was perceived to have evaporated, and the stories in the *London Journal* and in penny novelettes may all, according to Edward Salmon – himself not free from ready moralizing – "be characterised as cheap and nasty . . . utterly contemptible in literary execution; they thrive on the wicked baronet or nobleman and the faithless but handsome peeress, and find their chief supporters among shop-girls, seamstresses, and domestic servants."[41]

This taste for moral certitude can be traced across much Victorian fiction, even if it is not always as blatantly expressed as in the works targeted at a working-class or lower-working-class readership. It should be seen in tandem with the convoluted yet largely resolved plots that one encounters in Dickens and in Thackeray, in Wilkie Collins and other sensation novelists, in Hardy and Mrs. Humphry Ward. Although not every thread is invariably tied up, and although the sense of completion may be accompanied with feelings of depletion and loss, a particular type of satisfaction is promised to the reader by the long Victorian novel. Raymond Williams, in *The Country and the City*, writes eloquently of how most novels are, in some sense, "knowable communities." He explores the structure of Dickens's works, paralleling one's initial impression of seemingly random characters passing each other, as though in a crowded street. But below this surface, as his plots gradually reveal, there is a vast network (or web, as the Darwin-influenced George Eliot or Thomas Hardy might have it) of interconnections, and gradually, "as the action develops, unknown and unacknowledged relationships, profound and decisive connections, the necessary recognitions and avowals are as it were forced into consciousness."[42] The promise of underlying order and coherence, of knowability, is held out by fiction, or, as Robert Louis Stevenson put it: "Life is monstrous, infinite, illogical, abrupt and poignant; a work of art, in comparison, is neat, finite, self-contained, rational . . ."[43]

Reading is a curious activity. It is simultaneously a shared experience, and a highly private one. Whilst Victorians might discuss their reading with family or friends, join a reading circle based on the ideal of self-improvement, read literature according to syllabi prescribed by schools or, by the end of the century, by universities, what happened between them and the words on the page, as they entered into other lives and experiences, or as they condemned or praised the sentiments expressed, or as they puzzled with George Meredith's or Henry James's prose, is very hard to recover, except through hypothesis. It is, of course, possible to retrieve evidence of *what* people read. Although their reliability is on occasion questionable, publishers' archives, lists published in trade journals like the *Publisher's Circular* (founded 1837) and *The Bookseller* (founded 1854), and the records kept by some public and private libraries give one an idea of what was bought, what was borrowed. Dickens's novels, as has already been remarked, were enormously successful: the first number of *Nicholas Nickleby* (1838) sold 50,000 copies; Part 1 of *Our Mutual Friend* (1864) sold 30,000 copies in three days. G. W. M. Reynolds's melodramatic adventure tales – sold in penny or halfpenny numbers, with a largely working-class readership – were even more popular. The first two numbers of *The Soldier's Wife* (1852), retailing at 1d., each sold 60,000 on the day of publication; two years later, the equivalent figures for *The Bronze Soldier*, at $\frac{1}{2}$d. a number, were 100,000. The most notable sales in the mid-century were achieved by Harriet Beecher Stowe's *Uncle Tom's Cabin* (1852). Since ten different transatlantic editions of this were produced within two weeks, and forty within a year, it is hard to be exact about figures, but, including colonial sales, around 1,500,000 copies were sold to the British market. Providing an example of quite how dramatic an effect was produced by the dropping of the price of new novels was the publication, in 1897, of Hall Caine's *The Christian* – a story of love, religion, the London slums, and apocalyptic fervor – which sold 50,000 copies in a month.

To read and discuss those works of fiction which were runaway bestsellers (the term itself seems to have been coined in Kansas in 1889) went beyond the demonstration that one possessed what Pierre Bourdieu has termed "cultural capital," views about culture which demonstrated one's status in society, although the ability to converse about current literature was a component of educated middle- and upper-class life. Rather, becoming excited by these fictions was a means of asserting one's claim to be modern, to be in the know. "Novels," John Sutherland has reminded us, in the context of the gamble publishers undertook each time they invested money in a new work of fiction, "are things of a season and do not have the stamina of, say, text-books."[44] "Have you *Red Pottage?*" was the punning question in relation to Mary Cholomondeley's novel of that name which, appearing in 1899, combines highly contemporary debate about the role of women with an improbably sensational plot. At its most extreme, the excitement over new works spilled over into a commodification of the original conception which spread far beyond the book's covers. Dickens, Charlotte Brontë, and others had their novels dramatized. Wilkie Collins's 1860 novel prompted sales of "Woman in White" shawls and "The Woman in White" waltz. George du Maurier's *Trilby* (1894) was greeted somewhat indifferently when it first appeared in Britain, but was a runaway success in the United States: it circulated in about 200,000 copies of *Harper's Monthly Magazine*, and an American illustrated edition sold more than 100,000 copies. Returning to London as a stage dramatization, its popularity exploded. Lapel pins were sold in the shape of Trilby's beautiful foot; there were Trilby sausages and Trilby ice-cream molds as well as the Trilby hat.[45] The example of du Maurier's work, moreover, shows how fiction created communities of readers which spanned continents.

The issue of taste and consumption, which necessarily is suggested by sales figures, was discussed in more depth in magazine articles. Successive authors seized on the topic of working-class readership with the air of those exploring the faintly exotic: Thackeray, in 1838; Wilkie Collins, in 1858; James Payn, in 1881. "The luxuriance" of the growth of this unsuspected mass of readers, Payn remarks, "has become tropical."[46] Later pieces, bearing titles like "What English people read," "The reading of the working classes," "What do the masses read?," "The reading of the colonial girl," "What boys read," and "What girls read," relied, in some cases, not just on subjective impressions but on reader surveys. These were conducted, in fact, throughout the period. A couple of the earliest surveys published by the London Statistical Society looked at book ownership and readership among the working classes. Dickens and Scott came high on people's lists of preferences throughout the century, spanning classes, genders, and occupations. In a 1906 survey of the first large cohort of Labour Party members of parliament, 16 percent claimed that Dickens was the author or work which had influenced them the most strongly, a percentage point behind Ruskin, but two in front of the Bible.[47] Yet although he might represent a constant, journalists were fascinated by the phenomenon of changing preferences. Florence Low, writing in 1906 with what seems nostalgia for her own favorites when younger, laments that the "muscular Christian heroes" of Charles Kingsley are no longer popular; that the "wholesome and cheering" heroines of Louisa Alcott are now little known.[48] Reading material, once again, is unproblematically taken as apparently offering some kind of index to the general social and moral climate. A shift towards racy popularists like Marie Corelli, or L. T. Meade's formulaic, highly accessible stories about intense friendships and rivalries between adolescent girls, seemed particularly alarming, to a commentator like Low, in the context of the increased social freedoms and opportunities available to, and demanded by, women at the end of the century.

But *how* did people read fiction? What of the patterns of identification and resistance that were set up between individual readers and novels? What actual desires were invested and fulfilled? Here, it is far harder to be certain, however much one might hypothesize about the psychological desires which were invested. Reviews summarize the responses of those who turned leisure activity into paid work, and were invariably written with an eye to their *own* potential readership. They succumbed to a desire to sound morally upright, often in a way more likely to stimulate a reader's curiosity than to deter them, one might think (*Madame Bovary* [1857] "is not a work which we can recommend any man, far less any woman, to read").[49] The evidence provided in autobiographies, even letters and journals, must also be examined with caution, since it, too, is never innocent of self-construction and of an appeal to an audience, even if that audience is no broader than one's own ideal self. Those who hold particular religious or political or social briefs are anxious to bear witness to the texts which fired the compassion or conscience which informed their subsequent activities, recycling the didacticism. And one must bear in mind the fact that those who write autobiographies are frequently likely to be exceptional, in some way, in the first place.

It is in autobiography, nonetheless, that we find some of the most eloquent testimonies to the ways in which certain texts might move their readers, or indeed, in which the actual practice of reading is described. This can range from the candor with which Trollope describes his encounter with Eliot's increasingly obscure fictional prose, as manifested in *Daniel Deronda* – "there are sentences which I have found myself compelled to read three times before I have been able to take home to myself all that the writer has intended,"[50] through the evidence in the working-class testimonies recorded by David Vincent in *Bread, Knowledge and Freedom*,[51] to the mass transformation recollected by Annabel Grant-Duff Jackson. She tells how a fellow pupil at Cheltenham Ladies' College smuggled in a copy of Olive Schreiner's *The Story of an African Farm* (1883): "the whole sky seemed aflame and many of us became violent feminists."[52] The statistics for the sales of *Uncle Tom's Cabin* spring to life when, for example, one reads Lady Frances Balfour describe how "It did its work! A woman's pen, under Divine inspiration touched the iron fetters, the rivets fell apart and 'the slave where'er he cowers' went free."[53] The human and political liberation which Stowe describes seems to find its correlative in the awakening stimulated in Balfour's own mind.

Writing about the power that fiction can have over the reader, Robert

Louis Stevenson considers its capacity to make us let go of our conscious selves:

> In anything fit to be called by the name of reading, the process itself should be absorbing and voluptuous; we should gloat over a book; be rapt clean out of ourselves, and rise from the perusal, our mind filled with the busiest, kaleidoscopic dance of images, incapable of sleep or continuous thought. The words, if the book be eloquent, should run thenceforward in our ears like the noise of breakers, and the story . . . repeat itself in a thousand coloured pictures to the eye.[54]

This rhetoric of rapture hardly covers the cerebral challenges laid down by George Meredith's fiction, nor the psychological discrimination encouraged by Henry James's prose, nor the degree to which novels may be read as a means of acquiring factual information. But Stevenson's stress on the transformative power of fiction goes to the heart of the Victorian concern with novel reading. It was a practice which could consolidate one's sense of belonging to a particular sector of society, which could reinforce religious or gender norms: which could, in other words, confirm one's belief in the security, rightness, and communality of the life one led. On the other hand, it provided a space for exploring the self, trying out new thoughts, new possibilities, in private. Reading fiction, an activity which combined flexing the imagination with anticipating and reacting to the dynamics of a range of narratives, was a vicarious means of inhabiting other lives, and, potentially, changing one's own. Elizabeth Gaskell said that when she was reading, she was herself, "and nobody else, and [could not] be bound by another's rules."[55] Here, in the opportunity for the assertion of selfhood, lay both the perceived danger, and the very real power, of reading novels.

NOTES

1 Ed. Paul Jefferson, *The Travels of William Wells Brown. Narrative of William W. Brown, Fugitive Slave, and The American Fugitive in Europe. Sketches of Places and People Abroad* (Edinburgh University Press, 1991), 174.

2 William Alexander, "Literature of the People – Past and Present," *Good Words* 17 (1876), 92.

3 Mary Ann Evans to Maria Lewis, March 16, 1839, in Gordon Haight, ed., *The George Eliot Letters*, 9 vols. (New Haven: Yale University Press, 1954–78), 1:23.

4 William T. Stead, quoted in Amy Cruse, *The Victorians and Their Books* (London: Allen & Unwin, 1935), 67.

5 Edmund Gosse, *Father and Son. A Study of Two Temperaments* (1907; London: Oxford University Press, 1974), 24.

6 Anthony Trollope, *An Autobiography* (1883; London: Oxford University Press, 1923), 199.

7 Mary Braddon, *The Doctor's Wife* (1864; Oxford University Press, 1998), 30.

8 "To Those About to Write a Novel," *Saturday Review*, January 22, 1887, 122.

9 George Gissing, *Thyrza* (1887; Brighton: Harvester Press, 1974) 423.

10 Joseph Conrad to Edward Garnett, February 13, 1897, in Frederick R. Karl and Laurence Davis, eds., *Collected Letters I, 1861–1897*, eds. (Cambridge: University Press, 1983), 339.

11 See John Carey, *The Intellectuals and the Masses* (London: Faber, 1992).

12 Report of the annual meeting of the Newcastle-upon-Tyne Literary and Philosophical Society, *Library* 1 (1889), 178.

13 Agnes Repplier, "English Railway Fiction," *Points of View* (Boston and New York: Houghton and Mifflin, 1893), 209.

14 Matthew Arnold, "Copyright," *Fortnightly Review* ns 27 (1880), 28.

15 [G. H. Lewes], "Review of Books," *National Magazine and Monthly Critic* 1 (1837), 445.

16 Charles Dickens, "The Chimes" (1844), *The Christmas Books*, 2 vols., (Harmondsworth: Penguin, 1971), I:149.

17 Trollope, *Autobiography*, 132.

18 George Eliot, *The Mill on the Floss* (1860; Oxford: Clarendon Press, 1980), 168.

19 Thomas Hardy, 'Candour in English Fiction,' *New Review* (January 1890), reprinted in Harold Orel ed., *Thomas Hardy's Personal Writings* (London: Macmillan, 1967), 129.

20 Thomas Hardy to Edmund Gosse, November 10, 1895, in Richard Little Purdy and Michael Millgate, eds., *The Collected Letters of Thomas Hardy*, 7 vols. (Oxford: Clarendon Press, 1978– 88), II:93.

21 Elizabeth C. Gaskell, *The Life of Charlotte Brontë* (1857; London: Oxford University Press, 1919), 427.

22 Charlotte Brontë, *Villette* (1853; London: Penguin, 1985), 596.

23 Charles Dickens to John Forster, July 25, 1846, *Letters of Charles Dickens*, vol. IV, ed. Kathleen Tillotson (Oxford: Oxford University Press, 1977), 593.

24 Ella Hepworth Dixon, *The Story of a Modern Woman* (1894; London: Merlin Press, 1990), 183.

25 George Eliot, "Silly Novels by Lady Novelists," *Westminster Review* (October 1856), reprinted in A. S. Byatt and Nicholas Warren, eds., *George Eliot. Selected Essays, Poems and Other Writings* (London: Penguin Books, 1990), 140.

26 *Ibid.*, 141.

27 George Eliot, *Middlemarch* (1872; Oxford: Clarendon Press, 1986), 822.

28 John Ruskin, *Sesame and Lilies* (1865), in E. T. Cook and Alexander Wedderburn, eds., *The Works of John Ruskin*, 39 vols. (London: G. Allen, 1903–12), XVIII:129.

29 George Gissing, *The Odd Women* (1893; London: Virago, 1980), 54.

30 Sarah Grand, *The Beth Book* (1897; London: Virago, 1980), 373.

31 Charlotte Brontë's *Jane Eyre* provides a particularly strong case in point. See Patsy Stoneman, *Brontë Transformations. The Cultural Dissemination of* Jane Eyre *and* Wuthering Heights (Hemel Hempstead: Prentice Hall/Harvester Wheatsheaf, 1996).

32 "Our Female Sensation Novelists," *Christian Remembrancer* ns 46 (1863), 210.

33 See chapter 8, "Imperial Gothic: Atavism and the Occult in the British

Adventure Novel, 1880–1914," in Patrick Brantlinger, *Rule of Darkness. British Literature and Imperialism, 1830–1914* (Ithaca: Cornell University Press, 1988), 227–53.

34 Unsigned article, "Penny Novels," *Spectator*, March 28, 1863, 1808.

35 Lillian M. Faithfull, *In the House of My Pilgrimage* (London: Chatto and Windus, 1924), 32–3.

36 W. H. Davenport Adams, *Woman's Work and Worth* (London: John Hogg, 1880), 47.

37 Margaret Oliphant, *Miss Marjoribanks* (1866; London: Penguin, 1998), 3.

38 George Eliot, *Felix Holt* (1866; Oxford: Clarendon Press, 1980), 322.

39 George Eliot, *Daniel Deronda* (1876; Oxford: Clarendon Press, 1984), 140.

40 Unsigned review article, "Penny Novels," *Macmillan's Magazine* 14 (1866), 97, 101.

41 Edward G. Salmon, "What the Working Classes Read," *Nineteenth Century* 20 (1886), 112.

42 Raymond Williams, *The Country and the City* (1973; London: Paladin, 1975), 202, 191.

43 Robert Louis Stevenson, "A Humble Remonstrance," *Memoirs and Portraits: The Works of Robert Louis Stevenson*, 26 vols. (1884; London: Heinemann, 1922–23), XII:213.

44 J. A. Sutherland, *Victorian Novelists and Publishers* (Chicago: University of Chicago Press, 1976), 75.

45 See L. Edward Purcell, "Trilby and Trilby-Mania: The Beginning of the Bestseller System," *Journal of Popular Culture* 11 (1977), 62–76.

46 James Payn, "Penny Fiction," *Nineteenth Century* 9 (1881), 145.

47 Survey of Labour MPs' favorite authors in the *Review of Reviews*, 1906, table reproduced in Jonathan Rose, "How Historians Study Reader Response: Or, What did Jo think of *Bleak House*," in John O. Jordan and Robert L. Patten, eds., *Literature in the Marketplace. Nineteenth-Century British Publishing and Reading Practices* (Cambridge: Cambridge University Press, 1995), 204.

48 Florence B. Low, "The Reading of the Modern Girl," *Nineteenth Century* 59 (1906), 281.

49 Unsigned review, "Madame Bovary," *Saturday Review*, July 11, 1857, 40.

50 Trollope, *Autobiography*, 224–25.

51 David Vincent, *Bread, Knowledge and Freedom: A Study of Nineteenth-Century Working Class Autobiography* (London: Methuen, 1982). For bibliographic pointers to further autobiographies through which working-class reading habits may be traced, see John Burnett, David Vincent, and David Mayall, eds., *The Autobiography of the Working Class: an Annotated Critical Bibliography*, 3 vols. (Brighton: Harvester, 1984–89).

52 Annabel Grant-Duff Jackson, *A Victorian Childhood* (London: Methuen, 1932), 161.

53 Lady Frances Balfour, *Ne Obliviscaris: Dinna Forget*, 2 vols. (London: Hodder & Stoughton, 1930), 1:89.

54 Robert Louis Stevenson, "A Gossip on Romance" (1882), *Works*, XII:186.

55 Quoted in Jenny Uglow, *Elizabeth Gaskell. A Habit of Stories* (London: Faber and Faber, 1993), 45.

2

SIMON ELIOT

The business of Victorian publishing

For most of the eighteenth century the novel's physical form was highly variable: it might be published in one or two volumes, but it was equally likely to appear in three or more. Fanny Burney's *Camilla* (1796) was published in five volumes, Fielding's *Tom Jones* (1749) in six, Richardson's *Clarissa Harlowe* (1748) in seven, and Sterne's *Tristram Shandy* in nine volumes spread over eight years (1760–67). By the early nineteenth century things had started to stabilize, and the standard number of volumes for a first edition of a novel had settled down to three or four. Each volume was usually priced at five shillings or six shillings so a three-volume novel would normally retail at between fifteen shillings and eighteen shillings.

The author who changed all that was Sir Walter Scott. Scott's influence on both poetry and prose in the early nineteenth century was immense. He may be little read now, but in his time and for a few decades afterwards his poems and novels were probably more widely distributed and consumed than the work of any other serious contemporary writer. At the height of the Romantic movement, many more people read Scott's poetry than Wordsworth's. In terms of copies printed and copies read, Coleridge, Keats, and Shelley were negligible. Only Byron was sometimes able to rival Scott in terms of numbers of readers. It was later, during the Victorian period, that Wordsworth and Coleridge, Keats and Shelley acquired their belated and relative popularity.

Scott was to have a similar impact on the early-nineteenth-century taste for novels. Scott's long sequence of novels began with *Waverley* in 1814. This was published in three volumes but each volume was now priced at seven shillings, rather than five shillings or six shillings, thus raising the cost of a set of three volumes to twenty-one shillings, an almost unheard-of price. Scott and his publishers obviously knew their market for, despite the high price, his first novel went through eight editions in seven years (a total of 11,500 copies – a huge number for such an expensive book). Scott clearly had a captive market, and he and his publishers exploited it. By

1820 the newly published *Ivanhoe* cost the reader ten shillings a volume with the set retailing at thirty shillings.

A year later *Kenilworth* was published at ten shillings and sixpence a volume, its three-volume set selling for thirty-one shillings and sixpence, or a guinea and a half. It is difficult for modern readers, after nearly a century of inflation, to appreciate just how costly *Kenilworth* was in 1821. In the early nineteenth century most agricultural laborers earned between twelve shillings and eighteen shillings a week. Thirty shillings a week was a very comfortable working-class income. You could lead a modest middle-class life (with at least one servant) on about £150 per annum, or just under sixty shillings a week. A new Walter Scott novel in the 1820s cost more than most working-class men earned in a week, and half the gross weekly income of a modest middle-class family.

The price for a new novel in three volumes stuck at thirty-one shillings and sixpence. Between 1821 and 1894, despite inflation and deflation, criticism and attack, the price for a three-volume novel remained at thirty-one shillings and sixpence. Not all novels were published at this price, but for most of the nineteenth century the three-volume set, or three-decker as it was frequently called, was the fashionable, respectable, and high-status way of publishing the first edition of a novel. The publishing history of the novel for most of the nineteenth century is, at least in part, the history of how publishers, librarians, and readers adapted to, or got around, this price.

Price is, of course, a major determining factor in the distribution and consumption of novels. A high price means that few will buy and many will borrow. However, price is one thing, and cost to the individual reader is quite another. Two shillings may appear to be a low price for a reprinted novel, but if you are a junior clerk with only a few shillings a week to spare then two shillings might represent 20 percent or 30 percent of your weekly disposable income. Buying books also represented an opportunity lost. The Victorian period was one in which a whole host of new pastimes and entertainments became available to a much larger section of society: day trips (on the new railways), tourism, theaters, music halls, concerts, pubs, pleasure gardens. Unless you were very affluent and had lots of free time, in choosing to buy and read a book you were in practice giving up some of these alternative pleasures.

Book prices were rather fluid in the nineteenth century. Between 1829 and 1852 there had been an attempt by the publishers and booksellers to stabilize retail prices and stop large-scale discounting. In 1852 this practice was declared to be illegal, and all forms of retail price maintenance on books were abandoned.[1] From this time to the 1890s, most readers could expect a discount on the cover price of a book of between a penny and threepence in the shilling. In other words, a two-shilling novel might actually retail for as little as one shilling and sixpence. In the 1890s the publishing firm of Macmillan led the way in reintroducing retail price maintenance on books by devising the net book system, in which a "net" book was given a fixed price and then a standard discount on that was offered to booksellers. By 1901 this had become formalized under the "Net Book Agreement," a system that survived in the UK until the mid-1990s.

The era of free trade in books that ran from the 1850s to the 1890s happened to coincide with the great period of the Victorian novel, but there were deeper-seated economic reasons for this informal downward pressure on book prices. Between the mid-1860s and the mid-1890s the UK under-went a period of sustained deflation: that is, prices of many goods fell and the purchasing power of the pound actually rose. Roughly speaking, the pound increased in value by about 30 percent over these three decades. Any fixed price article, say a novel retailing at thirty-one shillings and sixpence in 1864 and at the same price in 1894, would in real terms be more expensive in 1894. The discounting of books during this crucial period for the Victorian novel could be seen as a way of compensating for this increase in the real cost of books.

In the twentieth century many of us are used to the idea of owning expensive items such as a house or a car. But in the nineteenth century renting, leasing and hiring expensive objects was much more common, even for the middle classes. Without building societies, installment plans or credit cards even many comfortably-off people simply could not afford to buy high-cost items outright. Thus the natural nineteenth-century response to an expensive object was to rent it. A three-decker novel was expensive so, on the whole, people did not buy it, they rented it. They were able to do this because of the circulating library. The circulating library had existed in one form or another for most of the eighteenth century, particularly in fashionable cities and spa towns, but it came into its own in the nineteenth century. The most famous of all was Mudie's. Charles Edward Mudie had opened his first "Select Library" in Southampton Row in Bloomsbury in 1842. The Mudie library system that the first branch gave rise to was to last for almost one hundred years, although its heyday was the mid- to late-Victorian period. There were many other circulating libraries but none was so closely allied to the three-decker novel both commercially and culturally. Despite having an enormous stock of non-fiction, over one-third of Mudie's's volumes were novels and, during our period at least, it was by the circulation of novels that Mudie's thrived. For an annual fee of a guinea a year, Mudie's subscribers were allowed to borrow one volume at a time.

This meant that, unless you paid a higher subscription that allowed three volumes to be taken out simultaneously, you would have to borrow and return three times to read a complete three-decker novel.

The combination of the expensive three-decker form and its tailor-made distributive system, the circulating library, imposed three restrictions on the novel: of price, of form and of content. We have already seen how the price shaped the way people read first book editions of many novels – by borrowing a volume at a time. But the three-volume form itself proved to be something of a Procrustean bed in terms of both form and content.

Novelists do, and always have, written at different lengths. Somehow these diversities had to be fitted into the three-decker system if it were to survive. Novels that were too short for three volumes tended to attract much lower prices from publishers. George Bentley, one of the largest publishers of novels during the period, offered Rhoda Broughton £1,200 for *Second Thoughts* (1880) if she could extend it to three volumes but only £750 if it ran to just two volumes.[2] When Emily Brontë published *Wuthering Heights* in 1847 it was bulked up to three volumes by its publisher Newby adding her sister Anne Brontë's novel *Agnes Grey* to it.

Mudie gave a very specific title to his library system: it always announced itself as "Mudie's Select Library," and the epithet "select" carried a great burden of meaning to his contemporaries. The minimum subscription of a guinea a year was not a huge sum, but it was enough to ensure that Mudie's was overwhelmingly middle class. But "select" applied to Mudie's stock as well as to his clientele. He inevitably acquired, and then cultivated, the role of censor. The exercise of this role also made commercial sense. In filtering out dangerous or corrupting literature, Mudie provided a safe and positive environment for middle-class women and children, always thought to be the most vulnerable. In providing a safe environment he stimulated custom. There was a similar happy confusion of a simple morality with solid profits among the publishers who relied on Mudie to buy their books. A three-decker novel he did not order would be one that struggled to clear its costs. A three-decker novel he did order was likely to make some sort of profit for the publisher, even if sales afterwards were disappointing. Quite naturally, when considering whether to issue a novel or not, many publishers or their readers would ask the question: "is there anything in this book that would deter Mudie from stocking it?"

Mudie was but a symptom of something that had been building throughout most of the nineteenth century. He gave these moral considerations of publishing a new financial significance. As the very successful late nineteenth-century writer Walter Besant observed, for a novelist risking exclusion from the Select Library it came down to "a question of money –

By the beginning of the nineteenth century there were at least two well-established forms of popular literature, that is, texts that sold extensively and continuously in large quantities. These were chapbooks and broadsheets. Neither was usually sold in a bookshop but instead hawked about the streets, fairs and markets by itinerant sellers. "Chapbook" means a book to be sold at a market (from the Old English "chepe" meaning market). Such books were usually little more than pamphlets of sixteen or thirty-two pages recounting the deeds of traditional and legendary heroes (such as Robin Hood). They usually sold for a penny or twopence. A broadsheet or broadside was a single, long sheet of paper, printed on one side only and giving an account of some exciting or horrendous event (a murder, an execution, or a monstrous birth). They were often "multi-genre" publications with a prose account, a poem on the subject (sometimes a song), and a woodcut illustration. They commonly sold for a halfpenny or a penny. Although not strictly fiction, many of these accounts were either fictitious or composite texts drawn from many traditional sources.

In the 1830s and 1840s a new working-class form emerged: a lengthy prose fiction serialized in one-penny or twopenny weekly parts. These were frequently concerned with adventures or with Gothic-like narratives. Many had the quality of soap operas in the sense that there was no close to the narrative; it just went on until the public lost interest. Some penny weekly novels in the 1850s and 1860s were serialized over four or more years. These implied a different readership: there was much more text and new text appeared relentlessly each week. Such a pattern of production could only be supported by an increasingly literate population.

Historians have always argued about literacy rates in the past, and will no doubt continue to do so. The main problem is evidence. The act of reading, unless it is a highly unusual one (such as the public readings of excerpts from his novels that Dickens gave in the 1850s and 1860s), does not leave any historical evidence behind it. Writing, of course, does, but until Hardwick's Marriage Act (1754) required all marriages to be recorded in a parish register by the signature of bride, groom, and two witnesses, there was no large-scale, consistent source of information on the ability to write. After 1754 historians can see the numbers of those who could sign their names in comparison with those who just made their mark. This is a crude technique for assessing literacy rates, but it is the best we have for the late eighteenth and early nineteenth centuries.

The biggest problem with this interpretation of the evidence is that it equates reading and writing. Until the late nineteenth century reading and writing were two distinct skills and were treated as such. Reading was taught first, and then writing. If you came from a low-income family, it might be able to afford to send you to school to learn to read, but could probably not afford to keep you there for another year or two to learn to write. By that time you would be old enough to work to supplement the family's income.

In most cases, until the last part of our period, reading and writing were not taught as good things in themselves. Reading and writing were skills that were taught for a purpose. Reading was usually taught to equip you for a job or, in Protestant countries, to save your soul. Most Protestant sects put a great stress on each individual achieving his or her own salvation through an understanding of God's word. God's word was in the Bible, so it was necessary to read it. Writing (and numeracy), however, were skills more associated with non-manual jobs: the filling of ledgers, the recording of bills, the writing of letters of credit, and so on. Most Sunday schools, which in the late eighteenth and early nineteenth century were the means by which many children from low-income families learned to read, would be concerned exclusively with reading as a means of spiritual exercise. To put it briefly, it is likely that more people could read than write, so any literacy study based on the signing of marriage registers is likely to underestimate reading rates. Literacy was not evenly spread in the nineteenth century. It was inevitably less common in low-income families. In Europe, literacy rates tended to be higher in Protestant than in Catholic countries. On the whole, more people were literate in towns than the countryside. Until around 1900 men were more likely to be literate than women.

Despite all the problems, by 1841 in England and Wales (until around 1900 literacy rates were always somewhat higher in Scotland) about 67 percent of men and 51 percent of women were able to sign a marriage register. By 1871 these figures were 81 percent and 73 percent respectively. By 1900 ninety-seven percent of both men and women signed the register. 1913 marked the first year in which over ninety-nine percent of both sexes could sign. The UK achieved a fully literate population just in time for everyone to be able to read the posted lists of the dead and missing in the First World War.

We ought to go back to 1850 for one important detail. In that year almost all marriages involving a middle-class groom were fully literate, that is, all four participants (bride, groom, both witnesses) could sign the register. But in marriages where the groom was an unskilled laborer only one marriage in thirteen had four literate signatories. However, in three-quarters of these unskilled laborer marriages, at least one participant could write. In other words, by 1850 at the latest, literacy and illiteracy were inextricably mixed socially. Most illiterates had at least one literate person in their immediate circle of family or friends. This is important because to experience text you do not have to read it. In the nineteenth century newspapers were read out loud in pubs, Dickens's novels were commonly read out loud to the assembled members of a family at home, and sometimes people were hired to read to workers in manual factories (such as cigar making) to keep them entertained. You did not need to be literate to enjoy literature.

Dickens was one of a number of authors who tried to break through the rigid system of the three-decker novel. He took the idea of novels in parts from the working-class form and went upmarket with it. Instead of weekly parts at a penny he offered monthly parts at a shilling. There was a strictly limited number of parts: twenty, which were serialized over nineteen months (the final part was a double issue at two shillings). Thus at the end of nineteen months the reader had an entire novel for a pound rather than thirty-one shillings and sixpence. It was still expensive, but the investment was spread. A shilling was still a middle-class price. However, even if the threepence a week that it represented was three times what most working-class fiction cost, it was still more within reach of those on lower incomes. In terms of sales, Dickens's novels certainly went much further down the social scale than most other serious novelists. Even so, Dickens's sales figures cannot begin to compare with the sales of genuine working-class texts. *Dombey and Son* (1846–48) sold on average about 32,000 copies of each monthly issue. Dickens's most successful novel, *The Old Curiosity Shop* (1840–41), was selling about 100,000 a month by the end of its run. But, in contrast, as early as 1828 a broadside, "Confession and Execution of William Corder," sold an estimated 1,166,000 copies.[8]

Dickens did publish novels in forms other than monthly parts. *Oliver Twist* (1837–39) was published in a shilling monthly magazine, *Bentley's Miscellany*; *Hard Times* (1854) was published as part of *Household Words*, a weekly twopenny magazine edited by Dickens himself; *A Tale of Two Cities* (1859) appeared in *All The Year Round*, another Dickens-edited weekly twopenny magazine; *Great Expectations* (1860–61) also appeared first in *All The Year Round*. Nevertheless, Dickens made monthly part-issue novels his own. No other novelist was able to make the cultural and economic success out of monthly parts that Dickens achieved, though many tried.

A whole host of minor or aspiring novelist attempted the form or something like it: William Harrison Ainsworth (*The Tower of London* 1840 [thirteen monthly parts], *Old Saint Paul's* 1841 [twelve monthly parts], *Mervyn Clitheroe* 1851–52 [twelve monthly parts]); Frederick

Marryat (*Poor Jack* 1840 [twelve monthly parts]); G. P. R James (*The Commissioner* 1841–42 [fourteen monthly parts]); Charles Lever (*Knight of Gwynne* 1846–47 [twenty monthly parts]); and R. S. Surtees (*Mr. Sponge's Sporting Tour* 1853 [thirteen monthly parts], *Ask Mama* 1858 [thirteen monthly parts], *Plain or Ringlets?* 1860 [thirteen monthly parts], *Mr Romford's Hounds* 1865 [twelve monthly parts]).

However, it was not just minor novelists who made this effort. Canonical authors also played variations on the Dickensian form: Thackeray (*Vanity Fair* 1847–48, *The History of Pendennis* 1848–50, *The Newcomes* 1853–55, *The Virginians* 1857–59 – the last three being in twenty-four one-shilling monthly parts each); and Trollope (*Orley Farm* 1861–62, *Can You Forgive Her?* 1864–65, *The Last Chronicle of Barset* 1867 [thirty-two sixpenny weekly parts], *He Knew He Was Right* 1868–69 [thirty-two sixpenny weekly parts], *The Way We Live Now* 1874–75 [twenty one-shilling monthly parts]). For most authors, this form was tempting and challenging mostly, one guesses, because Dickens had so obviously succeeded with it both culturally and financially. Many tried, but all finally abandoned it, leaving Dickens master of the field. When Dickens died in 1870 the form almost died out with him.[9]

Why did Dickens carry on with the form, long after most had given it up? Partly it was to do with Dickens's need to be reassured by an ever-present sense of an audience. The monthly or weekly serialized form kept a writer in frequent and regular contact with the audience he was addressing. The other reason was money. Successful serialization was a very effective way of generating income for a writer and sustaining that income over a long period. Quite apart from that, each part of a successful twenty monthly-part novel, such as *Dombey and Son*, would consist of thirty-two pages of the story plus a minimum of sixteen pages of advertisements. The "advertiser," as this supplement that surrounded and gave a context to the serialized novel was called, could itself be very profitable. Over the nineteen months of *Dombey and Son*'s run, the Dombey advertiser earned Dickens and his publishers, Chapman and Hall, £2,027 and one shilling.

There were various other ways of chopping up novels into affordable parts to be consumed over months or years. The most striking alternative was that adopted by George Eliot for *Middlemarch* (1871–72) which was published in eight separate volumes, one every two months, at five shillings each. This form, which had originally been suggested to Eliot's publisher John Blackwood by the novelist Bulwer Lytton as early as 1850,[10] was a way of coping with a text that was to be larger than even a long three-decker. To give authority to this attack on the three-decker G. H. Lewes, who acted as George Eliot's informal literary agent before there were such things as literary agents (John Forster did much the same job for Dickens), used Sterne's *Tristram Shandy* and the novels of Victor Hugo as parallels.[11] Despite misgivings, the experiment was a literary and commercial success, and Eliot's last novel, *Daniel Deronda* (1876), was issued in a similar form.

If the monthly or weekly issue of parts was not a form that was universally popular, what other means did novelists have at their disposal for dividing their novels up into manageable, cheaper units that could either bypass or defer the exorbitantly expensive three-decker form? The most common alternative was serialization not in a separate pamphlet but as part of a magazine or a newspaper. Such a form of serialization had considerable advantages. Apart from advertising revenue, it had most of the advantages of a part-issue novel without its vulnerability. A part-issue novel was on its own: if people did not like the story they would not buy it. Publishing a story in a newspaper or a magazine might reduce your public profile but it also hid you from direct observation. There were often other stories running in the periodical; there were certainly other things to entertain and distract the reader. If a story failed to be popular, readers might still buy the periodical for the rest of its content. Given these advantages, why were relatively few novels throughout the nineteenth century published serially in periodicals?

One explanation is that many periodicals and all newspapers were, for most of the earlier part of the nineteenth century, relatively expensive objects. Printed texts, particularly those that carried current news and comment had, since the English Revolution of the 1640s and even more so since the French Revolution of the 1790s, been regarded as potentially or actually subversive. During the period of political panic in Britain that followed the French Revolution and its Napoleonic aftermath, newspapers were subject to various forms of taxation that were designed essentially to price them out of the hands of the lower and potentially, it was thought, revolutionary classes.

In 1819 a Stamp Act was passed; this imposed a fourpence per copy tax on any periodical containing news or comment on the news which was published more frequently than every twenty-six days and cost less than sixpence. This was one of the notorious "taxes on knowledge," another one of which was on paper, which was at the rate of threepence a pound. A tax on newspaper advertisements of three shillings and sixpence each was a further restriction, for it reduced the indirect income of newspapers. The accumulated effect of these taxes was to ensure that newspapers carried an inflated price that meant that they were bought only by the affluent. The less well-off had either to hire them for a penny an hour from newswalks such as that run by the first W. H. Smith, or wait for them to be circulated through reading clubs days or weeks after their first publication. These taxes were progressively reduced and repealed during the second third of the nineteenth century: the newspaper tax was reduced to a penny in 1836 and finally abolished in 1855; tax on paper was finally abolished in 1861.

From the late 1830s, and coincidental with the rise of the mid-nineteenth-century novel, newspapers got cheaper and demand for them went up. As demand increased, newspaper owners had to find more efficient and effective means of production. It is not a coincidence that the first printing presses to be driven by steam rather than by human power were introduced to print *The Times* during the final years of the Napoleonic wars, when the demand for news, despite the taxes on knowledge, was huge.[12] Indeed, throughout the nineteenth century it was the newspaper trade rather than the book trade that pushed printing technology along: faster and faster powered machines, rotary printing, printing from a continuous roll (or web) of paper, and typesetting machines were all first introduced as ways of producing more newspapers more cheaply more quickly. The book trade finally benefited from many of these innovations, but that benefit was usually an accidental byproduct of the newspaper and periodical industry's expansion.

Even when taxation on newspapers was at its height after 1819, the demand for printed news kept on growing. Duty was collected by obliging each copy of a newspaper to be stamped, and the right to stamp had to be bought from a government office. This information about the number of stamps purchased can thus be used – for as long as it was recorded – to give some indication of demand for stamped newspapers. In 1801 16,085,085 stamps were issued. The imposition of a higher tariff on newspapers in 1814 and 1819 cut numbers in the period 1815–19 but by 1820 numbers of newspapers issued were 83 percent above the 1801 level. By 1824 the total was up to 26,308,003, an increase of 64 percent over the 1801 figures. The real surge came when newspaper tax was reduced to a penny in 1836. In 1837 demand for stamps rose to 53,897,926, more than three times the 1801 level. By 1846, when Charles Dickens began the *Daily News* as its editor, demand for stamps had risen to 78,298,125, a nearly fourfold increase over 1801.[13]

Although stamp duty on newspapers did restrict, or perhaps just slowed down, the rate of information exchange, it did have one advantage. Once the stamp was paid for, a newspaper could be sent free through the mail system, not just once but for as long as the paper survived. For this reason there was a great distribution and redistribution of used newspapers through the mails. Thus it is not that people did not have access to large quantities of print, but that their access was retarded. The way printed text was produced, printed, and distributed meant that there was a sort of "drag" or friction on information and entertainment: it was slowed down or delayed. This information inertia could have a significant effect on the readers of Victorian novels.

It has been observed that, at the height of the Romantic period, relatively few readers would have been reading Romantic poetry. This was because the owners of the copyrights of these works (commonly the publishers) usually wished to exhaust all the possibilities of sales of high-priced books before offering cheaper editions. Cheap editions of poetry were mainly restricted to poets originally published decades before the Romantics whose copyrights were, by that time, exhausted. Here again we can see price exerting a form of cultural friction that slowed down the transmission of new texts. While the price of novels was high, and while there was a longish delay between an expensive first edition and a much cheaper second edition, this same cultural drag can be seen in the reading of novels. It is only in the second half of our period that falling prices and the shortening of the gap between first and cheaper editions smooth out and speed up the transmission of new literature to a wider public. To put it another way: until the latter half of the Victorian period, the overwhelming majority of the reading public – who were too poor to read expensive new texts – read cheaper, older texts. The cultural environment we are used to in which new books are immediately and widely available in public libraries or soon afterwards in paperback, where the transmission of new texts is hardly impeded at all by cultural friction, is a creation of the late Victorian publishing industry.

Once newspapers and magazines were finally and fully liberated from fiscal restraints after 1861 their rate of growth was remarkable. Of course, with the abolition of taxes we lose information about the issue of stamps. However, we do have data about the number of periodical titles in existence in each year between 1864 and the end of Victoria's reign.[14] In 1864 *Mitchell's Newspaper Press Directory* recorded 1,768 titles; by the time of Victoria's Golden Jubilee in 1887 this figure had risen to 3,597 and by her death in 1901 there were no less than 4,914 periodical titles being published in the UK.

What must have been obvious to any aspiring novelist by mid-century was that Victoria's reign was not, in publishing terms at least, going to be characterized by the book, but rather by the newspaper and the magazine. This is confirmed by a census of production taken just after the end of our period. In 1907 printed books contributed about 5.3 percent to the total net value of the printing and related industries. In contrast, daily newspapers, non-daily newspapers and magazines contributed 28.2 percent.[15] The smart money went to the periodicals and so, on the whole, did the novelists. For every one successful novelist who first published in three-decker form or in weekly or monthly parts, there were many who would see their novel first appear in serialized form in a magazine or a local or a national newspaper.

Anthony Trollope, in terms both of selecting publishers and choosing publishing forms for his novels, was one of the most promiscuous novelists of the period. He experimented and shopped around, looking to maximize his popularity and his income. Indeed, the posthumous publication of his *An Autobiography* (1883) seriously damaged his contemporary reputation with its stress on authorship as a standard middle-class profession and the careful calculation of his income novel by novel. As such a self-conscious professional writer, Trollope's publishing history will give a good indication of the relative attractiveness of different means of getting a novel out into the public domain.

Trollope's novel-writing career stretched from *The Macdermots of Ballycoran* (1847) to *The Landleaguers* (1882–83). Using the final aboli-tion of the "taxes on knowledge" (1861) as a dividing line, we can see the shift in publishing methods before and after the periodical press was fully liberated. In the period 1847–61 Trollope published eleven full-length novels. Of these, nine were published directly in book form, overwhel-mingly as three-decker novels (eight out of the nine). One, *Orley Farm*, was first published in monthly shilling parts; and one, *Framley Parsonage* (1860–61) was serialized in a periodical – the *Cornhill*.

Between 1862–82 Trollope published some thirty-four full-length novels. Three were published directly in book form, seven were issued as various types of part novels (some in monthly one-shilling parts, others in weekly sixpence parts) and no less than twenty-five appeared first as serialized novels in a variety of periodicals including: *Cornhill Magazine*, *Fortnightly Review*, *Blackwood's Magazine*, *Macmillan's Magazine*, *Good Words*, *Graphic*, *Temple Bar*, *All The Year Round*, *Manchester Weekly Times*, and *Life*. As periodicals became cheaper and more widely distrib-uted, so Trollope gravitated ever more closely to them.

In practice, serialization did not inhibit later publication as a three-decker novel: indeed, by the 1870s and 1880s it was commonly the case that a novel, serialized in twelve monthly episodes in a magazine, would also appear as a three-decker when its run in the magazine was about three-quarters through. For instance, Walter Besant's novel *All Sorts and Condi-tions of Men* was serialized between January and December 1882 in Chatto and Windus's journal *Belgravia*. It was published by Chatto as a three-decker novel in October 1882, so those who wanted to know how it ended as soon as possible would be forced to borrow it from a circulating library rather than wait for its serialized conclusion in the December issue of *Belgravia*.

Although many observers have regarded the three-decker novel as the creature of the circulating libraries, and particularly of Mudie's, who usually took many more sets than did his rivals, there is a strong argument for suggesting that the three-volume novel was of equal significance to the publishers who churned them out. Indeed, we should remember that it was not the publishers who finally killed off this unwieldy form in 1894 – most of them were happy to go on producing three-deckers *ad nauseam* – it was the circulating libraries themselves who delivered the *coup de grâce*.

As part of a service industry, nineteenth-century publishers did not need a significant amount of capital as printers or papermakers or binders did (all three of whom needed to invest considerable capital in machinery and raw materials). Publishers would have to pay all three types of producer eventually, but not immediately on the publication of a novel. Commonly printers, papermakers, and binders would extend credit facilities to a publisher that would mean that bills might be settled months, or even up to a year, after the debts were incurred. There appears to have been a web of credit with the publisher sitting comfortably at the center of it. The publisher could get the paper, order the printing, and get the binding done on credit. He would then sell the 500–1,000 sets of the three-decker novel almost immediately to the circulating libraries. Being commonly a matter of fashion and immediate public demand, the three-decker was not a long-term, slow or steady seller: it would sell immediately or hardly at all. Even with the 50 percent discounts on the cover price required by the main libraries, a three-decker novel was still being sold at fifteen shillings, substantially above the cost of its manufacture. It is very likely that a publisher of a three-decker novel could get more than its production costs back before many of the bills had to be paid.

Thus, for the majority of novel publishers, the circulating library provided a safe, easy, and quick market for inflated-price goods. Even a third-rate novel, one that was never going to attract enough buyers to go into another edition, might nevertheless do more than clear its costs for a publisher. Many of the characters in George Gissing's novel *New Grub Street* (1891), including Reardon, the central figure, bumped along the bottom of the literary market by producing one or two three-deckers a year, most of which never achieved any other form and died almost the moment they were born, like Reardon's own sickly child.

For more successful novels, whether initially published as a part work, serialized in a periodical, or issued as a three-decker, a first edition was only the beginning of what might be a long and complicated publishing history. When the demand for that novel at the circulating library or in parts started to diminish, the publisher looked to the possibility of bringing the novel out in a single volume at a price that would make it buyable, at least by the sort of middle-class reader who would have been a subscriber to Mudie's. In the earlier part of our period the first cheap, single-volume reprint of a novel might have taken a number of years to appear and, when it did, might well have appeared in a reprint series that included older works regarded as "standard" or "classic" novels. Such series normally retailed at about five or six shillings. For instance, Colburn and Bentley's "Standard Novels" series, begun in 1831, had by 1855 expanded to a collection of 126 volumes which included works by Jane Austen, Fenimore Cooper, Marryat, Bulwer Lytton and Frances Trollope.

By the early 1850s, however, another form of cheap reprint was emerging. Printed matter has always been a very sensitive barometer of technical change (think of the huge number of magazines currently available on computers or mountain biking). In the 1840s and 1850s the new technology that was transforming Britain was the railway, and the printed word responded. The seasick-making motion of even the best mail coaches was now being replaced by smoother, better-lit travel in the compartment of a train. This was a much more hospitable environment for reading. Sometime between December 15–29, 1848, the publishing firm of George Routledge issued James Fenimore Cooper's *The Red Rover*. This was bound in boards covered with glazed paper on which was printed a picture. The book was small, easily slipped into a greatcoat pocket or handbag – and cheap. The Fenimore Cooper cost just a shilling. Routledge's "Railway Library" series survived until 1899 during which 1,277 titles were issued in it. Many other publishers followed suit in the 1850s and 1860s, and this cheap issue adopted what became a very common format: a book roughly 17.5 by 12.2 centimeters, covered often in yellow-glazed boards, carrying an illustration (frequently of a rather racy sort) on the front cover and commonly a picture-based advertisement on the back. Most cost between a shilling and two shillings and sixpence. Generically they became known as "railway novels" or "yellowbacks." They were the airport lounge paperbacks of their day.

Below the cheap yellowback were the first paperback novels. Paper-covered novels selling at a shilling and, even more significantly, at sixpence were a phenomenon also of the 1850s. Blackwood, Nathaniel Cooke, C. H. Clarke, and Bradbury & Evans all issued paperbacks at these prices, though it was the 1860s that saw the real paperback revolution with reprint novels series in paperback issuing from Chapman & Hall, John Camden Hotten, and George Routledge, who, in 1867, started a new series, "sixpenny novels," in which, yet again, Fenimore Cooper's novels led the way. Editions at two shillings or under from mid-century put more and more downward pressure on the first cheap reprint price of five or six shillings. By the 1870s and 1880s the first reprint price of many publishers had slipped, commonly to three shillings and sixpence.

We should not be surprised at finding novels written in the USA, such as Cooper's, featuring frequently as leading titles in these cheaper series. Before the US Congress passed the Platt–Simonds Bill (often called the Chace Act) in 1891, there was no legally binding copyright arrangement between the UK and the USA. British authors were frequently reprinted in the USA, and US authors in Britain, without any payment whatsoever. Even when some private arrangement had been made between publishers on both sides of the Atlantic, payments were usually very modest.

We should remind ourselves that most of the titles so far discussed were aimed mostly at the broad and growing middle-class audience. What of the even more rapidly growing literate working-class market? The yellowback format seems to have been a remarkably flexible vehicle both economically and culturally. It could function as a very cheap version of a high-status novel, but it could also be used as the first edition of a popular story aimed at a less sophisticated market. Many of the earliest detective novels (some even featuring female detectives) and lots of adventure stories were first published as yellowback series in the 1860s and 1870s. Indeed, it is possible to see the beginnings of the genre marketing of novels ("Mystery," "Detection," "Romance") in the way these yellowbacks were promoted. Yellowbacks could even flirt with faintly risqué novels concerning the deeds of stylish prostitutes; these could use the tradition of the come-hither covers commonly sported by even the most respectable yellowback novels for their own purposes.

From the 1860s to the 1890s there were a number of publications and series aimed at getting fiction of one sort or another down to those with the shallowest of pockets. In the 1860s the publisher John Dicks, who had started his career and made a lot of his money publishing the popular author G. W M. Reynolds (including his *The Mysteries of the Court of London* which ran from 1849–56), brought out Scott's novels at threepence a paperback volume. In 1884 his firm started the "Dicks's English Library of Standard Works," which offered the reader a compilation of up to five novels in a single paperback book retailing at one shilling and sixpence. In 1896, soon after the collapse of the three-decker novel, George Newnes began his "Penny Library of Famous Books," from which the reader could buy novels by Scott, Marryat, Reade, and Dickens for a penny (although the longest novels might cost up to threepence). It is perhaps significant that the innovator of the cheapest novel series was a newspaper and magazine entrepreneur, not a traditional book publisher.

By the 1880s there was a standard pattern of forms and prices through which a successful middle-class novel would evolve: from periodical serialization, through three-decker, through first cheap reprint at three shillings and sixpence, yellowback at two shillings, and paperback at sixpence. Not every novel went through every stage, and unsuccessful novels often got no further than the three-decker, but for a popular novel this system meant that it could exploit price elasticity to the full and, over its life, explore a range of markets. Our modern publishing system has nothing to compare with the price differential offered by the various incarnations of the Victorian novel. At best a paperback edition of a modern hardback book is about one-third the price of its first edition. But a first cheap reprint at six shillings represented less than one-fifth (19.05 percent) of the three-decker price. A first reprint at three shillings and sixpence was just over one-tenth (11.11 percent) of the price of a first book edition. A novel that then went into a yellowback edition at two shillings represented 6.35 percent of the original price. If the novel emerged as a paperback retailing at sixpence, it would end up costing only 1.59 percent of its original cover price. These sorts of percentage reductions are, in the late twentieth century, more reminiscent of the economics of the electronic than the book industry.

Over how long a period did this progressive price reduction occur? How long, in other words, was a Victorian novel's commercial life? This could vary from a novel that was never serialized and just crept into the circulating libraries for a short, fitful existence (rather like films that today are not distributed but go straight to video), to famous and canonical novels that have never been out-of-print since first publication. An average novel, if there were ever such a thing, would be likely to have a longer but less intense life in the earlier part of the century, and a shorter but more intense one in the later Victorian period. On the whole, novels waited longer in the 1840s and 1850s to go into cheaper editions than they did later in the century. This leisurely pace ensured that the circulating libraries were able fully to exploit their customers' demands without facing any cheap opposition. It made sure that the copyright owner (commonly the publisher) squeezed every last ounce of profit out of the expensive forms before moving downmarket. In the earlier Victorian period some novels waited five or ten years, or even longer, before they emerged in a cheaper form.

By the 1860s this pattern was beginning to change. More and more publishers were issuing first cheap reprints faster and faster. The gap was commonly down to a year or two, and as the decades passed that gap between the issue of a three-decker and its first cheap reprint at three shillings and sixpence, five shillings or six shillings got narrower and narrower. In January 1863, for instance, one of the most popular novelists of the period, Miss M. E. Braddon, issued her latest novel, *Aurora Floyd*, through the publisher Tinsley at thirty-one shillings and sixpence. Tinsley then reissued it as a single-volume reprint at six shillings in August of the same year, a mere seven months after first publication. In May 1880 Chapman and Hall issued Trollope's *The Duke's Children* at thirty-one shillings and sixpence; by November 1880 it was on sale in a single volume at three shillings and sixpence. As the 1870s gave way to the 1880s and then the 1890s, the reprint gap between first edition and first cheap edition narrowed, and the price at which these first reprints were being offered fell.[16]

It has been calculated that it would be extremely difficult for Mudie's and any other circulating library to make a profit on lending three-decker novels unless they had between nine months and a year of circulation without competition.[17] By the 1870s and 1880s this was clearly no longer the case for a significant number of novels. This must have been a particular problem for Mudie as his library system was more dependent on the three-decker novel than most others. Certainly by 1884 Mudie was complaining to the publisher (and Mudie shareholder) George Bentley that "not one in twelve of the 3 vol. novels pays its way."[18] This may have been a problem for Mudie's, but it certainly was not for the average novel publisher. With this new system of a narrow reprint gap between first edition and first cheap edition the publisher could, apparently, have his cake and eat it too. He could gain the security and quick return of the three-decker and then, using the publicity generated by the circulation of the title through Mudie's and Smith's, launch a cheap edition to cash in on the book-buying as well as the book-borrowing public. With such a convenient and profitable system on offer, it will come as no surprise that when, in 1864, Mudie's was threatened with bankruptcy, publishers flocked to his support and became the major shareholders in the circulating library company.[19]

One of the reasons that encouraged publishers to print novels more and more rapidly was, of course, the desire to realize their investment in the novel as quickly as possible. It has been pointed out that a three-decker version of a novel could probably pay for itself almost immediately, but unless it was a rip-roaring success at the libraries, it probably would not generate huge profits in and by itself. One of the problems was that, technically speaking, the three-decker was a one-off. The type for a novel would be set up by hand, and the novel would be directly printed from this type. Commonly 500–1,000 sets would be printed, although titles from popular authors might go as high as 1,500 sets. Apart from exceptional cases, the type would then be broken up, cleaned, and put back in the type trays from which it came (this process is called "distributing the type"). A publisher would then have to decide whether the popularity of the novel would justify a cheap reprint. If he did so decide, then the entire novel would have to be set again, this time for publication in a single volume. However, by the 1850s at the latest, this type would probably not be printed from. Instead it would be stereotyped: that is, each page of set type would have a plaster cast made of it. Molten metal would then be poured into that cast, creating a single metal plate from which the page could be printed. The original movable type could then be distributed for use elsewhere. As type was quite expensive and, except for very large or affluent printers, in short supply, this meant that printers could maximize their use of movable type. It also meant that they did not have to store huge settings of heavy and vulnerable movable type just in case another print-run was required. Instead they could store the sturdy stereoplates or even the plaster casts from which they were made. By the 1870s it was common for a publisher to order the three-decker and the first cheap reprint edition from his printer at the same time. In other words, by the time the three-decker edition had begun circulation, the publisher had the stereoplates ready for the first cheap edition. The temptation for the publisher to use them as soon as he could in order to recoup the investment in stereotyping as quickly as possible must have been difficult to resist.

The way novelists were paid during the Victorian period may also have had an effect on the process of distributing and selling novels. Of course, the most popular and most distinguished writers could dictate their terms to publishers. Dickens, after some early and traumatic experiences (partly of his own making), kept a very firm control over his books, often negotiating deals (which got tougher and tougher as his fame increased) edition by edition. But most novelists were not like Dickens. Even middling authors could lead rather hand-to-mouth existences and those at the bottom of the pile led lives of quiet desperation. The majority of novelists were not able financially or socially to negotiate from a position of strength. Although the concept of copyright, of the author owning literary property rights, had been enshrined in English law since the copyright Act of Queen Anne in 1710, in practice most authors sold this right as soon as they could out of necessity, desperation, or ignorance.

By the Victorian period there were roughly four ways in which an author could turn literary property into much-needed cash. The first was publishing "on commission": this meant that the author paid the publisher as an agent to organize production and publication; he or she also paid all the printing, binding, and other costs. The advantage was that if the book were a success the author could take all the profits. The extreme form of this was when the author was charged for virtually everything and got nothing back – "vanity" publishing was as common in the nineteenth century as now. The second was "half profits": in this the author offered the manuscript as capital and the publisher invested the cost of production and distribution. The publisher would periodically deliver an account to the author in which the profit, if any, was calculated and divided equally between them. This would be fine with an honest and efficient publisher, but a less principled one could run up all sorts of fictitious costs so that the profit would apparently vanish. The third was by "outright sale": in this the author was offered at the beginning a lump sum for the copyright of the book. In certain cases this would be an unconditional sale, in others it might be for a fixed number of years (usually five) after which copyright reverted to the author. Given that many authors would be on the bread line or near to it, the temptation of ready cash would often be irresistible. The fourth and final method was the newest and one of the most uncommon, "royalty": this had originated in the USA but by the end of the nineteenth century was beginning to percolate through to the UK. A royalty deal usually consisted of an arrangement either for a number of editions or a number of years during which the author would allow publication in return for the publisher paying the author a certain percentage of the cover price of each copy of the book sold. Half-profits and outright sale were the most common arrangement between publishers and novelists. Usually half-profits were calculated and paid either half-yearly or yearly. It was therefore in both the publisher's and author's interest to push ahead with the issue of the first cheap reprint as soon as possible, particularly if the publisher wished to publish the author's next book. This was even more emphatically the case if the publisher had bought the author's literary property outright. The sooner the publisher could increase turnover on the novel, the sooner he could recoup his investment in author fees.

Certain publishers, most notably Chatto and Windus, had a system in which they bought full book rights for the initial five years of a book's life. This arrangement put a high premium on the publisher running through as many stages of a novel's life as possible so as to maximize profits on his time-limited investment. If, at the end of the five years, the publisher could claim that the market for a particular novel was virtually exhausted, then he could buy all the remaining rights cheaply. Walter Besant, a very popular novelist of the 1880s and 1890s, might receive £1,200–£1,500 pounds for five years' book rights on a novel. (By the late nineteenth century serial rights of a novel were often worth as much if not more than book rights and were frequently sold separately.) After five years Besant was rarely offered much more than £150 for all remaining rights. Within those first five years Chatto would have commonly produced a three-decker edition, a "Piccadilly novel" edition (at three shillings and sixpence) and a "popular" edition (at two shillings) of a Besant novel and, by the 1890s, might well also have issued a sixpenny paperback as well.

Copyrights were also traded between publishers, and publishers would also offer to buy, at a cheap rate, copyrights of older novels from their author owners. Chatto, who launched his firm in 1873, invested wisely in a large number of copyrights of novels (sometimes paying only twenty-five pounds or thirty pounds a piece for them) during the 1870s and issued these in three shillings and sixpence and two shilling editions in print runs of tens of thousands.

Most print-runs were rather modest. Publishers were cautious and tended to prefer a larger number of shorter print-runs to a smaller number of longer print-runs. With stereoplates available for most cheap editions and with these plates usually being stored by printers, the overhead costs of ordering a new print-run were not great, so most publishers – not wishing to have large quantities of unsold stock – tended to err on the side of caution. Chatto and Windus, for instance, might order no more than 2,000 or 3,000 copies a time of a three shilling and sixpence reprint. Two shilling-reprints might well be printed at 4,000 to 6,000 at a time, but even these might, near the end of a novel's commercial life, have runs as low as 500 (for three shillings and sixpence) or 1,000 (for two shillings). Sixpenny paperbacks, at least by the 1890s, were somewhat different. With their coarse, newsprint paper, their small type in double columns, they were obviously being produced on fast, high-volume, newspaper and magazine presses, and these were not economic at very low print-runs. Commonly Chatto had print runs for sixpenny editions that ran from 25,000 right up to 100,000 copies, although print-runs as low as 10,000 have been recorded.

Certain novels were among the great bestsellers of the period, though it is doubtful whether any of them got anywhere near to the Bible or the New Testament, for these were printed in their tens of millions during Victoria's reign. However, a significant number of these religious texts were not produced for commercial reasons and they were frequently distributed at cost or below it, and sometimes for free. Nevertheless, production figures are impressive. To take the three-year period between 1848 and 1850: the queen's printer in England, the queen's printer in Scotland, Oxford

University Press, and Cambridge University Press between them produced 2,163,219 New Testaments and 2,471,055 Bibles. The work of fiction that got closest to these figures, at least in the short-term, was Harriet Beecher Stowe's *Uncle Tom's Cabin* (1852) which sold around 1,500,000 copies in its first spectacular year.[20] It was calculated that Dickens's *Pickwick Papers* sold, in book form alone, some 800,000 copies between 1836 and 1879.[21] A more modest bestseller would be represented by Mrs. Henry Wood's *The Channings*, which sold 180,000 copies between 1862 and 1898.[22] Walter Besant's most successful solo novel was *All Sorts and Conditions of Men* (1882). In total it sold 271,500 copies between its first publication and 1920, including 160,000 sixpenny paperback copies.

These large sales would not have been possible without the series of technical revolutions in printing and papermaking that run through the nineteenth century: the invention of the Fourdrinier papermaking machine in the 1800s; the introduction of powered presses in the 1810s; the extensive use of stereotype (particularly after the 1850s when a new, light robust substance called "flong" replaced the brittle, cumbersome plaster molds); the development of rotary printing in the 1870s; the development of type-casting machines in the 1860s and 1870s; and the development of hot metal type-composing machines in the 1880s and 1890s. All these innovations had a powerful general effect on book production. Just occasionally, however, a new technology could have a more precise impact on the way a novel was produced.

Until type-casting machines became widespread in the later nineteenth century, most type was hand-cast. This was an expensive and slow process. Very few printers could afford to set up a whole novel in type because they could not afford to have that much type locked up in the production of just one book. This meant that a novel had to be set up in type, proofed, and printed a few sheets at a time. The type would then be broken up and reused for the next few sheets, and so on. In other words, the form and content of a novel would be fixed as it went along, and the beginning could not be corrected in the light of the end. With the revolution in type-casting, which brought in cheap and plentiful movable type, the novelist had the chance to work with the entire novel before it was printed. This allowed the concern for tightly structured plots, consistent characterization, and avoidance of digression which so characterizes the novels at the end of our period (most notably in writers such as Henry James) to develop. The "loose baggy monsters" of the mid-Victorian period that James so disparaged were a product of the available technology, just as his own were.[23]

Novels, and fiction generally, were only part of the astonishing revolution in print communications that extended throughout the nineteenth century. How important a part? All discussions of particular genres in the past are bedeviled by both inadequate statistical information and problems of definition. What constitutes a novel? What is a work of fiction? How do you distinguish a story written for older children from a story written for a semi-literate adult? The Victorians who compiled subject lists of newly published books finally gave up, and lumped all forms of fiction and juvenile literature into one category, so this is the category that we have to use. A list covering the major books published in the UK between 1814 and 1846 indicated that about 16.2 percent of the catalogued titles fell in to this broad fiction category. By the 1870s this proportion had gone up to 23.3 percent, and in the 1880s it rose again to 26 percent. In the last decade of our period, the 1890s, fiction and juvenile books were claiming 31.5 percent of the total titles produced in the UK. In the year of Queen Victoria's death that percentage had risen to nearly one-third of all titles (33 percent).[24]

In 1850 William Ewart piloted the Public Libraries Act through Parliament. This allowed most local authorities to raise a halfpenny rate (later increased to a penny) to set up public lending libraries. There was no rush to do this, but by the 1870s momentum was increasing and in the period between Dickens's death and Victoria's hundreds of public lending libraries were established. Many were set up under the sound liberal principle that reading was the best form of self-education and that once you were exposed to the best you would shun the worst. There was a long-running debate among public librarians and those paying for the books as to whether or not fiction should be stocked at all. After all, the more puritanical argued, at best it was frivolous and at worst it was akin to lying. However, the liberal argument won out. It was that, although readers might start out reading fiction, they would naturally gravitate to weightier and more serious matters as their taste matured.

Readers, as they have done throughout recorded history, resolutely refused to fit into the educational pattern planned out for them. They went on demanding the novels of Ouida and Miss Braddon and did not move on to read Gibbon and Darwin. A survey of over eighty public library catalogues issued between 1883 and 1912 has revealed that, in terms of numbers of copies held, Miss Braddon, Mrs. Henry Wood, and Ouida remained the novelists most in demand.[25] Since then the names have changed and the subjects have become racier but the preference for popular fiction among the reading public has not changed. In that sense, the activities of the fiction industry and its readers in the nineteenth century were a good rehearsal for developments in our own and, no doubt, succeeding centuries.

NOTES

1 See James J. Barnes, *Free Trade in Books* (Oxford: Clarendon Press, 1964).
2 Guinevere L. Griest, *Mudie's Circulating Library and the Victorian Novel* (Bloomington: Indiana University Press, 1970), 55.
3 *New Review* 2 (January 1890), 6–12.
4 George Moore, *Literature at Nurse, or Circulating Morals* (London: Vizetelly & Co., 1885), 18.
5 *Ibid.*, 18.
6 *Ibid.*, 4.
7 Griest, *Mudie's Circulating Library and the Victorian Novel*, 172.
8 Richard D. Altick, *The English Common Reader: A Social History of the Mass Reading Public 1800–1900* (Chicago: University of Chicago Press, 1957), 382.
9 One of the last novels to be published in this form was William Black's *Sunrise* (1880–81).
10 John A. Sutherland, *Victorian Fiction: Writers, Publishers, Readers* (London: Macmillan, 1995) 109–11.
11 John A. Sutherland, *Victorian Novelists and Publishers* (Chicago: University of Chicago Press, 1976), 191–92.
12 John Walter, the editor and owner of *The Times*, introduced two Koenig steam-driven presses on the night of November 28–29, 1814. These machines were each capable of producing 1,100 printed sides an hour as opposed to the 250 sides that an iron manual press, such as the Stanhope (first used around 1800), could print.
13 See Simon Eliot, *Some Patterns and Trends in British Publishing* (London: The Bibliographical Society, 1994), 147.
14 *Ibid.*, 148.
15 *Ibid.*, 105, 157.
16 Simon Eliot, "The Three-Decker Novel and its First Cheap Reprint, 1862–94," *The Library*, sixth series, 7, 1 (March 1985), 38–53.
17 Simon Eliot, "Bookselling by the Backdoor: Circulating Libraries, Booksellers, and Book Clubs 1876–1966," *A Genius for Letters* (Winchester: St. Paul's Bibliographies, 1996), 152.
18 Quoted in Griest, *Mudie's Circulating Library*, 168.
19 See David Finkelstein, "The Secret: British Publishers and Mudie's Struggle for Economic Survival," *Publishing History* 34 (Autumn 1993).
20 Altick, *The English Common Reader*, 384.
21 *Ibid.*, 383.
22 *Ibid.*, 385.
23 See Allan C. Dooley, *Author and Printer in Victorian England* (Charlottesville: University of Virginia Press, 1992).
24 Eliot, *Some Patterns and Trends*, 127–29.
25 Simon Eliot, "A Measure of Popularity: The Public Library Holdings of Twenty-Four Popular Authors, 1883–1912," *History of the Book – On Demand Series*, no. 2 (Bristol: HOBODS, 1992).

3

LINDA M. SHIRES

The aesthetics of the Victorian novel: form, subjectivity, ideology

Lord Jim (1900) by Joseph Conrad and *Wuthering Heights* (1847) by Emily Brontë, published fifty-three years apart, ostensibly have little to do with each other aesthetically or ideologically. One is written by a man; one by a woman. One by an *émigré* and one by a native Briton. One is overtly a text of diasporic imperialism and the other a text of domestic colonizing. One is constructed leisurely in the impressionist-realist mode, with a fast-paced romantic, even gothic, finale; the other is a dramatically bifurcated text, a domestic hybrid of romance and realism. Conrad's is usually classified as modernist; Brontë's is classified as Victorian. While *Lord Jim* is considered aesthetically typical of its historical moment, *Wuthering Heights* is considered an aberration.

Yet these two novels, which may be said temporally to frame the Victorian novel despite its official beginning a decade before *Wuthering Heights* and despite the very real difference between them, can be connected through issues of form, subjectivity, and ideology. The topic for this chapter is, of course, large and even unwieldy. It reminds me, in its scope, of what the words "Victorian novel" usually summon up in our minds: huge casts of characters, complex plots, cliffhanger sections due to serialization, even three-decker novels. By using *Lord Jim* and *Wuthering Heights* as a window on aesthetic and ideological transformations in the era's fiction, I am concerned to trace permutations and innovations in the Victorian novel and to show how it both registers historic pressures and alters aesthetically under them.

The main subject matter of the Victorian novel is the relation between self and society, a topic that can be explored in many different ways. My interest lies in how, formally, the novel takes the emphasis on self and individualism that characterizes the Romantic period and shows it to be pressured by increasingly powerful ideologies of capitalism. I will not pursue this idea thematically or historically, however, as has been done briefly some years ago by Terry Eagleton in *Criticism and Ideology*. Rather,

I am interested in the relation of aesthetics to hermeneutics and epistemology – how form establishes varying degrees of knowledge or doubt and
how it alters in its demands of a reader whom it is ideologically shaping.
Instead of dwelling on a heroine's relation to her community, say, or even
on the historical explanation of the rise of an ideology of capitalism, I am
interested in noting how pressures of ideology begin to change radically the
form of the Victorian novel. For, in the last decades of the century, the
Victorian novel becomes aesthetically more impressionistic and more self-
conscious with its inscriptions of artistic practice and issues of communication.

Let me start at the far end of my frame with Conrad's novel. "I cannot
say I had ever seen him distinctly – not even to this day, after I had my last
view of him," confides Marlow to his tiny and ever diminishing audience in
Conrad's haunting *Lord Jim*, "but it seemed to me that the less I understood
the more I was bound to him in the name of that doubt which is the
inseparable part of our knowledge. I did not know so much more about
myself."[1] This striking passage could be a key to any novel, in the sense
that the reader's and narrator's desire to move through mysteries towards
knowledge serves as the propelling, hermeneutic impulse of reading fiction.
However, Marlow's highly self-conscious emphasis on epistemology,
through mystery, partial views, and doubt, as ties that bind audience
members to each other, registers an important development in the aesthetic
of fiction and in the ideology of the subject at the end of one century and at
the beginning of the next. In a sense, Marlow's statement is almost
desperate. We as individuals have no sure grasp on truth and little binds us
together in a community of readers except doubt and mystery.

Conrad's Preface to *The Nigger of the Narcissus*, published in 1897,
elaborates on his aesthetic credo as it is practiced in his novels. His desire,
primarily, is "to make you hear, to make you feel – it is above all to make
you *see*. That – and no more, and it is everything." Yet, as Virginia Woolf
and other high modernists would do later, Conrad goes on to isolate the
temporal moment and impressionistic fragment as significantly impregnated with meaning: "The task approached in tenderness and faith is to
hold up unquestioningly, without choice and without fear, the rescued
fragment before all eyes . . . it is to disclose its inspiring secret." If one is
fortunate, hopes Conrad, one can "awaken in the hearts of the beholders
that feeling of unavoidable solidarity . . . which binds men to each other
and all mankind to the visible world."[2] We should not, however, assume
from this credo that Conrad believes in a simplistic theory of easily
ascertainable meaning, as his equivalent statement in *Heart of Darkness*
(1902) affirms. As the narrator explains, when describing how Marlow

tells a sea yarn to his small audience on board ship: "to him the meaning of an episode was not inside like a kernel but outside, enveloping the tale which brought it out only as a glow brings out a haze, in the likeness of one of these misty halos that sometimes are made visible by the spectral illumination of moonshine."[3] Conrad recognizes reality, then, as multi-layered and covered in moving mists; he understands character as unpredictable and unable to be fully known. Perhaps even more central, he finds partial visions just as important and more truthful than omniscience. Indeed a collection of partial views may offer more than a single view, which must itself always be partial, even if it believes itself to be whole. What other authors might have understood as utterly fragmenting, Conrad views as a challenge. In his belief system, doubt serves to bind us all together.

Still, with such a treatment of vision, epistemology, mystery, and form, in the service of an encompassing solidarity, *Lord Jim* and other novels by Conrad, such as *The Secret Agent* (1907) or *Heart of Darkness* finely register a version of what has been called the crisis of nineteenth-century realism. As I will later suggest, realism, the dominant mode of representation and the dominant reading practice of the Victorian era, supposes a privileged epistemological point of view from which both knowledge and judgment can be truthfully and precisely issued to establish consensus among implied author, narrator, and reader. Yet in the last decades of the Victorian era, especially, an ideological break occurs which is mirrored in the novel's aesthetic, particularly in areas of point of view, the representation of reality, the construction of character, and the relationship to the audience.

Illustrating less certainty about the accuracy of observation and thus revising the treatment of subject matter, Conrad's fellow-novelists such as Thomas Hardy and even Rudyard Kipling, place a heavier reliance on impressions or possible views and on gaining truth from diverse vantage points, rather than relying on either one sure and ostensibly non-implicated point of view or on conventional ways of knowing. Responding to the changing nature of reality and to the increasing power of capitalist ideology to shape culture, novels take up as a subject the difficulties of accommodating the self to a world in which it no longer finds much security at all. Indeed sometimes, as in a novel such as *Dracula* (1897), the stable self is attacked both from within and without so forcefully that characters representing all the institutions of society must band together to defend that security. They become a corporation of selves in pursuit of a terrifying danger not only to the single self, but also to the nation.

Registering less certainty about any security selfhood might offer and about the newly vexed relationship between experience and value, late-Victorian novels have a hard time issuing clear judgment through a narrator or implied author. Indeed, like *Lord Jim*, published in the first year of the new century, the novel in the last two decades of the nineteenth century is overtly concerned with the status of fact, truth, multiple point of view, and subjective impressions. Thus the later Victorian novel registers a more challenging relation to an audience, who can no longer be passive consumers, but must become more active.

Yet the passage from *Lord Jim* I quoted above reveals more. "The less I understood the more I was bound" indicates that the subject Jim becomes more "real" in this novel by remaining unpredictable and even largely unknown. It is as if Marlow's act of attention, the claim of reality taken on faith, must be enough to convince us of Jim's realness. The basis for this claim to reality substantively differs from the tenets of classic realism as practiced either by a Regency period author such as Jane Austen or even by Victorian successors in this mode, such as George Eliot, Anthony Trollope, or Margaret Oliphant. The ideological fracture of experience and value within the narrator and central character, transmitted to the reader-subject, as registered through *Lord Jim* and novels similar to it, appears unprecedented and yet it has an ancestry worth pursuing.

Although a similar heightened sense of mystery and uncertainty also permeates the aesthetic of *Wuthering Heights*, it is that of a puzzle to be solved or an experience of the supernatural and unconscious to be accepted, rather than as evidence of secular epistemological fracture, as in *Lord Jim*. The initial narrator of Brontë's novel, Mr. Lockwood, finds himself in an awkward position: "1801 – I have just returned from a visit to my landlord – the solitary neighbour that I shall be troubled with."[4] Thus the visitor Lockwood opens the story of *Wuthering Heights*, a novel often considered distinctively different from most other Victorian novels. Critics have claimed it to be so different, in fact, that it has been described as closer to Elizabethan drama than to any fiction of its own time. It is a work of generic ambiguity. Yet it is this Brontë novel that provides in stark relief, I believe, the central paradigm of the Victorian novel.

With Lockwood, we are trying to enter a house, which resists the speaker, and yet he is the only guide we have into the structure. The structure is not only the building called "Wuthering Heights," which Lockwood finally does enter, but it is also the verbal structure of the novel also called *Wuthering Heights*, which starts "1801," as if it were a diary entry, a dateline, or a newspaper report. This house may be seen both as Brontë's own strange house of fiction and as suggestive of the frequent strangeness of Victorian fiction in general. While it seems an uncomplicated and inviting house, it proves quite dramatically deceiving. Lockwood meets a closed gate, a chain barring his entrance, and an interlocutor whose invitation to enter emerges through clenched teeth. As we see from Lockwood's many mistakes at interpretation and his inadequacies as both a rationalist and a man of feeling, the novel is already discrediting him as a narrator we can trust.

In terms of its relation to contemporary and complex realist conventions, *Wuthering Heights* is extreme in its presentation of threatening asocial energies and in showing up its narrator as highly limited. Lockwood's confusion in fathoming an alien world reproduces well the responses of early readers of the book. For unlike most of the Victorian novels we still read and teach such as Thackeray's *Vanity Fair* (1848), Dickens's *David Copperfield* (1850), and Eliot's *The Mill on the Floss* (1860), this one met confusion in its own day. It baffled Victorian readers and there were precious few who bothered to read it at all, until Emily's sister Charlotte, famous for *Jane Eyre* in 1847, wrote her 1850 Preface to *Wuthering Heights* in order to persuade readers of its distinction.

What did its first readers expect, before Charlotte defended it to make it more socially acceptable? I would argue that they expected something more in the vein of a novel by Jane Austen or Sir Walter Scott, fiction based largely on classic realist literary conventions, whether domestic or historic realism. Through the presentation of an intelligible history, classic realism calls forth certain conventional reading practices, precisely because of the text's aesthetic. Often a hierarchy of discourses, in which truth accrues to the implied author, the narrator, and the reader, it relies on third-person omniscient narration. This type of narration tends to efface its status as discourse and promotes a sense of organic, coherent form. Realism privileges a reading focusing on a central character or several central characters. It stresses a model of coherence or consistency not only in its form but also in the construction of characters. When the consistency or coherence of a character is challenged, through any number of disrupting desires or external events, the movement of the narrative usually reinstates order. The ending is normally that of marriage or death.

This form not only places the reader in a position of privileged knowing and moral judgment, thus shaping his/her subjectivity into middle-class Victorian norms, but often does so with the aim of creating conformity. The realist novel largely accepts middle-class ethics and mores. The emotionally complex hero or heroine is molded to the bourgeois ideal of the rational man or woman of virtue. Relying on a structure of psychological development, the classic realist novel allows lapses from a bourgeois code, but treats them as errors of judgment owing to immaturity. So, for example, just as Elizabeth Bennet in *Pride and Prejudice* (1813) learns to modify her prejudice and eventually marries Mr. Darcy, Jane Eyre monitors her potential lapse – loving a man she discovers to be married – and leaves Thornfield. Sometimes, as with Maggie Tulliver in Eliot's *The Mill on the Floss*, a moral lapse is but a preliminary to a tragic ending. Sometimes, as with Becky Sharpe in Thackeray's heavily satiric *Vanity Fair*, characters discover more about human nature, but do not radically change themselves or move on a continuum of maturity. The paradigm of maturing or refining one's relation to society to which I have been referring, however, explains why the novel of incremental self-knowledge is such a popular form during the Victorian period. Maturing correctly is a prerequisite for functioning well in Victorian bourgeois society.

Yet *Wuthering Heights* speaks what a realist novel knows, but does not usually tell so fully. It has a realist novel's understanding of the dangers of asocial energies, yet it is also a romantic, even sometimes a gothic fiction, with a desiring individualism so violent and transgressive that it crosses the material world into the spiritual realm. This novel is formally bifurcated right down the middle, according to the narratives of two generations, so that the first half is considered the asocial romance and the second is considered the realist socialization. While it is formally split, however, and has been read by critics such as Leo Bersani as a socialization of desire that endorses an adult point of view, it remains, in my view, ideologically dialectical. It illustrates continuous tensions between such opposites as nature and culture, the Grange and the Heights, consciousness and unconsciousness, location and dislocation, Romantic individualism and socialization. These tensions are kept in play, forcing readers to acknowledge the separate and powerful claims of each side.

Thus, although *Wuthering Heights* seems expressly divorced from the concerns and aesthetics of *Lord Jim*, I take it as paradigmatic of a structure that appears throughout the entire Victorian period. Let me explain more fully. While its aesthetic can be read in realist and coherent terms, this novel also points to unresolvable ideological fissures; it forcefully illustrates the ideological split between Romantic individualism and social consensus that rests at the heart of the novel form, which later Victorian novels will be increasingly hard pressed to heal aesthetically. It also mingles residual, dominant, and emergent forms that will be recombined and altered as the novel develops through the Victorian era. The first half of Brontë's novel (the residual) defends Romantic individualism through the intense relationship of Cathy I and Heathcliff; the second half of the novel (the dominant) defends realist socialization through the taming relationship of Cathy II and Hareton. The middle and the end of the novel do neither. The middle illustrates the strains of any ideological compromise between individualism and socialization through the very vexed relationship of Cathy II and Hareton. The finale, drawing out the emergent qualities of the text, ends with equal doubt and faith concerning the supernatural wanderings of Heathcliff and Cathy I.

To read this novel and most other novels of the period, then, one must set one perspective against another, rather than privileging one over another or collapsing them to an explanatory center. It is presumably this very hybridity and type of bifurcation to which Henry James so strenuously objected in his late-Victorian/early-modernist quest for a perfect organic form: "What do such large loose baggy monsters, with their queer elements of the accidental and the arbitrary, artistically *mean*?" he asks about *The Newcomes*, *Les Trois Mousquetaires*, and *War and Peace*. The context of his remarks underscores his need for a "structural centre" in fiction and his "mortal horror of two stories, two pictures, in one."[5] Although the British, French, and Russian examples to which he refers are panoramic, historical novels, his question has been applied as a judgment against the aesthetic of the typically large, highly detailed, double or multi-plotted, singly or multiply-narrated English nineteenth-century novel.

James's preference for a tight central coherence establishes a norm against which much Victorian fiction must seem inevitably to fall short or fail. If we were to judge the Victorian novel by James's criteria or others like them (thematic unity, tonal unity, logical construction), we would, as Raymond Williams suggests, end up ranking a writer such as Trollope over Eliot or Dickens.[6] Rather than follow James's lead by regarding accident and arbitrariness or skewed structures as failures of some kind, we should attend carefully, as did Emily Brontë, to separate elements of the novel and to the reframing offered by such attention.

Wuthering Heights holds in tension, without resolving that tension, both the vital and enduring power of Romantic individualism and the necessity of socializing such energies. Its ending questions whether or not the claims of individualism can last anywhere – if not in the natural, real world, then perhaps in the supernatural world. The text does not know and does not tell. This same dilemma between individualism and desire versus socialization is one that the Victorian novel takes up in its many permutations. Moreover, subsequent novels work often within the same general ideology, one lacking a sustained or coherent world view. In short, the Victorian novel's fractures, including the fractured subjectivities it records, demand as much of our attention as their ideological solutions. M. M. Bakhtin's postulation of "dialogism" in the novel form can assist us in this regard.

Bakhtin understands dialogism as the characteristic epistemological mode of a world in which there is a constant interaction between meanings, all of which have the potential of conditioning the others. Although the literary effect of coherent or unitary language or a single set of meanings is possible, such an effect is only possible relative to the fact of dialogism. Referring specifically to the heteroglossia of the novel form, Bakhtin argues that "The language of the novel is a *system* of languages that mutually and ideologically interanimate each other."[7] Peter Garrett notes that Bakhtin's oppositions are always based on relations between or among individual consciousnesses, not between language systems, and he rereads what he sees as a limitation in the work of Bakhtin by removing the notion of competing consciousnesses. In its place, he inserts the notion of competing structural principles. Victorian multiple narratives, Garrett proposes, develop dialogic tensions through diverging narrative lines, contrary narrative perspectives, conflicts within the narrative voice, and between characters and narrator.[8] From this historical vantage point, we are able to add dialogic languages and ideologies to Garrett's isolation of dialogic structural principles.

The Victorian novel comprises many sub-genres, as we learn from the different chapters in this volume, such as the historical novel, the domestic novel, the silver fork novel, the detective novel, the industrial novel, and the science fiction novel. Moreover, Victorian literary discourse intersects with many other important cultural discourses of the period, most prominently religion, science, and political economy. These discourses shape novel sub-genres even as they inform narrative texture and then enable us to place the Victorian novel in its historical context: some examples might include the novels taking up issues of racial difference, evolution and breeding, and labor unrest. Yet to historicize the aesthetic and political complexity of the Victorian novel – its critique of the very norms it also endorses, its complex relation to the reader as subject, and its departures from classic realism or structural centers – we should also, I think, make sure we place it in conversation, if briefly, with another key literary discourse of the period, poetry, which shares the ideological pressures felt by the Victorian novel.

We normally take up the novel and its aesthetic apart from the Victorian lyric, dramatic monologue, verse epic, or anti-narrative narrative poem. This persistent separation may be seen as a largely unquestioned inheritance from the Victorian period and as detrimental to our grasp of the novel's ideology and aesthetic. In the 1830s and after, as is commonly known, poetry ceased to be centrally important in the same way, for example, that it had been during the prior century or even the Romantic period. Despite Tennyson's popularity well into the 1850s and afterwards as the Poet Laureate, poetry moved further and further to the cultural margins.

However, this inheritance – poetry as not useful to society or even to cultural capital anymore – continues to perpetuate an almost unbridgeable critical gap between Victorian poetry and fiction. The fact that much nineteenth-century poetry is not simple lyric, but is dramatized or narrativized lyric is an important point. Unlike Romantic poetry, Victorian poetry illustrates a profound discomfort with a central "I" of unmediated experience, a coherent self, and with what James would call a structural center. Instead, this poetry repeatedly calls into question the status of point of view and the status of representation itself. It raises problems of how we make meaning.

Let me illustrate briefly what I mean with a very short poem and go on to establish connections to the novel aesthetic through particular fictional examples. The poem "Home" (1876) by Dora Greenwell, a still under-read Victorian woman poet, condenses in one set of words two entirely different readings.[9] It both presents and endorses the morals and ideologies of the Victorian middle class and exposes them to merciless questioning at the same time.

> Home
> Two birds within one nest;
>   Two hearts within one breast;
> Two spirits in one fair,
> Firm league of love and prayer,
> Together bound for aye, forever blest.
>
>   An ear that waits to catch
>   A hand upon the latch;
> A step that hastens its sweet rest to win;
>   A world of care without,
>   A world of strife shut out,
> A world of love shut in.

Ostensibly this poem is a hymn to domestic calm through the affective mode of sensibility popularized by two women poets of the Romantic period, Felicia Hemans and Letitia Landon. The fact that stanza one is missing a line in position six can refer to the fact that unity and blending have occurred, so there may have been two separate hearts originally, but they unite now in one marriage nest. This first reading is the affective, expressive reading.

However, these meanings are also put into radical question by a second reading, a commentary on the first, which does not annul it, but which exists in tension with it. In terms of subjectivity, one of the key lines is

"Two hearts within one breast." Not only does it refer to married union, but, rather, it indicates two sets of feeling in one breast, i.e. self-division. The same duality and splitting occur in the line "Two spirits in one fair" (line 3), which means person.

When one realizes, too, that there is no "I" in this poem, except a displaced one in the sound "for aye" (an "I," one might argue, displaced into eternity), one also wonders about that missing line in stanza one. Could it represent an absent person or refer to the fact that the speaker is, in some sense, not affectively present in the way she should be? The story of homecoming can also take on a reversal of meaning: not the woman waiting with joy for the man to come home and take his rest, but a woman who would rather go to her heavenly rest than open the door. Note the semicolon that divides lines two and three in stanza two – separating the sentiments and story of homecoming into two possible moments: daily ritual; one-time death.

There are many other textual issues, but the force of the last "shut" resonates. A tension between being shut out or in is reproduced in the alternating emphases contained in the last three lines' final words: "without," "out," "in," where the feeling of a love, not embraced, but "shut in" as a door closes, becomes an issue of captivity as well as security. The second reading of the poem, then, translates nest into cage, speaks of marriage as bondage, and seeks an alternative to "forever" in the here and now. There are many examples of Victorian poems that offer expressivity on one level and commentary on another.

The instance of "Home" relies on language to tell two stories. However Victorian poetry relies on other overt strategies to keep two readings in tension such as the dramatic monologue, the mask lyric, pendent poems, the female echoing and rewriting of male genres, or women's lyrics responding to specific poems by men about women. Yet no matter how dualism is established in or among poems, tensions of expressivity and commentary are kept alive, not resolved.

The dialectical nature of much Victorian poetry is matched by the dialectical play and tensions of ideological oppositions in a novel such as *Wuthering Heights*. The aesthetic of the Victorian novel repeatedly foregrounds and tries to heal such tensions in a variety of ways, until, with a novel like George Eliot's *Daniel Deronda* (1876), the fissures can no longer be smoothed over. Let me offer two examples from the mid-Victorian novel, however, before turning to how the novel develops towards modernism in terms of aesthetics, politics, and epistemology.

Elizabeth Gaskell's *North and South* (1855) is an industrial novel and a romance that has often been read by critics as one or the other genre.

Following the tenets of realism, it works to join two very different plots and spheres, private and public, into a (false) coherence through metonymy. As Catherine Gallagher has suggested, Gaskell does so through the use of the heroine Margaret Hale as a central ethical point of view. Gaskell connects social and family themes by Margaret's judging of ethical dilemmas as similar in both spheres.[10] This use of Margaret and this connection of spheres leads some critics to read the book as a novel of self-education. Yet, as Gallagher notes, the novel provides, as well, a "running ironic commentary" on its "official ideas."[11] It forcefully questions its narrator in a variety of ways. By way of example, as Margaret moves through the novel from her rural home to a factory town, she is consistently challenged in her moral views. Margaret's influence on the men and women around her "does not" as Gallagher points out, "form a recti-linear narrative pointing directly to social harmony."[12] In fact, as the novel continues, and particularly through the challenge posed to Margaret by the sexual appeal and moral ambiguity of John Thornton, the novel shows that a single standard of ethical behavior will not work to weld public and private worlds or self and society.

In spite of a realist closure, which integrates the domestic love plot with the public issues of factory control and revolt, the novel is still built on the separation of the private and the public – a problem it does not face directly. As Patricia Ingham explains, in her fine analysis of discourse and the use of dialect in this novel, *North and South* in fact produces no closure on a number of important social and personal questions it raises.[13] The marriage of Thornton and Margaret does not resolve the strife that has existed in their encounters; the cooperative relationship between Thornton and Higgins, one of his employees, cannot be reproduced, writ large, to sort out the problems of industrial society; the question of what is a strike? is transformed into: how can we avoid a strike? rather than ever being answered. In short, the ideological opposition between self and society in the novel is smoothed over aesthetically, by means of metonymy, but the ideological fissures remain as deep as ever.

Even George Eliot's *Middlemarch* (1872), which is considered by many critics the perfect example of aesthetic unity in the Victorian period, shows itself to be deeply skeptical about any ideological totalities. Idealism, scientific rationalism, Evangelical Christianity, and Romantic idealism, embodied and enacted in varying degrees of complexity, by Edward Casaubon, Tertius Lydgate, Nicholas Bulstrode, and Will Ladislaw, particularly, are all progressively shown to be not only partial, but also flawed.

George Eliot's narrator refers to his project in chapter 15 as significantly different from that of an eighteenth-century predecessor, Henry Fielding. "I at least have so much to do in unraveling certain human lots, and seeing how they were woven and interwoven, that all the light I can command must be concentrated on this particular web, and not dispersed over that tempting range of relevancies called the universe."[14] The image of the web, which Eliot draws upon to emphasize the organicism at the heart of her fictional undertaking here, is a three-dimensional spatial form which foregrounds surface connections. The novel's interlacings work through the movements of her characters, who are connected either by family ties, acknowledged or disavowed, and by what Eliot calls "the irony of events."[15] In this sense, the novel is comparable to many of Dickens's novels that rely on a huge canvas of characters, chance encounters, and intricate links through events. However, the plots of Eliot's *Middlemarch* are themselves organically shaped into overlapping spheres. Four separate but analogically-linked plots, the stories of Dorothea Brooke, the Garths, Lydgate, and Bulstrode, are set within the provincial life of Middlemarch, which is itself set within the larger sphere of the religious, scientific, historical, and social changes in the nation during the 1830s. As U. C. Knoepflmacher notes, however, to isolate the component ideological strains in this construct "is to the lose the impact of their joint effect."[16]

The central problem which *Middlemarch* poses but does not answer is the viability and place of a Romantic will and ideal in a world dominated by provincial awareness, on the one hand, and by empiricism, progress, and scientific rationalism on the other. As in *North and South*, another novel that takes up important social issues, *Middlemarch* betrays a formal bifurcation it does not heal, though unlike *Wuthering Heights*, it does not make an overt display of that bifurcation. Ethical moralizing replaces a substantial engagement with history and the real. As Terry Eagleton puts it, there is a mystification inherent in realism "which by casting objective social relations into interpersonal terms, constantly holds open the possibility of reducing one to the other."[17] This is particularly true, I would argue, of the mid-nineteenth century novel. As noted, we also find it prominently in novels like *North and South* and *Middlemarch*, on either side of that mid-point.

Eliot's last novel, however, *Daniel Deronda*, marks a major turn in the fortunes of realism as an aesthetic in the period. In its open split, so wide as ostensibly to harbor two different novels, and thus reminiscent formally if not thematically of *Wuthering Heights*, this novel commands our attention primarily for a total rewriting of realist character and action. It illustrates, even more dramatically than does *Middlemarch*, a crisis in value and interpretation about coherence itself. In other words, if realism as an aesthetic seeks to promote coherence – of character, of a reader-subject, of plot lines, of connections among social viewpoints – then *Daniel Deronda* questions the premises of realism, even as it questions whether coherence is possible at all in a fragmented culture.

Yet *Daniel Deronda* goes further; it also questions the very nature of the self by offering us characters who tend to be flat and one-dimensional, such as Henleigh Grandcourt, Daniel Deronda, and Ezra Mordecai Cohen, while at the same time giving us Gwendolyn Harleth, one of the most richly complex characters in Victorian fiction. A quotation about Grandcourt cannot serve to evoke Deronda and Cohen, but can, at least, point to the issues at stake: "How trace the why and wherefore in a mind reduced to the barrenness of a fastidious egoism, in which all direct desires are dulled, and have dwindled from motives into the vacillating expectations of motives: a mind made up of moods, where a fitful impulse springs here and there conspicuously rank amid the general weediness?"[18] Eliot articulates here a reduction of realist character to a collection of signs. We could, however, take this quote as a description of what occurs in the novel form between *Wuthering Heights* and *Daniel Deronda*, between 1848 and 1876. For Brontë, characters are filled with desire, clear motive, moodiness, and impulses they act upon. Yet Eliot's novel records character in terms of negativity or absence: dulled desires, expectations only of motives, a dominating moodiness in a weediness of mental, spiritual, and emotional confusion. Some of the major characters in *Daniel Deronda* do not know themselves, do not know each other, and are difficult to penetrate because they lack realist depth. Character in this book, like narrative event, is premised more on accident or mystery than anything else. Notably, the book opens with a gambling scene in which Gwendolyn is trying her luck at roulette and ends with the death of the Jewish character Cohen, who, of all the characters in the novel, most firmly believes in a mysterious, transcendental unity surpassing earthly fragmentation.

Although many have argued that the Christian/Jewish split in the plot points to a defect, and that the second half is a failure, my sense is that such a criticism comes only from a realist-trained perspective. F. R. Leavis, for example, would have done away entirely with the Jewish half. Eliot's project, however, fundamentally calls realism into question. For her, Judaism mixes the real and the ideal, the spiritual and the material, the traditional and the progressive. She tests it for its applicability to renovate her own society and she uses it to challenge the novel form itself. She sets world-view against world-view, type against type, and allows them to reframe each other, question each other, and even call each other to account, before she falls back on providence and Daniel Deronda as a new figure of messianism. In this important novel, the mystery of character, of self, of event, of society points to the ideological break in experience and value that is more fully realized formally in novels of the later Victorian period.

The fortunes of realism and the ideological break I have been situating formally can be illustrated even more dramatically by looking carefully at a novel of the 1890s: Thomas Hardy's *Tess of the d'Urbervilles* (1891), which more self-consciously confronts issues raised forcefully by *Daniel Deronda* and tackled head-on by *Lord Jim*: epistemology and interpretation. Hardy explores these issues by dwelling on the self and a world felt to be fragmenting or under attack.

Chapter 2 of *Tess of the d'Urbervilles* opens by describing Marlott, the village where Tess was born. But the passage goes beyond mere description by providing the reader with important aesthetic directives. After locating the village geographically in "the Vale of Blakemore or Blackmoor"[19] and noting that tourists and landscape painters have usually avoided the valley, Hardy's narrator predicts that its beauty will attract future viewers. Yet he quickly chills the enthusiasm of such prospective viewers. After initially asserting that the fertile spot never succumbs to dried-up springs or brown fields, he now calls attention to the droughts of summer only to recite further obstacles: poor ways to travel, difficult roads, and consequent disappointments one might want to avoid. The narrator then reverses himself once again by insisting that any traveler from the coast will inevitably be delighted by contrasts between the calcareous downs and lush cornlands (*Tess*, 22).

It would be easy to misread these oscillations in emphasis as something approaching equivocation. Yet here Hardy conditions his readers by exposing them to a multitude of conflicting impressions. Offering different reasons for coming to the valley, different routes, different kinds of walks, he then introduces further variables: the pace of arrival, the weather, vertical/horizontal positionality, time of year, and decisions about whether to travel with a guide or alone. Hardy's description is not simply figural or symbolic, but epistemological. He knowingly destroys a common literary convention from Romantic poetry and the realist nineteenth-century novel in which a landscape is presented and endowed with significance by a strong poetic "I" or a central, omniscient and omnipresent narrator. Instead, Hardy's narrator stresses the partiality and noteworthiness of every point of view.

With its emphasis on what we see, how we know and nominate, how we experience, how a thing can be viewed multiply, and how it affects us physically, mentally, emotionally, the description of Marlott glosses the aesthetic undertaking of *Tess*. Reminiscent of Marlow's fathoming Lord

Jim through a mist of impressions, Hardy's aesthetic demands that readers grasp reality as objectively varied, changing, and filtered by many and contradictory subjective impressions. At every narrative level – plot and event, the handling of time, narration, character, language use, and intertextual allusion – Hardy relies on multiplicity, seeming contradiction, incongruity, and dialogism, strategies he adapts within a general framework of tragic ambiguity. In so doing, Hardy questions the very foundations of representation and belief. He asks his readers to become conditioned into thinking simultaneously in terms that are multiple and even contradictory.

Hardy pushes readers, as does Conrad after him, to understand the relativity of their values and judgments. This does not mean that Hardy is a relativist. It does mean that he sees stereotypical values and judgments (such as blame the victim, or the seducer is a cad, or rape ends a woman's life) as being socially constructed, historically shaped, and often irrelevant to a particular situation. Certainly they should be irrelevant to a discriminating readership.

Tess of the d'Urbervilles is a particularly significant text to this discussion because it reproduces, through challenges to realism on every front, a divorce between experience and value. The novel assaults the reader with shocking materials that it does not soften. It is probably the only novel in the English language that allows a heroine to be raped, abandoned, thrown into poverty, arrested for murder, and hung. Unlike the work of Gaskell or Eliot, both of whom wrote novels about fallen women – Ruth in *Ruth* (1853) and Hetty Sorrel in *Adam Bede* (1859) – this novel offers no final explanation or satisfying closure for its events. Indeed, Hardy seems to mock a fulfilling closure by suggesting a perpetuation of tragic relationships in having Angel Clare marry Tess's sister, Liza-Lu, and the final scene is so heavily aestheticized by a Giotto painting analogy and jarring intertextual references, that it rings false.

By exploding conventions that previously cemented the bond between narrator and reader, Hardy undermines narrative community. He shatters narrative form to make his readers experience fragmentation, the "ache of modernism" (*Tess*, 140). But he does so in ways that make the bifurcation of *Wuthering Heights* appear tame in comparison, rather than radical. That breakage – aesthetic, ideological, and social – would eventually issue forth, during World War I and afterwards, in a fully developed, different aesthetic for fiction, modernism. Yet it is instructive to remember that the glaring differences once noted by critics between Victorian and modernist novels are conditioned as much by critical practice as by history. Just as we may connect *Wuthering Heights* and *Lord Jim*, so seemingly different from one another, through issues of aesthetic form, construction of subjectivity, and influences of dominant ideology, so, too, we may connect the conventionally disparate literary periods of Victorian and modernism.

NOTES

1 Joseph Conrad, *Lord Jim* (1990; New York: Penguin, 1981), 169.
2 Joseph Conrad, "Preface" to *The Nigger of the Narcissus,* known as "The Condition of Art," *The Portable Conrad* (New York: Viking: 1950), 708.
3 Joseph Conrad, *Heart of Darkness, The Portable Conrad,* 493.
4 Emily Brontë, *Wuthering Heights,* eds. William M. Sale, Jr. and Richard J. Dunn (1847; New York: Norton, 1990), 3.
5 Henry James, Preface to *The Tragic Muse, The Art of the Novel,* ed. R. P. Blackmur (New York: Scribners, 1934), 88, 84.
6 Raymond Williams, *The English Novel* (London: The Hogarth Press, 1984), 85.
7 M. M. Bakhtin, *The Dialogic Imagination,* ed. Michael Holquist, trans. Caryl Emerson and Michael Holquist (Austin: University of Texas Press, 1981), 47; see also the glossary for *dialogism* and *heteroglossia,* 426–28.
8 Peter Garrett, *The Victorian Multiplot Novel: Studies in Dialogical Form* (New Haven: Yale University Press, 1980), 8–9.
9 Janet Gray introduced me to the work of Greenwell in 1991 and offered a reading of "Home" similar to this one.
10 Catherine Gallagher, *The Industrial Reformation of English Fiction: Social Discourse and Narrative Form 1832–1867* (Chicago: University of Chicago Press, 1985), 170–71.
11 *Ibid.,* 171.
12 *Ibid.,* 172.
13 Patricia Ingham, *The Language of Gender and Class: Transformation in the Victorian Novel* (New York: Routledge, 1996), 70–71.
14 George Eliot, *Middlemarch,* ed. Gordon Haight (1872; New York: Riverside, 1968), 105.
15 George Eliot, *Quarry for Middlemarch,* ed. Anna Kitchel (Berkeley: University of California Press, 1950), 45.
16 U. C. Knoepflmacher, *Religious Humanism and the Victorian Novel* (Princeton: Princeton University Press, 1965), 72–73; 74.
17 Terry Eagleton, *Criticism and Ideology* (London: Verso, 1978), 121.
18 George Eliot, *Daniel Deronda,* ed. Graham Handley (1876; Oxford: Oxford University Press, 1984), 258.
19 Thomas Hardy, *Tess of the d'Urbervilles* (1891; New York: Signet, 1980), 22. See also Linda M. Shires, "The Radical Aesthetic of *Tess of the d'Urbervilles,*" in Dale Kramer, ed., *The Cambridge Companion to Thomas Hardy* (Cambridge: Cambridge University Press, 1999).

4

JOSEPH W. CHILDERS

Industrial culture and the Victorian novel

Among the vast array of goods and materials produced during the aggressive onset of industrialism in Britain in the early Victorian period, none was more widely disseminated, more instrumental to everyday life, more essential to the shaping of industrial culture than information. For along with the grand *mélange* of *things* that seemed to flow unchecked out of British factories, a river of knowledge (and questions) about how the world worked coursed through every aspect of Victorian life. The era's most conspicuous outward signs of unprecedented material change – steam engines, factories, railroads, urbanization – denoted even grander transformations in the way people thought and acted. Received notions about everything from gender to nationalism, from class to religion, from propriety to biology were open to question. Even assumptions about such fundamentals as space and time were challenged. Not only were people living differently, they were thinking differently, talking and writing differently, acting differently. They were *existing* differently. Such monumental changes and the effects they wrought became both the form and the substance of nearly all forms of inquiry. On the abstract level, thinkers like Mill, Carlyle, Ruskin, Morris, and Pater took up the issue of "progress" – or at the very least "change" – in terms of its political, moral, and aesthetic implications. Others, from novelists such as Gaskell, Dickens, Disraeli, Kingsley, and Frances Trollope to the new breed of social investigator like Edwin Chadwick, James Kay-Shuttleworth, and Henry Mayhew, while often fully aware of the abstract principles that grounded their work, were more directly invested in the concrete examples of change (as either progress or decline) that quotidian life provided.

The well-documented rise in literacy in Britain during this period underscores the mutual dependence of the cultures of information and industrialism. The novel, in its rise in popularity as well as in its participation in shaping cultural practices, is a particularly good example of this relationship. As a number of critics have pointed out in various ways, a neat separation of industrialism and the novel is nearly impossible in the years between 1832 and 1867.[1] Each looked to the other for models of effecting and controlling as well as understanding change. Novels turned to the "record of industrialism," for example to parliamentary reports and the press, for the details of everyday life that came to characterize their narratives, while the social investigations looked to the novel as the most effective way of organizing and presenting those details. The result is often a blurring of generic lines and practices, not to mention perceived intentions. For instance, one "bestseller" of the 1840s was not a novel at all, but Edwin Chadwick's *Report on the Sanitary Condition of the Labouring Population in Great Britain*, which, by at least one account, enjoyed a distribution of over 100,000 copies.[2] Clearly, the subject matter of such reports was of growing interest to the general reading population, and this in itself marks an important shift in how people were thinking about their world. Those who had previously been socially peripheral became symbolically central to the projects of novelists and social reformers alike; and it was these characters, whether from novel, bluebook, or newspaper report who captured the reading public's imagination. In fiction as well as in non-fiction it was the poor, the criminal, and the diseased who elicited the most interest – whether Fagin, Sikes, and Nancy in *Oliver Twist* (1838) or Carlyle's Irish widow dying from and spreading typhus in *Past and Present* (1843). Furthermore, the middle class's own relationship to this segment of society, a relationship fraught with ambivalence, generated a good deal of discussion about social responsibility. The "feeling [that] very generally exists that the condition and disposition of the Working Classes is a rather ominous matter at present; that something ought to be said, something ought to be done, in regard to it" was, as Thomas Carlyle dubbed it in "Chartism," the "Condition of England Question";[3] and it was around this question that many of the important novels of the early Victorian period congregated. The difficulty for social reformers and novelists alike, however, was what could and should be done to alleviate the opprobrious conditions of this relatively new, and seemingly ubiquitous, segment of society – the industrial working class.

As workers crowded into the cities – within a decade increasing by half again the populations of northern industrial towns like Manchester, Leeds, and Sheffield – the unease observed by Carlyle became apparent in all manner of writing about the poor. "The Great Unwashed" were seen as a threat to the stability of British life. Viewed as potentially violent – even revolutionary – and as carriers of both physical and moral disease, the working class was physically pushed into inadequate spaces for living and working within these cities, nearly to the point of being pushed out of sight of most members of the middle and upper classes. Simultaneously, they were discursively hauled into the white hot light of observation by private and parliamentary investigations that undertook the task of representing them to a reading public eager for detailed – but not necessarily first-hand – information. The novels, too, played heavily on the middle classes' lack of direct knowledge about either the conditions or the culture of the working classes, and both reports and fiction sometimes pushed the very limits of representation, deluging their readers with descriptions of deplorable conditions. No doubt it was much easier to read about these things than actually experience them, and as a result the novels and investigative reports acted as a sort of *cordon sanitaire* insulating the middle classes, defining and broadening the gap between the two nations. Yet, these writers' shared project of representing as fully and completely – and often as shockingly – as possible also meant that their works served as a bridge across that divide.

One of the early trusses of that bridge is Frances Trollope's 1840 *Michael Armstrong, the Factory Boy*. As in so many of the industrial novels that would follow in the 1840s and later, Trollope predicates a good deal of her project on the assumption that her reading public is both ignorant of and interested in the plight of the poor. In her Preface she states her intention "to drag into the light of day, and place before the eyes of Englishmen, the hideous mass of injustice and suffering to which thousands of infant labourers are subjected, who toil in our monster spinning-mills."[4] True to her word, the rhetoric and plot devices of hiding and discovery play crucial roles in the narrative. The novel begins with Michael's being taken out of the factory of his employer, Sir Matthew Dowling, as a reward for coming to the aid of Dowling and his guest, Lady Clarissa. Having saved them from an angry bull they encountered during a postprandial stroll, Michael, at Lady Clarissa's insistence, is taken into the Dowling household, ostensibly to be raised as one of the family. But the entire scheme is an elaborate pretense on Sir Matthew's part, allowing him to save face with Lady Clarissa. Instead, Michael becomes a prisoner of the mill owner's "charity," and is treated no better as a new member of the Dowling household than he was as a factory hand.

Set against Sir Matthew's charade of benevolence is the pure-hearted charity of the novel's heroine, Mary Brotherton, a young heiress whose attempts to rescue Michael from Dowling lead to her adoption of Michael's lame brother, Edward, and a young factory girl, whom she saves from the mill. Before Mary acts, however, she educates herself about the effects of industrialization on the working poor, especially the children, and it is in this gathering of knowledge that the novel defines the essence of the social problem it is addressing. The antagonism between Mary and Sir Matthew is the narrative engine of the first part of the novel; much of that antagonism is based in their differences about what should be known about the working conditions of the poor, and who should know them. Rosemarie Bodenheimer has remarked on the elaborately contrived schemes of the plot, which "pit heroine and villain against each other for possession of the guilty knowledge of what the factory system does to young children."[5] That guilt motivates the two very differently, however. For Sir Matthew, the grotesqueness of the factory and its "inmates" is to be hidden from polite society and from his family. The latter have never visited the factory, since Dowling will not indulge them "by exhibiting to them the secret arcana of that hideous mystery by which the delicate forms of young children are made to mix and mingle with machinery, from whence flows the manufacturer's wealth" (*Michael Armstrong*, 79). Mary, on the other hand, whose own wealth is also intimately connected to textile manufacturing, considers it "exceedingly wrong that [she] should be so profoundly ignorant on the subject" of the working classes and their circumstances (95). For her it is a moral obligation to know about the factory and its effects on those who work in it. When a friend observes that she cannot hold herself responsible for something she was never told, Mary replies that it was equally wrong for her never to wish to be told or for never having considered the subject (95).

These remarks by Mary forcefully voice a sentiment that had taken hold in Victorian England. Not only was it useful (or profitable) to know about the poor; it was morally expedient. Knowledge as a commodity had appropriated the force of a moral argument, and the line between "useful" and "needful" knowledge was significantly blurred. When Carlyle, and later Ruskin, or even Marx, write of the social whole and the necessity for understanding how entire sections of society stand at enmity with one another, at bottom one can observe the moral argument at work. Not only are there remnants of it in Marx's discussions of surplus value and exploitation, but the humanization of the utilitarianism of the early part of the period into the liberalism of later Victorian England also shares this moral impetus. In so much of the writing of the period, the sovereignty of the individual is squarely opposed to the requirements of the social. As the "millocracy," that new sector of the middle class rivaling the aristocracy in wealth and political power, rose to ever greater prominence, the doctrine of individualism seemed to emerge as the soul of industrial culture. Offsetting that creed, however, was the growing insistence by many that it was both politically and morally essential to understand the price of individualism paid by the "other nation."

The tension between these two positions lies at the narrative heart of novels like Elizabeth Gaskell's *Mary Barton* (1848) and Charles Kingsley's *Alton Locke* (1850), both of which have characters traveling across class boundaries to present the contrasts in the communities that exist on either side of that divide. Also, both novels participate in the discourse of individualism, as the quickest glance at the novels' titles immediately indicates. In both works, main characters come to an understanding about themselves in part because of the knowledge they have gained about the social whole. *Mary Barton* is particularly insistent on the necessity of the understanding of community, and Gaskell is careful to juxtapose the conditions of the working classes and the mill owners for the benefit of her readers. As in Trollope's novel, the poor are hidden away, not readily observed, and when seen not particularly noticed by the upper classes. We should remember that the subtitle of *Mary Barton* is "A Tale of Manchester Life" and that Gaskell, like Friedrich Engels, was well aware of that town's construction, which managed space so that mill owners could take "the shortest road through the middle of all the labouring districts to their places of business, without ever seeing that they [were] in the midst of the grimy misery that lurk[ed] to the right and the left."[6] But the poor are well known to each other, and as John Barton asserts, "it's the poor and the poor only" who care for and give aid to the poor.[7] In perhaps the most famous section of the novel, George Wilson and John Barton go on an errand of mercy to the Davenport household when the father, Ben, falls ill with typhus. As the two men descend into the cellar the Davenports call home, the "smell was so fetid as almost to knock the two men down." Peering through the gloom they discern the sick man, his exhausted and despairing wife, and "three or four little children rolling on the damp, nay wet, brick floor, through which the stagnant, filthy moisture of the street oozed up" (*Mary Barton*, 98). After several pages of similar descriptions, the reader is taken into the home of the factory owner, Carson, where George Wilson goes to seek an infirmary order for the dying Davenport. There life is light and fine. No one is dying of fever; food abounds; one of the Carson daughters cajoles her father for half a guinea in order to buy flowers. "Life was not worth having without flowers" (108).

One effect of the pairing of the descriptions of the squalor of the Davenports with the relative opulence of the Carsons is to emphasize the ignorance of Carson about his own workers. Carson does not even recognize Davenport's name when Wilson asks for the infirmary order. But for Gaskell, knowledge runs in two directions, and the novel is nearly as adamant about informing the workers of why layoffs and work shortages are necessary as it is about the responsibility of the middle classes to understand the plight of the poor. In *Mary Barton* rich and poor are ineluctably bound to each other, and as a consequence are also responsible for and to each other. And while individuals are the main concern of the narrative, the social danger lies in allowing these individuals to remain an aggregate rather than to meld together as a knowable and known community. Thus the strongest traits of the main characters, whether the undisciplined desire of Mary, the animosity of John, or even the ambition of Jem Wilson – the traits that define their individuality – are finally always linked to the successes or failures of larger social groups to know, and almost importantly to want to know, about each other.

The version of individualism that operates in *Alton Locke, Tailor and Poet* relies upon Alton's coming to terms with his own class position and the limits of it. Unlike the characters in *Mary Barton*, however, Alton, though working class himself, has to be introduced to the horrors of poverty. When he takes up poetry, trying his hand at a piece about corsairs and cannibal Pacific islanders, his mentor tells him to forget such drivel and write what he knows. The problem is that Alton does not really know very much and must be shown. Using the metaphor of light much as Trollope does to indicate observation and knowledge as well as hope, the chapter "Light in a Dark Place" is Alton's introduction to the wages of poverty – sin and death. In a foul London slum, he meets a starving family of four – an old woman and three young seamstresses. Unable to provide for their family by their needlework, two of the daughters have turned to prostitution. His initiation into the squalor and demoralization suffered by so many of the working classes transforms Alton from a lackluster imitator of Byron to a potentially effective writer, chronicling the conditions of poverty and the garment-making industry in London.

Alton thus becomes a conduit for this information, and more importantly he becomes a voice from within the prison-house of poverty that industrialism has constructed. The formation of his own subjectivity, his status as an individual, is conditioned both by his ability to act – in this case following the Gospel of Work elaborated by Thomas Carlyle of turning his hand to the work nearest him – and by his connection to his work. However, Alton struggles with the temptations of lionization as the new working-class poet as well as with the easy living to be made as a political hack for the *Weekly Warwhoop*, a radical newspaper closely modeled on the Chartist *Northern Star*. For Alton, whose identity and social status are forever unclear to him, the knowledge he has to impart is always ideologically tainted: it is either diluted remedies easily digested by the middle classes or bombast designed to incite civil unrest by the poor. Though Alton seems to yearn to be like Ruskin's unnamed Gothic stonemasons, contributing of themselves to the medieval cathedrals they helped to build, or Marx's pre-capitalist non-alienated laborer who has not forfeited his species being, it is not until Alton is able to confirm his own identity in Kingsley's Christian Socialism that the link between himself and his work can finally define him as an individual. By then, however, it is nearly too late, for he is dying. It is not too late for others, however. We have the record of his life, his "autobiography," that educates its readers as its protagonist learns who he is and what he can – and cannot – do. Through Alton, as well as through the characters in *Mary Barton*, the poor gain a modicum of identity: they get faces and names rather than occupations and characteristics. They also get human problems which are always on the verge of violating class boundaries to become the human problems of the middle class as well. And for the middle classes, perhaps chief among the threats posed by a disaffected laboring population was Chartism.

As a political movement, Chartism had a brief but influential life. Arising in the 1830s as an organized attempt to reform electoral politics in Britain and Ireland so as to include the working classes, Chartism became a kind of catch-all category for all sorts of class-based political unrest in the 1840s, and by 1849 had fairly evaporated as a formidable political organization. In its early years, however, it demonstrated the vigor with which many members of the industrial working classes were willing to work for political reform. It had its own newspaper, *The Northern Star*, which was owned and operated by Feargus O'Connor. First published in 1837, it specialized in the details of local struggles and catered to the interests of the more militant Chartist flange. By the end of 1838, the *Northern Star* was selling 50,000 copies a week, and it was soon evident to the working and middle classes alike that Chartism was a force to be reckoned with. Its leaders were educated working-class men, not unlike Alton Locke, who continually divided over the question of tactics: that is, whether to adopt a "moral force" philosophy that could bring around Parliament by the sheer force of numbers and arguments about the immorality of keeping such a large segment of the population excluded from wealth and political voice, or to align themselves with more militant tactics, including riots and strikes, for recognition. In 1839 and again in 1848, the Chartist leaders met to present their petition to Parliament: a six-point program of universal male suffrage, equal electoral districts, secret ballot, annual parliaments, abolition of the property qualification for, and payment of, Members of Parliament. Each time the Chartists met with little success, and after the 1848 convention, the movement essentially dissolved.

Despite the relatively small amount of actual damage the Chartists did to persons and property over the decade of their heyday, for the middle classes, the potential for Chartist violence was very real. Both *Alton Locke* and *Mary Barton* involve main characters in Chartist activities, and in each case those characters pay dearly for political violence gone dreadfully wrong. Carlyle comments on such matters in his 1839 pamphlet, "Chartism." There he writes of it as a kind of justifiable madness, a symptom of the illness of the social body, that threatens to hasten the devolution of social order into anarchy: "When the thought of a people, in the great mass of it, have grown mad, the combined issue of that people's workings will be a madness, an incoherency and ruin! Sanity will have to be recovered for the general mass; coercion itself will otherwise cease to be able to coerce" ("Chartism," 153). For Kingsley and Gaskell, writing of Chartism in 1850 and 1848, respectively, it was easy to point to its ultimate failure and to use it as an example of a poor solution to the problem of the two nations. But for Benjamin Disraeli, whose *Sybil, or The Two Nations* was published in 1845, the specter of Chartism still loomed large and ominous.

Unlike *Mary Barton* and *Alton Locke*'s Chartists, who are thoughtful and intelligent, if wrong-headed and desperate, *Sybil*'s version of working-class political activists is more closely related to the Tory tradition of anti-mob discourse that surfaced around the time of the French Revolution. While it is true that Sybil Gerard and her father, Walter, are sympathetic, representing the reasonable, moral-force wing of Chartism, they are quickly overrun by the noisy backdrop of the novel's lesser characters, whose affiliation is with the physical-force faction of the movement. For Disraeli, the social remedy must be a political one. Far less interested in depicting the plight of the poor than in quashing working-class radical and Whiggish liberal claims to political power and the promise of social amelioration, Disraeli portrays both of these positions as bereft of any real solutions. Instead, he holds out the offer of a union between the two nations that relies upon the emergence of a natural, enlightened aristocracy. As the heroine Sybil, buffeted about by the nascent violence of Chartism in scene after scene, loses much of her ideological connection with Chartism and its goals, her love interest Egremont learns that his own noble heritage is of more recent and common vintage than he had been led to believe. The result, for both, is a loosening of their class affiliations, Sybil becoming more receptive to the Tory paternalistic position, Egremont opening up to the arguments of the articulate and reasonable working class. The narrative conclusion, as in so many Victorian novels, leans heavily on the marriage plot – in this case the union of the noble Egremont to the commoner Sybil. In such a resolution the reader is offered an answer to the problem of the two nations, a problem described by one character as constituting an England where there is no community; "there is aggregation," he says, "but aggregation under circumstances which make it rather a dissociating than a uniting principle." Without a "community of purpose," he goes on, "men may be drawn into contiguity, but they still continue virtually isolated."[8]

Ostensibly, Disraeli's desire in *Sybil* is to replace contiguity with identification as the uniting principal of *one* nation. But Sybil Gerard turns out to be a dispossessed aristocrat and not the putative "daughter of the people." The union of Sybil and Egremont, then, is a consolidation of resources on the side of the aristocracy, but in a way that recognizes time-worn traditions – such as the Saxon lineage of the Gerards and their association with the land – as well as the wealth and interests of the parvenu nobility whose titles are a consequence of their commercial and industrial successes. Unlike *Alton Locke* or *Mary Barton* which paint sympathetic pictures of the plight of the poor and even the Chartists to encourage narrative solutions based primarily on the two nations each understanding the plight of the other, *Sybil* is much less interested in a compassionate depiction of the poor. As often as not, they are seen as heathenish or barbaric; only rarely are they the self-sacrificing factory hands of Gaskell's novel, or the autodidacts of Kingsley's. Consequently, Chartism is dismantled because of its political rather than its social failings. It cannot provide a form of government that is workable. Instead, Disraeli literally marries the past to the future of England as a way of ensuring that even as industrialism sweeps across the country, the conservative interests of those wishing to preserve Church and Crown, peasantry and nobility, are served.

It is well known that Disraeli depended rather heavily on parliamentary reports to inform his novel. Sections of the 1842 report of the Children's Employment Commission and of an 1843 report on the payment of wages find their way, verbatim, into *Sybil*. But, again, this was by no means either unusual or unethical. It was all part of the free flow of information about industrialism that was making its way among the reading public. As early as 1833, Chadwick and his collaborator Nassau Senior were furnishing sections of their Poor Law Report to Harriet Martineau to assist her in her writing of *Poor Laws and Paupers, Illustrated* (1833–34), a follow-up to her highly popular nine-volume, *Illustrations of Political Economy* (1832). Both of these titles sold extraordinarily well to Mechanics' Institute Libraries, helping them to reach their intended audience and educate the working classes in the rudiments of political economy. This goal of educating the laboring population informs a number of social ideas that gathered momentum throughout the century. From the middle-class perspective, it candidly commodifies knowledge, making it the entity which, above all else, has the power to civilize and level. It provides the means by which young men and women can challenge the limits of their lots in life; it offers a way of making the best of one's talents and of acquiring "useful knowledge." It is a ladder out of penury; it swings wide doors to opportunities that could not otherwise have even been imagined. With an education, one can move into circulation, make something of one's self. It also enlightens the poor to the moral and social dangers attendant to poverty. Armed with such insight one might even, as Chadwick wrote, come to realize that one has a character to lose.

Formal education and its consequences, both good and bad, are fundamental to many of Dickens's novels. From *Pickwick* (1837) to *Our Mutual Friend* (1865), he comments time and again on the role of schools in their connections to other social institutions. Sometimes, as in *Great Expectations* (1861), *Nicholas Nickleby* (1839), or *David Copperfield* (1850), education seems far removed from the hustle and bustle of industrialism and the utilitarian's conception of the "march of the mind." Yet even in these novels, schools are the places where future gentleman are trained, or tortured, or neglected; and these gentlemen become the professionals who exist on the accretions of industrialization, whether they be German-merchants, heirs to Australian fortunes, or aspiring novelists in their own right. Not only future gentlemen went to school, however. Factory schools and Sunday schools (which provided academic as well as religious instruction) were proliferating throughout England for working-class youth. In such institutions the connections between school and factory were readily apparent. It comes as no real surprise, then, that Dickens's own powerful industrial novel, *Hard Times* (1854), yokes the emerging educational system to factory life in the fictional Coketown.

The startling opening pages describe a classroom in Thomas Gradgrind's school, where the "one thing needful" is facts. According to Gradgrind, "you can only form the minds of reasoning animals upon Facts: nothing else will ever be of any service to them."[9] Even taste, which might belie the universal usefulness of facts and insert the possibility of subjective choice "is only another name for Fact" (*Hard Times*, 51). This, we are told, is "a new principle, a discovery, a great discovery" that has reconstituted what it can mean to "know" anything. No longer are students, or anyone for that matter, to "fancy" – "nothing of the kind" (51–52); information is no longer interpretable. Rather it is always correspondent to an empirical reality. Anything more is useless, unnecessary, spurious. The production of and dispensing of knowledge is reducible to a system that is regular, predictable, and dependable. The schoolmaster himself, Mr. M'Choakum-child, was a product of this system. He and "some one hundred and forty other schoolmasters" had been "lately turned at the same time, in the same factory, on the same principles, like so many pianoforte legs" (52–53).

This last description, of the schoolmaster and how he has been trained, speaks to Dickens's criticism of how the methods of industry had crept into facets of life seemingly divorced from the factory. For Dickens, industrial culture threatens to turn all of society into a kind of large factory, churning out fact while devouring beings who have lost the capacity for feeling and human connection, not to say imagination. This is a much more profound fear than that of Gaskell, Disraeli, or Kingsley for it goes beyond a concern about the violence and inequities that industrialism seemed to foster. It expresses instead what Dickens saw as the inflexibility of industrialism and the practices that sprang out of it. We see that rigidness in the novel's first scene as Sissy Jupe is silenced by Gradgrind when she admits that she would, if presented the opportunity, buy a carpet with flowers upon it or wallpaper decorated with pictures of horses; and we see that inflexibility's effects in the growing dysfunction of the Gradgrind family: Louisa's emotionless marriage to the blustering mill owner, Bounderby; her near seduction by the bored dilettante, James Harthouse; young Tom's turn to crime, and worse, his framing of factory worker Stephen Blackpool in order to clear himself. For Dickens, the social discourses that have grown up out of industrialism are so pervasive and inimical that the inevitable moment of reconciliation between father and daughter, when Gradgrind "sees" Louisa for the first time as something more than a repository for facts, cannot overcome the antipathy the young woman feels toward this human connection. As Catherine Gallagher has pointed out, melodramatic convention would have this scene conclude with an embrace; but Louisa cannot bear it: "He tightened his hold in time to prevent her sinking on the floor, but she cried out in a terrible voice, 'I shall die if you hold me! Let me fall upon the ground!' And he laid her down there, and saw the triumph of his system, lying, an insensible heap, at his feet" (242).

In contradistinction to the Gradgrind plot that is founded entirely on fact and the uses of facts – and thus at least for Gradgrind incapable of being analyzed in any other terms – is the Josiah Bounderby narrative, which is based upon bluster, bullying, and balderdash. A "self-made" man who denies his true origins and the nurturing and love he received from his mother so that he can embellish his fabulous story of self-help, Bounderby's version of industrialism allows him to forgo human affiliations and establish his relationships on the basis of profit. Although not precisely a form of reification or commodity fetishism since not all of his relationships are directly tied to labor, Bounderby's attachments to others are, nonetheless, dehumanizing – they are commodities that are at least partly defined by their "usefulness." Stephen Blackpool, Louisa, Mr. Gradgrind, Mrs. Sparsit, even his mother, are only valuable to the mendacious mill owner to the extent that they can corroborate, or embellish, his presentation of himself to the world. According to the rules by which Bounderby lives, there is no vantage point outside that of the individual whom industrialism rewards by increasing his wealth and power.

As far as knowledge and information are concerned in *Hard Times*, none that is associated with industrialism is trustworthy. Facts admit to no interpretation and thus foreclose all sorts of possibilities of knowing that are not contained within their rigid boundaries. Facts' companion in *Hard Times'* representation of the discourses of industrialism is the fabricated paean to the extraordinary individual. This too offers little satisfaction as a language of information, for its interpretive or representational statements provide no point of reference outside the self-interest of the one who utters them. Bounderby and Gradgrind embody twin pillars of industrial discourse in its failure to contribute to increased knowledge, tolerance, and understanding of others, that is, to human and humane progress.

Stephen Blackpool's and Sissy Jupe's stories stand in direct opposition to those narratives, but they too hold out little promise for amelioration. Blackpool, for instance, is completely at the mercy of the industrial system: his job, his wretched marriage to an alcoholic wife, his status as a fugitive for a crime he did not commit, his death by falling down a mineshaft, are outside the compass of his agency. His few attempts at self-assertion, such as his request for knowing the law that would grant him a divorce or his refusal to join the efforts of the union organizer Slackbridge, hardly fly in the face of industrialism and ultimately are inconsequential. And while Dickens depicts him as sympathetic, he is also the working-class everyman, a symbol of how the demands of the culture of industry have robbed the laboring population of the chance to lead contented, fulfilling lives. Blackpool is nearly allegorical in this respect, an abstraction or a cipher who is, finally, subject to the whims of those who do control the logic of industrialization: the Bounderbies and Gradgrind of the world. He has given up understanding; for him life can be lived and lamented, but it cannot really be made sense of. For Blackpool, for the working class, so far removed are they from the source of knowledge about what really makes the smoke pour out of Coketown's factory chimneys that their own situations can be summed up by Stephen's continually repeated observation, "Aw's a muddle."

As despairing and bleak a view as some of Dickens's other novels may present, *Hard Times* is especially unforgiving to its characters. For instance, the Gradgrind family, which is partially redeemed at the end of the novel, gets no opportunity to reproduce itself. The "whelp," Tom, escapes both the family and the consequences of his crime, never to return to England. Louisa is never to bear children. Bounderby, who is only tangentially a member of the family, suffers a more grotesque fate. His only "offspring" are the twenty-five "Humbugs" created by his will. These men, each "past five and fifty years of age," are to take on the name Josiah Bounderby, eat and sleep in Bounderby buildings, and "nauseate all healthy stomachs with a vast amount of Bounderby balderdash and bluster" (312). The industrialist's legacy to Coketown is these progeny, born in adulthood, who promise a "long career of quibble, plunder, false pretences, vile example, little service, and much law" (312). Bounderby himself, the narrator tells us, will die of a fit in the street. That same unforgiving spirit informs the novel's representation of the Coketown strike, where the workers are as self-deceiving as any Bounderby. Dickens's attitude was decidedly different in his *Household Words* article of April 1854, "On Strike." There he was much more sympathetic to the strikers – more than 20,000 of whom had been workless for twenty-three weeks. He portrayed them as good-humored but determined, amenable to receiving financial support or hearing useful remarks, but unwilling to countenance "politics and differences" among themselves, when what was wanted was "'armony, brotherly love, and concord."[10] That "On Strike" ran three weeks after the serialization of *Hard Times* had begun emphasizes the use he put this novel to as social critique. All things compromised by industrial culture, from the bestial drunkenness of Stephen's wife, or the saccharine goodness of Stephen and Rachel, to Harthouse's dilettantism or the decimated Gradgrind family are objects of Dickens's relentless mockery and scorn.

Hard Times stands as Dickens's contribution to the "industrial fiction" genre proper, but Dickens's texts are always engaged with the effects of industrial culture. Even historical novels like *Barnaby Rudge* (1841) or *A Tale of Two Cities* (1859) have an allegorical quality to them, making it difficult to dismiss their implicit commentaries on the political unrest linked to industrialization. Nor are the worlds of Dickens's novels ever very far removed from another result of industrial culture – the growing professional business class, those who make their money as lawyers, accountants, agents, international traders, and the like. Mr. Dombey, for instance, is no manufacturer, but his interests are closely allied to the steam-driven manufacturing world. They are fatefully tied to the railroads. His son's nurse, Toodles *cum* Richards, comes from the class that is building those railroads, refiguring and compressing London and the world. As the ironhorse inexorably marches across the city, the novel chronicles its progress. The venerable Staggs's Gardens once thought itself a "sacred grove not to be withered by Railroads."[11] But the "yet unfinished and unopened Railroad was in progress," trailing smoothly away from "dire disorder" upon "its mighty course of civilisation and improvement" (*Dombey and Son*, 121). Within only a few brief years, Staggs's Gardens is no more. The ancient neighborhood has been made over in the fashion of the new railway city; there are "railway patterns in its drapers' shops, and railway journals in the windows of its newsmen. There [are] railway hotels, office-houses, lodging-houses, boarding houses; railway plans, maps, views, wrappers, bottles, sandwich boxes, and time-tables; railway hackney coach and cabstands" and on and on (290). Through this new area people and goods move like "throbbing currents," as though its "life-blood." It is on these currents that Dombey manipulates his trading empire; it is on these currents that Carker and Edith escape him, and Dombey follows. And finally, it is in the path of a locomotive, the physical force of these currents, that Carker meets his grisly fate.

In *Dombey and Son* the railroads enact the profundity of industrialism, bringing with them new senses of time, new organizations of space, new personal tastes. In *Little Dorrit* (1857) industrial culture seems farther removed, but its impact is still greatly felt. This novel of the late 1850s turns its gaze on those who have most directly profited from the advent of industrialization, and those whose job it was to direct the "progress" accompanying it. Lionel Trilling once remarked that the prison is the organizing metaphor of this novel, but language and information are almost equally central. The Circumlocution Office, that collection of bureaucrats whose motto is "how best not to do it" epitomizes the effect of industrialization on all sectors of society. This office, which so much enters but nothing ever escapes, is made possible and even necessary by the success of industrialization. The Circumlocution Office is the regulator of social change, and it manages its charge by studiously avoiding doing anything that might hasten either social amelioration or social degradation. It is an enormous mechanism for, paradoxically, both granting and denying agency to individuals: granting inasmuch as anyone who would do any-thing that is in anyway connected with the public good (or ill), solicits the Circumlocution Office for the requisite permits, licenses, patents, etc; denying in that no (or very few) such authorizations are ever issued. The result is a maelstrom of misdirection and language, of activity and bustle, but very little movement either forward or backward. So effective is the Office at thwarting change of any kind that the forthright inventor, Daniel Doyce, is forced to the Continent to seek permission to patent and manufacture his creations.

Whether it is the railroads, Civil Service bureaucracies, or as in *Bleak*

House (1853) class and infection or philanthropy for the English poor (as opposed to proselytizing to the Empire), some effect of industrialization plays a significant role in Dickens's novels. Industrial culture reaches into the lives of all his characters in ways that often may seem trivial and innocuous, but upon closer inspection demonstrate the depth at which the presuppositions of this culture was lived. In a Dickens novel, the culture of industry, if not always the object of narrative observation, is always ubiquitous, saturating the narrative so thoroughly as to be, ironically, almost invisible. For George Eliot, who was less a novelist of the city than Dickens, the reverse is true. Eliot's novels, with only a few exceptions, are layered upon a quiet but insistent nostalgia for times that are not infused by the "spirit of industry." *Adam Bede* (1859), *The Mill on the Floss* (1860), *Silas Marner* (1861), and *Middlemarch* (1872) all comment on industrialization by its relative absence from their pages. Only in subtle ways does it seem to insert itself, such as in *The Mill on the Floss* where the reader is told of the ancient ways of St. Oggs or in *Adam Bede* through the carpentry of the Bede brothers. In *Silas Marner* it is Silas's profession as a handloom weaver, working out of his own home, that reminds us that industrialization has disposed of the need for such cottage industries; in *Middlemarch*, it is Mr. Brooke's decision to run for parliament and the peripheral discussions of the 1832 Reform Bill which point to the social changes that industrialism wrought.

In one of her works, however, Eliot takes up issues of industrialization directly and reads them through the lens of education, culture, and the importance of asserting one's "best self" familiar from the thinking of Matthew Arnold. Her 1866 *Felix Holt, the Radical* was published on the eve of the second Reform Bill, but set thirty-five years earlier, during the debates surrounding the passage of the first bill to extend the franchise. Unlike the social-problem novels of the "Hungry Forties," which focused on the conditions of the working classes, *Felix Holt* concerns itself with incorporating the working classes into a broader, more inclusive national culture. Resonating with many of the concepts expressed in Matthew Arnold's *Culture and Anarchy*, this novel similarly links culture to the political. Culture, as an expression of our best selves, "suggests the idea of the State."[12] Only through culture, conceived of in this way, is it possible to stave off the anarchy that accompanies democracy – or in this instance merely the extension of the vote. The novel's protagonist, Felix, symbolizes the potential for such a culture. Educated, intellectually capable of realizing a middle-class life for himself, Felix prefers instead to remain within his class, working as a watch repairer. But like Arnold's "aliens," Felix does not truly belong to any class. His vision and aspirations are fixed upon something much larger than class affiliation. He champions the lower orders, but not as an advocate for legislation that will extend the political rights of the workers. Instead, he argues for moral regeneration through education and a concern for the "common estate of society."

This shift from the sensational depictions of the conditions of the working classes in the novels of Frances Trollope, Gaskell, and Kingsley in the 1840s to considerations of a social totality founded on a conception of culture as an articulation of our best selves, and symbolized by Arnold's idea of the "best that has been thought and known" marked an emergent way of thinking about class difference. Certainly class issues persisted throughout the rest of the century, but the concept of a broader social experience that could be shared, regardless of class lines, introduces the possibility of a new kind of identity, one based in this shared social experience. In the "Address to Working Men, by Felix Holt," written by Eliot after the passage of the 1867 Reform Bill and published in *Blackwood's*, Eliot explores this possibility. In the persona of Holt, she writes that "just as there are many things" that working men can "know better and feel much more strongly than the richer, softer-handed classes can know or feel them," so too are there "many precious benefits" that the working classes are "not so likely to be aware of" – that "treasure of knowledge" which "yields a great deal of discovery that corrects error, and of invention that lessens bodily pain," and must at last make life easier for all."[13] What this identity may be labeled remained to be seen, but *Felix Holt* implies that the treasure of knowledge can only be obtained through a "certain patience . . . with many institutions" (*Felix Holt*, 621). By driving those classes who hold those "treasures of knowledge" into the background, the working classes "run the risk of injuring [their] inheritance and the inheritance of [their] children" (622).

In *Felix Holt* that inheritance is much more than the impossibly entailed Transome estate; it is the legacy of Englishness. When Harold Transome returns from Smyrna, declaring that he "is an Oriental," he implicitly renounces his claim to Englishness, while simultaneously claiming a greater insight into things English, especially politics, because he *is* an Oriental. This man, the outsider whose mother does not recognize him, who has sired a son by a Levantine woman, and whose name by all rights should not be Transome at all, but Jermyn, is juxtaposed to the stalwart and almost priggishly English Felix. Felix stands for those traditions and customs that mark the limits of Englishness, and unlike the rich "radical" Transome, Holt's form of radicalism puts right reason and moral purpose before quick-fix enfranchisement. Felix nevertheless is punished for his association with the mob – not to mention his inadvertent killing of a constable –

though the narrative ultimately exonerates him in his marriage to Esther Lyon, the true heir to Transome Court, who rejects that inheritance for a life with Felix.

Thirty years after the ascension of Victoria to the throne and nearly two decades after works like *Mary Barton* and *Alton Locke*, statements of industrial culture are still linked to information. In *Felix Holt* that information is those bits of knowledge and understanding that comprise English culture, and which are managed, for the most part, by the middle classes. This knowledge must also be acquired by the working classes. For without such an acquisition, "No political institution will alter the nature of Ignorance, or hinder it from producing vice and misery" ("Address to the Working Men," 623). That is not to say that control of such institutions was not still very much a part of both middle- and working-class participation in industrial culture toward the end of the century. Chartism had run its course by 1848; the political expressions concerning the effects of industrialism were increasingly recognizable as full-blown socialism. Works such as William Morris's *News from Nowhere* (1891) and George Gissing's *Workers in the Dawn* (1880), *Demos* (1886), or *The Nether World* (1889) are cases in point. Political agendas became more sophisticated, and doctrinal, but the didacticism characterizing earlier "social-problem" novels still existed. Relying on different aesthetic assumptions, as well as using startlingly dissimilar settings and narrative strategies, Gissing and Morris each make important cases for involving the working classes in the legitimized political activities of society. For instance, Morris's novel takes its narrator, William Guest, into a future of cooperation and idealized communal living. In this anti-industrial novel (or romance, or "dream vision"), Guest experiences a twentieth-century England that has thrown off the confusion, dirt, and speed of the industrial age to move forward to a simpler, cleaner, egalitarian future. Gissing's novels, on the other hand, are part of the tradition of exposing the conditions of the poor to the upper classes, a literary convention that never really lost its popularity, as Henry Mayhew's *London Labour and the London Poor*, published in four volumes in 1861–62, and Charles Booth's *Life and Labour of the People in London* (1892–97) attest. His first novel, *Workers in the Dawn*, is especially notable for its scenes of working-class destitution. His later work, however, is characterized by his social and political disillusionment, born of what Raymond Williams has called his negative identification with the working classes.[14] More in line with Gissing's social disillusion than Morris's optimism is H. G. Wells's *When the Sleeper Wakes* (1899), a cautionary tale of a Rip Van Winkle-like character who awakens after two hundred years to find himself the richest man in the world, his wealth having accumulated during his cataleptic nap. This world is ruled by technology and a totalitarian state-corporate regime. The protagonist, Graham, a socialist before his fateful coma, dies leading a doomed uprising of the proletariat.

Such works are the legacy of the mid-Victorian culture of industry and information that shaped so many of the novels of that era. And like those earlier texts, they often intend to shock, either through their naturalistic representations of working-class life or through their depictions of the logic of capitalism (or in Morris's case its alternative). However, these fictional descendants of those early industrial novels did not celebrate middle-class values as the answer to working-class woes. Rather, authors like Wells, Gissing, and Morris, despite their own stolid bourgeois roots, advocated political agendas that would indeed have looked like anarchy to Kingsley, Dickens, or Gaskell.

In a similar vein, but invested at least as much in the politics of gender as the politics of class, is another of the descendants of the early social-problem novels: New Woman fiction, and by extension the figure of the "New Woman" who also appears in works that would not, strictly speaking, be included in that sub-genre. The "New Woman" of the last two decades of the nineteenth-century is clearly a product of industrial culture inasmuch as its economic and educational effects created opportunities for women outside the domestic sphere and the outworn marriage plot of middle-class respectability. A tremendous amount of public commentary in the periodicals over the New Woman and the causes she championed began as early as the 1870s, and peaked in the 1880s and 1890s. In part at least, her emergence can be traced to the service economy that spun out of the massive production that flourished from the mid-century on. As more women entered this service economy, insisted upon university educations, and became financially independent, the issues informing the "Woman Question" of the last third of the century closely resembled many of the "Condition of England" issues of the 1840s. Voting rights, education, standards of morality and conduct, all surfaced again and moved to the center of public discussions, but this time with a decidedly gendered point of view. Among specific New Woman issues were appropriate or "rational" dress for women, contraception, the social purity movement – which advocated policing men's sexuality rather than women's (from 1864 to 1886 the purview of the Contagious Diseases Acts) – occupations for women, women abstaining from marriage, and the extension of the franchise to women. The fiction of the *fin-de-siècle* contributed substantially to this discussion. Novels such as *The Woman Who Did* by Grant Allen and *The Heavenly Twins* by Sarah Grand were tremendously shall he restrict his pencil or shall he restrict his purse?"[3] In addition, Meredith, Hardy, Gissing, and many other distinguished and less distinguished novelists had problems with Mudie's Select Library. The most notorious, and certainly the most vociferous, was George Moore. Moore had *A Modern Lover* (1883) rejected by Mudie. In retaliation he published a pamphlet, *Literature at Nurse, or Circulating Morals* (1885), in which he describes the literature of the past as a robust product of open competition between ideas, and contrasts it with present-day literature, reduced to an effete, childlike state in the over-protective, matriarchy of Mudie's Library; "literature is now rocked to an ignoble rest in the motherly arms of the librarian," he claimed.[4] The attack may be vigorous but the imagery and the rhetoric is quintessentially Victorian: the struggle between good and poor literature is Darwinian, the knockabout heartiness of the struggle sounds the theme of muscular Christianity, and Moore's accusation that "Mr Mudie possesses a monopoly, and he cannot be allowed to use that monopoly to the detriment of all interests but his own"[5] is straight out of orthodox Victorian liberal economic theory.

Moore rose to his own economic challenge by circumventing the three-decker novel entirely and publishing his next novel, *A Mummer's Wife* (1885), in a single volume priced at six shillings, and thus aimed at a buyer's rather than a borrower's market. In *Literature at Nurse* he claimed that this novel had proved a great success and was then (within a year of its original publication) "in its fourth edition."[6] In choosing a single volume selling at six shillings Moore was being prophetic. When Mudie's and Smith's finally abandoned the three-decker novel by sending what amounted to an ultimatum to novel publishers in 1894,[7] the form that replaced it as the first book edition of a novel was a single volume priced at six shillings.

Because the three-decker was so egregious, there is a danger of looking at the publishing history of the novel in the nineteenth century and seeing everything in the light of that unique form. This would be a mistake. The majority of novels, and certainly a substantial majority of fiction, were not published first as three-deckers. The most obvious example of this was fiction written for the working-class market. In this context, "working class" is a term of convenience. It has to cover all sorts of people from, on the one hand, the traditional agricultural laborer and his family who, certainly in the earlier part of our period, might be earning little more than ten to sixteen shillings a week, and may have been illiterate or only semi-literate to, on the other, an artisan or a skilled industrial worker who might be earning two to three times that amount and would almost certainly have been literate.

popular; Allen's novel went through nineteen editions in its year of publication (1895) and Grand's was easily the best seller of 1893. Other, more mainstream writers such as Gissing in *The Odd Women* (1893) and Hardy in *Tess of the d'Urbervilles* (1891) and *Jude the Obscure* (1895) also contribute to the end of the century fascination/fear of female assertiveness and desire. Mina Harker in *Dracula* (1897) is another good example of how prevalent a fictional – and social – type the New Woman had become.

By the end of the century industrial culture had left center stage while the information culture which had been ineluctably associated with it – indeed which had in part defined and was defined by industrialism – was on the threshold of refashioning itself with the advent of new information technologies, a refashioning that continues today. Questions of empire, nation, and identity seemed to have replaced the central concerns of industrial culture. Nevertheless, the residue of industrial culture remained apparent, for it had already established its connection to these issues. Thus in works like Conrad's *Heart of Darkness* (1902) or *Lord Jim* (1900), Kipling's *Kim* (1901), Doyle's Sherlock Holmes stories, or in the aesthetic theories of Pater and Wilde, one can easily trace thematic pedigrees back to concerns first voiced when the culture of industry was at its most dominant, and ways of knowing, thinking, and learning about such matters first established themselves. Somewhere in all these texts, however faint, is the outline of the Crystal Palace and the Great Exhibition of 1851, when England celebrated itself, its institutions, and its industry.

NOTES

1 See Catherine Gallagher, *The Industrial Reformation of English Fiction: Social Discourse and Narrative Form 1832–1867* (Chicago: University of Chicago Press, 1985); Patrick Brantlinger, *The Spirit of Reform* (Cambridge: Cambridge University Press, 1977); Louis Cazamian, *The Social Novel in England, 1830–1850*, trans. Martin Fido (1903; London: Routledge and Kegan Paul, 1973); Rosemarie Bodenheimer, *The Politics of Story in Victorian Social Fiction*, (Ithaca: Cornell University Press, 1988); Joseph W. Childers, *Novel Possibilities: Fiction and the Formation of Early Victorian Culture* (Philadelphia: University of Pennsylvania Press, 1995).

2 According to Chadwick's biographer, S. E. Finer, Chadwick reported to Lord Brougham in July 1842 (the month of its publication) that "upwards of 20,000 copies of the Report have been sold." In September of that year he inquired about advertising in the *Times* and the *Morning Chronicle*. S. E. Finer, *The Life and Times of Edwin Chadwick* (New York: Barnes and Noble, 1952), 55.

3 Thomas Carlyle, "Chartism," in Alan Shelston, ed., *Thomas Carlyle: Selected Writings* (Harmondsworth: Penguin, 1971), 149.

4 Frances Trollope, *The Life and Adventures of Michael Armstrong, the Factory Boy* (London: Henry Colburn, 1840), v.

5 Bodenheimer, *Politics of Story*, 12.
6 Friedrich Engels, *The Condition of the Working Class in England, 1844*, trans. W. O. Henderson and W. H. Chaloner (1845; Stanford, CA: Stanford University Press, 1968), 78.
7 Elizabeth Gaskell, *Mary Barton* (1848; Harmondsworth: Penguin, 1970), 45.
8 Benjamin Disraeli, *Sybil or the Two Nations* (1845; Harmondsworth: Penguin, 1980), 94.
9 Charles Dickens, *Hard Times For These Times* (1854; Harmondsworth: Penguin, 1969), 47.
10 Charles Dickens, "On Strike," *Household Words* 213 (April 22, 1854), 226.
11 Charles Dickens, *Dombey and Son* (1848; Harmondsworth: Penguin, 1985), 122.
12 Matthew Arnold, *Culture and Anarchy* (1869; Cambridge: Cambridge University Press, 1960), 95.
13 George Eliot, "Address to Working Men, by Felix Holt," in *Felix Holt the Radical* (1868; Harmondsworth: Penguin, 1972), 621.
14 Raymond Williams, *Culture and Society* (1958; New York: Columbia University Press, 1983), 176.

5

NANCY ARMSTRONG

Gender and the Victorian novel

The impact and tenacity of the argument launched in Thomas Malthus's famous *Essay on the Principle of Population* (1798) can mean only one thing: the nineteenth century opened onto a very different field of narrative possibilities than had preoccupied and entertained the previous century, possibilities in terms of which Victorian authors and readers would imagine their lives, write their novels, and hammer out domestic and colonial policy. Although infant mortality rates had changed little for most of the people and would not improve significantly throughout the nineteenth century, the English population was growing younger. Compounded by the fact that no bouts of plague, famine, or other natural disasters had limited the growth of the population, people were marrying at a younger age. Marry a man with whom you were emotionally compatible if you could, but marry a man of material means you must, such novels as *Pride and Prejudice* (1813) and *Emma* (1816) seemed to say, or else face the degradation of impoverishment or, worse, the need to work for a living. Given that the population under twenty-five years of age shot up from 46 to 58 percent of the population between the mid-eighteenth century and the beginning of Victoria's reign in 1837, courtship rituals to ensure that deserving women would meet and win the hearts of eligible men could not have been considered a frivolous activity. Nor could knowledge of the social rituals of the sort that fill Austen's pages be distinguished from the political power of a group of men and women who were neither aristocratic nor forced to work for a living.[1] The delicate nuances of feeling and elaborate rituals that gave those feelings both vigor and charm not only consolidated this group but also contained the secret of its perpetuation.

In this chapter, I will describe how the novel teamed up with the emergent human sciences to refine the rules governing the social and biological reproduction of those people who could belong to the respectable classes, as well as those texts, objects, and images, such people could safely consume. If the eighteenth-century novel had insisted on the value of an individual independent of birth and inherited wealth, a value that resided in such qualities of mind as reason, morality, sympathy, and the will to be oneself against all odds, then in the course of the nineteenth century, the novel problematized that individual and sought to contain, constrain, and normalize him or her in ways that at once created, reinforced, and updated a new and distinctively modern social classification system. The novel not only linked the fate of the emergent middle class, its norms, values, customs, and concept of nationality with the nation itself, it also insisted that fate in turn depended on biological reproduction.

For purposes of grasping the significance of this relatively uncharted shift in cultural categories and what it must have meant for individual self-definition as well as national identity, it is instructive to see how Malthus's *Essay on the Principle of Population* revised the relationship between individual and state that John Locke had formulated near the end of the seventeenth century. Locke's "Essay on Paternal Authority" imagines a prosperous household in which the son does not have to wait for his father to die and inherit his position as head of household.[2] The son can become head of his own household as soon as he has acquired the means of self-government, and self-government comes in the form of knowledge of the law, or a developed faculty of judgment. In representing the development of paternal judgment as the limit on inherited patriarchal authority, Locke countered a blood-based definition of authority with one based on gender, or masculinity. For the nineteenth century, however, this earlier distinction between patriarchy and paternalism was much less important than the difference between a model for distributing resources based on lineal descent and one based on reproduction. Malthus situates himself in the aftermath of the French Revolution and understands the epoch stretching before him "as a period *big* with the most important changes, changes that would in some measure be decisive of the future fate of mankind."[3] No sooner does he represent the nation's history as one pregnant with possibility, however, than he turns this optimistic metaphor over to expose a sinister underside. Food increases according to a simple linear calculus, he reasons, while hungry mouths increase exponentially, each reproducing itself several times over. Indeed, times of apparent plenty were especially dangerous, since these times promoted marriage and, with it, an even greater disparity between a growing population and a diminishing food supply.

At this point in his argument, Malthus calls on domestic respectability to put a curb on sexual reproduction. When a man's income places him on the bottom rung of this group to begin with, a wife and children would certainly push that family completely off the ladder:

The woman that a man of education would naturally make the object of his choice would be one brought up in the same tastes and sentiments with himself and used to the familiar intercourse of a society totally different from that to which she must be reduced by marriage. Can a man consent to place the object of his affection in a situation so discordant, probably to her tastes and inclinations? Two or three steps of descent in society, particularly at this round of the ladder, where education ends and ignorance begins, will not be considered by the generality of people as a fancied and chimerical, but a real and essential evil.[4]

Many inferences can be drawn from this passage, including its patent unfairness to those men who lacked the economic means to live according to the polite standard, not to mention those women who understood themselves as more than a population explosion waiting to happen. What must be stressed, however, is an overarching cultural logic that gathered persuasive force as Malthus rewrote Locke's model of the household to apply to the entire world population. Malthus's *Essay on the Principle of Population* translates an insurmountable problem in the domain of production (e.g. the growing of food) into a seemingly manageable problem in the domain of reproduction (e.g. the production of human beings). If heterosexual desire caused overpopulation, which is in turn the source of war and misery, then, he reasoned, it was imperative to bring such desire under control.

The solution that presented itself not only to Malthus but also to generations of concerned authors and intellectuals who followed him was to control the problem at its source – in the female body. The advantages of this rhetorical shift in the source of the problem would prove invaluable to proponents of industrial capitalism. As newly impoverished migrants from all over an agrarian England began to accumulate in the industrial centers, the blame for their deplorable physical condition could be deflected back onto the promiscuity of their women. Even someone so critical of capitalism as Friedrich Engels was sucked into this rhetorical trap in 1845, as he described the Irish quarters as the fecund center of an infernal Manchester.[5] There, in what he describes as the unregulated sexuality of Irish immigrants, he discovered the disintegration of differences between household interior and public street, between humanity and livestock, between parents and children, which he claimed to be infecting English workers. During the two decades leading up to the 1848 collapse of Chartism, an organized effort to command the votes and wages that would ensure adequate provisions for working-class families, fiction was busy reformulating sexual relations as the resolution and even adequate compensation for forms of violence done to the family by an economic system that fiction portrayed as an autonomous and self-willed machine.

Paradoxically, however, the very same fiction that represented the household as a haven in a heartless economic world also insisted that sexual desire rather than an unregulated economy brought about the human misery that accompanied capitalism. If a good woman could compensate for socio-economic inequities, then a bad one could be represented as the cause of economic disaster for the very reasons that Malthus spells out early on and that Father Time reiterates in Thomas Hardy's *Jude the Obscure* at the end of the century. Once a novel relocated the cause of economic inequity and the exploitation of labor in the female body, it was a relatively simple matter to resolve those problems symbolically by bringing that body under control, whether through that woman's reform, her incarceration, or her banishment from the text. Emily and Charlotte Brontë's fiction performs exactly this translation of social and economic change into emotional and sexual turbulence, as if to suggest that no end of destruction could issue from one apparently powerless human being, if that human being were female. In this historical milieu, the same form of femininity that had attracted men to women in Austen's fiction began to serve as a curb on female desire instead. In the fiction of the Victorian period, gender ceased to be the means of guaranteeing reproduction of the ruling class and provided instead the means of limiting sexual reproduction. Thus set in opposition to natural desire, or what might be called "femaleness," a woman's display of Victorian femininity marked the difference between middle-class reproductive practices and those specific to the working classes, the Irish, and so-called "native" peoples. Or so we might conclude from comparing Austen's fiction to that of Emily and Charlotte Brontë.

With this as my working hypothesis, I will use selected works of Victorian fiction to show how that culture bound gender to economics in a way that put the fate of the nation in constant risk from female desire. I will also suggest (1) how fiction made the constraints of gender seem natural and necessary, if not always desirable and right, to a geographically diverse and socially heterogeneous readership, and (2) how fiction simultaneously produced a range of violations of and resistances to gender capable of reverberating across the entire system of social categories. By generating such tension between the prevailing gender norms and what appeared to be the compelling demands of natural desire, as we will see, fiction transformed the gender distinctions specific to the modern middle class into an adaptable political rhetoric, capable not only of incorporating a critique of capitalism, but also of transforming gender norms in response to economic and social change. Thanks at least in part to Victorian fiction, middle-class sexuality – its moral norms, family structure, household organization, and marriage rules – grew uniquely capable of traveling almost anywhere the novel could, both up and down the social hierarchies organizing the modern metropolis and outward to the remote corners of an expanding Empire. If it is true, as many cultural historians say, that Western modernity cannot be distinguished from its distinctive brand of mass literacy, then neither can Western modernity be distinguished from the gender differences that indelibly mark a novel as Victorian.

The failure of middle-class masculinity

In writing the sequel to his *On the Origin of the Species by Means of Natural Selection* of 1859, Charles Darwin revealed a contradiction within his own definition of masculinity. He declared that contradiction a fact of nature and then explained its contradictory character as the difference between the sexes. Published in 1871, *The Descent of Man, and Selection in Relation to Sex* abandoned Darwin's concern with human superiority over other species, a concern which resulted in a theory of evolution that could be used to rationalize the demonstrably brutal economic triumph of the modern middle classes over other social groups. He turned instead to the question of how the modern ruling-class male could represent at once the strongest competitor in the natural struggle for food and women and the very embodiment of refinement and rationality as well. "The sexual struggle is of two kinds," he determined,

> in the one it is between the individuals of the same sex, generally the male sex, in order to drive away or kill their rivals, the females remaining passive; whilst in the other, the struggle is likewise between the individuals of the same sex, in order to excite or charm those of the opposite sex, generally the females, which no longer remain passive but select the more agreeable partners.[6]

According to this model, there is only one form of desire in all of nature. This desire compelled a man to beat out other men and attract women. Any man who lacks this implicitly masculine desire and any woman who fails to respond to it would have to be excluded by their unnaturalness from the rituals of reproduction.

Darwin's modification of his own theory of evolution broke down the masculine competition for the food supply and women into two separate actions. In the first, individual men compete against each other to dominate and thus improve the bundle of traits passed to future generations, and in the second, or feminine phase, men compete among themselves to "excite or charm" women. The feminine phase clearly tests a man's ingenuity in enacting courting rituals as well as his possession of physical beauty. Here, women are empowered to exercise what Malthus called "taste and refinement" and so choose a man who has not only proved his brute ability to survive but has also struck them as a pleasant partner. This passage creates a basic asymmetry between the sexes where men are both the agents of ruthless nature and the bearers of cultural rituals that constrain, sublimate, and aestheticize that nature. Moreover, this passage translates that asymmetry into a false equivalence between the genders. A woman is responsible for selecting her partner from among successful competitors. Thus, if ruling-class men are deficient either in the vigor required for successful competition or in the cultural accouterments necessary for a harmonious domestic life, whose fault could it be but that of the woman? She, after all, selected what she regarded as "the more agreeable" man. The law of natural selection allowed Victorians to understand a capitalistic economy as a machine that worked according to its own version of nature's law, namely, that the victor in economic competition was the fittest for social domination. To tamper with this law was to endanger the national economy and thus the welfare of its entire population. This understanding of political economy had, as Karl Marx observed, rigged the competitive struggle in favor of those men who owned money and against those who owned only their labor.[7] Indeed, even Victorian intellectuals who advocated a living wage, something like a welfare safety net, and enfranchisement for working-class men, still thought of the middle classes as the superior competitors and class of men most fit to rule.

Well before the publication of Darwin's theory of natural selection in relation to sex, however, the Victorian novel had radically altered earlier notions of bourgeois love based on natural sympathy and class affinity. The Brontës were not alone in reimagining these same principles as the means of ensuring that only those capable of governing their desires could assume a position among the respectable classes. Like the Brontës, Charles Dickens, William Makepeace Thackeray, and virtually every other Victorian author we revere today demonstrate that on an individual's ability to subordinate female desire to feminine taste and morality, whether in one's lover, wife, daughter, or oneself, depended the quality and perpetuity of domestic life. On these in turn depended the quality and perpetuity of the nation.[8] Indeed, we might say that Darwin, in revising his theory of evolution to include the factor of natural selection in relation to sex, was performing the same sleight of hand that novels had been performing for several decades. He provided the natural historical rationale for relocating the cause of economic exploitation and social inequity in individuals' lack of self-government and the poor quality of family life that inevitably resulted.

Were it not for the fact that Victorian fiction so often positions its heroines to choose the wrong man, we would surely notice the conspicuous failure of middle-class masculinity to prove itself against contenders across many decades and sub-genres of nineteenth-century fiction. The second Catherine may strike us as a mix of physical precocity and cultural literacy befitting a heroine created during the century of fiction Jane Austen inaugurated, but Catherine's creator, Emily Brontë, decided not to populate *Wuthering Heights* (1847) with a single man who measures up in terms Darwin only later described as the basis for natural selection in relation to sex. There is, to be sure, no lack of either competitive brutality or cultural refinement in the world of Brontë's novel, but to find in one package a man who can both compete successfully with other men and display the "taste and refinement" that pleases a woman, the second Catherine must educate the loutish Hareton Earnshaw herself. In the same year, Charlotte Brontë gave Jane Eyre what may appear to be a wider selection of men, but her heroine nevertheless rejects all candidates who could by any stretch of the imagination belong to the modern middle class, preferring, like Emily, a well-born mate for her heroine whom the novel cuts down to size and the heroine rehabilitates for a modern household. Even if we consider the Brontë sisters idiosyncratic in this respect, there is Charles Dickens to contend with. He goes to even more extravagant lengths than the Brontës to create a form for masculinity that is at once economically functional and attractive to women. Indeed, we can read Dickens's *Dombey and Son* (1848) as an anatomy of the same contradiction that Darwin later sought to resolve by assigning its component parts to two opposing sexes.

Dickens begins this novel with the consummate capitalist, Dombey, and a woman who is as passive as ever a woman should be. By providing her husband first with a daughter and then with a son and heir to his flourishing business, she fulfills her obligations as a Victorian woman. Having little other purpose in life according to the prevailing law of nature, she dies within a few pages of the novel's opening, and the loss of this source of love paradoxically produces a son who lacks the will to survive. We might be tempted to call this a case of gender confusion, whereby the son inherits his mother's feminine passivity and dies in childhood, were it not for the fact that the surviving Dombey child, Florence, is quintessentially feminine. Indeed, the scandal of this novel is that simply by exuding affection she competes successfully against her father for the affection of his son and his second wife. Indeed, Dombey muses resentfully, everyone seems to prefer her to him:

Who? Who was it who could win his wife as she had won his boy! Who was it who, unaided by his love, regard, or notice, thrived and grew beautiful when those so aided died! Who could it be, but the same child at whom he had often glanced uneasily in her motherless infancy, with a kind of dread, lest he might come to hate her; and of whom his foreboding was fulfilled, for he DID hate her in his heart.[9]

Thus Dickens places femininity in competition with masculinity and insinuates the possibility that femininity, contrary to natural law, makes one the more fit to survive in modern society. Dombey may have all the economic power of the successful capitalist and the social authority of the head of a prosperous household, but his ability to succeed in these terms makes him unattractive to his second wife Edith. Lacking what is required to be "agreeable" to women, he fails in his capacity as head of household, and for lack of the qualities that would earn him loyalty, Dombey loses his business as well.

This link between emotional lack and economic failure is not quite as wishful as it may seem, given the historical weight that historians Catherine Hall and Leonore Davidoff place on signs of family feeling. During the 1830s and 1840s, they contend, fiction and magazines sought to translate earlier models of domestic happiness into a lived reality for middle-class readers. Authors and publishers such as Harriet Martineau and John Loudon were among those who represented the family as the way to achieve not only social harmony but also individual fulfillment. "This democratization of domesticity was solidly rooted in the homes of the middle class and not in the country estates of the minor gentry," according to Hall and Davidoff: "It was no longer tied to a desire for retreat from the development of towns and industries and a return to a patriarchal rural idyll, but located in the towns and villages of England, among middling manufacturers, traders, professionals and farmers." During this period, those businessmen and entrepreneurs with good credit consolidated their hold on the British economy. Given the instability of the English currency at this time and "the fact that credit arrangements remained essentially local or at the most regional, personal reputation became a key to survival. The behaviour of the entrepreneur, his family and household, as well as their material setting, were tangible indications of financial as well as moral probity."[10]

His possession of a well-appointed home and wholesome family indicated that a capitalist possessed a masculinity that could both prevail competitively and make him agreeable to women, in short, not only the kind of masculinity that potential investors apparently felt they could trust but also the masculinity to which Darwin ascribed the success of any species in the natural struggle for survival. When we consider how conspicuously the Brontës and Dickens represent the natural dependency of femininity on masculinity as the relationship between object and owner, their apparent disagreement with Darwin begins to make sense. When he remodels his house for Edith, clothes her magnificently, and showers her with splendid things, Dombey transforms her into an object. Her transformation into a sign of his buying power resembles the process of commodification. In a section of *Capital* called "The Commodity Fetish and its Secret," Marx describes the commodity as a special kind of object that subsumes the labor that goes into making it as so many of its own physical qualities. To do so, moreover, the commodity substitutes an image of the object for the object itself. This image-object enters into an abstract economic relationship with other such objects, and that relation among objects replaces the social relationship among human beings.[11] Thus Dombey strives to make Edith part of the Dombey mansion, a showpiece for his success in relation to other men. In turning her into a reflection of himself, however, Dombey does not possess so much as lose control of her. Like Lady Dedlock, the fallen heroine of *Bleak House* (1853), Edith Dombey is both more than the object Mr. Dombey thinks he possesses (she is her "self," or a subject), and less (she has depreciated her value as an object of exchange among men by entering into an adulterous relationship with Dombey's subordinate, Carker). By way of contrast, Florence Dombey represents what Dombey himself lacks. By concealing his daughter from public view, moreover, he keeps her off the marriage market, inadvertently increasing her value as a feeling subject.

With such noble exceptions as Joe Gargery of *Great Expectations* (1861) or John Harmon of *Our Mutual Friend* (1865), Dickens's male protagonists can be incorporated within the family and rehabilitated by woman as subject only after they have been misled and brought low by woman as object. Like the rehabilitation of Hareton Earnshaw and Edmund Rochester, that of Dombey, Pip, David Copperfield, Mr. Gradgrind, Eugene Wrayburn, Sidney Carton, and so many others entails a loss of the very qualities that allowed these characters to compete with other Victorian men for money, position, and love. One would not have to construe their feminization as a loss of masculinity, however, were the women involved to remain economically dependent on their men, while the men in turn came to depend on their women for what Malthus called the "taste and refinement" appropriate to their social station. But such complementarity of genders does not inform Victorian fiction. With Heathcliff's demise, Catherine and Hareton both inherit the estates of their parents; Jane Eyre must become an heiress before she can return to Thornfield and rehabilitate

Rochester. Like Rochester, Eugene Wrayburn of *Our Mutual Friend* suffers a debilitating physical blow and reduced circumstances before the novel deems him a suitable match for Lizzie Hexam, and Dombey fulfills the parable that one must lose his financial empire in order to inherit the emotionally sustaining domestic kingdom that forms around his daughter Florence. As if to call attention to the contradiction posed by the two forms of competition in Darwin's paradigm, the Victorian novel demonstrates that the competitive masculinity required for economic success is not all that "agreeable" to women. Nor does it foster the kind of affective bond necessary to sustain a home. The fact that such masculinity cannot therefore reproduce itself becomes explicit in the deaths of Heathcliff's and Dombey's sons.

If George Eliot seems to offer a subtler version of the same paradigm, that is because we tend to read her work retrospectively through the lens of *Middlemarch* (1872), when in fact *Silas Marner* (1861) offers as stark a demonstration of the inverse relationship between (masculine) economic and (feminine) affective success as any we find in Dickens or Hardy. Like the eponymous hero of Hardy's *Jude the Obscure* (1895), Silas is head of a household embedded in a political economy sustained by masculine competition. Both lose out to those with social and economic capital, only to regain stature for the reader as they assume a reproductive role. To give Silas a chance to earn redemption through a maternal relationship to the golden-tressed Eppie, Eliot must set the story in a pastoral context that capitalism has not yet come to dominate. But Hardy battens down this same escape hatch in *Jude*, when he sets his story in the historical period following the industrial commodification of labor. Although *Middlemarch* seems to belong to an inescapably modern England, Eliot's reputedly realistic novel is more of a piece with Hardy's *Far From the Madding Crowd* (1874) than criticism acknowledges. Like *Silas*, *Far from the Madding Crowd* tends to be dismissed for the unabashed pastoralism which restores some of the symmetry to sexual selection that appears to govern courtship in Austen's fiction. Both Eliot's Dorothea Brooke and Hardy's Bathsheba Everdene have money, and they must consequently struggle to find another basis on which to subordinate themselves to a man. This struggle consists in their surveying and rejecting as inadequate for purposes of their self-definition a whole string of eligible suitors: doctors, intellectuals, gentlemen farmers, military men, and politicians. Having demonstrated the unacknowledged superiority of their heroines in relation to all these types, *Middlemarch* and *Far From the Madding Crowd* import forms of masculinity unavailable within the modern urban world. Eliot conjures up Will Ladislaw, a distant cousin of Dorothea's intellectually inferior scholar-husband, and Hardy early on introduces Gabriel Oak, an educated farmer and former landowner who serves as the manager of Bathsheba's farm. Both men combine the masculine vigor of the pre-industrial Englishman with the emotional receptivity of the feminized economic loser. In marrying these men, Dorothea and Bathsheba settle for a life more ordinary than each had hoped, more ordinary, as Eliot's closing salvo famously contends, than her heroine actually deserves.

Trollope characteristically carries the novel's interrogation of the Darwinian model of sexual selection through to its logical conclusion. *The Eustace Diamonds* (1872) makes it clear that women must select men for their money rather than for their agreeable qualities. Indeed, it is fair to say that any man whom women find agreeable in other respects will in all likelihood cost them dearly in economic terms, and there can be little emotional gratification in that. As Trollope collapses the masculine and feminine phases of sexual selection into one another, agreeability – indeed, intimacy itself – becomes an item of economic exchange designed only to capture a fortune. Trollope is less than interested in the man born to great wealth, as such a man might marry whom he will, or even not marry at all. Marriage is similarly uncomplicated for the poor man, since "his wife's fortune will consist in the labour of her hands, and in her ability to assist him in the home." But, he continues, "between these there is a middle class of men, who, by reason of their education, are peculiarly susceptible to the charms of womanhood, but who literally cannot marry for love, because their earnings will do no more than support themselves."[12] Rather than occupying the normative, moral center of a spectrum of masculinities, the man in the middle is forced to compete with other men for the most valuable women. Women, in this setting, fare somewhat better, but this is only because they are the products of masculine competition, objects whose value is determined in a marketplace that cannot be distinguished from the business world at large. Trollope allows us to admire Lizzie Eustace, as she attempts to hang onto the diamonds that give her value as well as notoriety in the eyes of the whole spectrum of eligible men, but he will not allow us to admire her for anything resembling femininity. Indeed, whenever she counts on a man, whether Lord Fawn, or her "Corsair," or even the quasi-heroic Frank Greystock, rather than on her own wits to determine her fate, she loses her grip on the diamonds, her value in the marriage market, and thus her ability to compete for those men. In a system of exchange where men compete for the economically successful woman, women cannot be feminine any more than men can be masculine. Presuming that a good share of the novel's readers were precisely these people in the middle, we must ask ourselves why the novel's insistence on the steady erosion of middle-class masculinity had such enormous appeal.

Judging by their fiction, this class of people authorized themselves by means of emergencies that periodically put the virtue of economically dependent woman at risk. The so-called India Mutiny of 1857–58 provided just such an occasion, as did the spread of venereal disease among military men that inspired the Contagious Diseases Acts of the 1860s, as well as the *fin-de-siècle* outbreak of hysteria. Although it dealt harshly with women who exceeded the limits set by bourgeois femininity, Victorian fiction also suggested that women behaved in this way only when the wrong kind of men were in charge. Indeed, Victorian novels are reluctant to offer anything like an adequate middle-class man. In nineteenth-century fiction, the regularity with which the reigning masculinity fails to make a world safe for femininity suggests that threatened femininity is not a disruption of the system but part and parcel of modern cultural logic and the guarantee of its success.[13] Victorian fiction offered the reader the figure of a feminine body – vulnerable to the forces of history and empowered to resist by passive means alone – and placed that body in a state of crisis. In so doing, fiction redefined the feminine body, the interiority that body was presumed to contain, and the household surrounding it, as that same fiction called forth new forms of bourgeois masculinity to resolve a problem created by an historically earlier ruling-class man.

The discrepancy between sex and gender

Victorian masculinity assumed that it took a fundamentally asocial desire to acquire wealth and rise in the social world. Unless he satisfied this drive, a man was not qualified to be head of household and reproduce his kind. If men do not make "agreeable" domestic partners in fiction, then we can assume it is simply because men are masculine rather than feminine. Along with this concern for the agreeability of middle-class men, Victorian novels maintained that most women do not make agreeable domestic partners either. But given the fact these women were women and not equipped by nature for the competitive struggle, novels had to ponder the source of disagreeability in women. Eighteenth-century England regarded such women as simply lacking the education, social acumen, emotional delicacy, and refined taste it took to attract and select the right man. Where Jane Austen portrayed a Lydia Bennet or Maria Bertram as lacking the cultural equipment that ensured a woman's femininity, Victorian novelists placed traditional femininity in an agonistic struggle with female nature. Such heroines as Catherine Earnshaw, Jane Eyre, Maggie Tulliver, Louisa

Gradgrind, and many others, pulsate with a desire capable of canceling out all signs of femininity and, with it, their economic basis for a position within the middle classes. If eighteenth-century fiction invented "femininity," then it is fair to say that Victorian fiction invented "femaleness."

The founders of British anthropology pushed Darwin's second phase of natural selection to the point where it contradicted Darwinian theory, identifying primitive cultures as polyandrous cultures in which their reproductive function gave women the authority, or "mother right," to establish the pecking order among men, several of whom were required to support a reproductive unit. Where Friedrich Engels saw this system as in some ways superior to a modern culture in which men competed with other men for control of women, most Victorians regarded anything else but the self-supporting, monogamous, paternalistic, heterosexual household as abnormal expressions of sexual desire that it was culture's business to suppress.[14] Indeed, even Engels felt that human desire, if left to its own devices, would eventually sort itself into monogamous heterosexual partners and their immediate families. He could imagine desire bringing about this comedic ending to the conflict between itself and social convention, however, only because he did not think that human beings were naturally promiscuous. Meanwhile, urban ethnographer Henry Mayhew was discovering how many working-class women were willing to exchange sexual favors for an economic livelihood outside the bounds of marriage and often to more than one man. By so violating the norms of paternalistic monogamy, these women had turned the great industrial cities of financial-industrial England into generative centers of poverty and crime. "In tracing the geography of a river," Mayhew claims suggestively, "it is interesting to go to its source, possibly a tiny spring in the cleft of a rock in some mountain glen . . . We proceed," he continues, "in a similar manner to treat of the thieves and swindlers of the metropolis. Thousands of our felons are . . . carried to the beershop or gin palace on the breast of worthless drunken mothers, while others, clothed in rags, run at the heels or hang by the skirts of their petticoats."[15]

Within four decades, Sigmund Freud and his collaborator Josef Breuer were discovering similarly blocked and diverted instincts as the suppressed content of the fantasy lives of respectable women, to account for which they concluded that the memory of a psychical trauma, sexual in nature, "acts like a foreign body" within the individual.[16] Like Mayhew, they describe their work in terms that invoke at once the urban detective and the imperial explorer, as they trace the hysterical symptom back to its source in the individual unconscious. By locating the source of urban poverty and crime in the bodies of working-class women, Mayhew followed the

Malthusian pattern and recast an insurmountable problem in the masculine domain of production as a manageable problem in the feminine domain of reproduction. Anthropology's sleight of hand was to represent alternative family structures as inversions of the natural family, thus the cause of that family's malfunction.[17] Similarly, by locating scenes of these "foreign" or "primitive" ways of organizing sexual relations in the modern unconscious, especially that of women, Freud attributed their hysteria – which rendered women unable to carry on sexual relationships – to a struggle between their female instincts and feminine acculturation.

For the half-century before Freud wrote up the results of his conversations with victims of hysteria, novels had been representing women's lives in terms of precisely this struggle between femaleness and femininity. What else if not such a struggle generates the interlocking fates of the two Catherines Earnshaw in *Wuthering Heights*, of Esther and Lady Dedlock in *Bleak House*, of Sissy Jupe and Louisa Gradgrind in *Hard Times* (1854), and of Lucy Morris and Lizzie Eustace in *The Eustace Diamonds*, to mention but a few? Desire rarely comes in its pure form, at least not in a flesh and blood Englishwoman; it takes such forms as Jane Eyre's nemesis Bertha Mason, the ghost of the first Catherine Earnshaw, Mary Barton's near-dead Aunt Esther who collapses into an unrecognizable heap outside her window (Elizabeth Gaskell, *Mary Barton*, 1848), or Estella's murderous working-class mother (*Great Expectations*). Indeed, although Victorian heroines tend to come in pairs, the protagonist within each couple carries on within herself a struggle between the extremes of femininity and femaleness that set her in opposition to her fallen sister or mother. There, but for having won this internal struggle, goes she. Victorian heroines can, like Jane Eyre, gratify their reproductive instincts only by triumphing over the female who lurks within. Alternatively, like Maggie Tulliver, the protagonist of George Eliot's *Mill on the Floss* (1860), they can lose this heroic struggle with desire, become virtually indistinguishable from their brothers, and be swept away into social oblivion. Any compromise between the two powerful drives – toward sexual gratification and social survival – tends to leave the Victorian heroine in the curiously diminished state that characterizes not only Thackeray's Becky Sharp and her reincarnation as Trollope's Lizzie Eustace, but the far more complex Dorothea Brooke as well, as Eliot submerges her in the collectivity of unacknowledged domestic saints in the closing paragraphs of *Middlemarch*. At one extreme of this spectrum, we find those curiously listless women who have simply capitulated without much of a struggle to femininity as enforced by bourgeois masculinity. Dickens's Mrs. Smallweed has to be plumped up daily like a pillow, for example, and Louisa's mother simply fades away, the rest of the family unable to recall the exact moment when she died, so unobtrusive was her presence in the day-to-day life of the Gradgrind household.

The heroine of Ellen (Mrs. Henry) Wood's *East Lynne* (1861) initially lacks a desire to call her own. The daughter of an unhealthy mother and benignly irresponsible aristocratic father, she is simply passed on along with her father's house to the delighted man who purchases the family estate shortly before her father's death. This novel proves, as do so many others, that nothing makes a man quite so desirable as his absence. After she leaves her husband and children in an equally passive manner for a life in Europe with a unrepentant rake, desire at last rushes in to fill the empty place in the bosom of Isabel Vane: "A stepmother at East Lynne, and one of her children gliding on to death! Oh to be with them! to see them once again! To purchase that boon, she would willingly forfeit all the rest of her existence."[18] As it turns out, the only way Isabel can satisfy this belated longing for husband and children is to return to East Lynne in disguise as governess to her own children. The natural components of her longing – maternal as well as sexual – must be completely suppressed if she wants to bask in the presence of her missing family at all. Two questions emerge from the popular theory of desire shaping this novel: how can the absence of natural desire that manifests itself as listlessness lead to a woman's promiscuity? How can the total suppression of natural desire, on the other hand, lend heroic stature to a sexually experienced woman, if only heroic stature of the very limited kind that Eliot allows Dorothea Brooke? In Victorian fiction, a woman's value as a woman no more depends on her lack of desire than on the machinations propelled by desire that lead to her gratification. True femininity depends on the subject's active suppression of desire. If readers tend to consider Lucy Snowe, the heroine of Charlotte Brontë's *Villette* (1865), peculiar, even perverse, it is simply because she carries this principle to its extreme but nevertheless logical conclusion. Lucy derives pleasure from simulating the listless Victorian woman. By refusing to give even the most modest expression to her consequently turbulent desire for human companionship, she intensifies her longing to be seen, heard, and loved.

And what of desire that cannot or will not be so suppressed? It is fair to say the Victorian novel never gives female desire a fully human form, in this way driving home the point that such desire, once it is allowed to take charge of a woman's body, distorts that body so that it cannot be placed within the categories of middle-class culture. Mr. Rochester's "mad, bad and embruted" first wife, Bertha Mason, in *Jane Eyre*, is perhaps the most memorable example of such disfiguration:

> In the deep shade, at the further end of the room, a figure ran backwards and forwards. What it was, whether beast or human being, one could not, at first sight tell: it groveled, seemingly on all fours; it snatched and growled like some strange wild animal; but it was covered with clothing; and a quantity of dark, grizzled hair, wild as a man, hid its head and face.[19]

It is important to notice that this description does not simply reduce Bertha Mason to an animal. In pushing her back down the evolutionary tree, Brontë also gives Jane's antagonist the markings of what Darwin called the "lower" races and Mayhew considered typical of the "criminal classes." Brontë performs this transformation on Rochester's Creole wife, despite the fact she was of pure European descent and the daughter of a wealthy landowner.

There is a reason why literary criticism has interpreted the monstrous figure of Bertha as Brontë's representation of Jane's passion for Rochester, on the one hand, and of colonial subjects, on the other, in defiance of the fact that no Victorian heroine could display the traces of a lower race while colonial subjects invariably did.[20] The link between the two female characters is hardly arbitrary. In figures so different as Catherine Earnshaw's ghost, Estella's murderous mother, and Mary Barton's bad aunt Esther, the middle-class woman has been physically disfigured so as to represent the intractable desires housed in savage and working-class bodies. Even the pre-pubescent protagonist of Lewis Carroll's *Alice's Adventures in Wonderland* (1866) knows that should she fail to regulate her appetite, her body will instantly and grotesquely grow out of control, pushing her out of her rightful place within the sanctuary of a middle-class home. These are the terms in which Alice admonishes herself upon failing to recite by rote the education that places her above the ignorant Mabel: "'I'm sure those are not the right words,' said poor Alice, and her eyes filled with tears again as she went on, 'I must be Mabel after all, and I shall have to go and live in that poky little house, and have next to no toys to play with, and oh, ever so many lessons to learn!'" To be degraded to the status of the relatively undisciplined Mabel is, for Alice, too awful to contemplate. "'No, I've made up my mind about it,'" she says, "'if I'm Mabel, I'll stay down here . . . until I'm somebody else.'"[21]

The Victorian novel certainly drew on arguments about the relationship between female nature and the characteristics called femininity that social scientists were attributing specifically to women of the Western European middle classes, but the novel did something with the relationship between female nature and feminine culture that only such a popular medium could do. Victorian fiction revised an earlier narrative that insisted a woman's quest for financial security and social respectability began and ended with her ability to attract an agreeable man and extract a promise of marriage from him. According to this narrative, in which a woman's desires determined her place in the intricate ranking system of the social world her femaleness and femininity were one and the same. In Victorian fiction, however, such closure becomes increasingly impossible over the course of the century. A woman did not necessarily desire the man who could both gratify her desire and provide her with a secure social position. Industrial novels such as *Mary Barton* and *Hard Times* indicate that the wrong object choice on the part of a woman could shake masculine authority over both household and nation to its foundation. Such sensation novels as *East Lynne* and *Lady Audley's Secret* (1862) pick up where Dickens left off with Edith Dombey of *Dombey and Son* and Lady Dedlock of *Bleak House*. Sensation novels exploit the possibility that even when a woman succeeds in marrying well, misinformation and deceit can make him appear a rake or her an adulteress, generating passions that destroy the most established families. During the 1850s and 1860s, in other words, fiction made the selection of a husband into the most important thing a woman did. On her choice of a love object, a man she could both marry and desire, depended not only her identity as a white, respectable English woman, but also the integrity of the family unit, on which in turn rested the well-being and longevity of the nation. To regulate the female body thus became imaginatively bound up with the internal order and external authority of Great Britain itself.

Bad reproduction

Literary criticism assumes that fiction whose character, setting, and narrative logic violate the principles of self-enclosure, materialism, and probability does so for purposes of representing the emotional extremes produced by fantasy and delusion. Such fiction is usually classified as "gothic" or "romance." Realism, in contrast, places material curbs on the inner operations of private fantasy so as to provide the reader, in the words of Georg Lukács, with a sense of "the organic, indissoluble connection between man as a private individual and man as a social being, a member of a community."[22] Our examination of the relationship between femaleness (those aspects of character subject to natural desire) and femininity (those aspects of character subject to the constraints of politeness, good taste, and greater concern for others) suggests, however, that Victorian social conventions sought to organize a far less stable social world than Lukács suggests, so that flare-ups of desire could destroy the most traditional home and destabilize the social position of its inhabitants. With the notable exception of George Eliot, novelists from Emily and Charlotte Brontë through Dickens to Eliot, Hardy, Trollope, James, and Conrad simultaneously won the approval or earned the scorn of Victorian readers on the basis of how they blended gothic effects with fiction that purported to carry out the mission of realism as Lukács defines it.[23] To understand the cultural logic and impact guiding and authorizing this collaboration between what only appear to be mutually exclusive fictional modes, it is instructive to think of that collaboration in terms of gender.

By offering a parable of the consequences of bad reproduction, Mary Shelley's *Frankenstein* (1818) provides an instructive step toward this objective. As in *Dombey* and *Hard Times*, the mechanized labor and instrumental rationality that accompany capitalism permeate the domestic and educational institutions designed to counter the competitive operations of the marketplace. Such interpenetration of the domestic and socio-economic worlds results in a failure of bourgeois masculinity, an eruption of female desire, or both, which dismembers the normal family. *Frankenstein* carries male production to an extreme where it completely usurps the female role of reproduction. Shelley's anti-heroic scientist Victor Frankenstein attempts to bypass both female nature and a feminizing culture by manufacturing a human being out of the raw materials of the charnel house. The result is a monstrous parody of so-called natural reproduction, a motherless ghoul who quite literally dismembers the extended Frankenstein family. Untempered by the feminine phase of natural selection in which the females select the most agreeable males, Frankenstein's excessive masculinity threatens to bring civilization itself to an end.

At the century's close, by way of contrast, Bram Stoker's *Dracula* (1857) creates its enduring gothic effect by shifting the threat to family and nation to the second, feminine phase of natural selection. This novel is as obsessed with consumption as *Frankenstein* is with production. *Dracula* is all about women's inability to select the right men. Lucy Westenra represents the traditional heroine who obeys desire and therefore fails to exercise the very principle of selection on which the future of Western civilization depends in this novel. Pursued by a number of suitors, she does choose the one born of English gentry, as well she should, but she wishes she could say yes to all of them. Her latent promiscuity blossoms into a tendency to wander at night, admit bats through her bedroom window, and drink the blood of English babies. With Dracula's arrival, the problem of promiscuous desire may have exponentially increased to nationally disastrous proportions, but the problem of wanton consumption is already in Lucy waiting to be put into practice. When it is, all traces of femininity are displaced by the features of racial taint and social decline, features with which the readership would by now have become all too familiar. Then out of the diseased, disfigured, and dismembered remains of the traditional heroine, a new kind of heroine emerges.

If any one scene from a novel could demonstrate how the gothic changes the relationship between femaleness and femininity at the end of the nineteenth century, it would certainly be the bedroom scene where Dracula forces Mina to perform a peculiar kind of oral sex:

> On the bed beside the window lay Jonathan Harker, his face flushed and breathing as though in a stupor. Kneeling on the near edge of the bed facing outwards was the white-clad figure of his wife. By her side stood a tall, thin man, clad in black. His face was turned from us, but the instant we saw all recognised the Count – in every way, even to the scar on his forehead. With his left hand he held both Mrs. Harker's hands, keeping them away with her arms at full tension; his right hand gripped her by the back of the neck, forcing her face down on his bosom. Her white nightdress was smeared with blood, and a thin stream trickled down the man's bare breast which was shown by his torn-open dress. The attitude of the two had a terrible resemblance to a child forcing a kitten's nose into a saucer of milk to compel it to drink.[24]

What governs this grotesque tableau, if not the figure of inversion? Here, Dracula turns the maternal function of nursing into a poisonous form of force-feeding designed to turn Mina into the kind of rapacious consumer Lucy was. Gothic fiction such as this simply dramatizes the magical thinking that inhabits the heart of realism, whenever an individual rubs up against something capable of eradicating that difference on which that individual depends for his or her identity as such. Charlotte Brontë's heroines Jane and Lucy undergo much the same disintegration of autonomy in the red bedroom and dormitory attic, respectively, as Emily's Lockwood experiences in Catherine Earnshaw's bed. Even George Eliot resorts to descriptions that erode the distinction inside and outside, or self and non-self. Indeed, by putting Maggie Tulliver through a sequence of such moments, each of which simultaneously expands her intellectual boundaries and threatens her autonomy as a woman, Eliot makes the point that there is no place within the categories of realism for an intellectual heroine.

At least through the 1850s, gothic forms of boundary dissolution – between male and female, white and racially marked individuals, English and non-English, human and animal – tend to work against normative definitions of masculinity and femininity in order to expand the possibilities for becoming a man or a woman. In the later Victorian period, however, dissolutions of these same boundaries are more likely to operate in the service of degeneration than in the service of self-production. As a theory, "degeneration" found perhaps its clearest expression in the protracted psycho-social treatise authored by Max Nordau. Nordau's *Degeneration* (1895) attempted to convince an international readership concerned with national purity that European individualism had passed its zenith and was generating consumer practices that obscured the difference between men and women. The result of *fin-de-siècle* consumerism was an illicit mixture that destroyed the autonomy of individual and type as well. In the fashionable sections of London and Paris, one consequently "seems to be moving amongst dummies patched together at haphazard in a mythical mortuary, from fragments of bodies, heads, trunks, limbs, just as they come to hand, and which the designer, in heedless pell-mell, clothed at random in the garments of all epochs and countries."[25] Here Nordau links the bad cultural reproduction effected by *fin-de-siècle* consumerism with Victor Frankenstein's inaugural act of bad reproduction. Clearly, what began as a solution to the problems of mass production – namely, the translation of those overwhelming problems into one of reproduction – no longer works by the end of the century.

H. G. Wells recast degeneration theory as a fictional narrative in *The Time Machine* (1895), where a time traveler hurls himself into the future to discover an apparently advanced, bucolic, but effeminate version of middle-class man whose every need is provided by a ruthlessly masculinized working class who labor invisibly beneath the ground. Ironically, these nasty creatures are the brains of this advanced civilization, where the elites are cultivated as livestock prized for their delectable flesh. Like Nordau, then, Wells revised Darwin's theory of evolution to demonstrate that excessive development not only feminized men but also set those men on the slippery slope to becoming objects. Both authors suggest that degeneration manifests itself as a disease of consumption that turns human beings, once producers of objects, into a commodity for consumption themselves. As the Western individuals become too cultured, they exchange their natural bodies and the qualities of race, class, and gender inherent in them for an identity based on the objects they consume. Earlier on in the century, there were indeed men and women – Thackeray's Becky Sharp, the Lammles in Dickens's *Our Mutual Friend*, for example – who could pass for members of a higher class than their background or income warranted, but these characters never leave the reader any room to doubt that the truth of natural identity can and will be acknowledged before novel's end. As early as the 1860s or thereabouts, however, fiction begins to display significant erosion of this faith that class will out, on the assumption that class is as fixed as race or gender. *Alice's Adventures in Wonderland* asks us to suspend belief in an *a priori* class identity for the duration of her ultra-literary dream. Even after Alice quits the dream for the security of middle-class domestic life, however, Lewis Carroll allows the suggestion to linger that this so-called reality is but one more byproduct of literature. Fact and fiction have traded places both within the dream and in the frame tale.

This inversion of traditional mimetic priorities is sometimes ascribed to "Bovarysm," a label containing the secret of fiction's enduring relationship not only to gender but to commodity culture as well.[26] Ever since the rise of the novel during the eighteenth century, women were considered far more susceptible than men to the influence of the new genre, as Charlotte Lennox's *The Female Quixote* (1752) and Austen's *Northanger Abbey* (1818) attest. But where the eighteenth-century woman was educated by the humiliation she suffered from applying novels to actual experience, the nineteenth-century heroine could lose her livelihood and even her life, as Gustave Flaubert's famous heroine, Emma Bovary, did when she attempted to realize a literary romance in her choice of sexual partners. Dickens's Lady Dedlock and Hardy's Tess come immediately to mind. Even in a novel so fond of deflating melodrama as *The Eustace Diamonds*, the consequences of living a novel lead the heroine to trust the wrong man with the secret of the theft of the eponymous jewels, simply because he fulfills her fantasy of a "corsair." In accounting for the diamonds, how she got them, her reasons for keeping them, the persecution she has suffered for so doing, as well as the time and place of their disappearance, Lizzie not only converts the diamonds into fiction in claiming to have acquired them legitimately when in fact she had not, but she also makes the diamonds the basis for her social position and value as a woman. Her imaginary jewels make her a desirable match for marriage, although she is woefully in debt. Under these circumstances, the diamonds are no longer her accessory so much as she is theirs; they not only threaten to drag her with them into the criminal economy, but also give their name to the title of the novel. By basing her identity on the jewels, Trollope thus suggests, his heroine becomes the victim of nothing else but her willingness to objectify her value as an object – a largely fictional object at that.

The gothic implications of this reversal of copy and original play themselves out in Oscar Wilde's *Picture of Dorian Gray* (1891). For Wilde, identity is not something forged in the internal struggle between innate desire and the gendered norms of one's culture. Nor is it a struggle restricted to women. Although Victorian culture allowed men more freedom to express their desires, those desires were themselves a literary effect, as we soon discover when Lord Henry's little yellow book sends Dorian on a road to experiences incompatible with the noble figure Basil

Hallward once captured in paint. Those desires inscribe themselves, not on anything resembling his hero's authentic nature, Wilde would insist, but merely on a previous and rather boring cultural stereotype:

> It was the strangest book that he had ever read. It seemed to him that in exquisite raiment, and to the delicate sound of flutes, the sins of the world were passing in dumb show before him. Things that he had dimly dreamed of were suddenly made real to him. Things of which he had never dreamed were gradually revealed . . . It was a poisonous book.[27]

This book immediately begins to revise the masculine type of the romance hero that initially informs his character. Like Lady Dedlock, Dorian strives to preserve the appearance of the type, despite the narrative of crime and punishment that inscribes itself at once on his interiority and on the portrait he has hidden in the attic. In contrast with even the most idealized characters we find in Dickens, the characters in Wilde's novel are just that, "characters," and being so, he contends, they are as much the basis of our own reality as of the novel's. *The Picture of Dorian Gray* dramatizes the degeneration of the gentleman who masquerades as a type into the type of the degenerate. Being equally types, these seemingly incompatible characters are ultimately interchangeable. As the concluding lines of the novel explain, "When they entered they found, hanging on the wall, a splendid portrait of their master as they had last seen him, in all the wonder of his exquisite youth and beauty. Lying on the floor was a dead man, in evening dress, with a knife in his heart. He was withered, wrinkled, and loathsome of visage. It was not till they had examined the rings that they recognized who it was" (*Dorian Gray*, 264). What makes this novel seem so thoroughly queer has less to do with the nature of the secret crimes that grotesquely mark Dorian's body, then, than with Wilde's use of a male to dramatize the logic of Bovarysm – where reading creates rather than reflects the sexual desire of a male. Victorian culture thought of this inversion of art and life as a female problem.

Now to review the cultural differences that gothic fiction seems intent on challenging. A novel by the Brontës or Dickens asks us to assume that a feminine character is by definition not masculine. Since working-class women and women of other races are assumed to be less than feminine, they are to varying degrees presumed to be masculine. Although the same principle holds true for masculinity, that it cannot incorporate elements of femininity without a loss of status, we find the social prerogatives and material privations that accompany gender difference to be far from symmetrical. If a character proves void of all signs of feminine passivity, for example, this is a good thing only if that character is male. On the other hand, if a character lacks all signs of masculine aggression, whether male or female, that character will be economically dependent. The moment a female character reveals a gram of competitive acuity, she becomes ineligible to participate in the second phase of natural selection, where, as Darwin tells the story, she is empowered to choose the man she finds most agreeable. What femininity loses in terms of socio-economic independence, it thus regains with a vengeance in symbolic terms, as women become the arbiters of taste and gentility. Moreover, the importance of "woman" within this second, strictly cultural domain appears to increase over the course of the century, as we can observe within the novel *Dracula* itself.

The story of Lucy Westenra assumes that a woman begins as a purely feminine being and is subsequently corrupted or not by forms of desire, whose traces are signs of masculinity (witness the rapacious look that comes over Lucy's features as she reaches out to clasp her human lover in a last lethal embrace). But the story of Mina Harker exactly inverts this model of identity formation. As a wife separated from her significantly overpowered husband and as a secretary to the vampire hunters, she assembles the information they collect, revealing the pattern of cultural behavior that allows them to know Dracula for what he is and overpower him. Her communication skills are enhanced by the fact she is infected by his bite and can telepathically read his mind and movements. As such, however, she is also a foreign agent among her closest friends and family, whose motives and movements the vampire in turn detects through her. It is almost as if by reproducing the thoughts and acts of others in writing, she has herself been reproduced as writing, a transparent medium, something that can be read. Thus she begins by containing a mix of categorical possibilities – neither male nor female, white nor racially-marked, of high status or low. Mina acquires the femininity befitting a heroine as she casts out of herself many of the features of race, class, gender, and nationality that late nineteenth-century British culture made available for precisely this purpose. Oscillating between a competence at managing information which often outstrips the ability of her masculine counterparts, on the one hand, and an utter dependence on masculine mastery of knowledge, on the other, Mina survives an elaborate purification ritual to give birth to Jonathan Harker's son. Thus where Lucy begins as a feminine woman and subsequently incorporates masculine desire, Mina becomes a feminine heroine through a purification ritual that externalizes the masculine behavior induced by bad blood and a flow of information that should be restricted to men. What Stoker separates into two heroines, those novels we consider examples of realism had already packed into one. Hardy's Tess and Eliot's

Dorothea Brooke, for example, owe their complexity to the interaction of these conflicting theories of identity formation. Both heroines follow what cannot be called the purest of feminine motives in selecting a mate, but both are nevertheless allowed to recover their femininity according to a very different principle: Tess, as the cultural logic guiding Lucy Westenra's fate overtakes the logic governing Mina Harker's, Dorothea, as she settles for being Mina after playing at being Lucy.

In their relentless feminizing of such intellectual heroines as Dorothea Brooke and Mina Harker, these novels are not primarily concerned with keeping English women pure for English men. They are more concerned with updating the difference between cultural tasks that can be considered feminine and those which are strictly masculine. Even though her compilation of information not only helps to slay the vampire but also provides Stoker himself with a device for conveying the story to us, his concluding chapter is careful to distinguish Mina's secretarial work from the intellectual labor of the various men who figure out and execute the solution to the problem posed by Dracula: "I took the papers from the safe where they had been ever since our return so long ago. We were struck with the fact, that in all the mass of material of which the record is composed, there was hardly one authentic document; nothing but a mass of type-writing" (*Dracula*, 382). The heroes of the tale achieve a form of masculinity capable of competing with the vampire's as Mina transfers her duties of information gathering and assimilation over to them; her fall as a secretary enables their rise as social scientists working to classify elements of an increasingly diverse population to curtail the growth of those considered hostile to the English way of life. Because fiction written during the early Victorian period naturalized and preserved the cultural division of labor as a masculine domain of production and a feminine domain of reproduction, later Victorian fiction redrew the gender line right down the middle of the feminine domain so as to distinguish biological reproduction as feminine from cultural reproduction as masculine. Characters so diverse as Hardy's Sue Bridehead, Trollope's Lizzie Eustace, Eliot's Maggie Tulliver, Charlotte Brontë's Lucy Snowe, or Dickens's Mrs. Jellyby dramatize the mutual hostility of the two forms of reproduction. But it is not until the 1860s and 1870s that femininity itself acquires its identity by casting off masculine characteristics rather than accumulating feminine ones.

The shift in concern away from the problem of overpopulation to the problem of degeneration marks the emergence of a new class of experts who took it upon themselves to oversee all those social responsibilities that had been identified as feminine and entrusted to the middle-class woman: childbirth, education, regulation of the emotions, home decorating, shopping, as well as many of the new social practices with the emergence of a modern institutional culture.[28] Among this cluster of cultural practices also belong the activities occupying leisure time, especially fiction. Still working within a Malthusian problematic, this new cast of experts turned Malthus on his head. In their view, the superior femininity of middle-class women could no longer be imagined as an example of and curb on the sexuality of the underclasses. On the contrary, the taste and refinement that Malthus had considered a primary inducement to self-restraint had completely backfired. In Olive Schreiner's *The Story of an African Farm* (1883), bourgeois femininity's phobic reaction to any intimation of the presence of masculine desire in women spilled over and assumed the form of a similar revulsion to signs of desire in men. Schreiner's enfeebled feminist heroine gives birth to a baby girl who dies almost immediately and then proceeds to die herself. Moreover, as she proceeds to do so, who should take care of her but a former lover, not the father of her child, who wears a nurse's dress and bonnet in order to nurture Lyndall in the manner she requests. As the end of the century approached, moreover, H. Rider Haggard's heroes joined Wilde's in celebrating the homosocial bond between men over the kind of heterosexuality that we associate with the term Victorian. The degeneration of the national population, from this late Victorian perspective, appeared to pose a far more serious problem than the "misery" and "vice" Malthus had predicted for the poor in nations whose reproduction outstripped their productivity.

Many different authors participated in the reflux whereby the very characteristics that had placed other people outside of middle-class culture reappeared at its core. Along with those bohemians who qualified as degenerates, eugenicists mounted a sustained argument that the quality of the nation depended on the quality of those men and women who reproduced themselves. These population scientists were troubled by the prospect that the bodies of respectable women seemed unfit for the work of biological reproduction, while the masses and people of other races seemed to have no trouble breeding at all. At about the same time, pioneers in the nascent science of psychology discovered that modern bodies were inhabited with the same desires and predilections associated with savage peoples; fear of these desires and predilections is what enfeebled them. It is entirely accurate to say that the novel spelled out this parabolic logic whereby the supposedly superior Western mind curved back and collapsed into its opposite decades before Freud used this same logic to elicit the discourse of the unconscious from women whose definition of gender had thwarted and distorted any semblance of sexual desire. The Victorian novel packaged this logic for a diverse and heterogeneous readership so that it came to seem natural and necessary, if not always desirable and right. But the Victorian novel also produced a range of violations and resistances with corresponding consequences capable of reverberating across the entire system of social categories. By creating this tension between the prevailing gender binary and what appeared, by way of contrast, to be the realities of human nature, desire, or the exigencies of social experience, fiction made gender into the extraordinarily flexible and pervasive set of cultural rules with which we are living to this day.

NOTES

1 In *The Best Circles: Society, Etiquette and the Season* (London: Crescent Library, 1973), Leonore Davidoff identifies this group: "The untitled gentry, on the one hand an intermediate group with ties to the nobility by marriage and similar life styles, on the other linked by family ties and farming interest to farmers and the middle class, has long been recognised as a crucial factor in the English social hierarchy . . . In England . . . formalised Society took the place of mobility controlled through legal classifications. By regulating yet allowing the flow of new personnel, it prevented the formation of angry, alienated newcomer groups barred from full social recognition" (21).

2 John Locke, *Two Treatises of Government*, ed. Peter Laslett (Cambridge: Cambridge University Press, 1988), II. 1:1–14.

3 Thomas Robert Malthus, *An Essay on the Principle of Population*, ed. Philip Appleman (New York: Norton, 1976), 16.

4 *Ibid.*, 34.

5 Friedrich Engels, *The Condition of the Working Class in England*, ed. David McLellan (New York: Oxford University Press, 1993), 72–77.

6 Charles Darwin, *The Descent of Man, and Selection in Relation to Sex* (Princeton: Princeton University Press, 1981), 398.

7 Karl Marx, *Capital*, vol. I, trans. Ben Fowkes (New York: Vintage Books, 1977), 279–300.

8 For an extended analysis of "Darwin's plots" and their influence on Victorian fiction, see Gillian Beer, *Darwin's Plots: Evolutionary Narrative in Darwin, George Eliot, and Nineteenth-Century Fiction* (London: Routledge & Kegan Paul, 1983).

9 Charles Dickens, *Dombey and Son* (1848; New York: Oxford University Press, 1966), 470.

10 Leonore Davidoff and Catherine Hall, *Family Fortunes: Men and Women of the English Middle Class 1780–1850* (London: Hutchinson, 1987), 208.

11 Marx, *Capital*, 162–77.

12 Anthony Trollope, *The Eustace Diamonds* (1872; Oxford: Oxford University Press, 1982), 329.

13 In "The 'Failure' of the Victorian Middle Class: a Critique," in Janet Wolff and John Seed, eds., *The Culture of Capital: Art, Power and the Nineteenth-Century Middle Class* (Manchester: Manchester University Press, 1998), 17–44, Simon Gunn notes how regularly attempts to account for the historical role of the middle class in modern British society "are linked by a single, pervasive theme:

the 'failure' of the middle class to realize its hegemonic ambitions" (p. 18). He offers two reasons for the lack of a history of the middle-class comparable to accounts chronicling the decline of a traditional aristocracy, the fate of the gentry, and the making of an English working class during the modern period: (1) the middle ranks were always absorbing various aspects of the classes they displaced, particularly the landed gentry, and (2) the middle classes never acquired a univocal and internally coherent class character. Thus, in deliberating any given issue, its clear sense of historical mission, associated with progress and individual liberty, was invariably subject to dispute and compromised. The novel is in large part responsible for our prevailing sense of the failure of the middle class. The novel promoted this theme, as I argue, so as to make bourgeois masculinity the best remedy for its own failures.

14 Friedrich Engels, *The Origin of the Family, Private Property, and the State, in the Light of the Researches of Lewis H. Morgan* (New York: International Publishers, 1972).

15 Henry Mayhew, *London Labour and the London Poor*, vol. IV (New York: Dover, 1968), 273.

16 Josef Breuer and Sigmund Freud, *Studies in Hysteria*, trans. James Strachey (New York: Basic Books, 1955), 6.

17 See George W. Stocking, Jr., *Victorian Anthropology* (New York: The Free Press, 1987), and Laura Ann Stoler, *Race and the Education of Desire: Foucault's History of Sexuality and the Colonial Order of Things* (Durham, NC: Duke University Press, 1996).

18 Mrs. Henry Wood, *East Lynne* (1861; London: J. M. Dent, 1994), 404.

19 Charlotte Brontë, *Jane Eyre* (1847, New York: Norton, 1972), 257ff.

20 For a classic reading of Bertha as the caged female in Jane, see Sandra Gilbert and Susan Gubar, *The Madwoman in the Attic: The Woman Writer and the Nineteenth-Century Literary Imagination* (New Haven: Yale University Press, 1979). For a reading of Bertha as the victim of colonial oppression, see Gayatri Chakravorty Spivak, "Three Women's Texts as a Critique of Imperialism," *Critical Inquiry* 12 (1985), 243–61. For a recent discussion of this issue, see Sue Thomas, "The Tropical Extravagance of Bertha Mason," *Victorian Literature and Culture* 27, 1 (1999), 1–18.

21 Lewis Carroll, *Alice's Adventures in Wonderland* (1866; New York: Norton, 1992), 16.

22 Georg Lukács, *Studies in European Realism* (New York: Grosset and Dunlap, 1964). For Lukács's influential description of how novels carried out this mission in nineteenth-century England and France, see "The Crisis of Bourgeois Realism," *The Historical Novel*, trans. Hannah and Stanley Mitchell (Lincoln: University of Nebraska Press, 1983), 171–250.

23 Charlotte Brontë's publisher rejected her initial attempt at novel writing, *The Professor*, because it lacked the gothic elements she proceeded to incorporate in her highly successful *Jane Eyre*. Emily's *Wuthering Heights*, in contrast, was an immediate success, but inspired reviewers' criticism for representations of Heathcliff and Catherine in terms that overstep the limits at once of realism and good taste. See Elizabeth Gaskell, *The Life of Charlotte Brontë* (Harmondsworth: Penguin, 1975). The reviewers of Hardy's *Jude the Obscure* condemned the novel as much for the gothic extremes of emotion it portrayed as for its

frank descriptions of female desire. Wherever we turn for evaluations of Victorian fiction, then and now, the terms of realism and gothic romance cast doubt on the quality of a novel if it swings too far in either the one direction or the other.

24 Bram Stoker, *Dracula* (1897; New York: Signet, 1992), 288.

25 Max Nordau, *Degeneration* (1895; Lincoln: University of Nebraska Press, 1968), 9.

26 Jules de Gaultier, *Bovarysm*, trans. Gerald M. Spring (New York: Philosophical Library, 1970).

27 Oscar Wilde, *The Picture of Dorian Gray* (1891; New York: Penguin, 1985), 156.

28 For historical accounts of the rise of this class of people and how they revised the notion of the middle class as capitalists, see W. J. Reader, *Professional Men: The Rise of the Professional Class in Nineteenth-century England* (New York: Basic, 1966); Philippa Levine, *The Amateur and the Professional* (Cambridge: Cambridge University Press, 1966); Harold Perkin, *The Rise of Professional Society: England Since 1880* (London: Routledge, 1989).

6

JEFF NUNOKAWA

Sexuality in the Victorian Novel

Victorian novels and the history of sexual desire

A history of sexual desire?[1] Are not the intimate intensities of mind and body that go by that name as insulated from the mass and massive public events that we commonly call history as hunger or pain? Is not the heart filled with passion always the same old story, a drama whose costume may vary from period to period, but whose script remains essentially unchanged? But while much that we experience as sexual desire seems a largely immutable condition of human (and perhaps not just human) existence, the scope and shape of the meanings that we attach to this experience are decided by a complex of historical forces, not least of which, for those of us who live in its aftermath, is the Victorian novel itself. Thus, for example, the great expectation, usually observed in the breach, that sexual bonds will culminate in marriage, or its contemporary cognate, the Permanent Relationship, finds its most eloquent propagations in what one of their critics calls "our books,"[2] the novels whose promise of romance we know by heart as surely as we have forgotten the details of their plots. If we continue to acknowledge, typically in the privacy of our own disappointments, as universal truth a vision of sexual desire as the engine and origin of a partnership at least lifelong, this is in no small part because of the sentimental education we receive from the Victorian novel and its afterlife in more recent narrative forms. If, against often overwhelming evidence to the contrary, we persist in perceiving the halo of "happily ever after" light up the object of our sexual affections, that is in no small part because books like *Jane Eyre* (1847) and *Middlemarch* (1872) have taught us so well to do so.

The question that we will take up here is not whether or where there is sexuality in the Victorian novel: generations of readers, including those who were present at their creation, have routinely detected all kinds of erotic energy even in the household words with which Dickens and

Thackeray entertained the whole family in the middle of the century, not to mention the tales of outlaw passion with which Hardy or Wilde scandalized even mature audiences at the end. Sexual desires are everywhere in the Victorian novel, either as an explicit topic or as a subterranean force close enough to the surface that it may as well be.[3] This chapter aims to consider not whether or where sexual desire is admitted in the Victorian novel, but rather how it is described and organized when it is; not whether the characters who inhabit the Victorian novel are allowed erotic passion, but rather how they, and through them we, are trained to define and discipline it. Taking a cue from the most influential investigations of sexuality conducted over the past century and a half, the method of this chapter will be the individual case study: we will trace the career of erotic desire in five more or less familiar novels written at the heart of the Victorian period: *Jane Eyre* (Charlotte Brontë); *The Tenant of Wildfell Hall* (Anne Brontë, 1848); *Vanity Fair* (William Thackerary, 1848); *Adam Bede* (George Eliot, 1859), and *Our Mutual Friend* (Charles Dickens, 1865). To cast these texts as exemplary is by no means to claim that they comprehend the character of sexuality in the Victorian novel, but rather to suggest the dense network of cultural cause and effect that surround the formation of desires that often feel as simple as the pangs of hunger.

For those familiar with the course of Victorian fiction, a decision to end a survey of its erotics at 1865, rather than to take up works that inhabited and indeed helped to ignite the climate of sexual controversy that characterized the later part of the nineteenth century will seem odd, even perverse. Why not an investigation of *Tess of the D'Urbervilles* (1891) or *The Picture of Dorian Gray* (1891), whose ostentatious *fin-de-siècle* erotics would seem to make them eligible, indeed perhaps inevitable subjects for an essay on sexuality in the Victorian novel? I want to suggest though that many of the central strains in the history of sexual desire that are dramatized in the works of Hardy, Gissing, Wilde, and for that matter Proust and Freud, strains of desire which help to define the way we live now, are predicted in the writings of the mid-Victorians scrutinized here. Thus, for example, the sense conveyed so fully in Hardy that erotic attraction, and in particular male heterosexual desire, has the destructive force and the aura of inevitability that we attach to a natural disaster or an industrial revolution, finds a crucial antecedent in the works of the texts taken up in this chapter. Or to mention another, more devious example, the effort that Wilde describes in his famous novel to immortalize homosexual desire in the portrait of the young man who incites it, may be read as an effort to reverse a mid-Victorian tendency, eloquently apparent in a work like *Jane Eyre*. Brontë's novel aims to identify such passions as an ephemeral and intermediate attraction, one which makes way for those that end in matrimony and family values. (It hardly seems necessary to remark, by the way, the enduring potence of this trend in an era when a health crisis has worked to encourage the proclivity of our culture to perceive the homosexual as little more than a picture of what must die young.)[4] As with everything else human, when it comes to sex, the past is prelude.

Anne Brontë and the disciplining of desire

Even the many who have never read the novel are more than familiar with the warning that *The Tenant of Wildfell Hall* delivers about the hazards of passion unchecked by judgment, the catastrophe that results when our assessment of someone is clouded by our desire for him; the often sounded "warn[ing] . . . against . . . fixing [our] affections where approbation d[oes] not go before, and where reason and judgement withh[o]ld their sanction."[5] Also, those who have never read *The Tenant of Wildfell Hall* will be able to guess that the admonition issued early and often in the novel – "[f]irst study; then approve; then love" (*Wildfell Hall*, 150) – falls on deaf ears: after all, who, apart from someone who has reason to know it already, could take such advice seriously? Certainly not the novel's young protoganist, to whom this warning is addressed, Helen Huntingdon, who can hardly hear her guardian's exhortations across the gulf that separates those who feel sexual "fascinations" from those who seem to have forgotten how. Like more recent admonitions to just say no, the guardian's exhortation pays no heed to the power of the attraction that it would simply subordinate to "reason and judgement."

At first glance, the distance between the guardian's cold perspective and the girl's passionate eye could not seem greater: while her aunt appears to inhabit a bloodless universe where the "attractions" of the "handsomest" are "nothing . . . Principle is the first thing; after all; and next to that, good sense, respectability, and moderate wealth" (150) – the girl herself belongs to a world where there is nothing else: "he is always in my thoughts and dreams. In all my employments, whatever I do, or see, or hear, has an ultimate reference to him" (168). But the difference between these estimates of attraction is smaller than it seems, since in her very condemnation of "the snares and wiles of the tempter," the guardian gives the devil his due; her anxious warning grimly acknowledges as all but irresistible the allure which her niece more happily admits:

> "Helen," said she, with reproachful gravity . . . "I know many . . . that have . . . through carelessness . . . been wretched victims of deceit; and some, through weakness, have fallen into snares and temptations terrible to relate."

"Well, I shall be neither careless nor weak."

"Remember Peter, Helen! Don't boast, but watch. Keep a guard over your eyes and ears as the inlets of your heart, and over your lips as the outlet, lest they betray you in a moment of unwariness. Receive, coldly and dispassionately, every attention, till you have ascertained and duly considered the worth of the aspirant; and let your affections be consequent upon approbation alone. First study; then approve; then love. Let your eyes be blind to all external attractions, your ears deaf to all the fascinations of flattery and light discourse. – These are nothing – and worse than nothing – snares and wiles of the tempter, to lure the thoughtless to their own destruction." (150)

The vigilance urged in this passage extends beyond wariness about "external attractions" to include as well wariness about the attraction *to* them; beyond the fascinating suitor to include as well the senses and affections that he targets: "Keep a guard over your eyes and ears as the inlets of your heart;" "let your affections be consequent upon approbation alone." And even so, what power of vigilance, no matter how broad its scope, could possibly withstand a temptation as insinuating as the one Helen's guardian fears? How to resist an enemy whose fascinations are as hard to avoid as the weariness that comes as surely as the sun sets, the weariness that overtakes even the most zealous apostle, who, at the moment of truth, despite his best intentions, cannot stay awake to save his soul?

Sexual temptation is as hard to withstand as the need to sleep, or as the thrill of what is forbidden: common sense tells us that the siege mentality the guardian elaborates ends up giving aid to the enemy. Everyone knows that the best fan for the flame of desire is prohibition, and that an eye ever keen for any sign of what has been prohibited does nothing so much as to illuminate and expand its allure. This irony informs Michel Foucault's influential *History of Sexuality*, whose subject is the spirit of surveillance that we hear in *The Tenant of Wildfell Hall*, a spirit which, taking as its point of departure the tactics and sense of seriousness attached to religious confession, articulates itself in modern methods and institutions of supervision (for example, what was called sexology in the nineteenth century and psychoanalysis in the twentieth), established to monitor and categorize sexual desire and practice. If, on one hand, the conviction that our sexual desires and the way we respond to them are matters of the utmost importance (crucial both to the management of society, as well as to the destiny and definition of the individual who inhabits it), justifies the networks of surveillance that Foucault considers a crucial version of modern political power, then these forms of supervision themselves function to promote the very centrality of sexuality which gives them their reason for being in the first place. According to the reciprocal development that Foucault traces, the institutions established to monitor sexuality are not merely reactions to the recognition of its central significance, they themselves help to make it so significant.

But there is another, more immediate explanation for the empire of the erotic that reigns in *The Tenant of Wildfell Hall*. If the power of sexual desire is amplified by the force of surveillance arrayed against it and because of it, this power is secured in the first place by the absence of competing attractions. The alternative that the aunt offers in place of the excitement of sexual love is hardly very enticing: "Here the conversation ended, for at this juncture my uncle's voice was heard from his chamber, loudly calling upon my aunt to come to bed. He was in a bad humour that night; for his gout was worse" (*Wildfell Hall*, 167). Who would choose to lie in such a bed, rather than the one that Helen makes for herself with the handsome reprobate she marries? Who would have the will power sufficient to withstand the temptation of unsafe sex when the alternative is a sensible marriage such as the one that Helen's guardian suffers, the passionless partnership whose terms are spelled out by the mother of another character in the novel?: "I'm sure your poor, dear father was as good a husband as ever lived, and after the first six months or so were over, I should as soon as expected him to fly, as to put himself out of his way to pleasure me. He always said I was a good wife, and did my duty; and he always did his – bless him! – he was steady and punctual, seldom found fault without a reason, and always did justice to my good dinners, and hardly ever spoiled my cookery by delay – and that's as much as any woman can expect of any man" (79).

The dullness of such a marriage has a name in Brontë's novel: that name is duty. "He always said I was a good wife, and did my duty; and he always did his." According to the terms of marriage set out here, a woman can hope for nothing other than doing her duty to a husband who can look forward to nothing other than the prospect of performing his to her in turn. This marriage contract reflects the bleak climate of obligation that prevails generally in *The Tenant of Wildfell Hall*, starting on its first page, in which the novel's hero describes the sacrifice of his own desires to satisfy the demands of his father:

> My father . . . was a . . . farmer . . . and I, by his express desire, succeeded him in the same quiet occupation, not very willingly . . . He exhorted me, with his dying breath, to continue in the good old way, to follow his steps, and those of his father before him, and let my highest ambition be, to walk honestly through the world, looking neither to the right hand nor to the left, and to transmit the paternal acres to my children in at least as flourishing a condition as he left them to me. (35)

The specific form that duty, or imposed obligation, takes in this passage – the protagonist's occupation – sounds like what Marx in his early manuscripts calls alienated labor: "the alienation of the worker . . . means . . . that it exists outside him . . . as something alien to him."[6] While Marx is describing a form of work quite opposed to the occupation of a "gentleman farmer," in either case, no matter how diversely, what one must do is severed from what one wants to do. For a school of thought that Marx founded, the spirit of alienation expands beyond the zone of labor where it begins to take hold in the culture more generally.[7] We may hear a symptom of this dissemination when praise of a husband sounds like the memory of a fair employer: "he seldom found fault without a reason"; or like a recommendation of a good worker: "he was steady and punctual." And whether or not the dutiful marriage takes its form from the workplace, its "steady and punctual" subject is certainly fit for it. He is ready in particular for the "steady and punctual" work required by the capitalist system whose "triumph" is, in one historian's phrase, "the major theme"[8] of the era in which Brontë wrote.

For those who inhabit the dull world of duty that Brontë surveys, the excitement of sexual desire is the only thrill in town. In a world like this, there is no counterweight to love: nothing can check its power since nothing can compete with its luster. But if desire cannot be displaced by another interest, it must nevertheless be contained. Accordingly, the novel seeks not to annul the fascination of sexual desire – how could this be possible when nothing can hold a candle to it? – but rather to discipline it. If the novel is powerless to extinguish the erotic drive, it can nevertheless inculcate the inclination to defer its indulgence.

This inclination is encouraged by the assurance the novel delivers that the denial of sexual desire is indeed only its deferral. The hard renunciation prescribed by and for the characters who appear in *Wildfell Hall* is softened by the faith that one will have in the future what one must relinquish for the present. For those who inhabit the novel, this faith is founded explicitly on a familiar religious belief in a paradise that comes at the end of their lives: "We shall meet in heaven. Let us think of that" (409). For its readers, though, such faith is implicitly conducted by the no less familiar ending of the novel itself. The miracle at the end, the union of two lovers who had given up all hope of ever being together in this life, is routine enough in, and then beyond the Victorian novel, that it can come as no surprise to anyone. It is routine enough to take up tenancy within its reader as the unspoken article of faith by means of which the work of mourning is silently annexed by its opposite, an article of faith felt in the buried hope that we will have again the lost lover at the moment we have given him up for good.

Finally freed from its embrace, *Vanity Fair*'s most long suffering fool of love, George Dobbin, sums up its damages:

> I know what your heart is capable of . . . it can't feel such an attachment as mine deserves to mate with, and such as I would have from a woman more generous than you. No, you are not worthy of the love which I have devoted to you. I knew all along the prize I had set my life on was not worth the having; that I was a fool, with fond fancies too, bartering away my all of truth and ardour against your little feeble remnant of love. I will bargain no more: I withdraw. (776)

Whether it be the virulent strain signified by the fever of "uncouth convulsions" caused by Becky or the lighter but finally no less debilitating mutation that takes the shape of "fond fancies" prompted by Amelia, the problem with desire is a failure at the bottom line: simply put, love is a bad bargain; the return that it offers is no match for the investment it requires. More exactly, the problem with desire that *Vanity Fair* diagnoses is a failure to consider the price. It is only when he is cured of his passion that the lover can figure out that the cake is not worth the candle: only then, can he perform the simple arithmetic which reveals that the cost of Amelia is not worth the price that he must pay for her. Like a sign of returning health after a long illness, Dobbin's inclination to perform such calculations announces that the force of his desire for the woman he has loved throughout the novel has finally dissipated.

The disaster of desire fans out from the privacy of bedrooms and closets, and spills into the broader avenues of society in the novel. Thus, the "passion" for gambling that possesses the denizens of *Vanity Fair*: "the mania for play was so widely spread, that the public gambling-rooms did not suffice for the general ardour, and gambling went on in private houses as much as if there had been no public means for gratifying the passion" (430). If the "general ardour" for getting money breaks into the private houses where the transactions of sexual passion are usually conducted, Thackeray's very rendering of the drive for money as a form of passion describes the opposite movement: it leaves no doubt that erotic drives have already left their private domains, and come to electrify the current of greed.

Like the sexual desire that it comes to duplicate, the love of money is an impulse powerful enough to prompt irrational expenditures; it is powerful enough to overwhelm the inclination to balance the cost of an investment against the benefit that results; powerful enough to overwhelm the capacity to know when expenditure is wasteful because it is powerless to secure the object of desire. Thus, the problem with the drive for money in *Vanity Fair* is not that it is too much engrossed in the cool rational calculations of the marketplace, but that it has become too little so. It is not that the gambler is too greedy, but rather that his desire for gain overwhelms his capacity to secure it: like the lover who fails to recognize a bad bargain when he sees it, the gambler fastened to the roulette wheel or card table is too ardent to consider his chances carefully enough to quit while he is ahead.

Its infection by the forces of sexual passion disables what an important tradition of political theory regards as the signal virtue attached to the profit motive. In *The Passions and the Interests: Political Arguments for Capitalism Before its Triumph*, Albert O. Hirschman traces in the writings of figures such as Hume, Montesquieu and Dr. Johnson a line of thought which praises the motive of moneymaking as a calm desire that works to counteract passions such as anger and lust.[11] While by the lights of this tradition, the economic interest in acquisition opposes other, less governable passions, in Thackeray's novel this interest has been overtaken by the impulses that it is supposed to contain. The result is the general ardour of *Vanity Fair*, an overheated passion or a quiet delusion that debases, impoverishes or destroys everyone it touches.

But while economic interest cannot be relied upon to contain the vicissitudes of desire in *Vanity Fair*, the novel counts on desire to absorb the rule of interest sufficiently well to regulate itself. If the extinction of Dobbin's desire for Amelia is the condition that enables him to see her clearly in the end as a poor purchase, it is also the effect of that calculation; if the heat of passion has deranged the rationality of economic interest, the rationality of economic interest in turn casts its cooling light upon the heat of passion. The calmness that prevails at the end of the novel, the quiet afterglow that succeeds the intensity of desire, is the achievement of a sexual subject who has taken to heart the lessons of an economic principle that has ceased to prevail in the precincts of a stock exchange as much given over to the general ardor as the compulsive gambler or the drunken lover. It is the achievement of a sexual subject who has taken to heart an economic principle which is now nowhere else in sight.

Jane Eyre: homosexuality as history

The cases we have examined so far allow us to recognize two kinds of history written by the Victorian novel. If, as I suggested at the outset, the Victorian novel helps to make the history of our sexuality, spelling out the plots by which we define and thus experience its pleasures and hazards and showing us our unconscious inheritance of their history, such stories are no less made *by* history. The dramas of desire staged by the Victorian novel are enacted against the epic backdrop that Eric Hobsbawm calls the "global triumph of capitalism . . . the major theme of history in the decades after 1848.'[12] Sometimes what Anne Brontë calls "the frenzy of ardour" is posed by the novel as a threat and an exception to a dull sense of duty allied with the common sense of capitalism; sometimes this frenzy appears to merge with economic interests, as it does in *Vanity Fair*: in either case, though, whether sexual passion is defined by its distance from the economic interests at the heart of the capitalist system or by its closeness to them, the specter of market society everywhere haunts the scenes of desire that everywhere haunt the Victorian novel.

But if the sexual desire featured in the Victorian novel is always part of a broader social history that it absorbs and disseminates, it also has a history all its own. Novels like *David Copperfield* (1850) and *Jane Eyre* tell a story of sexual education whose hero is prepared for mature love by the youthful infatuations he experiences on his way there, a story as familiar as the reassurance that a species of sexuality whose enduring power to alarm is "just a phase." In the history of desire written by the Victorian novel, various forms of homoerotic passion make a brief but crucial appearance; the sexual education conducted by the Victorian novel includes a typically forgotten course of homoerotic enthusiasm which teaches heterosexuality its lessons. Such education is not confined to the novel. The particular course we will audit takes place in *Jane Eyre*, but its cognates range from the homosexual desires that psychoanalytic theory casts as the prolegomena to heterosexuality, to the famous predisposition of a sophisticated song writer whose best-known lesson in love teaches the greater glory of the birds and the bees.

Jane Eyre, though, warms the heart with a story of man and wife which could not be less like the cool festal glamour imagined by the Cole Porter song, where good looks are as prerequisite as evening clothes. Plain Jane progresses to the heights of a metaphysical romance where looks do not matter, or matter only because to love them requires the insight to see past them. He was not easy on the eyes, Jane Eyre declares upon first meeting Rochester, and that was just as well, for, of course, she was not much to look at herself: "I had a theoretical reverence and homage for beauty, elegance, gallantry, fascination; but had I met those qualities incarnate in masculine shape, I should know instinctively that they neither had nor could have sympathy with anything in me, and should have shunned them as one would fire, lightning, or anything else that is bright but antipathetic."[13]

The raised voice of a "Mighty Spirit" that manages to rouse a lover miles out of earshot is only the most ostentatiously metaphysical feat of an affair of heart and soul that everywhere surpasses the boundaries of the body. No less wonderful, only more familiar than the transcendent powers of love recorded in *Wuthering Heights*, desire in *Jane Eyre* shows its genius by choosing an object with little to show for itself. A devotion maniacal enough to reject the impediments of mortality is no more miraculous than the passion inspired by a woman who is not "pretty" and a man who is not "handsome" (*Jane Eyre*, 163); a romance high enough to rise above death has nothing over an earthbound one that flourishes in the face of home-liness or harshness. Phrenology, not astrology, is the conceit that guides this courtship; Rochester and Jane Eyre find each other's signs not in the stars, but in bodily forms rendered immaterial by their reading.

If the object of desire in *Jane Eyre* is not the body, neither is it strictly the soul; it is rather a figure found passing from the province of the first to the second. What is admired here is not what is already abstract, but what becomes so: Jane cherishes Rochester neither by adoring nor by ignoring his formidable physique, but by tracking its sublimation; before her loving eyes, his rough features are ignited into a trinity of metaphysical forces "more than beautiful": "Most true it is that 'beauty is in the eyes of the gazer.' My master's colourless, olive face, square, massive brow, broad and jetty eyebrows, deep eyes, firm, grim mouth – all energy, decision, will – were not beautiful, according to rule; but they were more than beautiful to me" (203–4). For his part, Rochester returns the abstracting tribute of this regard; rejecting the "gazelle eyes" of "the Grand Turk's seraglio," his passion is reserved instead for the "something glad" he detects in the "glance" of the most ordinary of English girls; for the "becoming air" he witnesses her become: "Although you are not pretty any more than I am handsome, yet a puzzled air becomes you" (163).

Like the penchant for flogging from which some public schoolboys never seemed to recover, Jane's taste for the disincarnated begins at school; her longing for the metaphysical is defined by the original objects of her desire, Maria Temple and Helen Burns. Their bodies, unlike the too solid flesh of the hated John Reed, "dingy and unwholesome skin; thick lineaments in a spacious visage, heavy limbs and large extremities" (41), are forever disappearing: "she looked tall, fair, and shapely; brown eyes with a benignant light in their irids, and a fine penciling of long lashes round;" "on each of her temples her hair a very dark brown, was clustered in round curls . . . Let the reader add, to complete the picture, refined features; a complexion, if pale, clear; and a stately air and carriage, and he will have, at least as clearly as words can give it, a correct idea of the exterior of Miss Temple – Maria Temple, as I afterward saw the name written in a Prayer Book entrusted to me to carry to church" (79–80). As Jane enumerates Maria Temple's qualities, the lady, or at least her body, vanishes; the eclipse that begins as the parts of her body give way to a transparent aspect and an abstract disposition, becomes total when Maria Temple becomes a name; the "steps" that Jane's "organ of veneration" "trace" with "admiring awe" go all the way, in the course of this passage, from the sphere of the body to the pages of a book.

For Jane Eyre, and for us as well, such translations of the body are less the dismissal of sexual excitement than the source of it. We would be hard pressed to deny the erotic value of the "interest" that Rochester's features hold for Jane Eyre, at the moment they are stripped of the garments of the body, "an interest, and influence that quite mastered me – that took my feelings from my own power and fettered them in his" (204), even without Freud's suggestion that sexual excitement starts in the swerve away from bodily needs; even without the more common sense view that sex really gets started when it gets into the head.[14]

As it does when, alone at night with Maria Temple, and the girl she loves even more, Jane's "organ of veneration expand[s]" beyond all limit as she watches "powers within [Helen Burns]" arise from "her own unique mind" to displace her frail body:

> they shone in the liquid lustre of her eyes, which had suddenly acquired a beauty more singular than that of Miss Temple's – a beauty neither of fine colour nor long eyelash, not pencilled brow, but of meaning . . . of radiance. Then her soul sat on her lips, and language flowed, from what source I cannot tell; has a girl of fourteen a heart large enough, vigorous enough to hold the swelling spring of pure full, fervid eloquence . . . my organ of veneration expand[ed] at every sounding line.   (*Jane Eyre*, 104–5)

A compulsion to repeat stations the sublime object of Jane's first love as the model for subsequent ones. If Jane speaks less and less during the course of the novel of the teacher and the classmate she adored, she has nonetheless taken them in as the definition of what is to be loved; if she puts away the objects of her schoolyard passion with other childish things, she finds them again in the body of a man made fabulous by its change into "energy, decision, will."

But while the object of Jane Eyre's homosexual enthusiasm survives as the ghostly paradigm for her heterosexual passion, the course of disembodiment that defines this figure ensures that it survives *only* as such. For the path of sublimation trodden by Helen Burns is another name for the drive towards death; her eloquence another name for her epitaph. A rumor of morbidity encrypted in the graveness of Maria Temple's countenance and her mention in a book of prayers, is substantiated by Helen Burns's headlong progress to the grave. When she speaks of "the time when we shall put off our cumbrous flesh, and only the spark of the spirit will remain" (91), she speaks for herself; the look that Jane would die for: "What a smile! I remember it now, and I know that it was the effluence of fine intellect, of true courage; it lit up her marked lineaments, her thin face, her sunken gray eye, like a reflection from the aspect of an angel" – is the look of one near death, the glance of a "passing martyr, imparting strength in transit" (99).

This drive towards death is determined by a Victorian pattern legislated in and beyond *Jane Eyre*, a pattern that ensures that all passion leads, one way or another, to Church; a pattern which ensures that all passion leads either to the altar, where Jane and Rochester are finally married, or to the graveyard where Helen Burns is buried. The thought that Rochester will marry another woman, and the subsequent discovery that he already has, is death for Jane: "I am not talking to you now through the medium of mortal flesh," she remarks to Rochester at the moment when she believes he will marry someone other than herself, "it is my spirit that addresses your spirit; just as if both had passed through the grave." "I can but die," she declares later, at the end of her suicidal flight from the man she loves after the revelation that he is already married, and her rejection of his proposal that she live as his mistress.

Such melodramatic sentiments, surprising from a heroine whose speech is normally as plain as her face, conform to a law of desire inscribed in more books than *Jane Eyre*. A law with two clauses: where the telos of the marriage plot falters in and beyond the Brontë novel, that of the death drive takes over; when passions are accidently or constitutionally prevented from reaching the altar, they come instead to the bleakest of houses. Barred at the nuptial door, those taken up by such passions must cross a different bar, the one that an unmarried missionary nears at the close of *Jane Eyre*: "St. John is unmarried: he will never marry now . . . The last letter I received from him . . . anticipated his sure reward . . . 'My Master,' he says, 'has forewarned me' . . . he announces more distinctly, 'Surely I come quickly!' and . . . I more eagerly respond, 'Amen; even so, come'" (477).

Extramarital passions may be less heated than those that confirm St. John Rivers's bachelor status, but they always tend to the same conclusion. When Jane and Helen finally sleep together, they do so in a deathbed: "Miss Temple had found me laid in [the] little crib; my face against Helen Burns's shoulder, my arms round her neck. I was asleep, and Helen was dead" (114). And with this, Jane has learned all she can from the girl she loves, who dies defining the criterion for desire; the tutor who, like a "martyr in transit," takes the hit not only for herself, but for her partner in passion, as well. For Jane is only asleep; she will arise and go now to put what she has learned into practice: the transubtantiated body of the man she finally marries is the ghost of the girl who dies because she can't marry Jane herself. "Her grave is in Brocklebridge Churchyard: for fifteen years after her death it was only covered by a grassy mound; but now a gray marble tablet inscribed with her name, and the word '*Resurgam*'" (114).

Sexuality and solitude in *Adam Bede*

With *Adam Bede* we return to the relation between sexuality and its social context, at first to notice a basic aspect of that relation, overlooked in the socio-economic genealogies of sexual desire that we sought to assemble through *The Tenant of Wildfell Hall* and *Vanity Fair*: namely that in one simple sense, there is no relation between them at all. None, that is, except for mutual exclusion: when it comes down to it, sexual desire and sexual intercourse in and beyond *Adam Bede* typically takes place behind the closed doors or secret hideaways of private houses or fantasies; when it comes down to it, sexual intercourse is usually conducted only in the absence of broader society, usually only when those who are not involved directly with the lovers have been removed from sight, or mind, or both. Except for those whose particular passions involve public venues, or those whose straitened circumstances offer them no other, sex is generally a private affair.

"They were alone together for the first time. What an overpowering presence that first privacy is!"[15] You do not have to know *Adam Bede* to know this story: the scene alone, the scene in which two people find themselves alone, provides all the cue that is required to surmise what is about to happen here. (Eliot's readers will have an additional advantage figuring out the erotic dimensions of this scene: her novels are filled with situations like this, situations in which the pressure of potential sexual intercourse between two people arises solely from the fact that they are alone together.) You *do* have to know *Adam Bede* to know that the sexual encounter that is about to take place between Arthur Donnithorne and Hetty Sorrel "alone together"destroys their relations with everyone else in the book. Only those who have read the novel can be aware that as a result of what takes place here, Arthur loses his best friend – Adam Bede will soon happen upon this scene, and things will never be the same between the two men; only those who have read the novel will know that, as a result of their affair, Arthur Donnithorne and Hetty Sorrel are forced away from the community that had been their home. (No wonder that, "for the rest of his life," Adam Bede "remembered" the moment before he discovers his best friend with the woman he wanted to marry "as a man remembers his last glimpse of the home where his youth was passed, before the road turned, and he saw it no more" [*Adam Bede*, 341]; no wonder, since so much exile arises from the scene he is about to encounter of "two figures . . . with clasped hands . . . about to kiss" [342].)

But if you have to read *Adam Bede* to glean all the ways that the intercourse between Arthur and Hetty drives them apart from other people, the most basic one is as familiar as the lock on the bedroom door, or the lie that is told to conceal what goes on behind it. You do not have to read *Adam Bede* to recognize the most anti-social element of sexuality in the world of the novel, since it is the same in our own: "The candid Arthur had brought himself into a position in which successful lying was his only hope" (344–5); "Arthur was in the wretched position of an open generous man, who has committed an error which makes deception seem necessary;" "Arthur had impressed on Hetty that it would be fatal to betray, by word or look, that there had been the least intimacy between them." The couple keep their secret as long as they can, and so does the narrator, who declines to reveal it even to the reader, whom she elsewhere flatters with special access to the inside story. No one else knows how far things have gone between Arthur and Hetty until the scandal of the pregnancy makes it impossible to hide it any longer.

And then there is another zone of sexual privacy in Eliot's novel even more isolated than the spot in the forest where Hetty and Arthur meet, a zone that escapes detection altogether, a realm of desire that cannot be exposed because it cannot be communicated. We hear of it when the narrator joins the rakish squire as he stops his tour of a family farm to admire "a distractingly pretty girl of seventeen,"

> standing on little pattens and rounding her dimpled arm to lift a pound of butter out of the scale.
>
> Hetty blushed a deep rose-colour when Captain Donnithorne entered the dairy and spoke to her; but it was not at all a distressed blush, for it was inwreathed with smiles and dimples . . . [she] tossed and patted her pound of butter with quite a self-possessed, coquettish air, slyly conscious that no turn of her head was lost.
>
> There are various orders of beauty, causing men to make fools of themselves in various styles, from the desperate to the sheepish; but there is one order of beauty which seems made to turn the heads not only of men, but of all intelligent mammals, even of women. It is a beauty like that of kittens, or very small downy ducks making gentle rippling noises with their soft bills, or babies just beginning to toddle and to engage in conscious mischief – a beauty with which you can never be angry, but that you feel ready to crush for inability to comprehend the state of mind into which it throws you, Hetty Sorrel's was that sort of beauty. Her aunt, Mrs. Poyser,

who professed to despise all personal attractions and intended to be the severest of mentors, continually gazed at Hetty's charms by the sly, fascinated in spite of herself . . .   (89–95)

As it comes to rest in this passage with "a beauty like that of kittens, or very small downy ducks . . . or babies just beginning to toddle," the sexual luster that is concentrated on "a distractingly pretty girl of seventeen," is dispersed, but it is hardly canceled. While the universal attraction that dominates this scene drifts from the particular species of sexual desire (male, heterosexual) where it originates in this passage, it is hardly detached from sexual desire altogether. Like the girl who arouses it, "slyly conscious that no turn of her head was lost," the force of attraction that turns every head, "not only of men, but of all intelligent mammals, even of women" is animated by an erotic element as hard to deny as it is to define: "Her aunt . . . continually gazed at Hetty's charms by the sly, fascinated in spite of herself."

Even if she could do so herself, how could we take the dimensions of sexual desire in Mrs. Poyser's sly, fascinated gaze? The universal attraction for Hetty Sorrel is paradoxically quite private:

> It is of little use for me to tell you that Hetty's cheek was like a rose petal, that dimples played about her pouting lips, that her large dark eyes hid a soft roguishness under their long lashes . . . of little use, unless you have seen a woman who affected you as Hetty affected her beholders, for otherwise, though you might conjure up the image of a lovely woman, she would not in the least resemble that distracting kitten-like maiden.   (128)

Those who know her will recognize that the doubt that Eliot's narrator expresses here about her ability to convey the experience of someone else is as fugitive as any of her moods. Elsewhere she could hardly be more at home with the task of communicating the inmost impulses of others; elsewhere she is sufficiently certain of her qualifications for this task, that she mounts a virtual science out of sympathy. Here, though, all of that confidence is lost in a sense of the distance between self and other – how can I describe the experience of someone else to you unless you have had the experience yourself?; how, therefore is communication possible unless it is redundant, and therefore not really communication at all? – here, when it comes to conveying how "Hetty affected her beholders."

More than a barrier that defines one limit of sympathy, the case of sexual attraction provokes a recognition of those limits more generally:

> I might mention all the divine charms of a bright spring day, but if you had never in your life utterly forgotten yourself in straining your eyes after a mounting lark, or in wandering through the still lanes when the fresh-opened

blossoms filled them with a sacred, silent beauty . . . what would be the use of my descriptive catalogue? (128)

Like a universal attraction that descends from a particular one, the general problem of other minds that Eliot invokes when she connects her inability to convey the attraction of Hetty Sorrel to her inability to convey the pleasures of a spring morning begins with the specific case of sexual desire, the specific case whose details are never quite worked out of the abstract principle which arises from it: "I could never make you know what I meant by a bright spring day. Hetty's was a springtide beauty; it was the beauty of young frisking things, round-limbed, gambolling, circumventing you by a false air of innocence" (128).

The solitude of the desiring subject in Eliot's novel makes her a stranger to the society that Foucault studies, and that we have touched upon before in this chapter, a society of supervision where the powers of discernment convene first of all on sexuality; a society of surveillance in which sex is "*the* secret" that must be known, and moreover a secret that can be known: "What is peculiar to modern societies, in fact, is not that they consigned sex to a shadow existence, but that they dedicated themselves to speaking of it *ad infinitum*, while exploiting it as *the* secret."[16] A fascination for "a distractingly pretty girl of seventeen," a sly attraction that must remain private, not because it is culturally unacceptable but rather because it is simply incommunicable, defeats, as if by the force of a natural fact, the intrusions of "modern societies" committed to and even constituted by the task of putting sex in view by putting it into "discourse."

But if the loneliness of Eliot's sexual subject liberates her from one aspect of modern society, it is only to inscribe her in another. If this illegible character resists a social power that consists of seeing over and through its subject, she is quite fit for the climate of alienation that Durkheim and Weber called modern society, an urban and capitalist society where anonymous, or nearly anonymous associations have replaced personal attachments. Such relations, Georg Simmel remarks, require minimal knowledge about the other party: "The modern merchant who enters business with another; the scholar who together with another embarks upon an investigation; the leader of a political party who makes an agreement with the leader of another party . . . all these know . . . only exactly *that* and no more about their partner which they *have* to know for the sake of the relationship they wish to enter."[17]

Hetty Sorrel, towards the end of the novel, venturing to the city with the secret of her pregnancy, is a model citizen of this society. "'Ah it's plain enough what sort of business it is,'" says the wife of the landlord at the inn where she stays. But what is plain to her, apart from the broadest sense that Hetty has been done wrong by the man she loves, is only the aspect of the girl that is relevant to another sort of business, the sort that she and the landlord have to conduct with her:

> "She's not a common flaunting dratchell, I can see that. She looks like a respectable country girl, and she comes from a good way off, to judge by her tongue. She talks something like that ostler we had that come from the north: he was as honest a fellow as we ever had about the house – they're all honest folks in the north."
>
> (*Adam Bede*, 423)

Glimpsed in this exchange is the brave new world of modern society, one where the mysterious subject of sexuality, frightened and lonely perhaps, but with her secret still intact, could not be more at home.

Our Mutual Friend and the erotics of downward mobility

Far from the madding crowd in Eliot's novel, a man sees no social difference between himself and the woman he wants: "While Arthur gazed into Hetty's dark beseeching eyes, it made no difference to him what sort of English she spoke; and even if hoops and powder had been in fashion, he would very likely not have been sensible just then that Hetty wanted signs of high breeding" (178). Stationed at the heart of society in Dickens's novel, a man sees little else: "so hard to touch, so hard to turn!" the hero laments in *Our Mutual Friend*, as he gazes from his lowly station at the haughty goddess he adores, "[a]nd yet so pretty, so pretty!".[18]

And yet? Would it not be more candid for the passion-struck John Harmon to say *and thus* so pretty? For it is not just that sexual desire leaves intact the sense of social distinction that separates its subject and object in *Our Mutual Friend*, rather sexual desire requires it. How would it be possible to disentangle John Harmon's fascination with the "scornful" Bella from the cuts he suffers at her hands? His longing, if not his love for her, is only whetted when she reminds him that they are separated by a social gulf as great as any; his longing, if not his love for Bella is only made vivid by the sight of "the proud face with the downcast eyes, and . . . the quick breathing as it stirred the fall of bright brown hair over the beautiful neck" (*Our Mutual Friend*, 432).

We have reasons to suspect a strain of sexual desire here that inverts the more familiar Victorian privileged male taste for lower-class girls or boys. More exactly, we have reasons to suspect that John Harmon is excited by Bella's social altitude, less as a thing in itself than by how low it makes him feel by comparison; reason to suspect that whatever his announced motives for doing so, the situation that John Harmon goes to extraordinary lengths to set up for himself in the novel – designated by his father's will to inherit his vast fortune and to marry Bella Wilfer, he instead shams his own death, disguises himself as a penniless stranger named John Rokesmith, takes lodgings at the Wilfer's house and a secretarial position with the couple who have inherited his fortune and brought Bella to live with them "upon equal terms" (257) – is tailor-made for a sexual taste that, submitting to the taxonomical spirit of nineteenth-century sexology, we could call "class masochism."

We may suspect that the sense of abjection with which Bella leaves him is the very point of his elaborate exercise in declassment; we may suspect that the eager hand he lends her in putting him down is animated by the pleasure of pain: "He went down to his room, and buried John Harmon many additional fathoms deep . . . And so busy [was] he all night, piling and piling weights upon weights of earth above John Harmon's grave . . . [until he] lay buried under a whole Alpine range; and still the Sexton Rokesmith accumulated mountains over him, lightening his labour with the dirge, 'Cover him, crush him, keep him down!'" (435) (Signs of a sexual taste for class denigration surface all over Dickens's novels, as when the brokenhearted Pip recalls the origin of his socio-economic discomfort in *Great Expectations*: "Truly it was impossible to dissociate her presence from all those wretched hankerings after money and gentility."[19] The girl he desires is entangled less with the desire to get money and gentility than with the sense of wanting it, with "wretched hankerings after" these things rather than the determination to get them.)

The suspicion that Harmon's desire for Bella is caught up with the sense of abjection that she provides for him is confirmed rather than contradicted by the satisfaction of that desire in the honeymoon household where the Harmons and the Boffins finally dwell together. Confirmed, because this is the end of his desire in both senses of the term: the wedded bliss finally achieved by John and Bella Harmon may be more joyful, but it is no less erotically impoverished than the passionless marriage advocated by Helen Huntingdon's grim guardian or the frightening domesticity projected by Bella's sadly ridiculous parents. If, as Nancy Armstrong declares in *Desire and Domestic Fiction*, class differences in the eighteenth- and nineteenth-century novel "are . . . represented as a struggle between the sexes that can be completely resolved in terms of the sexual contract,"[20] this resolution, at least in the Dickens novel, comes at the cost of the sexual element in the sexual contract. Too busy playing house, "Bella, putting her hair back with both hands, as if she were making the most business-like arrangements . . . enter[ing] the [domestic] affairs of the day" (*Our Mutual Friend*, 749), has no time now to let her hair down long enough for her former role as class sadist.

We need only weigh the difference between John Harmon's fantasy of social abjection and Lizzie Hexam's fantasy of social ascent to sense what will probably be obvious anyway, that the category of class masochism in *Our Mutual Friend* is a species of male sexuality:

> "I wonder if anybody has . . . captivated . . . [Mr Wrayburn], Lizzie!"
> "It is very likely."
> "It is very likely? I wonder who!"
> "Is it not very likely that some lady has been taken by him, and that he may love her dearly?"
> "Perhaps. I do not know. What would you think of him, Lizzie, if you were a lady?"
> "I a lady!" she repeated, laughing. "Such a fancy!"
> "Yes. But say: just as a fancy, and for instance."
> "I a lady! I, a poor girl who used to row poor father on the river." (401)

Thus an irony as common as the greener grass on the other side: while the desires of the entitled man are bound up with a hankering to be taken down the class ladder, the desires of the river dredger's daughter are condensed in a dream of upward mobility. And if the difference between the desires of John Harmon and Lizzie Hexam seems only a matter of class rather than sex, consider that the most virulent strain of social masochism recorded in the novel appears well below the upper reaches of the novel's social anatomy, in a man who dwells at the bottom edge of respectability:

> Bradley Headstone, in his decent black coat and waistcoat, and decent white shirt . . . He was never seen in any other dress, and yet there was a certain stiffness in his manner of wearing this, as if there were a want of adaptation between him and it recalling some mechanics in their holiday clothes. He had acquired mechanically a great store of teacher's knowledge . . . From his early childhood up, his mind had been a place of mechanical stowage. The arrangement of his wholesale warehouse, so that it might be always ready to meet the demands of retail dealers – history here, geography there, astronomy to the right, political economy to the left . . . had imparted to his countenance a look of care. (266–7)

The drive for social improvement that engrosses Bradley Headstone, whose threadbare respectability requires infinite pains to sustain, illuminates by contrast the downward trajectory of his sexual compulsion. Consider his anguished declaration to Lizzie:

> I love you. What other men may mean when they use that expression, I cannot tell; what I mean is, that I am under the influence of some tremendous

attraction which I have resisted in vain, and which overmasters me. You could draw me to fire, you could draw me to water, you could draw me to the gallows, you could draw me to any death, you could draw me to anything I have most avoided, you could draw me to any exposure and disgrace.

(454–5)

Headstone's "tremendous attraction" pulls him to a hideous death, but also to the social ruin at least as bad as that in the book of the anxious *arriviste* "who had toiled hard to get what [he] had won, and . . . had to hold it now that it was gotten" (267). Drawn on by his "tremendous attraction," Bradley Headstone falls not only to the bottom of the river, "under the ooze and scum" (874), but, no less horribly, to the bottom of the social order.

And the downward pull of Bradley Headstone's attraction manages to defeat the drive upward that is also confided there. In her study of the social intercourse between men routed through the channel of a common desire for the same woman, Eve Kosofsky Sedgwick remarks that "the link of rivalry between himself and Eugene Wrayburn," his upper-crust competitor, is the closest that Bradley Headstone comes to "patriarchal power," and, we might add, the cultural capital that his rival possesses in abundance.[21] But, as Sedgwick suggests, this is a miss as good as a mile – there is no way that the downtrodden schoolteacher can keep up with his entitled competitor, who amuses himself by inciting and frustrating Headstone's hunger to emulate him: "I tempt him on, all over London . . . Sometimes I walk; sometimes, I proceed in cabs, draining the pocket of the schoolmaster, who then follows in cabs . . . [I] tempt the school master to follow" (*Our Mutual Friend*, 606).

The gulf made vivid by Bradley Headstone's humiliation by a man who can afford things that he cannot may seem less a matter of masochism than the simple fact of class difference. But if Bradley Headstone is set up by the social order to lose the race for Lizzie Hexam from the start, he also appears to relish his loss. Like John Harmon, Headstone goes to considerable trouble to arrange a drama in which he stars as Social Inferiority:

"You think me of no more value than the dirt under your feet," said Bradley to Eugene, speaking in a carefully weighed and measured tone, or he could not have spoken at all.

"I assure you, Schoolmaster," replied Eugene, "I do not think about you."

"That's not true," returned the other; "you know better."

"That's coarse," Eugene retorted, "but you *don't* know better."

"Mr. Wrayburn, at least I know very well that it would be idle to set myself against you in insolent words or overbearing manners. That lad who has just gone out could put you to shame in half-a-dozen branches of knowledge in half an hour, but you can throw him aside like an inferior. You can do as much by me, I have no doubt, beforehand."

"Possibly," remarked Eugene.   (344)

And the downward direction of Bradley Headstone's sexual drive is more than a matter of its practical effects in the novel; more even than its entanglement with a taste for social denigration. It is not just that his desire drives him downward on the social scale, or, like his upper-class counterpart John Harmon, that he desires to be so driven; it is also that his desire is socially inferior in its very nature:

> He held as straight a course for [Lizzie's house] as the wisdom of his ancestors, exemplified in the construction of the intervening streets, would let him, and walked with a bent head hammering at one fixed idea. It had been an immovable idea since he first set eyes upon her. It seemed to him as if all that he could . . . restrain in himself he had restrained, and the time had come – in a rush, in a moment – when the power of self-command had departed from him. Love at first sight is a trite expression quite sufficiently discussed; enough that in certain smouldering natures like this man's, that passion leaps into a blaze, and makes such head as fire does in a rage of wind, when other passions, but for its mastery, could be held in chains.   (396)

The passion that is released in this "smouldering nature," the passion embodied in "a bent head hammering at one fixed idea," takes the form of labor – not the respectable occupation of the schoolteacher, but rather the labor of the blacksmith or the factory worker, the work that is done by those whose unchaining Marx saw as the start of a conflagration that would bring down the socio-economic order.

But if the return of the repressed in Bradley Headstone raises briefly the specter of revolution, it works as well to contain another kind of threat to society, a threat posed not by smouldering masses who seek to incinerate it, but rather by climbers who seek to enter it. They are everywhere in the novel. The dogged efforts of Bradley Headstone at respectability are matched by the delirious machinations of those who seek to enter a higher society: "Mr. and Mrs. Veneering were bran-new people in a bran-new house in a bran-new quarter of London. Everything about the Veneerings was spick and span new. All their furniture was new, all their friends were new, all their servants were new, their plate was new, their carriage was new, their harness was new, their horses were new, their pictures were new" (48). And such machinations are matched by virtually everyone else in the social gulf between Headstone and the Veneerings.

The clamor of improvement heard everywhere in *Our Mutual Friend* that originates in a capitalist economy providing unprecedented opportunities for class ascent, at least to some Victorians, is the social unrest that the class-defined and defining character of Bradley Headstone's sexuality helps to contain. It is in the context of a drive for upward mobility as incessant in the world of *Our Mutual Friend* as sexual desire itself that we can most fully understand Dickens's defense of traditional class distinctions, a defense that Franco Moretti describes: "Dickens succeeds in keeping alive the taxonomical rigidity of 'traditional-feudal' thought even after the erosion of its material bases . . . What marks the vast majority of Dickensian characters is, after all, the very same impossibility to 'escape from oneself' which in *Tom Jones* was the result of one's 'trade', and in Dickens, who is writing about a socially more fluid world, is connected to something strictly personal."[22]

And what could be more strictly personal than sexual passion? What better way to secure a wavering sense of someone's social rank than by translating it into the intimate idiom of his desire? The class position from which Bradley Headstone seeks to rise haunts his very efforts to do so, in "the stiffness of manner" that makes him in "respectable" dress like a "mechanic" in his "holiday clothes"; in the stiffness of mind that makes his exertions to transcend that position only a sublimated version of the labor that defines that position in the first place. But the ghost of the mechanic returns most fully in the passions that a "respectable" man cannot deny forever, the passion that sets him on a "course" set out for him by "his ancestors," "with a bent head hammering at one fixed idea." And here we return to the sexuality in the Victorian novel that has concerned us all along, the propagations of passion through which the forces of history make themselves felt.

NOTES

1 Those familiar with it will recognize that the phrase that begins and the thought that informs this paragraph are drawn from Michel Foucault's *History of Sexuality: An Introduction – Volume 1*, trans. Robert Hurley (New York: Random House, 1978).

2 Franco Moretti, "Kindergarten," *Signs Taken for Wonders*, trans. Susan Fischer, David Forgacs, David Miller (London: Verso, 1983), 181.

3 Although to phrase it this way is to risk obscuring how significant the particular forms of indirection are in determining the course and character of sexual desire in and beyond the Victorian novel. For an exemplary recent consideration of this question, see William A. Cohen, *Sex Scandal: The Private Parts of Victorian Fiction* (Durham, NC: Duke University Press, 1996).

4 On the definition of the homosexual as a form of desire and then later a mode of identity associated with early extinction in the Victorian period and beyond, see Jeff Nunokawa, "*In Memoriam* and the Extinction of the Homosexual," ELH 58.2 (1991), 427–38; "All The Sad Young Men: AIDS and the Work of Mourning,"in Diana Fuss, ed., *Inside/Out: Lesbian Theories, Gay Theories*

(New York: Routledge, 1992). On Wilde's efforts to invert this trend, see Jeff Nunokawa, "The Importance of Being Bored: The Dividends of Ennui in *The Picture of Dorian Gray*" in Eve Kosofsky Sedgwick, ed., *Novel Gazing: Queer Readings in Fiction* (Durham, NC: Duke University Press, 1997), 151–66.

5 Anne Brontë, *The Tenant of Wildfell Hall*, ed. G. D. Hargreaves (1848; London: Penguin, 1979), 165. All subsequent citations of the novel refer to this edition.

6 Karl Marx, *Economic and Philosophic Manuscripts of 1844*, trans. Martin Mulligan (Amherst, NY: Prometheus Books, 1988), 72.

7 See, for example, Georg Lukács, "Reification and the Consciousness of the Proletariat" in *History and Class Consciousness*, trans. Rodney Livingston (Cambridge, MA: The MIT Press, 1971), 83–222; Henri Lefebvre, *Critique of Everyday Life*, trans. John Moore (New York: Verso Press, 1991); Herbert Marcuse, *Eros and Civilization: A Philosophical Inquiry into Freud* (Boston: Beacon Press, 1955).

8 E. J. Hobsbawm, *The Age of Capital, 1848–1875* (New York: Scribner, 1975), xiii.

9 Max Weber, *The Protestant Ethic and The Spirit of Capitalism*, Introduction by Randall Collins; trans. Talcott Parsons (Los Angeles: Roxbury Publishing Company, 1996).

10 William Makepeace Thackeray, *Vanity Fair*, ed. J. I. M. Stewart (1848; London: Penguin, 1985), 93. All subsequent citations of the novel refer to this edition.

11 Albert O Hirschman, *The Passions and the Interests: Political Arguments for Capitalism Before Its Triumph* (Princeton: Princeton University Press, 1977).

12 Hobsbawm, *The Age of Capital*, xvii.

13 Charlotte Brontë, *Jane Eyre*, ed. Q. D. Leavis (1847; New York: Penguin, 1966). All subsequent citations refer to this edition.

14 Sigmund Freud, "Three Contributions to the Theory of Sex," *The Basic Writings of Sigmund Freud* (New York: Random House, 1938), 553–629.

15 George Eliot, *Adam Bede*, ed. Stephen Gill (1859; London: Penguin, 1980), 176. All subsequent citations of the novel refer to this edition.

16 Foucault, *History of Sexuality*, 35.

17 Georg Simmel, *The Sociology of Georg Simmel*, trans. and ed. Kurt Wolff (New York: The Free Press, 1950), 319.

18 Charles Dickens, *Our Mutual Friend*, ed. Stephen Gill (1865; London: Penguin, 1971), 257. All subsequent citations of the novel refer to this edition.

19 Charles Dickens, *Great Expectations*, ed. Angus Calder (1860; London: Penguin, 1985), 257.

20 Nancy Armstrong, *Desire and Domestic Fiction: A Political History of the Novel* (New York: Oxford University Press, 1987), 49.

21 Eve Kosofsky Sedgwick, *Between Men: English Literature and Male Homosocial Desire* (New York: Columbia University Press, 1985), 168.

22 Franco Moretti, "The Conspiracy of the Innocents," *The Way of the World: The* Bildungsroman *in European Culture*, trans Albert Sbragia (London: Verso, 1987), 193.

7

PATRICK BRANTLINGER

Race and the Victorian novel

"All is race; there is no other truth." So says Sidonia, Benjamin Disraeli's fictional Jewish sage and *alter ego*. The novel in which Sidonia makes this pronouncement is *Tancred* (1847), the third in Disraeli's Young England trilogy.[1] Even during his years as Prime Minister, Disraeli continued to believe in race as an all-encompassing explanatory category. Thus, in his novel of 1870, *Lothair*, Paraclete, a Syrian, tells the young protagonist:

> God works by races . . . The Aryan and the Semite are of the same blood and origin, but when they quitted their central land they were ordained to follow opposite courses. Each division of the great race has developed one portion of the double nature of humanity, till after all their wanderings they met again, and, represented by their two choicest families, the Hellenes and the Hebrews, brought together the treasures of their accumulated wisdom and secured the civilisation of man.[2]

The metaphor of "choicest families," suggesting divinely chosen branches of the one "great race," provides Disraeli with a formulaic – indeed, stereotypic – explanation of Western civilization and its two ancient sources, classical Greece and Judaeo-Christianity.

That Disraeli, through Sidonia and Paraclete, is expressing a widely held Victorian view of race as the mainspring of world history is evident from *Culture and Anarchy* (1869), in which poet and critic Matthew Arnold employs "Hellenism" and "Hebraism" as racial terms to distinguish the chief tendencies of Western civilization. Arnold believed that he was echoing the latest findings of "ethnology," an early version of physical anthropology that scholars today treat as a pseudo-science of racial difference. "Race is everything: literature, science, art, in a word, civiliza-tion, depend on it": so, sounding like Sidonia, declared Dr. Robert Knox in *The Races of Men* (1850).[3] Foreshadowing Count Gobineau's influential *Essay on the Inequality of Human Races*, published in France in the early 1850s, Knox argued that historical change is due to the physical and mental inequalities among races; that race hatred and conflict are inbred

The blessings of its happy ending are cast beyond the last pages of Anne Brontë's novel into the culture of capitalism where it is inscribed. Like a religion that justifies those who are enriched by the profits of the capitalist system,[9] or one that counsels resignation to those who labor to produce them, the secular scripture of desire promulgated by novels like *The Tenant of Wildfell Hall* promotes a faith that renders more tenable the sacrifices of desire exacted by that system. In the novel's closing scene of lovers together at last, an icon is born to ease the daily labor of renunciation exacted from the worker who must leave her own wishes at the door of the factory or office; in the closing scene of lovers together at last, an image arises that lights the path away from the pleasures that we want by the promise that we can return to them.

The passions and the interests in *Vanity Fair*

The strain of sexual desire entertained in Brontë's novel takes place outside the sphere of the economy; it takes form as an impulse whose suspension is demanded by a capitalist regime sufficiently established by the middle of the nineteenth century to count as a principle of reality, a regime which depends upon and demands steady, punctual labor, or at least the habit of pulling out of bed and showing up to work on time. Elsewhere though, as in Thackeray's famous novel, the trouble with desire is not how little it has to do with economic values, but rather how much. *Vanity Fair* records the contamination of the cool motives associated with the marketplace by the heat of a passion that will pay any price, no matter how inflated, to have what it wants, a passion too blind to see the price it pays will not secure the prize in any case, a passion Thackeray and others identify as the essential style of sexual love.

A passion which puts those who are touched by it in the most embarrassing positions: for anyone who has read the novel, the spectacle of Jos Sedley at Vauxhall, drunk enough to make his move on Becky Sharp, clings like the memory of a personal humiliation: "'Stop, my dearest, diddle-diddle-darling,' shouted Jos, now as bold as a lion, and clasping Miss Rebecca round the waist. Rebecca started, but she could not get away her hand."[10] His death, probably by the same hand near the end of the novel merely literalizes the mortification he suffers for it near the beginning. And while Jos Sedley, "that fat *gourmand*," (*Vanity Fair*, 93) furnishes the broadest target for the "barbed shaft of love," no one is exempt from it: "[Rawdon Crawley] raved about [Becky] in uncouth convulsions. The barbed shaft of love had penetrated his dull hide" (173). "'I'll make your fortune,' she said; and Delilah patted Samson's cheek" (204).

factors in human nature; that war and imperial expansion are the results of this hatred; and finally that, where climate does not affect the outcome, the fair, stronger races invariably defeat and either enslave or exterminate the dark, weaker races.

Knox's ideas about race may have been extreme, but they contributed to an emergent, pseudo-scientific orthodoxy – one that Charles Darwin both partly supported and partly contested in *Origin of Species* (1859) and *The Descent of Man* (1871). Knox favored polygenesis, or the theory that "the races of men" were distinct species with separate primeval origins.[4] The Darwinian position, which in this one way, at least, brought science into line with the biblical account of creation, treated mankind as a single species with a single evolutionary origin (monogenesis).

In stressing the unity of mankind, Darwin viewed the apparent physical differences among the races as much less significant than their similarities, the conclusion of scientists today. But evolutionary theory still maintained that there were huge chronological and therefore cultural differences among the races. Early cultural anthropology, represented by Edward Burnett Tylor's *Primitive Culture* (1872), sharply divided human societies into three evolutionary stages: savagery, barbarism, and civilization.[5] This chronological hierarchy in turn supported the "civilizing mission" of imperial expansion: it was "the white man's burden," as a poem by Rudyard Kipling famously put it, to try to raise "savages" and "barbarians" – the world's "new-caught, sullen peoples, Half devil and half child" – up to the level of white civilization. But, Kipling and many other Victorian intellectuals believed, many savage and barbarian "races" were incapable of becoming fully civilized, and at least some appeared doomed to inevitable extinction.

History, anti-semitism, and racial stereotypes

The belief that "all is race" was hardly scientific, but it seemed so to Knox, Arnold, and many Victorian novelists including Disraeli. The standard Victorian accounts of British history treated its main outlines as a series of racial migrations and conquests: the Britons and Celts; the Romans; the Angles, Jutes, and Saxons; the Danes; the Normans. The Norman invasion of 1066 was the subject of a number of historical novels that depicted the creation of modern England as the result of clashing races. The most famous and influential of these, Sir Walter Scott's *Ivanhoe* (1819), served as a model for several later depictions of English history, including Edward Bulwer-Lytton's *Harold, The Last of the Saxon Kings* (1848), Charles Kingsley's *Hereward the Wake* (1866), and to some extent also Disraeli's

Sybil (1845). *Ivanhoe* portrays the new Norman aristocracy lording it over the unhappy Anglo-Saxon race; the return of Richard the Lionhearted from the Crusades helps set matters right. Portrayed as the unifier of the two races, Richard overcomes the machinations of his brother, Prince John, and helps to celebrate the marriage of Ivanhoe, son of Cedric the Saxon, and Rowena, the direct descendant of Alfred the Great. Just as Saxon Ivanhoe had allied himself with Norman Richard during the Crusades, so now Richard allies himself both with downtrodden Saxon nobility and with the Saxon outlaw hero Robin Hood and his merry men to defeat the conspiracy of the Norman aristocrats who threaten his rule. *Ivanhoe* thus adumbrates the future fusion of the Norman and Saxon races and, partly through this racial harmonization, the emergence of modern Great Britain. Scott's "historical romance" suggests that racial intermingling, when it occurs between two white, European races, is or can be a source of historical progress.

In *Sybil*, focused upon industrialization and the working-class Chartist movement of the 1840s, the heroine and her father, Chartist leader Walter Gerard, discover that they are the descendants of Saxon nobility. Sybil's union with the aristocratic protagonist, Charles Egremont, symbolizes the overcoming of class conflict and also, albeit less logically than in *Ivanhoe*, of the racial division between Norman and Saxon. Disraeli draws from Scott the standard equation of the common, authentic English people (the mainstay of the working class) with the Anglo-Saxon race. He interprets Chartism, whose main goal was universal (male) suffrage, as in part an effort to restore the lost rights and freedoms that the Anglo-Saxon race supposedly enjoyed before the Norman Conquest.

Ivanhoe also depicts the romantic attachment of the Jewish heroine Rebecca to the hero, and the trials and tribulations of her money-lending father, Isaac. At the novel's end, Isaac and Rebecca go into exile from turbulent, Jew-persecuting England, thus making way for the union of Ivanhoe and Rowena. Scott's treatment of his Jewish characters is at once anti-Semitic (Isaac as cowardly usurer) and sympathetic (the dark Rebecca as a more active, interesting heroine than the fair Rowena). Scott's ambivalence toward the Jewish "race" is echoed by several later novelists. Thus, when Charles Dickens was accused of anti-Semitism because of his portrayal of the diabolical Fagin, master criminal in *Oliver Twist* (1838), he later tried to make amends through the gentle, innocent Mr. Riah and some other sympathetic Jewish characters in *Our Mutual Friend* (1865). Toward the end of Dickens's last completed novel, old Riah condemns anti-Semitism: "Men say, 'This is a bad Greek, but there are good Greeks. This is a bad Turk, but there are good Turks.' Not so with the Jews. Men find the bad among us easily enough – among what peoples are the bad not easily found? – but they take the worst of us as samples of the best . . . and they say 'All Jews are alike.'"[6]

To counteract the anti-semitism that Disraeli had to combat throughout his career as both a novelist and a politician, his fiction expresses an idealized, positive version of the cultural phenomenon informed by racist ideology that Edward Said has called "orientalism." While anti-Semitism can be understood as a version of orientalism, the latter term refers more generally to a set of stereotypic beliefs about the entire "orient" – all of the Middle East and Asia – according to which the highly diverse cultures and societies from Egypt to China are all mired in irrational, non-progressive customs and superstitions and in an inbred (that is, racially inherited) indolence and sexual indulgence (polygamy and the prurient motif of the harem).[7] But in *Tancred* and elsewhere, Disraeli asserts that all the world's great religions and empires originated in the orient, inspired by "the genius of Arabia," and he attacks anti-Semitism by substituting positive oriental virtues (wisdom, sophistication, generosity) for stereotypic negatives.

Partly in response to what she saw as Disraeli's shallow if positive treatment of history in racial terms, George Eliot focused on Judaism in her final novel, *Daniel Deronda* (1876). After saving the beautiful Jewess Mirah Lapidoth from suicide, Daniel encounters her brother Mordecai, through whom he begins to learn about Judaism and the history of the Jews. Daniel is attracted to the cultural and historical solidarity that he comes to identify with Judaism, and when he learns from his mother that he is in fact Jewish by birth, the stage is set for his marriage to Mirah and for their proto-Zionist journey to Palestine. Daniel's attraction to Judaism, however, is not primarily either racial or religious, but cultural. Judaism in *Daniel Deronda* represents a sort of trans-national nationalism, through which Eliot critiques both anti-Semitism and narrow versions of nationalism or patriotism that were often indistinguishable from racism (the English as the best race and nation in the world).

Later Victorian novelists also sometimes tried to counteract anti-Semitism, though not always successfully. In *Reuben Sachs* (1888), Jewish novelist Amy Levy attempted to portray Jews realistically, although her realism seemed anti-Semitic to some of her first critics. Another realistic portrayal of Jews and Judaism is Israel Zangwill's *Children of the Ghetto* (1892), an account of recent immigrants from eastern Europe to London. But more common than either idealistic or realistic portrayals are stereotypic representations of Jews as an inferior, often criminal, sometimes even diabolical race. The Rev. Joseph Emilius in Anthony Trollope's *The Eustace Diamonds* (1872), for example, is a hypocritical, smooth-talking con-man who charms Lizzie Eustace with his lies. Lizzie eventually marries the "nasty, greasy, lying, squinting Jew preacher," as the narrator calls him,[8] and he shows up again in Trollope's *Phineas Redux* (1873), where he murders the politician Mr. Bonteen, a crime for which the protagonist, Phineas Finn, is at first arrested. It also turns out that Emilius has committed bigamy – no crime too *outré* for this latter-day Shylock, it seems – although, to give him his due, he does not steal the diamonds in the earlier novel. That is instead the work of the equally criminal Jew, Mr. Benjamin. And in *The Way We Live Now* (1875), at the center of the web of dishonesty and corruption that Trollope presents as "the way we live now" is the fraudulent stockbroker and forger Augustus Melmotte, who is in all likelihood Jewish, though he has concealed that fact along with others from his shady past.

If race could provide a pseudo-scientific explanation for the entire history of Great Britain and, indeed, of the world, in Victorian fiction it more commonly provided a ready-made taxonomy for characterization. Thus, in William Makepeace Thackeray's *Vanity Fair* (1848) racial stereotyping helps to predict and explain the behaviors of many characters. The black servant of the Sedleys is named "Sambo" and has, like most black characters in Victorian novels, only a minor role. Also, we know that the wealthy West Indian mulatta, Miss Swartz, will not be a good match for George Osbourne – her silliness matches her dark complexion – despite her money and despite George's father's greed. As soon as we learn that Becky Sharp's parents are French, we know that she will play fast and loose with sexual mores, marital fidelity, and honesty. And we also know that Major O'Dowd and his family, because they are Irish, will be raucous, vulgar, and, though generous and sympathetic, also silly. This is not to deny that Thackeray's English characters are often vulgar, vain, or even vicious – in *Vanity Fair*, no one is more selfish, at least, than George's father, unless it is Sir Pitt Crawley, presumably of ancient English stock.

Jos Sedley may be an Englishman, moreover, but he is effeminate, overweight, and cowardly, so the backwaters of the empire – Bogley Wallah in India – is a good enough place of exile for him. Thackeray was born in Calcutta, and he would have been a wealthy man had it not been for the collapse of an Indian banking house in which his family had invested. This loss of fortune is reflected in *The Newcomes* (1855): good Colonel Newcome and his son, Clive, have invested their savings in the great Bundelcund Bank of India, only to see it collapse. Thackeray blames the bankruptcy on the machinations of an oriental villain, Rummon Loll, a "confounded old mahogany-coloured heathen humbug."[9] In one early episode, the "heathen gentleman" flirts with "the handsomest young

[English] woman" at a social gathering, and provokes both Col. New-come's and Thackeray's wrath (*The Newcomes*, 1:83). For Thackeray and many other Victorian novelists, the social mixing of races could seem improper, and the biological mixing of white with any of the "colored" races seemed almost unthinkable, taboo.

Besides the racially mixed Miss Swartz in *Vanity Fair*, in *Philip* (1862) Thackeray mocks the rich mulatto, Captain Woolcomb, for aspiring to the same social status as whites. Deborah Thomas comments that "'the tawny Woolcomb'" is "a reflection not just of Thackeray's personal thinking but of the widespread view among his contemporaries . . . that blacks could not be gentlemen."[10] To use a nineteenth-century term that was simulta-neously cultural and biological (and, hence, racial), Thackeray believed that blacks like Sambo and mixed-race people like both Miss Swartz and Captain Woolcomb lacked genuine "breeding," which money could not buy. Moreover, a widely accepted fallacy, at least before Darwin, was that racial hybrids such as mulattoes were or would become infertile, unable to reproduce. This fallacy implied also that mixed-race people were somehow even more inferior than racially "pure" people of any race. Racism in all its forms depends upon a fantasy of a pure origin, when a race was untainted by inferior "breeds" or "bloods." But, as modern scientists have demon-strated, all contemporary human populations are the results of long-term interactions that might well be labeled historical miscegenation or hy-bridity.[11]

Slavery and anti-slavery

When, in *Philip*, Captain Woolcomb runs for Parliament, his campaign slogan is, "Am I not a man and a brudder?"[12] Thackeray is mocking the slogan of the anti-slavery movement, "Am I not a man and a brother?" In abolitionist propaganda, this was the question of an African in chains, pleading for freedom. Led in Britain by such humanitarians as John Clarkson and William Wilberforce, the anti-slavery movement had resulted in outlawing the transatlantic slave trade in 1807 and in abolishing slavery in all British territories in 1833. Yet abolitionists did not necessarily believe in the equality of Africans with Europeans. And their humanitarianism was often attacked by social critics such as William Cobbett and Thomas Carlyle, who held that to be more concerned about black slaves abroad than about white "wage slaves" at home was hypocritical.

Both in his *American Notes* (1842) and in *Martin Chuzzlewit* (1844), Dickens expressed outrage over the violence visited upon slaves in the United States, but he clearly also believed that Africans (and all other "dark-skinned" peoples of the world) were racially inferior to whites, and like Thackeray he condemned what he considered to be hypocritical humanitarianism. In an 1848 essay on the failed Niger Expedition of 1841, which had been sponsored by evangelical abolitionists, Dickens lambasted "the heated visions of philanthropists for the railroad Christianisation of Africa, and the abolition of the Slave Trade," and declared: "Between the civilized European and the barbarous African there is a great gulf set." The "ignorant and savage races" of Africa should be left in their savage condition. In a later essay, Dickens debunked what he saw as the dangerous myth of the noble savage: there were only "ignoble savages," who should be swept from the path of civilization.[13] Dickens thus aligned himself with Carlyle, who in "An Occasional Discourse on The Nigger Question" (1849) defended slavery in part by condemning abolitionist and philanthropic activities that looked overseas rather than attending to poverty and exploitation in Britain. Thus, in *Bleak House* (1853), Dickens portrayed Mrs. Jellyby's philanthropic interest in the Borrioboola-Gha mission on the banks of the Niger River as evangelical hypocrisy.

In one of the American episodes of *Martin Chuzzlewit*, when Martin meets Mark Tapley outside a newspaper office, a third character is present, "a man of colour" named Cicero, who, Mark indicates, is also a "man and a brother, you know, sir." With that phrase, slavery comes to the fore, and Cicero's story illustrates its horrors. Mark tells Martin that, though Cicero is now a freedman, when he was young "he was shot in the leg; gashed in the arm; scored in his live limbs, like crimped fish; beaten out of shape; had his neck galled with an iron collar, and wore iron rings upon his wrists and ankles" and so on. But it is Mark Tapley who tells Cicero's story, not Cicero himself; and the scene ends when "the negro grinning assent from under a leathern portmanteau, than which his own face was many shades deeper [i.e., darker], hobbled downstairs" and away with Martin's luggage to Mrs. Pawkins's boardinghouse.[14]

Cicero may be an ex-slave, but he remains in "grinning," silent servitude, and the same is true of other "coloured" characters in Dickens's novels. Thus, in *Dombey and Son* (1848), boastful Major Bagstock employs a servant from India who serves mainly as the object of the Major's verbal and physical abuse. Dickens is critical of the abuse, but nevertheless treats the servant as a joke. Known only as "the Native," he "had no particular name, but answered to any vituperative epithet" from the "choleric" Major such as "villain."[15] Like Cicero, the Native gets no word in edgewise. Just as Dickens is critical of the institution of slavery, and yet makes it clear that Cicero is not deserving of full respect and sympathy, so too with Major Bagstock's "Native."

The novel that, a decade prior to the American Civil War, made the most influential case for abolition was *Uncle Tom's Cabin* (1852), by American Harriet Beecher Stowe, a bestseller which sold more copies in Britain than in the United States. But the abolitionist cause was also taken up by a number of British novelists both before and after the Civil War. Thus, Sarah Lee Wallis's 1847 novel, *The African Wanderers*, condemns the violence of the slave trade – "that horrible traffic" – within Africa.[16] And Harriet Martineau was both an early feminist and an ardent abolitionist. *Demerara*, in Martineau's series of short fictions, *Illustrations of Political Economy* (1832–34), makes the case for free trade and supposedly free labor versus slavery; and her historical novel, *The Hour and the Man* (1841), is an attempt to provide an heroic account of the Haitian leader Toussaint L'Ouverture and the revolution that defeated slavery in San Domingo (now Haiti and the Dominican Republic) in the late 1700s.

After the 1833 legislation that abolished slavery in the British colonies, British writers often expressed their abhorrence of slavery and their moral superiority to the upstart, hypocritical former British colonies, the United States, which boasted of liberty and yet allowed slavery to continue until the Civil War. British moral superiority in the struggle against slavery quite easily, however, turned into a justification for imperialist exploration and expansion in Africa. Even after the Civil War, the idea of an heroic crusade against slavery is expressed in numerous imperialist adventure novels, including a few written by prominent white explorers of "the dark continent," as Africa was often called.

The most famous, indeed revered, British explorer of Africa was missionary David Livingstone, whose journals of his various treks into central Africa became bestsellers.[17] Another bestselling narrative, *How I Found Livingstone*, was published in 1872 by American explorer, Henry Morton Stanley, who had been commissioned by the *New York Herald* to create a journalistic scoop by finding Livingstone after he had supposedly disappeared. Perhaps more than any other author, Stanley in his exploration journals, including *Through the Dark Continent* (1878) and *In Darkest Africa* (1890), helped to create the myth of "the dark continent." Even though both explorers made abolishing the slave trade within Africa one of their goals, in contrast to Livingstone's more positive portrayals of African tribal societies, Stanley's tend to be negatively stereotypic: slavery may be a bad thing, but Africans are not fit for anything better than servitude and obedience to heroic white men like Stanley.

My Kalulu: Prince, King, and Slave (1889) is an adventure novel that Stanley wrote to express, as he claims, "the evils of the slave trade in Africa," though obviously also to promote his various imperializing projects (Stanley wound up in the Congo working for King Leopold of Belgium, the horrors of whose private empire Joseph Conrad exposed in *Heart of Darkness*, 1902).[18] In any event, other white explorers of Africa also wrote adventure novels about their experiences. These include Samuel Baker's *Cast Up by the Sea* (1866) and Joseph Thomson's *Ulu: An African Romance* (1888). Like *My Kalulu*, Baker's and Thomson's novels, while seeming to champion Africans and anti-slavery, in effect do just the opposite. By depicting Africans as benighted savages, as unable to end the slave trade within Africa by themselves, and as generally inferior to Europeans, all three explorer-novelists make the case for the expansion of British imperialism in Africa.

The novels by Stanley, Baker, and Thomson reproduce rather than challenge the racist stereotyping, formulaic plot devices, and binary rhetoric of the hundreds of imperialist adventure stories written mainly for boys between the 1830s and 1914. Often these novels take the form of quest romances, as in H. Rider Haggard's *King Solomon's Mines* (1885) and *She* (1887). Like Stanley, Baker, and Thomson, Haggard had lived, worked, and traveled in Africa – in his case, as an official in the British colony of Natal in South Africa – and yet his novels, rather than following the conventions of social realism, are romances that spill over into the fantastic, and in doing so reinforce the stereotypes of Africa as "the dark continent" and sub-Saharan Africans as benighted savages. In *King Solomon's Mines*, two Englishmen, Sir Henry Curtis and Captain John Good, team up with South African hunter Allan Quatermain, and with Quatermain's noble-savage sidekick, Umbopa, in a quest ostensibly for Curtis's long-lost brother. The search leads to their discovery of the remains of an ancient civilization, centered around King Solomon's fabulously rich diamond mines. This ancient white or, at any rate, Semitic civilization has been overrun by the Kukuanas, a savage, black tribe ruled by the sadistic tyrant, Twala. Though ignorant about the earlier civilization and perhaps incapable of becoming civilized themselves, the Kukuanas can at least be better ruled. Their true king proves to be Umbopa, and after an epic battle in which Sir Henry kills Twala, Umbopa stays to rule Kukuanaland while the white adventurers return to civilization. In *She*, the quest that takes the white protagonists through shipwreck and cannibals into the "dark" center of Africa again leads to the discovery of an ancient, lost civilization, this time Egyptian in origin. The supposedly immortal witch-queen Ayesha or "She" rules by magic over the light-skinned but savage Amahagger race, now living among the ruins of the ancient kingdom of Kôr, which is distinctly not the product of either the Amahaggers or sub-Saharan Africans. When Horace Holly, narrator of *She*, speculates about lost civilizations in central Africa, he credits these to Egyptians, Babylonians, Phoenicians, Persians, and Jews.[19] In 1871, Karl Mauch discovered the ruins of Great Zimbabwe, but rather than attributing them to sub-Saharan Africans, he and other Europeans, including Haggard, chose erroneously to believe that they must have been constructed by some supposedly superior, lighter-skinned race.

Most of the plethora of boys' adventure novels, from Captain Frederick Marryat's *Mr. Midshipman Easy* (1836), through Mayne Reid's *The Scalp Hunters* (1851) and Robert M. Ballantyne's *Coral Island* (1858), down to G. A. Henty's journalistic potboilers (*With Clive in India*, 1884, *The Dash for Khartoum*, 1892, and so on), are more realistic or at least more factual than Haggard's romances.[20] But this does not mean that they are aesthetically superior. On the contrary, Haggard skillfully exploited the fantasy element in the quest romance tradition, including its regressive, childlike impulse to hark back to the most elemental aspects of experience. Even when written for adults, the quest romance simplifies reality by rendering it in terms of absolute, Manichaean antitheses: good versus evil, light versus darkness, white versus black. This is not to say that the quest romance is inherently racist, but rather that its conventions map easily onto the polar oppositions of racism: us versus them, civilized versus savage, white versus black. In this way, Haggard makes better aesthetic use of the narrative conventions of romance than do most other Victorian writers of adventure fiction.

Captain Marryat, however, heads the list of adventure novelists both chronologically and because he helped establish the conventions that later writers followed. Many of his novels are fictionalized versions of his own sometimes heroic experiences during the Napoleonic Wars. Valorizing the bravery, honor, and self-sacrifice of both the officers and the ordinary sailors in the Royal Navy, Marryat also depicts reality as rigidly hierarchical, every man at his post. *Mr. Midshipman Easy* is in part a satire against the wrongheaded egalitarianism of the hero's father. As an apprentice officer, Jack Easy quickly learns that, while all men may be brothers in an abstract sense, in practice all men are not equals. The shipboard hierarchy from deckhand to admiral mirrors the various hierarchies of the larger social order and, indeed, of nature. Though Jack acquires a black sidekick, a noble savage rather like Haggard's Umbopa, the nobility of this West African is, for Marryat, only a comic caricature of white, European nobility. His very name, "Mephistopheles" ("Mesty" for short), gives him a comic diabolism that matches his filed teeth and cannibal past. Though a "prince" back in Africa, Mesty is happy to be ship's cook and later a corporal, and also to be Jack's loyal follower instead of leader.

Though once Ashanti royalty, Mesty was sold into slavery, from which the Royal Navy freed him. When he recounts his life to Jack, his story can be read as a slave narrative, like the hundreds that were recorded and published by both white and black abolitionists. Yet, partly because Mesty, while still a prince, had also been a slave-trader, his story does not clearly support abolition. Indeed, in *Newton Foster* (1832), Marryat depicts the happy and healthy lives of slaves on a plantation in Barbados, a sort of pro-slavery pastoral. And in *Peter Simple* (1834), Marryat's midshipman hero observes how both the slaves and the free blacks of Barbados arrange themselves in an elaborate hierarchy of color, whereby "a quadroon looks down upon a mulatto, while a mulatto looks down upon a *sambo*, that is, half mulatto half negro, while a *sambo* in turn looks down upon a *nigger*." Near the top of this racial pecking order is the "one-eighth black" or "mustee," whose child with a white person is a "mustafina, or one-sixteenth black. After that, they are *whitewashed*, and considered Europeans," although Peter Simple has his doubts about the legitimacy of such "white-washing."[21] In any case, in Marryat's fiction, the hierarchy of races, with Englishmen at the summit and Africans somewhere near the bottom, parallels other hierarchies of both nature and society. Marryat's insistence on hierarchy, moreover, adds another simplifying ingredient to the Manichaean antitheses both of racism and of romantic as opposed to realistic narrative.

Racial monsters and atrocity stories

Race and empire were major factors in the juvenile fantasy world constructed by the Brontë sisters and their brother, Branwell.[22] This world was centered in an imaginary British colony – Glasstown, later Angria – on the Niger River. The earliest stories celebrate without irony the British conquest, enslavement, and extermination of the "Ashantees" and other "cannibals." But in the hundreds of pages that Charlotte Brontë wrote about Angria over fourteen years, there is a general development from simple affirmation of conquest to a far more complex, critical preoccupation with both racial and gender oppression. As Susan Meyer notes in analyzing the Brontës' African stories, "the gender positioning of British women writers required them to negotiate an association with 'inferior races'"[23] – a negotiation evident in *Jane Eyre* (1847) and *Wuthering Heights* (1847), among many other stories by women. Bertha Mason, "the madwoman in the attic" in Charlotte Brontë's *Jane Eyre*, is a Jamaican Creole, and though perhaps white, her passionate nature connects her to blackness, slavery, and the tropics.[24] Jane, however, associates her own subordinate status as a woman and a governess with slavery, and she identifies with the plight, at least, of the Creole madwoman.

In Emily Brontë's *Wuthering Heights*, similar analogies between gender, race, and social class domination are evident in the story of the "gypsy" Heathcliff, whose unclear but "dark" racial identity is linked both to his untamable passions and to the slavery-like oppression he experiences after the death of Mr. Earnshaw, who rescued him from the slums of Liverpool. Because Liverpool was the major British port for the slave trade, perhaps Heathcliff has some connection to slavery and abolition. But in *Heathcliff and the Great Hunger*, Terry Eagleton makes the equally plausible case that the "gypsy" hero-villain of *Wuthering Heights* may be an Irish outcast. After all, though it is set in the eighteenth century, *Wuthering Heights* was written and published during the Irish Famine of 1845–50. Yet, writes Eagleton, "Heathcliff may be a gypsy, or (like Bertha Mason in *Jane Eyre*) a Creole, or any kind of alien. It is hard to know how black he is, or rather how much of the blackness is pigmentation and how much of it grime and bile."[25] Rather than associating Heathcliff with a specific oppressed race, whether gypsy, African, or Irish, it perhaps makes more sense to associate him with all racially oppressed groups.

A similar ambiguity marks an at least equally famous fictional outcast, the Monster in Mary Shelley's Gothic romance, *Frankenstein* (1818). Like Heathcliff, perhaps the Monster reflects the abolitionist struggle.[26] It is at least reasonable to interpret the story of Frankenstein's rejected creature as a general criticism of social exclusions of all sorts, including racism and slavery. In any case, rather than with the abolition of African slavery, Victorian readers more frequently associated the Monster with Ireland and the Irish – the "Irish Frankenstein," a phrase that elides the distinction between the Monster and his creator. And while Mary Shelley and the Brontës align themselves sympathetically with their outcast characters (whether gypsy, African, or Irish, and whether female or male), racially-marked outsiders in most Victorian novels are far more likely to be either comic stereotypes or figures of monstrosity meant to repel rather than to evoke sympathy.

Before the Famine, Irish characters in English fiction were usually treated as harmless but also drunken, ignorant, comic "Paddies," a stereotype that even Irish novelists such as William Carleton retailed, as in his *Traits and Stories of the Irish Peasantry* (1830, 1833). But Carleton began to focus more seriously on Ireland's social problems in the 1840s, and his *The Black Prophet, A Tale of the Irish Famine* (1847), though melodramatic, is also grimly tragic. Both before and after the Famine, Thackeray treated Irish characters as comic stereotypes. Besides the O'Dowds and other minor characters, the narrator-protagonist of *Barry Lyndon* (1844, 1856) exemplifies the blarney that Thackeray saw as a chief racial characteristic of the Irish, a penchant for irresponsibility and verbose dishonesty that, in his view, rendered them unfit for self-government.[27] *Barry Lyndon* is not an overtly political novel, but whenever Irish agitation for independence from England comes to the fore, then, rather than harmless Paddy, versions of the Irish Frankenstein are likely to appear. This is the case, for instance, with the perpetrators of terrorist violence in Trollope's last, unfinished novel, *The Landleaguers* (1883). So, too, in Robert Louis Stevenson's Gothic romance, *Dr. Jekyll and Mr. Hyde* (1886), the doctor's demonic *alter ego* matches the stereotype of the Irish hooligan (Stevenson probably had Fenianism in mind).[28] And both Fenianism and eastern European anarchism figure in a number of late Victorian novels and early twentieth-century novels about terrorist bombings (Conrad's *The Secret Agent* [1907] for instance), often with racial implications.

Like the Monster in *Frankenstein*, the demonic characters in Victorian Gothic romances such as *Dr. Jekyll and Mr. Hyde* are often, at least implicitly, racial others. Thus, in Bram Stoker's *Dracula* (1897), the Count, carrying the scourge of vampirism from Transylvania to England, reflects several aspects of late-Victorian racism: anxieties about immigration, especially from eastern Europe; the anti-Semitism that such immigration aroused; and the fear of racial degeneration among the English themselves.[29] *Dracula* expresses some other anxieties, however, particularly those relating to "sexual anarchy": homophobia, fear of the "New Woman," and so on. Fictional monsters often serve multiple scapegoating purposes.

In *Wuthering Heights*, Heathcliff is likened to a vampire, a ghoul, and a cannibal – the last, a gothic metaphor that associates him with the "dark races" of the world. All three terms are monstrous metaphors for Heathcliff's "savage" rage, passion, and behavior. But there are also literal rather than metaphoric cannibals in Victorian fiction, and perhaps the most notorious of these literal man-eaters is the Irish "demon barber," Sweeney Todd.[30] Most fictional cannibals, however, appear in adventure stories set in Africa, the South Pacific, and sometimes also the Americas. Wherever it occurs, cannibalism is treated as the worst, most savage of savage customs, the absolute antithesis of civilization. From Daniel Defoe's *Robinson Crusoe* (1719) down to Conrad's *Heart of Darkness*, it hardly mattered to the writers of such fiction whether cannibalism was an actual practice and, even if it was, whether it was frequent or infrequent, indiscriminate blood-thirstiness or an aspect of religious ritual. In *The Coral Island*, Ballantyne's boy-heroes run the gauntlet of savagery, including the threat of being captured and eaten by cannibals. As Jack explains to Peterkin, "all the natives of the South Sea Islands are fierce cannibals, and they have little respect for strangers."[31] Whether the setting is the South Pacific or Africa, much the same is true of the "natives" in many other adventure stories written for male, adolescent readers. In Henty's *By Sheer Pluck, A Tale of the Ashanti War* (1884), for example, Mr. Goodenough tells Frank that "the other tribes all have a species of terror of these cannibals", the Fans, even though the Fans who accompany the white characters seem to be reformed cannibals.[32] But "the other tribes" are no better: the Dahomeyans and Ashantis are bloodthirsty savages whose main motivation for warfare is to take as many captives as possible for human sacrifice.

Well into the twentieth century, in the Tarzan stories by American Edgar Rice Burroughs and in the fiction of Edgar Wallace, Cutliffe Hyne, and other writers, central Africa especially is represented as cannibal territory, an aspect of the myth of "the dark continent." In *Sanders of the River* (1911) and Wallace's other stories about a British official policing Africans, Commissioner Sanders rules over "cannibal folk" – a phrase that implies that all Africans are cannibalistic unless prevented from being so by the law and order of white civilization. Most adventure stories that deal with cannibalism treat it as an ultimate atrocity that demands imperial policing of the sort provided by Sanders.

In contrast to Wallace, Stanley, Henty, and many other writers who depict "the dark continent" as a land of cannibals, fetishistic superstition, and perhaps uncivilizable savagery, Conrad in *Heart of Darkness* offers a partial critique of European imperialism and of the racism that was one of its ideological corollaries. When Marlow, the main narrator, sails up the Congo River to the Inner Station and its chief, Mr. Kurtz, the crew of his steamboat are "cannibals" who, however, exhibit what Marlow sees as a paradoxical moral restraint. Though their hippo meat is rotting, the cannibal crew do not turn on the whites on board and devour them. Marlow decides instead that they are morally more restrained than either the hypocritical, greedy European traders or Kurtz, who "lacked restraint."[33] "Fine fellows – cannibals – in their place," Marlow opines (*Heart of Darkness*, 35). Indeed Kurtz, supposed "emissary" of civilization, has betrayed it by "going native" and establishing himself as petty tyrant over the Africans in his territory, who have apparently taken to worshiping him as a god or devil at certain "unspeakable rites" (51), a phrase that hints at cannibalism, human sacrifice, or perhaps both. As the title *Heart of Darkness* implies, however, Marlow's tale does not directly contest the racist myths of "the dark continent" and of sub-Saharan Africans as cannibals, but it does condemn European imperialism as just as violent and rapacious as African savagery: "The conquest of the earth, which mostly means the taking it away from those who have a different complexion or slightly flatter noses than ourselves, is not a pretty thing when you look into it too much" (7).

In other imperial contexts, other savage or barbarian customs are figured in the same way as cannibalism, as atrocities that only European intervention can eradicate. In the Indian context, both *sati* (also spelled suttee: the immolation of Hindu widows on the funeral pyres of their husbands) and *thuggee* (an Anglo-Indian transformation of the Hindi word *thagi*, thought to mean ritualized robbery and murder) were the focal points for early Victorian intervention, and both figure prominently in Victorian novels.[34] Indeed, the most influential novel about India prior to Kipling's *Kim* (1901) was Philip Meadows Taylor's 1839 bestseller, *Confessions of a Thug*.[35] As a police superintendent in the service of the Nizam of Hyderabad, Taylor had begun to detect evidence of widespread highway robbery and murder, which proved to be the work of "thugs," members of a secret cult who worshiped Kali, Hindu goddess of destruction.

Taylor claimed that *Confessions* was a slightly fictionalized account of his interviews with captured thugs. The story is "confessed" to a listening "sahib" by an imprisoned master thug. The detailed, gruesome, yet exciting account of the hundreds of robberies and murders committed by Ameer Ali and his gang provided sensational reading for early Victorians, including the queen. Its documentary, first-person narrative gives it an ethnographic realism that even *Kim* lacks. Its focus on *thagi*, however, made that criminal cult a central feature of Victorian perceptions of India. On the basis of *Confessions*, a reader might conclude that *thagi* was rampant and would require a huge policing effort by the British to end it. Yet Taylor aimed to be realistic rather than sensational; he himself did not view Indians – not even thugs – in terms of simplistic stereotypes. Indeed, after the success of *Confessions*, Taylor wrote a series of novels focused on major events in Indian history, all of which feature sympathetic portrayals of Indians. The most important of these are *Tipoo Sultan: A Tale of the Mysore War* (1840), *Tara: A Mahratta Tale* (1863), and *Seeta* (1872), which deals with the Indian Mutiny of 1857–58. Of the dozens of novels written about the Mutiny by British authors, *Seeta* alone offers a halfway credible account of the motives for the Mutiny, and it is also almost unique in its sympathetic portrayal of an interracial love affair and marriage (Taylor himself had married a mixed-race descendant of Moghul royalty). Seeta, however, too conveniently sacrifices herself to save her English husband from a rebel spear, and the novel ends with his supposedly more proper marriage to an Englishwoman.

The effect of *thagi* on the Victorian imagination, coming partly through *Confessions of a Thug*, is evident in Dickens's last, unfinished novel, *The Mystery of Edwin Drood* (1870), in which John Jasper seems to have had some involvement with that dark and desperate cult, and also in Wilkie Collins's *The Moonstone* (1868), although the Indians haunting the fringes of that mystery novel turn out not to be thugs.[36] If *thagi* fades away in late Victorian fiction about India, that is perhaps because the Mutiny took central stage as *the* atrocity that seemed to prove the necessity of British imperial control over the subcontinent. The Mutiny spawned numerous specific atrocity stories (on both sides), like that of Nana Sahib and the infamous Well of Cawnpore. British reactions were often hysterical, and produced a hardening of racist attitudes toward Indians; such racist hysteria is evident in most novels about the Mutiny. To take just one example, James Grant's *First Love and Last Love: A Tale of the Indian Mutiny* (1868) dishes up stories of violence and of the rape of white women by mutineers that the investigations following the Mutiny had already discredited. In Grant's novel, "women were outraged again and again, ere they were slaughtered, riddled with musket balls, or gashed by bayonets; and every indignity that the singularly fiendish invention of the Oriental mind could suggest, was offered to the dying and the dead."[37]

The intensification of racist attitudes toward Indians is evident also in Flora Annie Steel's *On the Face of the Waters* (1896), which is, nevertheless, the most interesting Mutiny novel after *Seeta*, as well as in Kipling's many stories and poems about India. Like Taylor, both Steel and Kipling lived many years in India, and all three writers developed an appreciation for the diversity of Indian cultures, religions, and individuals that keeps their works from being merely, negatively racist. In *Kim*, Kipling's boy-hero, though culturally just as Indian as any of the Indian characters he encounters (he knows multiple languages, goes everywhere, assumes many disguises, and becomes adept at espionage, in the service of the British), is an Irish orphan. And, while Kipling, like his boy-hero, enjoys the exotic, colorful peoples and customs of the subcontinent, he obviously believes that the Irish are a racial cut above the Indians (of any race), but also that the English are a racial cut above the Irish, because otherwise Kim would not be an orphan, and "a poor white of the very poorest," as the first paragraph announces. All of Kim's adventures, moreover, aid and abet Colonel Creighton's Ethnographic Survey, the British espionage machine that, through native collaborators such as Mahbub Ali and Hurree Babu, helps to secure the British Raj, for the good of all Indians (according to Kipling), into the new century and perhaps well beyond.

The future of the race

Darwin's theory of evolution supported the widely held belief that, even if *homo sapiens* was one species, its multiple races had evolved in very different ways, and that the white, European races (especially the English) were in the vanguard of nature's evolutionary progress. So-called social Darwinism, applied to situations both at home (poverty, the Irish) and abroad (the British rule over millions of non-white, non-Western peoples), told its believers that, because of biological laws of nature, the fittest races necessarily dominated and sometimes extirpated the unfit. But evolution was ongoing; it did not come to a halt just because Britain had reached the summit of its imperial power and glory. So, for some novelists, the question became: how would the fittest, most powerful race the world had ever known evolve in the future? How would it surpass itself? In Germany, Nietzsche was predicting the evolutionary emergence of the *Übermensch* or superman, perhaps as an entire new race or even species, a thought anticipated by Bulwer-Lytton in his 1871 science fiction fantasy, *The Coming Race*.

The narrator of Bulwer-Lytton's novella discovers the subterranean realm of the Vril-ya, a race far superior to *homo sapiens* (and yet all-too-human in many respects: for instance, they still use money). The Vril-ya have acquired the power-knowledge of vril, a mysterious form of energy very much like electricity, and they are also rather angelical – large, beautiful, and equipped with mechanical wings. Just how they are the *future* race is a bit unclear, however. Perhaps they are incubating underground, waiting to hatch out of mine-shafts after humanity's course has ended in disaster. Or perhaps the surfacing of the Vril-ya will be the disaster for humanity. Or perhaps the inferior race of humans is evolving into the Vril-ya (though, given the story's premises, this is the least logical interpretation). The narrator speculates that the Vril-ya will one day emerge "into sunlight [as] our inevitable destroyers," but his guess is as good as the reader's.[38] Whatever the case, the Vril-ya are an infinitely superior race compared to mere Victorian mortals, even though one of their all-too-human aspects is their racism: "Nations which, not conforming their manners and institutions to those of the Vril-ya, nor indeed held capable of acquiring the powers over the vril agencies . . . were regarded with more disdain than citizens of New York regard the negroes" (*The Coming Race*, 725). The Vril-ya use vril without compunction to exterminate any creatures (human or otherwise) whom they consider both inferior and inimical to themselves.

A later, more influential work of science fiction, H. G. Wells's *The Time*

Machine (1895), does not predict the evolutionary surpassing of *homo sapiens*, but just the reverse. Some 800,000 years into the future, the Time Traveller comes upon the entropic ruins of humanity, which has evolved into two hostile types. Though he suspects that the Elois and Morlocks are the products of class conflict, they are also distinct "species" (and not merely separate races). The effete, childish Elois live above ground in a condition of blissful ignorance; the cannibalistic Morlocks dwell troll-like in a hellish underground and come up at night to feast on the Elois. Though the two species in their murderous symbiosis reflect class conflict, they seem just as clearly to reflect the violence and insanity of racial conflict. The contrast between Bulwer-Lytton's equivocally utopian *The Coming Race* and Wells's unequivocally dystopian *Time Machine* suggests that the future of the human species, or of any specific race or nation of humans, is uncertain; but also that racism is, unfortunately, likely to remain an influential aspect of human cultures well into the future.

NOTES

1 Benjamin Disraeli, *Tancred; or, The New Crusade* (1847; Westport, CT: Greenwood, 1970), 149. The other two novels in the trilogy are *Coningsby*, 1844, and *Sybil; or, The Two Nations*, 1845.
2 Benjamin Disraeli, *Lothair* (1870; London: Oxford University Press, 1975), 316.
3 Dr. Robert Knox, *The Races of Men* (1850; Miami: Mnemosyne, 1969), 90.
4 Knox does not explicitly advocate polygenesis, but he does believe in the permanence of races, perhaps as separate species: "Men are of various Races; call them Species, if you will; call them permanent Varieties; it matters not" (9–10).
5 On Victorian "race science," see Michael Banton, *Racial Theories* (Cambridge: Cambridge University Press, 1987); Nancy Stepan, *The Idea of Race in Science: Great Britain 1800–1960* (Hamden, CT: Archon Books, 1982), and George Stocking, *Victorian Anthropology* (New York: Free Press, 1987).
6 Charles Dickens, *Our Mutual Friend* (1865; Oxford: Oxford University Press, 1989), 726.
7 Edward Said, *Orientalism* (New York: Random House, 1978).
8 Anthony Trollope, *The Eustace Diamonds* (1872; Harmondsworth: Penguin, 1973), 710.
9 William Makepeace Thackeray, *The Newcomes*, 2 vols. (London: Everyman's Library, 1962), II:331.
10 Deborah Thomas, *Thackeray and Slavery* (Athens: Ohio University Press, 1993), 167.
11 For ideas about hybridity in nineteenth-century biology and culture and also in post-colonial cultural theory today, see Robert Young, *Colonial Desire* (London: Routledge, 1995), 9–11. And see Dr. Robert Knox, *The Races of Men* 107: "I do not believe that any mulatto race can be maintained beyond the third

or fourth generation by *mulattoes merely*; they must inter-marry with the pure races, or perish. Nature creates no mules, nor will she tolerate them."

12 William Makepeace Thackeray, *The Adventures of Philip* (1862; London: Oxford University Press, 1912), 642.

13 Charles Dickens, "The Niger Expedition," *The Examiner*, August 19, 1848, reprinted in *Miscellaneous Papers*, National Library Edition of Dickens's Works, 20 vols. (New York: Bigelow, Brown, 1903), XVIII:64. Dickens's "The Noble Savage" appeared in *Household Words* 7 (11 June 1853), 337–39.

14 Charles Dickens, *Martin Chuzzlewit* (1844; Oxford: Oxford University Press, 1989), 282–84.

15 Charles Dickens, *Dombey and Son* (1848; Oxford: Oxford University Press, 1989), 273. For Major Bagstock's "Native," see also Deirdre David, *Rule Britannia: Women, Empire, and Victorian Writing* (Ithaca, NY: Cornell University Press, 1995).

16 Mrs. R. Lee (Sarah Wallis), *The African Wanderers; or, The Adventures of Carlos and Antonio* (London: Grant and Griffith, 1847), 230.

17 David Livingstone, *Missionary Travels and Researches in South Africa* (London: John Murray, 1857), and *Narrative of an Expedition to the Zambesi and Its Tributaries . . .* (London: John Murray, 1865).

18 Henry Morton Stanley, *My Kalulu: Prince, King, and Slave* (London: Sampson, Low, Marston, Searle, and Rivington, 1889), viii.

19 H. Rider Haggard, *Three Adventure Novels: She, King Solomon's Mines, Allan Quarterman* (New York: Dover, 1951).

20 For boys' adventure novels, see Joseph Bristow, *Empire Boys: Adventures in a Man's World* (London: Harper-Collins, 1991), and Jeffrey Richards, ed., *Imperialism and Juvenile Literature* (Manchester: Manchester University Press, 1989).

21 Captain Frederick Marryat, *Peter Simple* (1834; London: Gollancz, 1969), 260.

22 See Susan Meyer, *Imperialism at Home: Race and Victorian Women's Fiction* (Ithaca: Cornell University Press, 1996), 29–59.

23 *Ibid.*, 11.

24 In *Rule Britannia*, Deirdre David argues that, though Bertha Mason's ambiguous racial identity is ambiguous, if she is "a white creole who behaves like a demented black person," that makes her even more "monstrous" than if she were black or mulatto. In that case, she would be an instance of a white person in the colonies "going native," like Kurtz in *Heart of Darkness*. But also the figure of "a white woman engorged with the rage and sexuality attributed to West Indian black women," David argues, makes *Jane Eyre* "an even more racist text than if Bertha were merely a mad half-caste Rochester had carted back to England" (109).

25 Terry Eagleton, *Heathcliff and the Great Hunger: Studies in Irish Culture* (London: Verso, 1995), 3.

26 See Howard Malchow, *Gothic Images of Race in Nineteenth-Century Britain* (Stanford, CA: Stanford University Press, 1996), 19–20.

27 *Barry Lyndon* first appeared as a serial in *Fraser's Magazine* in 1844. Thackeray published it in volume form in 1856.

28 Stevenson and his wife, Fanny, wrote a series of "dynamiter" stories in their *New Arabian Nights* which also reflect anxieties about Fenianism.

29 On anxieties about racial degeneration, see Daniel Pick, *Faces of Degeneration* (Cambridge: Cambridge University Press, 1989).

30 Immortalized in Thomas Prest's *Sweeney Todd, the Demon Barber of Fleet Street*, originally published as *A String of Pearls* (1846). See Malchow, *Gothic Images*, 45–48.

31 Robert M. Ballantyne, *The Coral Island* (1858; Oxford: Oxford World's Classics, 1990), 171.

32 G. A. Henty, *By Sheer Pluck, A Tale of the Ashanti War* (Federal Book Co., 1900), 132.

33 Joseph Conrad, *Heart of Darkness* (1899; New York: Norton, Norton Critical Editions, 1963), 58.

34 For *sati*, see David, *Rule Britannia*, 89–95.

35 See my introduction to Philip Meadows Taylor, *Confessions of a Thug* (1839; Oxford: Oxford World's Classics, 1997), vii–xvii.

36 See Tim Dolan, "Race and the Social Plot in *The Mystery of Edwin Drood*," in Shearer West, ed., *The Victorians and Race* (Aldershot: Scolar Press, 1996), 84–100, for an important analysis of how Dickens employed racial categories in his last novel.

37 James Grant, *First Love and Last Love: A Tale of the Indian Mutiny*, 3 vols. (London: Routledge, 1868), II:3–4.

38 Edward Bulwer-Lytton, *The Coming Race*, in *The Works of Edward Bulwer-Lytton*, vol. II (1871; New York: P. F. Collier, n.d.), 765.

8

RONALD R. THOMAS

Detection in the Victorian novel

In her otherwise favorable review of Wilkie Collins's *The Woman in White* (1860), novelist Margaret Oliphant cautioned that novels that focused their attention upon the detection of crime as insistently as this one did represented a significant threat to the integrity of Victorian literature: "What Mr. Wilkie Collins has done with delicate care and laborious reticence, his followers will attempt without any such discretion," she predicted. "We have already had specimens, as many as are desirable, of what the detective policeman can do for the enlivenment of literature: and it is into the hands of the literary Detective that this school of story-telling must inevitably fall at last."[1] Mrs. Oliphant's prophecy about the impending (if undesired) dominance of the field of Victorian fiction by the literary detective proved to be quite accurate. As she noted, several such figures had appeared on the scene already, and there would certainly be many more to come. Indeed, if we are to take *The Woman in White* as an example, where the detective work is carried out not by a policeman or a professional detective but by a drawing instructor who transforms himself into a collector of evidence and a solver of mysteries, the terms "detection" and "the Victorian novel" increasingly become synonymous as the nineteenth century progresses. From the discovery of Mr. Rochester's secret imprisonment of his wife in *Jane Eyre* (1847), to the revelation of Uriah Heep's elaborate scheme of forgery and extortion in *David Copperfield* (1850), to the exposure of Dr. Lydgate's unwitting complicity in a murder plot in *Middlemarch* (1872), to the tracking down of Tess Durbeyfield for the brutal stabbing of her ex-lover in *Tess of the D'Urbervilles* (1891), almost every Victorian novel has at its heart some crime that must be uncovered, some false identity that must be unmasked, some secret that must be revealed, or some clandestine plot that must be exposed. By the century's end, the most recognizable and popular figure of all English literature, surpassing any character created by Chaucer, Shakespeare, Milton, or Dickens, would be a professional detective, Arthur Conan

Doyle's remarkable Sherlock Holmes. The invention of this figure, the literary detective, is arguably the most significant and enduring contribution to the history of English literature made during the Victorian era.

The invention of "detective fiction" as a distinct literary form is also generally attributed to this period, coincident with the development of the modern police force and the creation of the modern bureaucratic state. This context was crucial in shaping the way detective fiction developed and in determining the kind of cultural work it performed for a society that was increasingly preoccupied with systematically bringing under control the potentially anarchic forces unleashed by revolutionary movements, democratic reform, urban growth, national expansion, and imperial engagements. This chapter will read those conditions back into the story of Victorian detection, tracing them to fundamental transformations in the Victorian conception of character during this period and to the influence that the emergence of criminology and forensic science had on these developments. One of my principal goals is to demonstrate how the classification of detective fiction as a marginal literary form may be read as an outcome of the culture of knowledge and power that produced it, effectively disguising the crucial fact that the detective narrative is integral rather than peripheral to the Victorian novel's crucial project of modern self-fashioning. A case might even be made that traditionally classic novels of high Victorian realism like *Mary Barton* (1848) or *Great Expectations* (1861) or *Daniel Deronda* (1876) turn themselves into detective stories in the end, not merely by coming to focus on an act of criminal detection or the discovery of a secret identity late in their complicated plots, but in the way they dramatize the gradual containment and policing of individual characters by the pressure of social and professional forces. This is not to claim that every nineteenth-century novel is a detective story or that the distinctions between these different kinds of narrative are unimportant. Rather, it points out that the historical conditions that brought the form into being have found their way (more or less) into virtually every other kind of literature in the period as well. In this sense, "detection" is both a quality of all Victorian novels and a distinctive kind of Victorian novel in its own right. Because it stakes out and enforces the limits of individual autonomy as it was realized in the biographical novel, Victorian detective fiction is at once critical of and collaborative with the nineteenth-century novel's fundamental achievements, providing as it does a potent set of discourses and techniques for identifying the individual in the modern world.

The importance of the detective story for the period is based in its crucial role in the process of making and monitoring suspect individuals. Detective stories convert every character into a suspect, and by so doing render suspect the categories by which character itself is defined. Theorists of the novel commonly define the genre as a biographical form that came to prominence in the late eighteenth and nineteenth centuries to establish the individual character as a replacement for traditional sources of cultural authority. The novel, Georg Lukács argues, "seeks, by giving form, to uncover and construct the concealed totality of life" in the interiorized life story of its heroes.[2] The typical plot of the novel is the protagonist's quest for authority within, therefore, when that authority can no longer be discovered outside. By this accounting, there are no objective goals in novels, only the subjective goal of seeking the law that is necessarily created by the individual. The distinctions between crime and heroism, therefore, or between madness and wisdom, become purely subjective ones in a novel, judged by the quality or complexity of the individual's consciousness. This condition comprises the novel's "givenness," according to Lukács, a condition in which telling the story of the quest for form is the story itself. In that story, the individual subject is a kind of romantic rebel or criminal who constructs (or fails to construct) his or her own authority, as we see in the great autobiographical novels of the nineteenth century like *Jane Eyre, David Copperfield,* or *Jude the Obscure.*[3]

The almost simultaneous invention of this other kind of biographical form during the nineteenth century – the detective story – maps the limits to the subjective authority of the biographical novel, imposing what Edward Said might call the "molestation" of its "authority."[4] In this respect, the detective novel may be seen as a corrective countergenre evolving along with *and* within the biographical novel. By reasserting an objective – even if unofficial – social authority over individual freedom, the detective story imposes restrictions on the autonomy of the self by identifying certain kinds of behavior as criminal and arresting or even punishing them. In the detective story, a designated cultural authority – the literary detective – rises to power to replace the rogue or rebel, corresponding in time to the introduction of the modern police force in England and to the invention of the science of criminology. This figure stakes out the precise place where heroism ends and criminality begins for the individual – the very boundary obscured by the subjective focus of the biographical novel as defined by Lukács. The introduction of the literary detective into the history of the novel converts the romantic tradition of a criminal biography that celebrates individual freedom into the Victorian account of criminal detection that subjects the self to some objective social authority. Seen in this light, detective fiction must be regarded as an equal accomplice in the important cultural work often ascribed to the biographical novel in this period. It is the expression of bourgeois democratic forces policing and disciplining the subversive energies of an earlier revolutionary era.

In this context, it is appropriate that the text generally recognized as the first modern detective story, Edgar Allan Poe's "Murders in the Rue Morgue" (1841), should appear in America at a time often recognized as the last decade of the revolutionary age in Europe, and that it should be set in the streets of Paris – the city commonly associated with both the achievements and the excesses of the revolutionary spirit. It is equally fitting that this story should be a mystery based in the problem of distinguishing the suspect's nationality, and that the mystery should be solved by the detective's use of forensic evidence to identify the suspect as someone or something without any national affiliation and therefore without the right to claim human liberty, equality, or fraternity. If Poe is the acknowledged inventor of the detective story in America, his English counterpart and mentor, Charles Dickens, is recognized as the originator of the detective story in Britain. The criminal in Dickens's first detective novel, *Bleak House* (1853), is also a foreigner – a French working-class woman – who is explicitly compared to the reign of terror that followed the revolution in France. But while in Poe's "Rue Morgue" the murder victims had been French working-class women – the most potent popular symbol of the revolution in France – that figure becomes the foreign criminal force in *Bleak House* that must be arrested and contained by the London police. With revolutionary France forming the background against which a new national order is defined and established by, respectively, the private detective Dupin and the police inspector Mr. Bucket, these very different representatives of an emerging bourgeois class of experts take on the authority of ascribing legitimate identities to individuals who are otherwise no more than suspects. The rise of this new literary hero thereby indicates a moment of fundamental social and political transition, signaling the end to what many historians have called "the age of revolution" in Europe in favor of a more conservative period of middle-class ascendancy and controlled democratic reform commonly referred to as "the age of capital."[5]

The immediate literary predecessors of the detective novel in Britain demonstrate this cultural shift. In the early decades of the nineteenth century, a group of reform-minded novelists developed a new genre known as the Newgate novel or the "rogue" novel. Named after a particularly harsh London prison, the Newgate novel commonly featured a criminal as its central character, portraying that figure as the sympathetic victim of a repressive legal system. The tone of these texts borrowed from the atmosphere of psychological oppression, mystery, and criminality that characterized the gothic fiction of late eighteenth-century writers like Ann Radcliffe and Matthew Lewis. But more in the spirit of William Godwin's turn-of-the-century propagandist novel *Caleb Williams* (1794), the rogue, or criminal, of the Newgate novel was romanticized as a rebellious individual posed against relentless social forces, widely admired for his courage and prowess, sometimes even by the police. To varying degrees, novels like Edward Bulwer-Lytton's *Paul Clifford* (1830) and *Eugene Aram* (1832), William Harrison Ainsworth's *Rookwood* (1834) and *Jack Sheppard* (1839), and Charles Dickens's *Oliver Twist* (1838) and *Barnaby Rudge* (1841) manifested these reformist principles, protesting (explicitly or implicitly) against the "bloody code" of British criminal law and its brutal forms of punishment while celebrating the willful spirit and energetic impulses of criminal protagonists. Emerging as the hopes and disappointments surrounding the Reform Bill of 1832 were becoming manifest (which ultimately denied the working class the right to vote) and extending into the decade of the 1840s, the life span of the Newgate novel corresponded almost precisely to the period of radical political activism stemming from the Chartist movement in Britain. Along with the industrial novels of Elizabeth Gaskell and Benjamin Disraeli later in the 1840s, these Newgate novels were the principal literary expressions of early nineteenth-century British reform.

Newgate Prison offered an appropriate site with which to associate these novels and these political ideas. Newgate was the place of confinement for many notorious eighteenth-century criminals before their execution. It had been burned down in a gesture of defiance by political activists during the Gordon riots of 1780. Once rebuilt, it became a kind of unintended gathering place for the British Jacobin cultural resistance in the 1790s, when a number of prominent radical thinkers were arrested and imprisoned there for their seditious political views. Newgate combined within its walls the romance of the rebellious individual along with the romance of revolutionary politics, therefore. Accordingly, it came to be popularly regarded as "the English Bastille" – as potent a symbol for resistance to political oppression in London as was the infamous French prison in Paris, in this case opposing an extraordinarily repressive criminal code in England that by 1819 would require capital punishment for over 200 offenses, more than any other modern European nation.

But the Newgate novel did not emerge as a literary form directly from Newgate Prison so much as it did from an intermediary quasi-literary phenomenon called *The Newgate Calendar*. Published in various cheap editions from the late eighteenth century through the 1820s and sometimes sold to the huge crowds that gathered for the spectacle of public executions at Newgate and elsewhere, these immensely popular texts consisted of "interesting memoirs of notorious characters who have been convicted of offenses against the laws of England," according to the title page of one 1816 edition.[6] Offered as factual accounts of the great criminal lives of the eighteenth century, *The Newgate Calendar* was itself a kind of romantic biographical genre that included, together with the scandalous life story of notorious outlaws, "moral reflections and observations on particular cases," "explanations of the criminal laws," a "correct account of the various modes of punishment of criminals," and the purported "confessions and last exclamations of sufferers" as they were about to be hanged. By bringing together sensational memoir, moral instruction, and legal history into one text, *The Newgate Calendar* provided its numerous avid readers with ethical warnings about the consequences of a life of crime while at the same time it romanticized the rebellious outsider through a titillating and morbidly entertaining glimpse into the intrigues of London's criminal underworld.

The plots of all the principal Newgate novels of the 1830s were drawn directly from the criminal biographies that appeared in *The Newgate Calendar*, narratives which these novelists transformed from stern moral lessons against a life of crime into more sympathetic accounts of society's criminal victims. In *Eugene Aram*, for example, Bulwer romanticized the case of a shrewd schoolmaster convicted of murder who finally confessed his guilt and attempted suicide before his public execution. The novel renders this story as a psychological profile of a tragic, Byronic hero and brilliant scholar driven to murder by his justifiable hatred of a corrupt society. Similarly, Ainsworth's *Rookwood* would feature the *Calendar*'s condemned "highwayman, horse-stealer, and murderer" Dick Turpin, recast as an ingenious gentleman-highwayman and master of disguise whose prowess in the face of oppression earned him the admiration of all, including those seeking to arrest him for his offenses. In much the same way, Ainsworth's *Jack Sheppard* sentimentalized the fate of the notorious Jonathan Wild, the cunning house-breaker, escape artist, and thief-catcher who had been memorialized in the previous century by no less than ten criminal biographies (including one by novelist Daniel Defoe) in addition to receiving a featured entry in the *Newgate Calendar*. Even though Dickens dismissed many contemporary critics' association of his early work with the Newgate novelists and refused to admit that his work in any way glamorized criminality, his *Barnaby Rudge* took as its subject the infamous 1780 Gordon Riots and the attendant burning down of Newgate Prison, events that were also recounted in several versions of the *Newgate Calendar*. As if to acknowledge both his debt to and his departure from that tradition, Dickens's *Oliver Twist* showed the victimized young orphan-protagonist actually reading in horror the pages of the *Newgate Calendar* as the boy became entangled in a gang of London thieves, many of whom might someday earn a place in that book's annals. After Oliver finally extricates himself from those criminal associations, the novel concludes, appropriately, with Fagin, the mastermind of the novel's criminal underworld, awaiting execution in his Newgate Prison cell.

Like many critics of detective novels after him, W. M. Thackeray condemned the Newgate novelists for their prurient and misguided sensationalizing of outlaw life, for their pandering to the most base of public appetites, and for their sentimental distortion of the immorality of the criminal classes. Thackeray not only published a series of diatribes against the form in *Fraser's* magazine in 1839–40, he also serialized a parodic Newgate novel of his own at the same time titled *Catherine*. He depicted this novel's characters with ironic contempt, introducing them as being "strictly in accordance with the present fashionable style and taste; since they have already been partly described in 'The Newgate Calendar'; since they are (as shall be seen anon) agreeably low, delightfully disgusting, and at the same time eminently pleasing and pathetic."[7] As his parody makes clear, from Thackeray's viewpoint such works were to be regarded as no more than "absolute drugs on the literary market."[8] Like other contemporary critics, he did not take these novelists' reformist impulses seriously.

The fact is, however, that the short vogue of Newgate fiction corresponded not only to the most active period of political activism associated with the Chartist movement in Britain, but also with the sweeping reforms of the English criminal code that took place in the early part of the century. Under the leadership of Home Office Secretary Sir Robert Peel, the criminal justice system would be thoroughly overhauled and rationalized during the same decades in which the Newgate novel reached the peak of its popular success. Between the 1820s and the 1840s, scores of capital offenses would be eliminated from the list of crimes that called for the death penalty; a complex series of laws on theft would be consolidated; abuses and corruption among constables and magistrates would be sharply reduced; and the police act of 1829 would institute the "new model" modern police force, a highly disciplined professional preventive force that replaced a patchwork of improvised (and often corrupt) private security agencies. Perhaps most importantly, by 1842 that preventive force would be supplemented by a Detective Office within the Metropolitan Police Department. This new group of public professionals supplanted the less efficient and sometimes corrupt band of "thief-takers" known as the "Bow Street Runners" which had been initiated in the previous century by Bow

Street magistrates John and Henry Fielding. In short, the transition to a modern police force was firmly established in Britain during the period of the Newgate novel, and the criminal code would be reformed to the condition in which it would essentially remain until the middle of the twentieth century.

Whatever involvement the Newgate novels may have had in these reforms, their principal contribution to the history of the British novel was their establishment of crime as a legitimate subject for serious literature. This achievement would be crucial for the development of the detective novel by figures like Dickens and Collins in the decades to come, just as it would for the industrial novel, the sensation novel, and even the novel of high Victorian realism of mid-century, where crime and intrigue continued to serve as important if not central plot elements. But with the introduction of the detective into these narratives – whether policeman or civilian, official representative of the law or freelancing amateur – the status of the criminal would undergo a sociologically significant transformation. The protagonist would no longer be the criminal who was being pursued, but the detective who was doing the pursuing. The hero would not be the one who broke the law, but the one who enforced it. In the post-Benthamite world of what Michel Foucault called the "panoptical machine," where the individual is not so much repressed by the social order as fabricated and scrutinized in it, the literary detective provides a new kind of hero, dramatizing the powerful and productive role of the social order in the process of making modern citizens.[9]

Because of the way this shift is reflected in its narrative structure, Dickens's *Bleak House* may not only be the first English detective novel, it may also be – despite its sprawling complexity – the most perfectly constructed version of the form. Significantly, *Bleak House* does not begin as a detective novel or a mystery story, but gradually evolves into one, as if responding to the political and sociological conditions the text documents. Dickens's great novel opens in the manner of a large-scale social epic, grandly portraying the pervasive fog and mud that cover all of London as expressive of a general condition of confusion and obscurity that spreads like a disease from the corrupt heart of English legal authority – the High Court of Chancery. In a society in which everyone becomes consumed by an unresolvable legal case that seems to have no beginning and no end, the opening of *Bleak House* shows the historic laws of England no longer protecting and ordering the body politic, but killing and confusing it.

This magisterial tale of social critique then abruptly shifts its subject and its narrative voice. In her own uncertain words, the orphan Esther Summerson begins to tell her personal story of being a victim of this broken-down legal system and corrupt society. That intimate narrative continues, alternating with the more formal and professionalized third-person narrative of invective aimed at larger social conditions. Once the detective, Inspector Bucket, enters both narratives, this novel juxtaposing accounts of fundamental legal corruption with sentimental autobiography changes once again, this time bringing the two parts of the story together into a murder mystery and a tale of mistaken identity. In that story, the detective acts as the principal unifying force, ultimately restoring faith in the law and, in the course of tracking down the murderer of a corrupt lawyer, restoring to Esther Summerson her true identity. In this and in subsequent detective novels, the literary act of transferring the authority to tell the secret story of the individual suspect to a designated professional expert is also a political act, one that corresponds historically to the reform of the English criminal code, the decline of aristocratic power, and the insistent rise of the modern professional police force in England.

The Inspector Bucket of *Bleak House* is generally recognized as Dickens's version of Inspector Charles Frederick Field, one of the early distinguished members of London's detective police force. Both before and after writing *Bleak House*, Dickens published a number of admiring articles about London's detectives in his magazine *Household Words*, some of which expressed his esteem for and amazement over Inspector Field himself. In those articles and in his treatment of Inspector Bucket, Dickens not only praised the detective's remarkable intelligence, strong character, and talent for observation and analysis, he also managed to appease many of the public's fears about the dangers posed by a new, invasive secret police force like the detective branch, offering these figures as heroic models of a dutiful social reform ideal rather than as calculating spies set on enhancing their own power or prestige. Significantly, however, Bucket is not the first representative of the law we encounter in *Bleak House*. The most significant legal figure of the first half of the novel is the cruel solicitor Mr. Tulkinghorn, who clearly aligns himself with the elitist regime of the old families of London and bases his considerable authority upon the strategies of secrecy, privilege, and manipulation. In contrast to the evil, self-centered Tulkinghorn, Bucket is presented as a duty-bound public servant who performs his job honestly and dispassionately without preference for any particular class and without undue concern for himself. "Duty is duty, and friendship is friendship," he reminds one of his friends he is compelled to arrest. "I never want the two to clash, if I can help it."[10] Just as Tulkinghorn has "treasured up within his old black satin waistcoat" secrets to use in a calculating way against his own clients and for his own profit, Bucket informs his clients in his disinterested, professional manner only what "it becomes my duty to tell" (*Bleak House*, 583).

The detective plot of *Bleak House* invites us to view this new kind of novel as an allegory for the transition of social power from a heartless and unjust aristocratic society dominated by privilege and secrecy to a more democratic world ruled by a sense of justice and duty. Accordingly, the official representative of the first of these versions of English law is the victim in the novel's murder mystery, and the representative of the second is the middle-class hero who solves that mystery and restores order. The detective not only replaces the cruel and corrupt lawyer as the exemplar of English law in the plot, he brings justice to the criminal condition that the lawyer had helped to create. Equally important to this reformist allegory is the identity of Tulkinghorn's murderer, who is described as "some woman from the streets of Paris in the reign of terror" (286). In her very first appearance, Mademoiselle Hortense is described by the narrator as a "She-Wolf imperfectly tamed," and is noted for "something indefinably keen and wan about her anatomy" (143). Her guilt "flashed upon me," Mr. Bucket explains in the course of tracking the murderer down, "as I sat opposite to her at the table and saw her with a knife in her hand" (649). The professional detective not only replaces the old tyrannical English legal establishment as the representative of justice in the plot, he also arrests the brute-like excesses that are embodied in this vision of working-class revolution originating from abroad. The association of criminal threats with foreign insurgency was a typical strategy used by advocates of a stronger police force in England with wider discretionary powers during the period immediately following the revolutions of 1848. In light of fears on the part of the public mind "lest the peace of Europe should suddenly break up with an invasion of our country," for example, Inspector of Prisons Fredric Hill argued in his 1853 opus on the modern problem of crime, "what difference in principle can there be in defending one's pocket and throat from a native robber or murderer, and in resisting an aggressor who speaks a foreign language?"[11]

Mr. Bucket is not the first detective to appear in the English novel, but he is the most important early representative of this emerging literary and cultural hero. Earlier novels contained characters who performed criminal investigations but occupied a less prominent place in the narrative. Dickens's Mr. Nadgett of *Martin Chuzzlewit* (1844), for example, is distinguished for his powers of observation when he investigates the murder of Anthony Chuzzlewit: "He saw so much," we are told of Nadgett, that "every button on his coat might have been an eye" (chapter 38). Elizabeth Gaskell's *Mary Barton* also includes a minor character who is an officer in the Detective Service and appears in the narrative as it devolves into a murder mystery. In addition to these novelistic treatments of the detective figure, quasi-fictional "memoirs" structured around the cases of Bow Street Runners or the early detective police appeared in this period as well.[12] While these texts were little more than picaresque adventure tales centering on a character who happened to be a policeman, they participated in a growing popular romance around the figure of the detective. Dickens's Inspector Bucket, the first detective from the Metropolitan District Police to play a significant part in an English novel, galvanized these trends and helped to create the new recognizable literary form that emerged from, respectively, the mid-century "mysteries novel" and the "enigma novel." Plots of crime and detection would continue to play a central part in Dickens's later novels like *Great Expectations* (1861), *Hard Times* (1854), *Little Dorrit* (1857), *Our Mutual Friend* (1865), and in his final unfinished work, *The Mystery of Edwin Drood* (1870). But it would be Dickens's friend and protegé Wilkie Collins who would be credited with writing what T. S. Eliot would call "the first, the longest, and the best of modern English detective novels." "In detective fiction England probably excels other countries," Eliot would argue, "but in a genre invented by Collins and not by Poe."[13] If Dickens introduced detection into the Victorian novel as a fundamental feature of the form with *Bleak House*, Collins made it into a genre unto itself with *The Moonstone* (1868).

Before writing *The Moonstone*, however, Collins's importance to the history of Victorian detection was based in the critical role he played in creating the sensation novel, another fictional genre closely related to the evolution of the Victorian detective novel which rose to prominence in the interval between *Bleak House* and *The Moonstone*. Generally thought to be inaugurated in 1860 with Collins's *The Woman in White*, and followed by dozens of sensationally popular books published during the 1860s by writers like Mary Elizabeth Braddon, Ellen (Mrs. Henry) Wood, Charles Reade, and Collins himself, sensation fiction was known for its elaborately complex plots. These tales of murder, sexual betrayal, and double identity combined elements from gothic fiction, the Newgate novel, and Victorian stage melodrama. As was true of *The Woman in White*, Wood's *East Lynne* (1861), and Braddon's *Lady Audley's Secret* (1862), these sensational and sometimes tortured plots characteristically focused on a menacing secret that threatened to expose the identity of a prominent individual: an illegitimate son passes himself off as a baronet and imprisons the true heir to his fortune in an asylum; a working-class woman murders her husband and changes her name to marry a gentleman; a servant woman and her barren mistress exchange identities to provide the master with a child he wrongly believes to be his own. As these story lines suggest, this fictional form that caused such a popular sensation among the middle class worked directly on middle-class anxieties about the status and stability of class identity in the period leading up to the renewal of Chartist sympathies and the passage of the second Reform Bill in 1867.

Even as they were awed by the elaborately constructed plots of sensation fiction, leading literary critics of the time were inclined to condemn this tremendously popular form – not just for its morally sensational content, but for its favoring of complex plot construction over complex character development. This same accusation would invariably be leveled against almost every expression of Victorian detective fiction. A chapter in the autobiography of prolific Victorian novelist Anthony Trollope dedicated to evaluating the other "English Novelists of the Present Day" illustrates the point. Trollope summed up what troubled him most about the works of both Dickens and Collins by pointing to the central plot motif of *The Woman in White*: "The author seems always to be warning me to remember," he says, "that a woman disappeared from the road just fifteen yards beyond the fourth milestone. One is constrained by mysteries and hemmed in by difficulties, knowing, however, that the mysteries will be made clear, and the difficulties overcome at the end of the third volume. Such work gives me no pleasure."[14] These stories of disappearance and detection did not impress him. Indeed, Collins fell so far down in Trollope's ranking of Victorian novelists because he thought his labyrinthine plots precluded the rendering of character with any degree of "truth" or "reality" at all. "With Collins," Trollope says dismissively, "it is *all* plot".[15] For such critics, the characters who were always disappearing from sensation novels seemed to suggest a widespread disappearance of the importance of character itself. It may be argued, however, that this very "failure" comprises the most significant contribution to the history of the novel made by the sensation novelists and the detective writers who would follow them. It was not their construction of sensational plots at the expense of character, but their discovery that modern characters were tangled up in very complex social plots of class and pretense – mysteries that required a specialized expertise to expose and clear up.

In virtually every sensation novel, this story of turning conventional characters into plots to be figured out begins as it does in *The Woman in White* – with the unexplained appearance or disappearance of a body. The plots tend to conclude in essentially the same way as well – with the recovery or reconstruction of that body in the form of an official text that authenticates the person's "true identity" once her "character" has been called into question. The outcome of that plot often depends upon reading

in the body-in-question physiological information that can be made legible
only by professional experts and can be made legitimate only by the official
documents they generate. In the case of *The Woman in White*, the living
body of Laura Fairlie (Lady Glyde) is finally distinguished from the dead
body of her mysterious double (Anne Catherick), when, with the impri-
matur of the family lawyer, the romantic hero and principal detective figure
of the novel makes a public presentation of the legally endorsed texts that
prove Laura's true identity. He also uncovers the legal and medical
documents proving that the cruel baronet who had perpetrated the fraud,
Sir Percival Glyde, was actually no baronet at all, but a bastard child with
no legal claim to his title or estate. If the representation of characters as
"recognizable realities" is (as Collins claimed in the novel's preface) the
essential condition of his ingenious plots, those characters are consistently
being made both "recognizable" and "real" in roughly the same way: a
collaboration of professional and private individuals collect a set of legal
documents that reconstruct a legitimate public "identity" for a person who
has lost or been robbed of her rightful "character" by some devious
criminal conspiracy.[16]

This conceptual transformation of character from a natural inheritance
of class into a legal construction takes place consistently not only in Wilkie
Collins's novels, but in those of his counterparts as well. In some of the
most popular sensation novels of the 1860s, lawyers play the part of the
heroic protagonist rather than the powerful background role they play in *A
Woman in White*. This is the case in two of the most famous sensation
novels, Ellen (Mrs. Henry) Wood's immensely popular *East Lynne* and
Mary Elizabeth Braddon's *Lady Audley's Secret*. In *East Lynne*, a successful young lawyer and politician defeats an aristocratic scoundrel in a
parliamentary election, bringing his opponent's double identity and criminal past to light as well. In *Lady Audley's Secret*, the solicitor Robert
Audley takes on the role of private investigator to look into the mysterious
disappearance of his best friend's wife and the subsequent vanishing of his
friend as well. He eventually discovers that his own aunt, Lady Audley, is
actually the missing wife of his missing friend. She has, the young lawyer
finds out, forsaken her husband, abandoned their child, created a new
identity for herself as a governess, and tried to murder her husband to
preserve the secret of her past in defense of her new-found wealth and
status. When the lawyer confronts his aunt with the results of his investigation and presents her with the evidence he has gathered, he threatens her
with the power of a legal procedure that will unequivocally determine her
identity for her: "I will gather together the witnesses who shall swear to
your identity, and at peril of any shame to myself and those I love, I will

bring upon you the just and awful punishment of your crime."[17] Together with a physician friend of his, the lawyer then extorts a confession from the suspect, gives her a new name, and confines her in an asylum for the rest of her life.

This containment of the criminal subject by a lawyer who transforms himself into a detective over the course of the novel reflects the emerging social bureaucracy for producing truth and defining modern citizens which Michel Foucault has described as one of the fundamental achievements of bourgeois capitalist society in the nineteenth century. At the very moment when the idea of natural rights was being advocated by the leaders of reform to dismantle patriarchal privilege, sensation fiction shows a declining patriarchy of title merely being reconfigured into an equally privileged professional elite. The consistent elevation of the authority of the lawyer over the individual in the sensation novel is consistent both with the rising power of the legal profession in Victorian culture and with a corresponding change in the conception of subjectivity during the period. Nineteenth-century psychology would define individual character as something constructed by the accumulation of sensations and impressions, effectively rendering all human perception "subjective" and therefore suspect from an evidentiary point of view. In courts of law, accordingly, the application of rational principles of evidence to verbal testimony increasingly required substantiation by material and circumstantial evidence. Guidelines for a new "science of proof" received their most ambitious reformulations in Anglo-American legal theory at the beginning of the nineteenth century in Jeremy Bentham's *Rationale of Judicial Evidence* (1825) and at the turn of the century in John Wigmore's *Principles of Judicial Proof* (1913), both of which cast doubt upon the dependability of individual testimony and enhanced the role of lawyers and experts in the presentation and substantiation of evidence. At least in the popular imagination, the nineteenth-century figure who most elaborately and successfully stages this transformation is not the lawyer, but the literary detective. He may be an attorney, a physician, a drawing master, or a professional detective; but his central action is the transfer of power over establishing a person's true identity to an authority outside the individual self by revealing how suspect every character in the story is.

That the mystery at the heart of almost every sensation novel is based in the disappearance and subsequent reidentification of some "character" reflects these parallel shifts in the realm of subjectivity and in the realm of the law: the replacement of the entire ideologically laden notion of Victorian moral character (something we associate with Victorian realism) with the more physiologically-based but socially defined conception of

Victorian identity (the commonly contested issue in a detective plot). Persons, that is, become defined most urgently in these forms of literary detection not as autonomous moral selves, or as members of a family or class, or even by the sum of their achievements; rather, they are defined through a plot of identification that attends most closely to documenting the material facts of physical embodiment as overseen by the law and by the detective-expert. In this respect, Mrs. Oliphant's comment about the dangers of novels like *The Woman in White* may have been more true than she realized. Her prediction about the inevitable progression from the mysteries of crime and detection in the sensation novel to the dominance of the literary detective would be effected in large measure by Wilkie Collins himself when he wrote *The Moonstone*, a novel in which the mystery is solved not by the legal expertise of an attorney nor even by the ingenious detective, but by the diagnostic brilliance of a physician. In this text, the rise of the scientific expertise of the medical profession is shown to be both collaborative and competitive with that of the legal profession, a development that corresponded to the emergence of criminology and forensic science as important new disciplines in the treatment of crime and to the establishment of detective fiction as a distinct and popular literary genre.

In the character of the brilliant but eccentric Sergeant Cuff, *The Moonstone* offers one of the great literary detectives in the genre. His keen powers of observation, his uncanny judgment of character, and his acute deductive reasoning impress everyone when he discovers a crucial, overlooked piece of evidence at the scene of the crime. Nevertheless, these talents are not adequate in bringing the case to a close. While he correctly predicts the outcome of the case and offers indispensable clues to its solution, proof of the perpetrator's guilt requires scientific knowledge outside of his expertise. The attorney Mr. Bruff plays an essential part in solving the mystery as well, but is also not adequate to the task. It is the young romantic hero, Franklin Blake, who makes himself into the principal detective in the novel; and he does so by combining the contributions of the lawyer and the detective with the critical evidence provided by a scientific expert. In the climactic scene of *The Moonstone* the mysterious theft of the diamond – which also serves as a symbol of the imperial conquest of India in the novel – is revealed to have taken place when the sleeping body of the unwitting thief, Blake himself, was operating under the influence of opium. The perpetrator and detective figure is presented as a victim of his own bodily processes and the plotting of a physician who wanted to demonstrate the power which the body wields over the mind. This mystery can only be solved when the controversial medical theories of another physician reveal that essential fact to the detective himself.

To solve the mystery and recover the missing gem, Blake must agree to the "bold experiment" of this second physician, who calls for a reenactment of the crime by subjecting the suspect's body to the same physiological conditions under which he functioned on the night in question. Here the successful act of detection depends as much upon the laws of science as it does on the skills of lawyers or policemen. The profound implications of scientific expertise in this case are demonstrated when this experiment proves to the protagonist that he was also (unwittingly) the criminal. Even the detective figure is suspect, that is to say, and must subject himself to the superior authority of science, which is able to reveal secrets about us that are otherwise unknowable even to ourselves. *The Moonstone* makes clear that to solve crime and the mystery of identity – to understand the truth about modern subjectivity – requires scientific expertise. This may explain why Henry James referred to Collins's novels as "not so much works of art as works of science."[18] The mystery of *The Moonstone* may have at its heart the exposure of a fraudulent aristocrat and the critique of the political crime of British imperialism. But by bringing together scientific and legal expertise to detect those social and political crimes, this text transforms them into questions of scientific inquiry. The "exact science of detection" as it was invented by the scientific detective Holmes with his physician partner Doctor Watson two decades after Collins's novel represents the fruition of this juridical-medical collaboration as it was established in *The Moonstone*.[19]

There would be other contributions to Victorian detection before Sherlock Holmes appeared, though none would as significantly influence the shape of Victorian writing or approach his level of popularity. These other works were usually comprised of a congeries of factual criminal cases presented in the conventional modes of gothic or sensation fiction, commonly appearing as serials in the popular press or monthly magazines. Andrew Forrester introduced an early popular version of New Woman fiction in this mode with the character of Mrs. Gladden in *The Female Detective* as early as 1864, to be followed only six months later by W. Stephens Hayward's *The Experiences of a Lady Detective* and, at the turn of the century, by C. L. Pirkis's *The Experiences of Loveday Brooke, Lady Detective* (1894). The Irish writer Sheridan LeFanu would write significant novels of crime in *Wylder's Hand* (1864) and *Checkmate* (1871), while in the following decade the Australian Fergus Hume would publish thrillers like *The Mystery of the Hansom Cab* (1886). Inspector of Prisons Major Arthur Griffiths wrote tales of criminal life under the titles *Fast and Loose* (1885) and *Locked Up* (1887) in this period, based upon his professional experience among criminals. These and other works like them would earn a wide range of popular success and critical respect. Whatever their literary merits, however, they all exploited a growing demand for stories of suspense and detection that would reach a culmination in Arthur Conan Doyle's immensely popular figure whose scientific expertise would make him into a virtual national hero as well as an unprecedented literary phenomenon.

Doyle first introduced Sherlock Holmes to the English reading public in 1887, the same year in which Alphonse Bertillon, a clerk in the office of the Paris Prefect of Police, was gaining notoriety for introducing a method for identifying criminals based upon the careful measuring and quantifying of certain anatomical parts. In the same period, researchers from other disciplines were exploring additional ways to detect the criminal in the body through such means as photography, fingerprinting, serology, toxicology, and forensic medicine. By the 1880s, for example, police departments in Europe and America alike had adopted Bertillon's combination of such techniques with his anthropometric principles into an archival system for organizing and indexing suspects into what we now call the mug shot – or the "*portrait parlé*," as Bertillon referred to it. The *portrait parlé* consisted of a photograph of the criminal printed on a card and accompanied by a set of vital statistics with which the suspect could be identified with certainty. At around the same time that these developments were taking place, Sherlock Holmes was inventing a parallel branch of criminology that would become integral to actual police work throughout Europe. By availing himself of all the chemical, biological, physical, and technological methods springing up at the turn of the century, Holmes became a kind of imaginative composite of these new criminological technologies. As much forensic device as he was human character, Doyle's detective would be introduced in the first of the *Adventures of Sherlock Holmes* (1892) as "the most perfect reasoning and observing machine the world has ever seen," a "sensitive instrument" in possession of "high-power lenses" capable of "extraordinary powers of observation."[20] Watson would even sometimes refer to his brilliant, machine-like companion as a walking calendar of crime.

As such characterizations suggest, the Sherlock Holmes stories not only provided good entertainment for their middle-class readers, they also anticipated and popularized contemporaneous advances in criminological practice as well. Indeed, both Bertillon and Edmond Locard, another pioneer in forensic medicine and criminology in France, attributed some of their own innovations to their reading of the Sherlock Holmes stories. In developing what he called "a new police science" that focused on the examination of microscopic particles on the criminal body, Locard would even instruct his colleagues and students "to read over such stories as 'A Study in Scarlet' and 'The Sign of the Four'" in order to understand the basis of the practices he was recommending.[21] Doyle himself acknowledged the relation between his fictional detective and the forensic scientist Bertillon in his "The Adventure of the Naval Treaty" (1893), where Holmes "expressed his enthusiastic admiration of the French savant," and again in *The Hound of the Baskervilles* (1902) where the client referred to Bertillon and Holmes as the two "highest experts in Europe" in the field of criminal investigation.[22]

To demonstrate the point, Holmes would use the new scientific advance of fingerprint evidence in several cases before any European police force had adopted it and even prior to the publication of Sir Francis Galton's pioneering book on the subject, *Finger Prints* (1892). In the very first Holmes text, *A Study in Scarlet* (1887), the detective claimed to have written and published his own theories on this subject in a magazine article that Watson stumbles upon in the detective's apartment as they are about to investigate their first case together. "By the callosities of his forefinger and thumb," Watson reads in this article with some incredulity, "a man's calling is plainly revealed."[23] In his next case, Holmes would maintain that the most important branch of "detective science" is the ability to read "footmarks," claiming, in words that directly anticipated the language in which Galton described the tremendous significance of fingerprints and footprints, "to my trained eyes every mark upon its surface had a meaning."[24] In a much later case, "The Norwood Builder" (1905), published after fingerprints had been instituted into regular law enforcement practice, Holmes discerns that what the police had regarded as compelling fingerprint evidence was in fact a counterfeit used to frame an innocent man. Holmes brought the true perpetrator to justice by showing the difference between the authentic fingerprint and the fake. As these and many other instances suggest, Holmes is consistently portrayed as the paradigm of a new kind of law-enforcement expert that came to be called the forensic scientist. His frequent pronouncements on the subject – which always set his unconventional scientific methods above the less-effective procedures of Scotland Yard – echo Watson's first meeting with Holmes. Surrounded by test tubes, microscopes, retorts, and other scientific paraphernalia, the detective exults over his discovery of "an infallible test" for the presence of human blood, a discovery he calls "the most practical medico-legal discovery for years."[25] In Sherlock Holmes, the Victorian detective and the Victorian scientist become one.

Many of the developments in police practice during the 1890s, both real and literary, may be traced to the founder of criminal anthropology in

Europe, Cesare Lombroso, and to his popularizer and explicator in England, Havelock Ellis, both of whom concentrated their research upon the body of the criminal in explaining the reasons for criminal behavior. Less than three years after Sherlock Holmes made his first appearance in 1887 in England, Ellis published England's first major contribution to forensic science, *The Criminal* (1890). Ellis wrote *The Criminal* to "present to the English reader a critical summary of the results of the science now commonly called criminal anthropology" at the very time when social scientists and even legal reformers would begin to look with increasing frequency for the causes and remedies of crime in the biological pathology of the offender rather than in the political or sociological circumstances of the crime.[26] As a trained physician himself, Arthur Conan Doyle's detective stories were consistent with this development. He not only provided his detective with a doctor for a partner, he modeled Holmes after his own medical professor from the University of Edinburgh Medical Faculty, Doctor Joseph Bell. Refining the medical model of investigation developed in *The Moonstone*, Doyle's application of the detective's use of observation and deduction closely resembles those of modern diagnostic medicine as they were being perfected in the latter half of the nineteenth century.

It should be noted that the extensive use of scientific techniques in the Holmes stories was as much a product of rising political concerns about controlling the vast British Empire as it was a result of advances in medical and criminal science. This conclusion is suggested by the number of stories that relate crimes at home to troubles in the colonies and to the invasion of London by foreigners and foreign influence. Most of the stories were written in the early 1890s expressly for the newly established *Strand Magazine*, where they often appeared side by side with articles about actual police cases, developments in criminology, miscellaneous news stories, political commentary, and reports from the empire. Doyle's use of the Indian Mutiny as the historical event behind the murders in *The Sign of Four* (1889) reinforces the connection between science and politics in these texts, since this was the very incident that had provoked civil servant Sir William Herschel to implement fingerprinting as a means to register Indian natives under his governance in the colonies. The same concerns had provoked Sir Edward Henry to do so first as Inspector General in Bengal and then in London, when he became the head of Scotland Yard's Criminal Investigation Department at the time it instituted its first fingerprint department. It was when Sir Francis Galton was visiting these same civil servants in the colonies that he was inspired to establish the scientific basis for such a system with which "to fix the human personality, to give to each human being an identity, an individuality that can be depended upon with certainty, lasting, unchangeable, always recognisable and easily adduced."[27]

In addition to appropriating (and sometimes anticipating) the modern medical model for the diagnosis of crime, Arthur Conan Doyle also perfected a literary form for Holmes that owed its origins to the medical profession as well – the case history. The new discipline of pathological anatomy as a form of medical diagnosis in the period brought with it a new epistemological imperative for the physician to observe carefully every detail of the patient's environment and physical condition, and to record that information in the form of a case study that would explore the network of possible connections between the seemingly insignificant details. In the case history, the physician would test and retest every conceivable set of relations until the cause of the patient's illness made sense, much as Holmes would do in his explanations of cases to Watson. Medical diagnosis became based upon a principle of "differential" semiological examination of the patient's body in the form of the medical case history.

Dramatized in novels written after mid-century ranging from *The Moonstone* to *Middlemarch* to *Dr. Jekyll and Mr. Hyde* (1886), the gradual acceptance of this diagnostic approach coincided with the establishment and growth of professional medical organizations throughout Europe, and with regular annual exhibitions hailing the invention of medical instrumentation in all the major European cities. These scientific developments also coincided almost precisely with the rise of the detective narrative as a popular literary genre and with Doyle's perfection of the case study as the most appropriate form in which to tell that story. Although the Sherlock Holmes canon began with two novellas, a form to which Doyle would occasionally resort later on, the great success of the master detective was realized in the collection of short "cases" Doyle wrote for the *Strand* magazine, stories in which Holmes made literary detection into what he called "an exact science" that imitated the form of the medical case history. In the popular imagination, Doyle took part in the wider drama occupying the culture at large: the transformation of the "glance" of the professional into what Foucault called the ever more penetrating "gaze" into the private life of the individual citizen.[28]

From the Newgate novel, to the sensation and enigma novel, to the detective story, nineteenth-century writers of detective fiction developed an immensely popular literature of such intricately constructed plots that it was often dismissed by critics for failing to meet the standards established by the great practitioners of high Victorian realism for rendering the complexities of human character. The detective story, as even the detective writer Dorothy Sayers would concede, "does not, and by hypothesis never can, attain the loftiest levels of literary achievement"; in its effort to achieve a perfection of plot and lend "a machine-like efficiency" to its detective, she confessed, it depends too much on types, caricatures, and clichés to properly represent "the heights and depths of human passion."[29] And yet, for all its investment in elaborate plotting, the typical detective narrative of the nineteenth century came to focus most attentively – by way of its meticulous investigations of the criminal body – upon a fundamental transformation taking place in the representation of human character during the period. The various devices of investigation and identification these narratives deployed to investigate a suspect body participated in a significant way in the century-long process in which modern urban and industrial societies began defining persons in terms of their identities rather than their characters. In this respect, Victorian detective fiction chronicles the disappearance of the Victorian character in the modern bureaucratic world of professional expertise.

Corresponding to the "inward turn" of psychological realism by figures like George Eliot, Henry James, and Joseph Conrad, these narratives demonstrate an equally powerful and opposing "outward turn" in the direction of a more materialist conception of the person as machine – a development that would come to fruition in modern literary movements like naturalism, the new realism, and postmodernism. Indeed, the special talent of the Victorian literary detective is his capacity to resist seeing the person primarily as a public character with a certain status in society, a moral reputation in the community, a knowable history of accomplishment, or a complex self-consciousness. The detective is most effective when he is most suspicious of those qualities and can recognize the hidden truth beneath those social constructions. The Victorian detective story not only makes this shift of emphasis the central act in its investigation, it also offers the account of this transformation of persons into identities (and the necessity of professional expertise to discern them) as the central story of modern civilization. It is in part for this reason that "detective fiction" is difficult to contain within the limits of a single sub-genre of Victorian fiction, but pervades even the most realistic and "character-centered" novels of the century.

In the modern spy story, the science fiction genre, and in the recent popularity of historical detective novels set in the nineteenth century, the fascination with the devices of forensic science and personal identity with which Victorian detective fiction began continues unabated. While hundreds of literary detectives have been invented since Sherlock Holmes, the man who made the profession into an "exact science" at the turn of the century remains the quintessential figure in the entire genre. So much did he embody a cultural fantasy for the period that when Doyle tried to kill him off in his infamous encounter with Professor Moriarity in "The Final Problem" in 1893, the British reading public went into mourning and demanded that the great detective be brought back to life. Doyle was compelled to oblige, and revived Sherlock Holmes for three more decades of life in print. Through this great Victorian detective, and through the detective genre in which he played such a crucial and culminating role, the modern world of DNA fingerprinting, satellite surveillance, and crime-scene computer simulation have become imaginable to us. In those technologies, and in the literary genre that remains today the most popular form of writing in the English-speaking world, the Victorian literary detective continues to police the way we perceive ourselves and are perceived by our society.

NOTES

1 Margaret Oliphant, "Sensation Novels," *Blackwood's Edinburgh Magazine* 91 (May 1862), 564–84; 568.
2 Georg Lukács, *Theory of the Novel*, trans. Anna Bostock (1920; Cambridge, MA: MIT Press, 1971), 60.
3 *Ibid.*, 60–61.
4 See Edward Said, *Beginnings: Intention and Method* (New York: Basic Books, 1975).
5 See E. J. Hobsbawm, *The Age of Revolution: 1789–1848* (New York: New American Library, 1962).
6 George Theodore Wilkinson, *The Newgate Calendar* (London: R. Evans, 1816).
7 W. M. Thackeray, *Catherine*, Biographical Edition of Thackeray's *Works*, 26 vols. (London, 1898), IV: 519–20.
8 Quoted by Keith Hollingsworth, *The Newgate Novel 1830–1847: Bulwer, Ainsworth, Dickens, & Thackeray* (Detroit: Wayne State University Press, 1963), 149.
9 Michel Foucault, *Discipline and Punish: The Birth of the Prison*, trans. Alan Sheridan (New York: Vintage Books, 1979), 217. First published in 1975 (in French).
10 Charles Dickens, *Bleak House: An Authoritative and Annotated Text*, ed. George Ford and Sylvere Monod (1853; New York: W. W. Norton, 1977), 597.
11 Fredric Hill, *Crime: Its Amount, Causes, and Remedies* (London: John Murray, 1853) 385–86.
12 See, for example, *Richmond: or Scenes in the Life of a Bow Street Officer*, 1827; and "Thomas Waters," *The Recollections of a Policeman*, 1849.
13 T. S. Eliot, "Wilkie Collins and Dickens," *Selected Essays of T. S. Eliot* (New York: Harcourt, Brace, and World, 1960), 409–18. See p. 413.
14 Anthony Trollope, *An Autobiography* (New York: Oxford University Press, 1950), 257.
15 *Ibid.*, 251.

16 See the preface to the second edition of Wilkie Collins, *The Woman in White* (1860; Harmondsworth: Penguin, 1974), 32.

17 Mary Elizabeth Braddon, *Lady Audley's Secret* (1862; New York: Dover, 1974), 227.

18 Henry James, "Mary Elizabeth Braddon," *Henry James Literary Criticism: Essays on Literature, American Writers, English Writers* (New York: Library of America, 1984), 741–46. See p. 743. First published in *Nation*, November 9, 1865.

19 Arthur Conan Doyle, *A Study in Scarlet*, in *The Complete Sherlock Holmes*, 2 vols. (Garden City, NY: Doubleday and Company, 1930), I: 33.

20 Arthur Conan Doyle, *The Adventures of Sherlock Homes*, *The Complete Sherlock Holmes*, I: 161.

21 Quoted in Jürgen Thorwald, *The Century of the Detective*, trans. Richard and Clara Winston (New York: Harcourt, Brace and World, 1965), 281.

22 Arthur Conan Doyle, "The Adventure of the Naval Treaty," *The Hound of the Baskervilles*, *The Complete Sherlock Holmes*, I: 460, II: 672–73.

23 *A Study in Scarlet*, *The Complete Sherlock Holmes*, I: 23.

24 *The Sign of Four*, *The Complete Sherlock Holmes*, I: 84.

25 "The Norwood Builder," *The Complete Sherlock Holmes*, I: 18.

26 Havelock Ellis, *The Criminal* (London: Scott, 1890), xix.

27 Sir Francis Galton, *Finger Prints* (London: Macmillan and Co., 1892), 169.

28 Michel Foucault, *The Birth of the Clinic*, trans. A. M. Sheridan Smith (New York: Pantheon Books, 1973), 164.

29 Dorothy Sayers, "The Omnibus of Crime," in Howard Haycraft, ed., *The Art of the Mystery Story* (New York: Carroll and Graf, 1974). Sayers's essay was first published in 1928–29.

9

LYN PYKETT

Sensation and the fantastic in the Victorian novel

By the late 1970s it seemed to have become a universally acknowledged truth that the typical form of the nineteenth-century English novel was the "classic realist text," a conservative literary form concerned to reinscribe a commonsense view of things as they are, whose formal and ideological characteristics were adumbrated (and frequently castigated) by a host of critics bent on a radical critique of literature and its institutions.[1] This account of the hegemony of realism in the Victorian novel has been interrogated by critics with varying theoretical and political preoccupations who have explored the non-realist or anti-realist aspects of canonical Victorian novels, or redirected literary historical attention to the cultural significance of a range of bestselling and sometimes controversial nineteenth-century fiction texts such as the sensation novel of the 1860s and a number of fantastic narratives from the *fin-de-siècle* which do not conform to the tenets of "classic" "bourgeois" realism, and which have tended, hitherto, to be pushed to the margins of literary critical attention, or treated as aberrant.

Although one might easily list a range of "fantastic" literary genres or sub-genres, or, like Tzvetan Todorov, attempt to theorize a transhistorical genre of the "fantastic," the literary fantastic is perhaps best seen as a mode of representation which assumes a variety of different generic forms at different historical junctures,[2] rather than as a discrete genre. During the Victorian period the forms of the fantastic proliferated into a range of fictional genres and sub-genres, many of which originated in the various strands of late eighteenth-century gothic romance. Indeed gothic (broadly defined) might almost be described as the paradigmatic form of the fantastic in Victorian fiction. In its various mutated forms, it remained a significant presence in the nineteenth-century novel long after the waning of the vogue for gothic romances in the years around the turn of the eighteenth to nineteenth century. "Gothic traces"[3] were embedded in a range of popular fictional genres: in crime novels in the 1830s and 1840s;

in the ghost story from the 1840s to the end of the period; in the sensation novel which dominated the bestseller lists and critical columns in the early 1860s; in the rise of the modern detective story, such as Charles Dickens's *Bleak House* (1853), Wilkie Collins's *The Moonstone* (1868), and Sir Arthur Conan Doyle's Sherlock Holmes stories, beginning with *A Study in Scarlet* in 1887; in a range of *fin-de-siècle* degenerationist fantasies and imperial romances, and in what H. G. Wells called the scientific romance. This chapter will be concerned to explore some of these mutations, transformations, and modernizations of gothic.

The extent to which the fantastic pervaded Victorian fiction can be seen in the success of novelists such as Charles Dickens, Wilkie Collins, Elizabeth Gaskell, and Margaret Oliphant (like Gaskell, better known now as the author of realistic chronicles of family life) as writers of ghost stories and other tales of terror and the supernatural. Even George Eliot, the doyenne of realism, produced a tale of the supernatural in her strange and disturbing occult novella, *The Lifted Veil* (1859), whose narrator and central protagonist develops clairvoyant powers following an illness, and is subsequently haunted by his ability to read the minds of others and by his (fore)knowledge of the fate that awaits him. Perhaps even more interesting as an indication of the pervasiveness of sensation and the fantastic in Victorian fiction than these forays into fantastic sub-genres is the irruption of sensation and the fantastic into novels (some of which have been cited as examples of Victorian realism) which cannot easily be assigned to a single generic category. For example, in the demonic characters, gothic scenes, and dreams in the novels of Emily and Charlotte Brontë; in Dickens's frequent use of gothic or ghostly scenes, interludes, or interpolated tales; in the melodramatic excess and sensational plotting in Dickens's fiction generally, in Gaskell's social problem novels, in the work of George Eliot, whose *Felix Holt the Radical* (1866), *Middlemarch* (1872) and *Daniel Deronda* (1876) all employ sensation plotting and sensation effects, and in the novels of Anthony Trollope and Thomas Hardy. Hardy, who was later to deny (somewhat unconvincingly) his indebtedness to the sensation novel was the author of a thoroughgoing example of the genre, *Desperate Remedies*, published anonymously in 1871. Hardy's description of this novel might serve as a template for the mid-Victorian sensation novel: a "long and intricately inwrought chain of circumstance," involving "murder, blackmail, illegitimacy, impersonation, eavesdropping, multiple secrets, a suggestion of bigamy, amateur and professional detectives."[4]

What and how does the prominence of sensation and the fantastic in Victorian fiction signify? For many commentators sensation and the fantastic in fiction are forms of the personal or political unconscious; the return of the repressed in which "subconscious psychic energy bursts out from the restraints of the conscious ego,"[5] or in which subjugated, silenced, or invisible social groups or impulses rise up against the social institutions or forces which seek to deny or contain them. The literature of the fantastic is "all that is not said, all that is unsayable, through realistic forms."[6] Sensational and fantastic literature confront taboo, they are associated with excess, with the irrational, non-rational or supernatural, and with carnival or misrule. Fantastic literature stages a confrontation between opposing models of reality, and, according to Todorov, is characterized by the period of "hesitation experienced by a person," whether it be a fictional character or the reader, "who knows only the laws of nature, confronting an apparently supernatural event."[7] In its various guises the fantastic problematizes or interrogates perception, language, time, space, and the conception of unified character; it disrupts linear narrative.

If there is a difficulty for the modern critic in establishing the boundaries between the fantastic and the realistic, or between the different generic forms and transformations of the fantastic in Victorian fiction, that is because the fantastic is itself a liminal and transgressive mode, concerned with and moving between borderlands and boundaries: the boundaries of the conscious and the unconscious; the rational and the irrational; the "civilized" and the "primitive"; the religious and secular; the material and the numinous; the natural and supernatural; the self and the not-self. The fantastic is an interrogator of established categories: not least those of sexuality, gender, and social class. Even the category of art itself comes under question as the literary fantastic very often raises questions about the boundaries between high art and low art.

Much recent critical discussion of sensation and the fantastic has focused on the nature of their relationship to realism and on the question of their subversiveness. Some critics have seen both of these modes as challenging, interrogating, and disrupting the conventions of realism and the social conventions (presumed to be conservative) which realism supposedly reinscribes. Some would argue that this interrogation of realism is an inherently radical move, since it opens up a space for subversive desire or radical critique; others would contend that Victorian sensation fiction or the Victorian fantastic opens up this space only to retreat from it, or to close it up by managing desire and recontaining critique. Some would argue that sensation and the fantastic merely interrupt realism, or punctuate it with question marks; others, that they are symptomatic of realism's contradictions and signal its imminent collapse. The following sections will examine a range of examples of sensation and the fantastic in Victorian fiction, from the ghost story to the *fin-de-siècle* tale of horror, and will explore both their relationship to their literary antecedents and their engagements with contemporary culture. In doing so they will suggest that sensation and the fantastic in Victorian fiction cannot simply be read as transgressively subversive of a supposedly monolithic dominant discourse, nor written off as a subserviently conservative reinscription of it. Rather, both modes should be seen as integral to the ways in which Victorian writers and readers constructed their world, and both confronted and evaded their fears and desires.

Sensation and the fantastic: the ghosts of gothic

> Take – An old castle, half of it ruinous.
> A long gallery, with a great many doors, some secret ones.
> Three murdered bodies, quite fresh.
> As many skeletons, in chests and presses . . .
> Mix them together, in the form of three volumes, to be
> taken at any of the watering places before going to bed.[8]

This recipe gives us the staple plot elements and favourite locations of eighteenth-century gothic fiction, and conveys, too, something of the critical ridicule which the genre attracted: it was clearly marked, for many of its contemporary critics, as a formulaic genre designed as a luxury commodity for fashionable consumer society. For Wordsworth, writing in the 1800 preface to *Lyrical Ballads*, the taste for such sensational tales was one of the symptoms of the degeneracy of a modern urban industrial culture. The heyday of the first phase of gothic fiction occurred between the 1760s and the 1820s. Among the best-known gothic romances were Horace Walpole's *Castle of Otranto* (1764), Ann Radcliffe's *The Mysteries of Udolpho* (1794) and *The Italian* (1797), Matthew Lewis's *The Monk* (1796), Charles Maturin's *Melmoth the Wanderer* (1820), and Mary Shelley's *Frankenstein* (1818). Although very different in style and emphasis these novels share a penchant for mysterious, archaic settings, which include isolated and possibly haunted castles, dungeons, or sublime land-scapes. They also share a preoccupation with the monstrous and super-natural, and make frequent use of dreams, visions, hallucinations, metamorphoses of various kinds, and, in some cases (for example, James Hogg's romantic gothic novel *Private Memoirs and Confessions of a Justified Sinner* (1824)) the psychological splitting or doubling of charac-ters. Their plots turn variously on dynastic ambition and intrigue, and Faustian overreaching, and they frequently involve violence, tyranny, imprisonment, and persecution (especially of women).

Although its origins lie in an eighteenth-century medievalism, gothic and its later mutations became one of the characteristic literary forms of modernity, the vehicle of a fragmented modern subjectivity, and detached, often politically and/or psychologically alienated individuals. Generically gothic is a hybrid, a Frankensteinian form assembled from fragments of other forms.[9] Above all gothic is concerned with feeling: from its inception it has been concerned to depict and explore feeling in character, but also (perhaps mainly) to create feeling or affect in the reader. The main feelings gothic fictions seek to arouse in their readers are those of fear and terror. Their common aim is the production of fear as a series of bodily effects: "to get to the body itself, its glands, muscles, epidermis, and circulatory system, quickly arousing and quickly allaying the physiological reactions to fear."[10] As well as producing the effects of fear in their readers, gothic and its Victorian transformations might be said to be forms which are produced by fears and anxieties shared by late eighteenth- and nineteenth-century writers and their readers, and by common cultural anxieties: about sex and gender and relations between the sexes; about power (and its gendering); about the nature of the self.

The ghost story and tale of the supernatural

One of the ghosts of gothic that developed a distinctive identity in the Victorian period was the ghost story. Its origins lie in a variety of traditional forms such as folk tales, tales of terror and the supernatural, as well as the gothic romance. In its modern form the ghost story begins with an interpolated tale – "Wandering Willie's Tale" – in Sir Walter Scott's *Redgauntlet* (1824). Subsequently one of Scott's great admirers, the Irish writer, Sheridan Le Fanu, helped to develop a market for magazine stories of ghosts and the supernatural, beginning with "The Ghost and the Bone-Setter" in the *Dublin University Magazine* (January 1838) which he was later to edit. Le Fanu is an important figure in the history of the Victorian ghost story and tale of the supernatural, contributing a wide range of novels and stories about the occult and hallucinatory spiritual possession (the most famous of which is "Green Tea"). He is also the author of the widely anthologized "Carmilla," the tale of a female vampire who befriends and preys on Laura, the young woman who narrates most of the tale. Both "Carmilla" and "Green Tea" were published in Le Fanu's collection *In a Glass Darkly* (1872), where they ostensibly belong to the casebook of Dr. Hesselius, a German practitioner of "metaphysical medicine." This narrative device, character type, and the concept of "metaphysical medicine" or "transcendental science" were used to even more disturbing effect by *fin-de-siècle* exponents of the super- or supra-rational tale, such as Robert Louis Stevenson, Arthur Machen, and Bram Stoker.

Dickens was another key figure in the development of the ghost story, as author, commissioning editor, and as an entrepreneur who developed the market for this particular kind of magazine story in *Household Words* and *All the Year Round*, and in particular in the special Christmas editions of (later Christmas supplements to) these periodicals. Wilkie Collins, Elizabeth Gaskell, Sheridan Le Fanu, and Edward Bulwer Lytton all wrote ghost stories and tales of the supernatural for (or with) Dickens in the 1850s. Dickens was himself the author of a new kind of "anti-gothic" ghost story with a contemporary setting, in which the supernatural erupts into the ordinary, everyday world. In his Christmas books *A Christmas Carol* (1843) and *The Haunted Man* (1848) supernatural machinery is pressed into the service of moral allegory in stories which trace the redemption of protagonists who have attempted to suppress memory and deny the past, and have made pacts with evil forces. In *A Christmas Carol* Scrooge, who has allied himself with Mammon, is shocked into human sympathy by the ghostly emanations of his past and future. Redlaw, the scientist at the centre of *The Haunted Man*, makes a bargain with his Evil Genius to be released from the memories of sorrow and past wrongdoing that haunt him, on condition that he passes on this power of forgetfulness to everyone he meets. The horror of the story derives from Redlaw's recognition that the erasure of memory also erases the sources of sympathy, tolerance, gratitude, and repentance from his own and others' lives. In later stories such as "The Trial for Murder" (1865) and "The Signalman" (1866), which impart "subjective," "psychological experiences . . . of a strange sort,"[11] the meaning of supernatural, as in many later Victorian ghost stories or tales of the supernatural, is tantalizingly indeterminate, and it is not so self-evidently part of a moral schema, nor so concerned with speculations about the sources of selfhood.

Dickens also provided a taxonomy of traditional types of the ghost story. In "A Christmas Tree," he outlined a range of plot scenarios which, despite their surface variety, fall into two main types: "unconscious ghosts" (or other uncanny phenomena, such as an indelibly bloodstained floor) which perpetually repeat or reenact some past wickedness or wrongdoing, and "conscious ghosts" which usually appear only to a particular individual or group in order to "right some ancestral wrong . . . to seek redress or retribution," or to presage future harm.[12] Dickens did not address the question of why such stories should have been so interesting to both readers and writers in the nineteenth century. However, subsequent analysts of the form have argued that the ghost story and the tale of the supernatural filled a cultural and psychological gap left by the rise of positivistic science and the decline of the supernatural and magical aspects of religion in an increasingly secular age. Freud, the author of his own kinds of modern ghost stories in his psychoanalytic case studies of the "hauntings" of the unconscious, suggests in *Totem and Taboo* (1913) that a preoccupation with ghosts and spirits is a survival from more "primitive" stages of cultural and individual development, and a way of dealing with fears about death and sex.

The ghost story, like the gothic, also offers a particular perspective on history or the past. In its refusal to regard "the past as a closed book," the Victorian ghost story, as Michael Cox has noted, "offered a way of anchoring the past to an unsettled present."[13] Ghost stories are also, in many cases, stories about power, in which the seduced, betrayed, persecuted, wronged, or dispossessed return to right or avenge their wrongs or repossess what has been taken away. This preoccupation with the consequences of unequal power relations may account for the interest of women writers in the genre: in addition to the writers already mentioned, Mary Elizabeth Braddon, Rhoda Broughton, Amelia Edwards, and Charlotte Riddell all wrote ghost stories. However, there are also material reasons for women writers' interest in the ghost story: there was a great demand for them in the growing market of fiction magazines.

Female gothic and the sensation novel

Gothic is a genre which has been, from its inception, closely associated with women writers and readers. As several feminist critics have demonstrated, "Gothics are particularly compelling fictions for the many women who read and write them because of their nightmarish figuration of feminine experience within the home."[14] Ellen Moers coined the term "female Gothic" to describe that tradition of women's writing, which she traced back to Ann Radcliffe, which used the gothic's "paraphernalia of claustrophobic castles, villainous dominating men, and beleaguered heroines to thematize women's sense of isolation and imprisonment within a domestic ideology fast becoming hegemonic by the end of the eighteenth century."[15] In the Victorian period female gothic became an increasingly complex and contradictory genre which not only represented women's fears of domestic imprisonment, but also enacted, and, simultaneously, or by turns, managed and recontained their fantasies of escape from the physical and psychological confinements of the domestic and conventionally defined femininity. Another contradictory aspect of the various transformations of female gothic in this period is the fact that by the 1860s the category had come to include work by male novelists, such as Wilkie Collins, who appropriated many of its preoccupations and devices. Certainly for fiction reviewers in the 1860s the kind of writing that has been retrospectively labeled as female gothic was not simply a tradition of writing *by* women, it was also a feminized form of writing.

There is more than a trace of gothic in the novels of Charlotte, Emily, and Anne Brontë, all of whom were avid readers of the gothic tales published in *Blackwood's Edinburgh Magazine*. Each of the Brontës, even the creator of that extraordinary uncategorizable novel *Wuthering Heights* (1847), contributed to the process of modernizing gothic – by both domesticating and psychologizing it – which occurred in the Victorian period. They domesticated gothic by locating their tales of female imprisonment, confinement, or persecution (whether physical or psychological) in everyday, domestic settings among the middling classes of society. Indeed, much of the strange power of their novels derives precisely from this juxtaposition of the domestic and the fantastic, as one of their first reviewers noted: "in spite of its truth to life in the remote corners of England – *Wuthering Heights* is a disagreeable story. The Bells [the Brontë pseudonym] seem to affect painful and exceptional subjects – the misdeeds or oppression of tyranny, the eccentricities of 'woman's fantasy'."[16]

In the fiction of each of the Brontë sisters it is usually the English home (rather than some remote castle) that is the locus of terror and the uncanny, a threatening place of physical and psychological violence, a prison rather than (or as well as) a place of shelter. Every reader of the Brontës will easily call to mind numerous scenes from their novels whose uncanniness is "unhomely" (one of the English translations of "*Unheimlich*," Freud's term for the "uncanny," discussed further below): the violent, barbarized household of *Wuthering Heights* into which Lockwood unsuspectingly stumbles at the beginning of Emily Brontë's novel; the oppressive marital home from which Helen Graham flees in *The Tenant of Wildfell Hall* (1848); the domestic torture chamber that is the Reed household, and the Bluebeard's castle of Rochester's Thornfield Hall (complete with apparently disembodied ghoulish laughter, later revealed as the ravings of the monstrous madwoman incarcerated in the attic) in *Jane Eyre* (1847); the claustrophobic place of surveillance that is Madame Beck's school and Lucy Snowe's home in *Villette* (1853). In this latter case Charlotte Brontë appears to be adhering to the conventional gothic use of a foreign location and a Roman Catholic culture as the site of oppression, but her choice of bourgeois Lebassecour (Belgium) as the location of her heroine's gothic experience is, in part, parodic or anti-gothic.

As well as domesticating the genre, the Brontës were also key figures in the psychologizing of gothic, a process in which gothic devices were used to figure and explore the psychological interiority of fictional characters. This shift towards a materialist supernaturalism, in which "terror" grew out of realistic psychological and physiological devices and processes used to achieve "Gothic effects,"[17] had begun at the end of the eighteenth century and was developed further by William Godwin (*Caleb Williams*, 1794), his daughter Mary Shelley, James Hogg, and Edgar Allan Poe. This movement from what Todorov, in *The Fantastic*, labels the "marvelous" (in which there is a complete break with the real) and the "fantastic-marvelous" (in which inexplicable occurrences have supernatural causes or associations), towards the "fantastic-uncanny" (in which such occurrences are subjective in origin) and the "uncanny" (in which they derive from unconscious projection), may be observed variously in Emily Brontë's representation of the ghostly dream figure of Catherine Earnshaw-Linton at the beginning of *Wuthering Heights*, and the demonic (but nevertheless entirely human) figure of Heathcliff; in the "ghost" of her uncle Reed which appears to Jane Eyre in her nightmare terror when she is incarcerated in the Red Room, or the voice of her dead mother which she hears prior to her departure from Thornfield after the revelations about Rochester's wife; in Lucy Snowe's "visions" of the nun , and in her defamiliarizing, opiate-induced hallucinations which embody both her acknowledged and unacknowledged fears and desires, in chapter 39 ("Old and New Acquaintances") of *Villette*.

The use of the term "uncanny" to designate a domain of threatening strangeness and uncertainty coincided with the rise of gothic, and recurs in fantastic literature throughout the nineteenth century. It seems to have made its first appearance in William Beckford's Oriental tale, *Vathek* (1786) and it recurs in James Hogg's disturbing tale of *doppelgängers*, *The Private Memoirs and Confessions of a Justified Sinner* (1824), and in Jonathan Harker's anxieties about the Count's castle in Bram Stoker's *Dracula* (1897) ("This was all so strange and uncanny that a dreadful fear came upon me").[18] As some of the examples given above suggest, instances of the uncanny in literature include an indefinable sense of dread or horror, madness, double selves, involuntary repetitions, or figures returning from the dead.

Freud's 1919 essay on *das Unheimlich* (the uncanny) offers an invaluable theoretical framework for the analysis of the uncanny in nineteenth-century fiction, not least because, as was so often the case, the pioneer of psychoanalysis was exploring by a different route the same terrain as his near contemporaries among the novelists. Central to Freud's analysis of the uncanny – and to its usefulness for exploring the operations and transformations of the fantastic in nineteenth-century fiction – is the double meaning of *das Unheimlich*. *Das Heimlich* signifies, on the one hand, the homely, familiar, cosy, intimate; in short that which gives a sense of being "at home" in the world. The negation of this is the unhomely, that which is unfamiliar, strange, or uncomfortable; in short that which gives a feeling of being not "at home" in the world. However, *das Heimlich* also signifies that which is hidden, obscured, or secreted. The negation of this sense of *das Heimlich* is that which uncovers or dis-covers what is normally concealed. For Freud the uncanny is "that class of the frightening which leads back to what is known to us and long."[19] The uncanny is also the effect of projection – of projecting unconscious fears or desires onto one's environment or other people. For Freud, the uncanny object is 'something familiar and old-established in the mind which has become alienated from it only through the process of repression," something "which ought to have remained hidden but has come to light";[20] it is (as Kelly Hurley glosses it) "*heimlich* within the occluded level of the unconscious, *unheimlich* to the conscious mind . . . a moment of near-rupture, wherein the repressed contents of the unconscious struggle to come to the surface and are repressed again."[21]

Charles Dickens succinctly anticipated Freud's definition of the uncanny when he described Wilkie Collins's *The Moonstone* as "wild yet domestic."[22] Dickens's phrase could be applied with equal aptness to the fiction of the Brontë sisters and to the sensation novel, a fictional sub-genre which enjoyed a sensational popular success and critical notoriety in the 1860s, and another of the heirs of gothic. Wilkie Collins is generally credited with initiating the sensation vogue with *The Woman in White* in 1860, although the Brontës might also be seen as early sensation novelists. Margaret Oliphant certainly linked the rebellious self-assertive heroines of the sensation novel and other unpleasant developments in nineteenth-century fiction to Charlotte Brontë's *Jane Eyre*, which "dashed into our well-ordered world, broke its boundaries, and defied its principles – and the most alarming revolution of modern times has followed."[23] However, it is Anne Brontë's *The Tenant of Wildfell Hall* that most obviously anticipates both the matter and manner of the sensation novel. Its complexly layered narrative, consisting of letters, the heroine's journal, and a commentary by the hero (a dispersal of narrative voices developed further by Collins), makes it the archetypal "novel with a secret" about a woman with a secret history, and it shares the sensation novel's preoccupation with the sufferings of women that arise from the iniquities of marriage customs and the inequities of the marriage laws and the laws concerning the custody of children.

For a brief period in the 1860s the sensational was deemed to have displaced domestic realism as the dominant fictional form. As well as Collins, those counted among the sensationalists at this time included Dickens (whose *Great Expectations* [1861] was reviewed alongside *The*

Woman in White as a less accomplished example of the genre), Mary Elizabeth Braddon, Ellen (Mrs. Henry) Wood, Rhoda Broughton, "Ouida" (Marie Louise de la Ramée), Sheridan Le Fanu, and Charles Reade. In fact the sensation label fits some of these authors better than others: Wood and Broughton both deal with racy subject matter and employ sensation plotting (which relies on narrative concealment, a great variety of incident and extraordinary coincidences), but in many ways their novels belong to the sin and sentiment school of domestic melodrama; Ouida's exotic novels of high life are a racy updating of the silver fork romance, and Reade uses sensation techniques (many of which were familiar to him from his work in the theatre) to sugar the pill of his novels with a social purpose. Braddon exploited the sensation label in a stream of novels from *Lady Audley's Secret* (1862) to *Run to Earth* (1868), but she also disavowed and satirized that "bitter term of reproach, 'sensation'"[24] in *The Doctor's Wife* (1864), a reworking of Flaubert's *Madame Bovary*. Sheridan Le Fanu explicitly remonstrated "against the promiscuous application of the term 'sensation'" in his "Preliminary Word" to *Uncle Silas* (1864), preferring to see his novel as belonging to the "legitimate school of tragic English romance." In fact *Uncle Silas* is a good example of female gothic: it is a claustrophobic tale (with intimations of the occult and supernatural in the Swedenborgianism of two of the characters and in the mysterious death which precedes the novel's action), in which a young and wealthy orphan, Maud Ruthyn, is effectively imprisoned by an unscrupulous uncle, a religious fanatic who wishes to marry her forcibly to his loutish son in order to gain control of her wealth.

Uncle Silas did, however, make common cause with the sensation novel in its British setting. In sensation novels the archaic, exoticized, foreign settings of gothic are replaced by the English country house, or the bourgeois villa. As Henry James put it, sensation novels were concerned with:

> those most mysterious of mysteries, the mysteries that are at our own doors. This innovation gave a new impetus to the literature of horrors. It was fatal to Mrs. Radcliffe and her everlasting castle in the Appenines . . . Instead of the terrors of Udolpho, we were treated to the terrors of the cheerful country house, or the London lodgings. And there is no doubt that these were infinitely the more terrible.[25]

Sensation novels were also close to home in their subject matter. Sometimes described as newspaper novels, and often borrowing their plots from sensational newspaper reports of criminal or divorce cases (such as the sensational trial of the teenaged Constance Kent for the murder of her young half-brother, and the complicated and colourful Yelverton bigamy and divorce case), they addressed contemporary anxieties and fantasies about marriage and the family, and about changing gender and class relations. Cross-class marriages, and, more generally, the relations between a declining aristocracy and a rising professional middle class figured prominently, as did relations between the aristocracy (or, even more commonly, the rising middle class) and their servants: for example, there were numerous plot situations which involved servants spying on or becoming involved in the plottings of, or plottings against, their masters and mistresses. Sensation novels focused on gendered social and familial roles (women's roles as wives and mothers, and men's roles as husbands and their relation to the public world of wealth and/or work), on the law's regulation of social and sexual behaviour, and on the tendency of contemporary marriage laws and customs to imprison and victimize women (even if, in the end, most sensation novels "redeem" marriage by locating their heroine in – or restoring her to – a happy marriage).

Murder, blackmail, fraud, adultery, and bigamy are common plot components in the sensation novel's unveiling of the secrets of respectable society. The effect of sensation plotting is to suggest the duplicitous nature of social reality, and to make both readers and characters into detectives. The history of Robert Audley, the detective-hero of Mary Elizabeth Braddon's *Lady Audley's Secret*, is a good example of the process by which the sensation novel creates universal suspicion. Robert is transformed from the idle reader of morally suspect French novels, to the active and suspicious reader of Lady Audley's behaviour. The question and answer that Robert addresses to his aunt, as a kind of warning that he is on her trail, neatly summarizes some of the main preoccupations of sensation fiction:

> "What do we know of the mysteries that may hang about the houses we enter? If I were to go tomorrow into that commonplace, plebeian, eight-roomed house in which Maria Manning and her husband murdered their guest, I should have no prescience of that bygone horror. Foul deeds have been done under the most hospitable roofs; terrible crimes have been committed amid the fairest scenes, and have left no trace upon the spot where they were done ... I believe ... that we may walk unconsciously in an atmosphere of crime and breathe none the less freely. I believe that we may look into the smiling face of a murderer, and admire its tranquil beauty."[26]

Like the gothic, sensation novels were generic hybrids, in this case combining the journalistic and the fantastic, the domestic and the exotic, realism and melodrama. Their complicated plots, like those of gothic romances, were concerned with terror, mystery, suspense, secrecy, deception and disguise, and they frequently (although not invariably) involved

the persecution and incarceration of the heroine. Like their gothic predecessors, sensation novels aimed at the production of affect, as contemporary reviewers were quick to point out, writing disapprovingly of the
sensation novelists' penchant for "preaching to the nerves," and appealing
to the reader's animal instincts.[27] Others parodied the sensationalists'
devotion to "Harrowing the Mind, making the Flesh Creep . . . Giving
Shocks to the Nervous System, Destroying Conventional Moralities, and
generally Unfitting the Public for the Prosaic Avocations of Life."[28]

As in the gothic, the sensation novel's creation of the *frisson* of terror or
the uncanny often had sexual overtones or undertones. This is fore-
grounded in the first sensation scene in Wilkie Collins's *The Woman in
White*, which reproduces for the reader the sexualized *frisson* of fear
produced by the physical touch, sound, and appearance of the mysterious,
dreamlike, ghostly (but nevertheless real) woman who seems to have been
conjured from the fantasies of Walter Hartright, the scene's narrator, the
"editor" of the narrative, and its hero. Much of the contemporary hostility
to the sensation novel originated in anxieties about its representation and
anatomizing of sexual feeling (especially the sexual feelings of women), and
in anxieties about the effects on readers (especially women and young men)
of such representations; a concern which resurfaced in the debate about the
so-called Fiction of Sex and the New Woman novel of the 1880s and
1890s. Among the most shocking aspects of the sensation novel (to
contemporary reviewers) were its focus on bodily sensations – of fear,
anxiety, and embarrassment as well as sexual feeling – and its representation of its female protagonists not simply as passive victims of male power
and their own feelings, but also as actively desiring and, in some cases self-
consciously manipulating the desires of others in order to circumvent the
usual constraints of their gendered roles and get what they want: for
example, Collins's disinherited Magdalen Vanstone in *No Name* (1862);
Lydia Gwilt and Lucy Audley, the socially aspiring *femmes fatales* in
Collins's *Armadale* (1866) and Braddon's *Lady Audley's Secret*; the eponymous heroine of Braddon's *Aurora Floyd* (1863); and Olivia Arundel in
John Marchmont's Legacy (1863). What these woman want (but for
interestingly different reasons) is marriage, and the plots of these novels
turn, in part, on their attempts to obtain, keep, or dispose of husbands.
Such novels may be read symptomatically as authorial and/or cultural
fantasies or anxieties about women, sex, and power, but some of them may
also be read as self-consciously anatomizing such fantasies, and offering an
element of critique of existing power relations.

Fantasy and the fantastic, the non-rational or irrational, as well as the
contents of the sensational newspaper press, provided the *mis-en-scène*,

plot components, and the subject matter of sensation fiction. Sensation novels constructed their secretive narratives, and opened up to investigation that which is normally hidden, obscured, or secreted through their depiction and exploration of "uncanny" psychic phenomena such as premonitory dreams (Collins's *Armadale*); through hallucinatory or uncanny scenes (for example, the various appearances of Anne Catherick in *A Woman in White*, Ozias Midwinter's first meeting with Lydia Gwilt in *Armadale*, or the invasion of Lady Audley's boudoir and the examination of her unfinished portrait in *Lady Audley's Secret*); through unconscious projections of various kinds (for example, Franklin Blake's concealment of the diamond in Collins's *The Moonstone*); through the depiction of extreme emotional states, such as hysteria, jealousy, sexual obsession, paranoia; and, most important of all, through their representation of madness, and other forms of social or sexual transgression or deviance which respectable society (mis)labels as madness. The sensation novel's repeated use of madness was a means of moving beyond (and, at points, engaging in a critique of) both social conventions and the conventions of literary realism. It was also a way of gaining access to and exploring "primitive," pre-social or anti-social drives, or, as a *Spectator* article on "Madness in Novels" put it, "the undeveloped wild beast in one's own heart":

> Miss Braddon perceived this, and it is to her credit that she discerned a mode of restoring the lost sensational effect to character. Madness may intensify any quality, courage, or hate, or jealousy, or wickedness, and she made Lady Audley mad. Thenceforward she was released from the irksome regime of the probable . . . Probability becomes unnecessary, *vraisemblance* a burden, naturalness a mistake in art, everything was possible, and the less possible the emotion, the greater the surprise and pleasure.[29]

Late-nineteenth-century male gothic: the "undeveloped wild beast in one's own heart"

The spectre of the "undeveloped wild beast in one's own heart," or, as the late nineteenth-century cultural critic Max Nordau put it, "the unchaining of the beast in man,"[30] lies at the heart of a group of late nineteenth-century tales of monstrosity: Robert Louis Stevenson's *The Strange Case of Dr. Jekyll and Mr. Hyde* (1886); Oscar Wilde's *The Picture of Dorian Gray* (1891); Arthur Machen's *The Great God Pan* (1894); H. G. Wells's *The Island of Dr. Moreau* (1896); and Bram Stoker's *Dracula* (1897). This is not an exclusively male tradition. Mary Elizabeth Braddon was the author of a vampire story, "Good Lady Ducayne" (1896), and in Marie Corelli's bestseller *The Sorrows of Satan* (1895), the writer-hero makes a pact with the protean Prince Rimanez, the devil (*inter alia*) in literary agent's clothing.

These strange tales revisit earlier nineteenth-century gothic and sensation, and rework them (sometimes in decadent form) for the *fin-de-siècle*. *Dracula's* ancestors include John Polidori's "The Vampyre" (1818), J. M. Rymer's penny gothic serial *Varney the Vampire* (1845–47), and Sheridan Le Fanu's "Carmilla" (1872). Each of the other novellas is haunted by Mary Shelley's *Frankenstein*, one of the key myths of post-Romantic culture, in which an overreaching scientist manufactures and then rejects a monstrous creature who returns to persecute his creator and (as his creator's monstrous double) to act out the scientist's own fears and guilts. The other gothic ghosts which hover over these *fin-de-siècle* fantasies include Charles Maturin's *Melmoth the Wanderer* and James Hogg's *The Private Memoirs and True Confessions of a Justified Sinner*. Maturin's novel is the story of a man who has bartered his soul for the promise of enduring life, and who wanders the world offering to relieve the sufferings of a series of characters (whose dreadful stories are told in succession) in exchange for their taking on his bargain with the devil. Hogg's *Memoirs* is a double story about *dopplegängers*; a twice-told tale, comprising an account by an impersonal editor and the confession of Robert Wringhim (the sinner), which turns on a diabolic, protean character, who assumes various identities and ultimately drives Robert to self-destruction. One interesting point of continuity between earlier nineteenth-century Gothic and its *fin-de-siècle* mutations is a narrative complicatedness, manifested in the widespread use of layered, framed, and embedded narratives including journal extracts and other ostensible documentary records. The effect of the latter devices is, in part, to create an illusion of verisimilitude; the effect of the former is to disperse narrative authority and to disrupt narrative causality and problematize origins.

Like *Frankenstein*, *The Strange Case of Dr. Jekyll and Mr. Hyde* is the tale of the overreaching of an ambitious scientist who seeks to move beyond material to transcendental science. Stevenson's tale, like Shelley's, has become a powerful modern myth, which (like *Dracula* as well as *Frankenstein*) owes its mythic status and continuing popularity to its suggestive indeterminacy, and its failure (or refusal) to resolve the various ideas it puts into play. However, *The Strange Case* also functions as an historically specific moral allegory about Victorian hypocrisy and repression. Dr. Jekyll inhabits a sterile, self-consciously repressed world of male professionals. As Jekyll pompously puts it in his "Full Statement of the Case" (which looks back to Hogg's *Confessions*):

> the worst of my faults was a certain gaiety of disposition . . . [which] I found
> . . . hard to reconcile with my imperious desire to carry my head high, and
> wear a more than commonly grave countenance. Hence it came about that I

concealed my pleasures . . . I stood already committed to a profound duplicity of life . . . It was thus rather the exacting nature of my aspirations, than any particular degradation in my faults, that made me what I was, and, with even a deeper trench than in the majority of men, severed in me those provinces of good and ill which divide and compound man's dual nature.[31]

Stevenson's novella is, among other things, a tale of civilization and its discontents, which conjures up the dark underside of the repressed world of the male professionals (doctors, scientists, and lawyers) who form Jekyll's circle. Jekyll's *alter ego*, Hyde, is a version of the id, acting out the libidinal desires which Jekyll's superego (or Jekyll *as* superego) would suppress. Hyde is a demonic creature of the night, a primitive pre- or anti-social energy.

Stevenson's tale of Jekyll and his *doppelgänger* not only exemplifies that preoccupation with doubles and dualism that characterizes nineteenth-century versions of gothic, but it also theorizes the double. Jekyll's experiment derives in part from his theory of the fractured, multiple modern subject: "man is not truly one, but truly two. I say two, because the state of my own knowledge does not pass beyond that point . . . [but] I hazard the guess that man will be ultimately known for a mere polity of multifarious, incongruous and independent denizens" (*Strange Case*, 82). Like Jekyll, Wilde's Dorian Gray makes a kind of Faustian or Melmothian bargain: he gambles on the possibility of self-splitting, of – as it were – separating the ego from the id and letting them go their independent ways. Wilde's novella, too, is a tale of the discontents of civilization, and of the double bind of repression: it would appear that both the repression of desire and its enactment turn man into a beast. Lord Henry Wooton seduces Dorian into his aesthetic experiment with life by arguing that if we repress our desires in conformity with social mores, "we degenerate into hideous puppets, haunted by the memory of the passions of which we were too much afraid." For Lord Henry repression is not the *sine qua non* of civilization but a primitive survival: "The mutilation of the savage has its tragic survival in the self-denial that mars our lives." Lord Henry argues that the 'soul grows sick with longing for the things it has forbidden to itself, with desire for what its monstrous laws have made monstrous and unlawful."[32] However, Dorian's soul grows sick with indulging in the things it has ceased to forbid itself in a narrative which turns into a simple moral allegory about the evils of narcissism, and the perils of aestheticism.

Jekyll's horrific metamorphoses into Hyde, and the double metamorphosis of Dorian's portrait, are echoed in the shape-changing of Helen Vaughan, the hideously beautiful woman at the centre of Arthur Machen's *The Great God Pan*. Helen is the unnatural offspring of a young virgin, who, as a result of a surgical experiment in "transcendental medicine," has the experience of "seeing Pan" and, by implication, is impregnated by him. In life Helen adopts a variety of identities and aliases, and (like Wilde's Dorian Gray) engages in unspecified infamies which lead to an outbreak of suicidal mania among the upper-class bachelor set. In her death throes she is described as "changing and melting" from "woman to man, from man to beast, and from beast to worse than beast."[33] The most complicated in narrative structure of these late Victorian gothic tales, and certainly one of the most bizarre, Machen's novella is nevertheless typical of the genre in "figuring sexuality as horrific, identity as multiple, the boundary between science and supernaturalism as permeable, and the 'normal' human subject as liable to contamination, affective, moral and physical, by the gothicized subject."[34]

H. G. Wells's scientific romance *The Island of Dr. Moreau* returns to the overweening scientist theme. Moreau is another example of the hubristic scientist who seeks to outdo nature by trying to create human beings from the body parts of animals. His Island is "peopled" by the strange hybrid creatures which result from his experiments, who are kept in line (in a grotesque parody of human society) by the Law, "certain Fixed Ideas implanted by Moreau in their minds, which absolutely bounded their imaginations . . . beyond any possibility of disobedience or dispute."[35] The novel relates the events which ensue from the disturbance of Moreau's rule of law by the arrival of an outsider, Prendrick, from whose point of view the narrative is told. Prendrick's narrative enacts a degeneration or reversion fantasy, as the creatures lapse back into animality, their natural, instinctive animal violence having been rendered more grotesquely violent by Moreau's tampering with it.

An animalistic bloodlust also lies at the heart of Bram Stoker's *Dracula*. Stoker's reworking of the vampire myth is a densely packed psycho-history of late nineteenth-century culture, which puts into play a range of contemporary fears and fantasies about modernity, about class, race, empire, sex, and gender. Count Dracula is both an aristocratic gothic villain and an uncanny otherworldly demon. He is a liminal creature who crosses boundaries: between life and death; man and monster; male and female; past and present; East and West. The Count, with his insatiable bloodlust signifying pure desire, is the repressed which always returns. As the last of his ancient Transylvanian aristocratic line the Count is represented as both primitive and ultra-civilized. He is the foreign, Eastern, "other" which threatens to invade the West (specifically England) in a form of reverse colonization. Stoker's plot enacts both a haunting and an exorcism, as the Crew of Light (the band of blood brothers assisted by Mina, the maternal woman who inspires them) remove the sexual and cultural threat the Count poses.

All of these tales dramatize the degenerationist fears that arose from late nineteenth-century evolutionary thought in the natural and social sciences. On the one hand, there was a fear of degeneration as regression: the fear that evolution was not a simple, one-way progressive process; that civilization was only skin-deep and that there was a savage beneath the skin of every civilized man, waiting to reclaim him. On the other hand, there was a fear that degeneration was the consequence of evolutionary "progress," the result and symptom of over-civilization, and of the peculiar pressures of urban modernity. Either way, fears of degeneration produced fantasies about reversion or "going native," some of which can be seen in these tales about the unchaining of the beast in man. It is, perhaps, not entirely coincidental that fears about "going native" should be so prominent in an imperialist country that regarded its colonial subjects as primitive savages, and grounded its colonialist project in the concept of civilizing the savage. Insofar as they both embody and explore such fears, these tales of monstrous men might be placed alongside Rider Haggard's romances, *King Solomon's Mines* (1885) and *She* (1887), as examples of imperial gothic. Certainly, Stevenson, Wells, and Stoker all to some extent racialize their "monsters": Hyde is a dark, hairy dwarfish savage, Dracula has Semitic features, and Moreau's beast-men are represented as savage, primitive, black, colonized subjects.

Imperial gothic is Patrick Brantlinger's term for the combination of adventure story and gothic which flourished from the mid-1880s and whose rise he links to the curious co-existence of the apparently scientific, progressive ideology of imperialism with a belief in the occult – a form of belief described by Theodor Adorno, the Frankfurt School cultural analyst, as a "regression to magic under late capitalism."[36] Brantlinger includes within the broad category of imperial gothic: atavistic fantasies about the reversion of whole civilizations to barbarism, as, for example, in Richard Jefferies's apocalyptic fantasy *After London* (1885); invasion narratives – such as *Dracula* and *She* – in which London is threatened with invasion by otherworldly representatives of ancient civilizations who wish to colonize the heart of empire; and narratives of reincarnation and spiritual possession. Some of these latter narratives (for example some of Kipling's stories) were also variations of the invasion narrative, in which the English colonizer is invaded or possessed by the spirit of the East or Africa, sometimes after he has returned to England.

This reverse colonization or return of the colonial repressed to disrupt the order of "civilized" English life links imperial gothic to earlier Victorian traditions of gothic and sensation, from Bertha Rochester in *Jane Eyre* to the colonial legacies of greed and violence in which the narratives of Collins's *Armadale* and *The Moonstone* have their origins. However, the moment of imperial gothic is also the moment in which, according to Judith Wilt, Victorian gothic underwent a crucial paradigm shift: "In or around December, 1897," she argues, "Victorian Gothic changed – into Victorian science fiction."[37] The occasion was the publication of H. G. Wells's *The War of the Worlds*, an event which heralded the development of distinctively twentieth-century forms of the fantastic in fiction.

NOTES

1 See, for example, Catherine Belsey, *Critical Practice* (London: Methuen, 1980), and Colin MacCabe, *James Joyce and the Revolution of the Word* (London: Macmillan, 1978).

2 See Rosemary Jackson, *Fantasy: The Literature of Subversion* (London: Methuen, 1981), 5.

3 Fred Botting, *Gothic* (London: Routledge, 1996), 113

4 Thomas Hardy, *Desperate Remedies* (1871; London: Macmillan, 1975), 37.

5 Maggie Kilgour, *The Rise of the Gothic Novel* (London: Routledge, 1995), 3.

6 Jackson, *Fantasy*, 26.

7 Tzvetan Todorov, *The Fantastic: A Structural Approach to a Literary Genre*, trans. Richard Howard (Ithaca, NY: Cornell University Press ,1987), 25.

8 Unsigned, "Terrorist Novel Writing" (1797), quoted in Botting, *Gothic*, 44.

9 Kilgour, *The Rise of the Gothic Novel*, 4.

10 Ellen Moers, *Literary Women* (London: The Women's Press, 1978), 90.

11 "To be taken with a grain of salt," from "Doctor Marigold's Prescriptions," sometimes published as "The Trial for Murder" (the first of "Two Ghost Stories"), in Charles Dickens, *The Christmas Stories*, ed. Ruth Glancy (London: Dent, 1996), 588.

12 Michael Cox, ed., *The Oxford Book of Ghost Stories* (Oxford: Oxford University Press, 1986), xv.

13 Michael Cox and R. A. Gilbert, eds., *Victorian Ghost Stories* (Oxford: University Press, 1991), ix.

14 Tamara Heller, *Dead Secrets: Wilkie Collins and the Female Gothic* (New Haven: Yale University Press, 1992), 14.

15 *Ibid.*

16 *Athenaeum*, December 25, 1847, reprinted in Miriam Allott, ed., *The Brontës: The Critical Heritage* (London: Routledge & Kegan Paul, 1974), 218.

17 Jenny Bourne Taylor, *In the Secret Theatre of Home: Wilkie Collins, Sensation Narrative and Nineteenth-Century Psychology* (London: Routledge, 1988), 6–7.

18 Bram Stoker, *Dracula*, ed. A. N. Wilson (1897; Oxford: Oxford University Press, 1983), 14. The strange, mysterious person that attended Robert Wringhim is described by another character as "uncanny." See James Hogg, *The Private Memoirs and Confessions of a Justified Sinner*, ed. John Carey (1824; Oxford: Oxford University Press, 1970), 186.

19 Sigmund Freud, "The Uncanny," *Standard Edition of the Complete Works*, trans. and ed. James Strachey (London: Hogarth, 1955), XVII:217–52; 220.

20 *Ibid.*, 241.

21 Kelly Hurley, *The Gothic Body: Sexuality, Materialism and Degeneration at the Fin de Siècle* (Cambridge: Cambridge University Press, 1996), 40.

22 Letter to W. H. Wills, June 30, 1867, in Norman Page, ed., *Dickens: The Critical Heritage* (London: Routledge & Kegan Paul, 1974), 169.

23 Margaret Oliphant, "Modern Novelists – Great and Small," *Blackwood's* 77 (May 1855), 554–68; 557.

24 Mary Elizabeth Braddon, *The Doctor's Wife*, ed. and intro. Lyn Pykett (1864; Oxford: Oxford University Press, 1998), 11.

25 Henry James, "Miss Braddon," *The Nation*, November 9, 1865, 594.

26 Mary Elizabeth Braddon, *Lady Audley's Secret*, ed. David Skilton (1862; Oxford: Oxford University Press, 1987), 140.

27 See [H. L. Mansel], "Sensation Novels," *Quarterly Review* 113 (1863), 481–514, and an unattributed review "Our Female Sensation Novelists," *Christian Remembrancer* 46 (1863), 209–36.

28 Quoted by Kathleen Tillotson in her Introduction to Wilkie Collins, *The Woman in White* (1860; Boston: Houghton Mifflin, 1969), xiii.

29 "Madness in Novels," *Spectator*, February 3, 1866, 135.

30 Max Nordau, *Degeneration* (1895; Lincoln: University of Nebraska Press, 1968), 5.

31 Robert Louis Stevenson, *The Strange Case of Dr. Jekyll and Mr. Hyde, and Other Stories*, ed. Jenni Calder (1886; London: Penguin, 1979), 81.

32 Oscar Wilde, *The Picture of Dorian Gray*, ed. Isobel Murray (1891; Oxford: Oxford University Press, 1981), 18.

33 Arthur Machen, *The Great God Pan* (1894; London: Martin Secker, 1926), 86.

34 Hurley, *The Gothic Body*, 13.

35 H. G. Wells, *The Island of Dr. Moreau*, ed. Brian Aldiss (London: Dent, 1993), 78.

36 Patrick Brantlinger, *Rule of Darkness: British Literature and Imperialism, 1830–1914* (Ithaca, NY: Cornell University Press, 1988), chapter 8. For Adorno on late nineteenth-century occult, see Theodor Adorno, "Theses against Occultism," *Minima Moralia: Reflections from Damaged Life*, trans. E. F. N Jephcott (London: Verso, 1978), 240.

37 Judith Wilt, "The Imperial Mouth: Imperialism, the Gothic and Science Fiction," *Journal of Popular Culture* 14 (1981), 618–28.

JOHN KUCICH

Intellectual debate in the Victorian novel: religion, science, and the professional

The Victorian novel was predominantly a novel of domestic manners, not a novel of ideas. As a general rule, Victorian novelists did not give intellectual propositions the status of themes, or employ characters to debate them – unlike later writers such as Thomas Mann or André Gide. In fact, Victorian reviewers and readers put serious pressure on novelists to downplay intellectual subjects, which were often regarded as anti-aesthetic. Intellectual life was also considered a male preserve, and intellectual subjects a threat to "masculinize" the novel.[1] The strict separation of private and public spheres in Victorian culture necessarily set the domestic novel apart from intellectual concerns. Nevertheless, an influential branch of intellectual fiction was sustained by a few major Victorian novelists – most notably, George Eliot, George Meredith, and Thomas Hardy. Close attention to the work of these writers (which I will provide later in this chapter) can help define a set of intellectual engagements that were, in fact, broadly shared by other novelists – even if those engagements often took place beneath the surface of domestic fiction, in matters of form and method, or in the intrusion of non-literary discourses, or in novelists' ambivalent fascination with the figure of the intellectual. In fact, intellectual debates informed so many aspects of Victorian fiction so powerfully that it would not be inaccurate to say that those debates governed both the form and the substance of the genre.

The veiling of intellectual debate is, however, an important issue – not simply because of the effort it now takes to recognize how, despite appearances, Victorian novels engaged intellectual life, but also because the sublimation of ideas in Victorian fiction helped shape them in particular ways. For example, fiction was one of the few cultural domains in which women could legitimately express themselves, which meant that the novel could inflect ideas with women's perspectives – often covertly. The novel was also a medium in which the impact of ideas on private life, or on non-privileged social groups, could be dramatized. And the novel, given its natural tendency to embody ideas within a social drama, could reveal the dynamics of social power entwined with supposedly disinterested speculation. In other words, the Victorian novel did not simply engage intellectual debates, either directly or indirectly. It also embodied them in the social relations that made up its primary subject matter. For that reason, I will focus this chapter, first, on "purely" intellectual controversies; and, second, on the figure of the intellectual in fiction – as one efficient way to explore the complex fit of Victorian intellectual life within social relations.

The debates that occupied Victorian intellectuals, literary or non-literary, primarily concerned two subjects: religion and science. As George Eliot once put it: "The supremely important fact" of the period was "the gradual reduction of all phenomena within the sphere of established law, which carries as a consequence the rejection of the miraculous [and] has its determining current in the development of physical science."[2] Like Eliot, John Stuart Mill saw the relationship between religion and science as essentially an agonistic one: "The war against religious beliefs, in the last century was carried on principally on the ground of common sense or of logic; in the present age, on the ground of science."[3] As the victor in this war, science was quite clearly a central – perhaps the central – arena of intellectual life. As Beatrice Webb claimed, in 1926:

> [W]ho will deny that the men of science were the leading British intellectuals of that period; that it was they who stood out as men of genius with international reputations; that it was they who were the self-confident militants of the period; that it was they who were routing the theologians, confounding the mystics, imposing their theories on philosophers, their inventions on capitalists, and their discoveries on medical men; whilst they were at the same time snubbing the artists, ignoring the poets and even casting doubts on the capacity of the politicians?[4]

On the evidence of Victorian fiction, Webb's caricatures are exaggerated, as we will see; but her estimate of the prominence of science is not.

It may be less obvious that religion remained a dominant influence on Victorian fiction. But religious concerns saturate the fiction, and religious doubt, in particular, helped shape the way novels represented scientific ideas themselves. Although religious doubt is a common theme of histories of the Victorian period, it has, perhaps, been overstated. Church attendance held steady over the course of the century, and there were a number of lively, public exchanges within religious circles that led to popular reforms of the Established Church. Still, religious doubt was both widespread and vocal in a way it had not previously been in England, and it was particularly pronounced among the intellectual classes. Important manifestoes of doubt, like Charles Hennell's *An Inquiry Concerning the Origin of*

Christianity (1838), or the scandalous *The Nemesis of Faith* (1849), by J. A. Froude and Frank Newman, were widely read and much discussed; Arthur Clough and Matthew Arnold, in their confessional poetry, meditated on their religious doubt, as did the Poet Laureate, Alfred Lord Tennyson; and a number of leading intellectual figures, like John Henry Newman and Mill, wrote autobiographically about their crises of faith. One cause of Victorian doubt was a growing sense that moral sensibility was no longer served by the religious and social institutions that were supposed to represent it. This disjunction had a number of different sources, including: the growing humanitarianism and optimism about social reform of the Victorian age, which clashed with what was perceived by many to be the cruelty, punitiveness, and indifference of the Christian God; distaste over squabbles within and between the various English churches; the evangelical movement, which was both more strict and more passionate than the doctrines that spawned it, thereby causing adherents to look beyond the Church from their very excess of moral zeal; and the spirit of cultural relativism that arose from the Victorians' fascination with history and, late in the century, with anthropology.[5] A second, more properly intellectual cause – about which I will have much more to say – was the series of scientific discoveries (primarily those of geology and astronomy in the first half of the period, and those of evolutionary biology in the second) that seemed to put into question accounts of divine creation and the division between man and animals.

Loss of religious faith was seldom considered a subject appropriate to raise in the pages of a novel. But it was reflected in Victorian fiction through a remarkably pervasive theme: the breakdown of a sense of social wholeness. The disorienting, sometimes hellish urban landscapes of Charles Dickens, the anarchic passions found in novels by the Brontë sisters, the sexual scandals unwittingly perpetrated by Hardy's characters – all betray novelists' preoccupation with the loss of spiritual stability in a morally incoherent world. A very strong element in this lament, beginning in the 1840s, was novelists' concern with deepening alienation between the various social classes, especially in "working-class novels" like those of Charles Kingsley, Benjamin Disraeli, and Elizabeth Gaskell.

The relationship between generalized visions of an unstable or amoral world and the loss of religious faith is often expressed elliptically in fiction, as my examples have suggested. One direct sign of doubt, however, is the widespread treatment of the clergy in satirical terms. In novelists who otherwise profess a strong sense of spiritual yearning, we find malicious portraits of evangelicals, like Brocklehurst in *Jane Eyre* (1847), or Chadband in *Bleak House* (1853), or Murdstone in *David Copperfield* (1850);

or negative representations of religious devotees, like Joseph in *Wuthering Heights* (1847); or exemplary ministers who have lost their faith, like Mr. Hale in *North and South* (1855). In Margaret Oliphant's Carlingford series, the ambiguities in Oliphant's portrayal of clergymen ultimately make the Church, whether high or low, seem irrelevant to the moral lives of her characters – an irrelevance that is even more marked in the fiction of William Thackeray or Anthony Trollope, where the complete absence of religion in the psychic or emotional lives of their characters contrasts with their satires of clergymen (particularly savage in Trollope's Barchester novels). Representations of official religion in Victorian fiction, in one way or another, always show a sense of strain – an uncertainty about religion's value, or about exactly what aspects of religious institutions need correction – even if that strain rarely proceeds to an open confrontation with faith itself. This kind of strain is most evident in the work of Dickens, who, on the one hand, is the most grandiosely Christian of Victorian novelists (in *Bleak House*, for instance, Allan Woodcourt teaches the orphan Jo a few phrases from the Lord's Prayer, while Jo lies dying); but who, on the other hand, consistently attacks clergymen as humbugs, and, more importantly, makes it devastatingly clear that God is absent from the world and uninvolved in his creation. In a few novels, religious doubt was expressed openly, but was transformed into the grounds of a deeper faith. This is the theme of the most popular Victorian poem, Tennyson's *In Memoriam* (1850), and it appears as well in novels like Mrs. Humphrey Ward's *Robert Elsmere* (1888), or in minor novels Robin Gilmour has called "cassock-rippers."[6] But, in general, explicit references to religion in Victorian fiction, as well as veiled allusions to it, raised the specter of a world that had lost its foundation in a spiritual sense of order.

Perhaps for this very reason, when the Victorians did appeal to religious values – stripped of their theological or institutional moorings – those appeals were often fused with non-religious discourses of social or moral ordering. These discourses were so various that they escape coherent ordering themselves. For example, Victorian political rhetoric – of whatever party, and on whatever issue – was saturated with moral appeals. Religious rhetoric was often used to represent certain social groups as spiritual communities – whether to argue that downtrodden groups deserved political recognition, or to advocate that powerful classes be given yet more authority. The religious values that working-class advocates like Gaskell or Kingsley associated with the poor, for instance, helped to affirm radical politics; but Trollope was able to marshal such rhetoric in his affirmation of the class of British "gentlemen." Novelists of both sexes also used religious imagery in their representation of women – which could have either empowering or repressive effects. Maggie Tulliver's saintly martyrdom at the end of *The Mill on the Floss* (1860) has often been taken as an heroic act on a public stage; but Dickens's angelic women were meant to exemplify the quietistic virtues of domestic service. Messages of reconciliation between social classes were also framed in the language of religion, as in *Mary Barton* and *North and South*. And fictional polemics over colonialism were often enwrapped in religious appeals, either to advance the colonial cause (as in the novels of H. Rider Haggard), or to problematize colonialism (as in Robert Louis Stevenson's *The Ebb-Tide* [1894] or *The Beach at Falesá* [1893]). Most important of all, perhaps, religious attitudes saturated Victorian thinking about private life, and profoundly shaped the daily rituals and roles of the family, as well as shaping ideas about sexuality – to either ecstatic or ascetic ends, as one might see by comparing the rhetoric of David Copperfield's heavenly love for Agnes Wickfield to Maggie Tulliver's reading of Thomas à Kempis in her efforts to renounce her passions. The diversity of the interchanges between sexual and religious discourses in Victorian culture is, in fact, one of the most striking refutations of the notion that there was *one* Victorian discourse of sexuality. In general, the multivalence of religious discourse is an important corrective to the views of those who, like Terry Eagleton, see religion in Victorian fiction only as a repressive force, a means of pacifying the masses.[7] The mantle of moral order and authority religion provided was put to all kinds of uses.

Many novelists, especially early in the period, also tried to recreate a consoling sense of social wholeness through the secularization of traditional religious values. Victorian fiction was a deeply moralistic genre, and the moral principles it espoused – self-sacrifice, humility, honesty – were clearly Christian in origin. But the secularization of religious values and principles went far beyond the level of thematics. The providential love plots of Dickens, Thackeray, and the early Trollope, for instance, all implicitly suggest a bedrock faith in the power of Christian love – though they are divorced from religious orthodoxies or institutions of any kind, and not always self-evidently about religious values. The providential organization of Victorian fiction extends as well to the use of dreams, omens, or portents (as in novels like *Jane Eyre* or *Great Expectations* [1861]), and to the reassuring voice of an omniscient narrator – who becomes a truly God-like figure in Dickens or Trollope. Providential thinking is also instanced in Victorian fiction's widespread concern to demonstrate the "connectedness" of everything. In Victorian fiction, the prominence of coincidence and unexpected kinship implicitly affirms that what might appear to be meaningless social agglomeration is, in fact, a web of interdependent relations.

Nevertheless, such displacements of religious thinking were precarious in a scientific age. The revolutionary discoveries of science may have done as much as anything else to shatter Victorian faith in theological order, but many philosophers and writers turned to science itself to provide a secure source of moral and social unity. Although they are commonly thought to have been antithetical to one another, Victorian religion and science can actually be seen to coincide in their quest for some grounds of consoling belief in either social or moral order.

The accessibility of Victorian scientific writing, among other things, was a remarkable stimulus to this mutual quest. Nineteenth-century science shared a common language with the educated public, and scientific writing was read avidly by lay readers and writers. Victorian novelists were often familiar with the work of the evolutionist Charles Darwin, the geologist Charles Lyell, the physicist John Tyndall, and others. Conversely, scientists often drew on literary texts and metaphors. Both Tyndall and the scientific moral philosopher Thomas Huxley testified to the effect on their early careers of reading Thomas Carlyle, for instance, and Darwin frequently employs traditional narrative devices – metamorphosis, origin, teleology – in addition to his frequent allusions to literary classics. One function of these literary allusions, in Darwin and in other scientists, was simply the assertion of their cultural credentials, and one reason for the accessibility of scientific writing was the dependence of many Victorian scientists on magazine writing and the lecture circuit for their livings (before scientific research became integrated into the universities late in the century – after it had overcome Anglican resistance). Nevertheless, scientists also incorporated literature directly into the argumentative structure of their writing (Lyell does this with Ovid, and the physicist James Clerk-Maxwell with Tennyson). Tyndall, Clerk-Maxwell, the mathematician William Clifford, and others also explicitly recognized the imaginative aspects of their work. In "Matter and Force," Tyndall claimed: "Besides the phenomena which address the sense, there are laws and principles and processes which do not address the sense at all, but which must be, and can be, spiritually discerned."[8] Gillian Beer and George Levine have thoroughly demonstrated the dependence of Victorian scientific writing on literary tropology, as well as the self-consciousness of many Victorian scientists about that linguistic and epistemological dependence; Levine has gone so far as to argue that Victorian literature and science were not in any significant way separate cultures.[9]

The connections between scientific and novelistic discourse – in particular, in their common efforts to replace religious order with another, more objective kind of order – are quite extensive. They might usefully be separated into three general areas: formal or epistemological; philosophical; and professional. The formal or epistemological conjunction shows itself most plainly in the realist aesthetic of Victorian fiction. Realism was, in most instances, a complex, highly self-conscious attempt to produce knowledge of the real world. Realists decried distortions of reality they associated with the poetic, the ideal, or the metaphysical, and one aspect of their epistemological rigor was the standard of naturalistic "correspondence" that governed Victorian fiction – the assumption that novelistic action must be coherent with the facts of nature or psychology. Georg Lukács has pointed out, however, that this standard of correspondence does not mean that Victorian novelists naively believed they were presenting definitive facts or unmediated reality. Rather, they saw themselves – like scientists – to be engaged in the process of discovering or exploring the world.[10] In *Middlemarch* (1872), for example, Eliot claims to explore "the history of man," showing "how the mysterious mixture behaves under the varying experiments of time," and even the novel's section titles ("Two Temptations," "Three Love Problems") parallel the spirit of laboratory experiment. Both Victorian science and Victorian fiction were also preoccupied with ordering through typology. A great deal of novelistic characterization, in particular, derives from the classificatory schemes of nineteenth-century medicine, especially medicine's fascination with pathological types. The novels of Dickens, Wilkie Collins, and other writers constitute typologies of various kinds of monomania, for instance, and much Victorian fiction played with medical classifications of neurosis, such as hereditary insanity (crucial in *Jane Eyre* and Mary Elizabeth Braddon's *Lady Audley's Secret* [1862]), or the physiognomic display of criminal or sexual pathologies.

A number of scientific ideas or metaphors kept writers away from naive assumptions about representation – what Hardy scorned as mere "copyism" – while providing formal or epistemological principles of order for their work.[11] In addition to emphasizing the process of discovery in narrative, or the production of typological systems, novelists sometimes saw themselves to be in pursuit of natural, sociological, or psychological laws – as opposed to empirical facts. In some writers, the controlling methodological metaphor was detection – in the sensation fiction of Collins, Braddon, Charles Reade, and others, for example, or in the fabulously popular *Adventures of Sherlock Holmes* (1892) by Arthur Conan Doyle. Certainly, these methodological overlaps did not prevent writers like Dickens from repudiating the scientific spirit in literary realism

– even though Dickens himself did more than most to celebrate the deductive, scientific intelligence of characters like Bucket or Woodcourt in *Bleak House*, or like Jaggers in *Great Expectations*. But they did eventually lead to recognition of science's affinity with creative fantasy in a genre like science fiction (usually traced back to H. G. Wells), and they enabled literary philosophers from John Ruskin to George Henry Lewes to contemplate the epistemological methods science might borrow from fiction. For all these reasons, Victorian realism was the first literary aesthetic to be comprehensively shaped by the methods, the procedures, and the analytical goals of science, and to make a sophisticated awareness of scientific epistemology the basis for formal ordering.

The philosophical relationships between fiction and science are, of course, directly related to the formal or epistemological connections between the two. In both cases, novelists and scientists were acutely concerned with the correspondence of natural order to human society. Most of their concerns focused on scientific naturalism (as the principal philosophy of Victorian science came to be known by the end of the century), which was based, for the most part, on the philosophical "positivism" of Auguste Comte. Above all else, naturalism affirmed an harmonious relation between the structure of the human mind and nature. Thus far, it echoed Romantic philosophy. But naturalism rebelled against romanticism's idealistic metaphysics, which gave pride of place to the aesthetic imagination, in favor of the positivist's emphasis on rationality and objectivity. Positivism was concerned not so much with the discovery of empirical truth – as is often assumed by contemporary caricatures – but with the articulation of a system of rational laws that link phenomena together beneath the level of appearances. The systematic ordering of positivistic science, more so than its belief in empirical verification, promised a rejection of theological or metaphysical order that might nevertheless avoid relativism, by producing a theory of naturalistic law. Darwinian theory, for instance, was compatible with positivism in its insistence on the regularities of natural law; in its claims about the inextricability of human and natural order; and in its repudiation of any divine hand in this order. Tyndall evoked this harmonious, systemic confluence of human and natural order brilliantly when he declared: "all our philosophy, all our poetry, all our science, and all our art – Plato, Shakespeare, Newton, and Raphael – are potential in the fires of the sun."[12]

Positivism was also a profoundly reformative philosophy: it sought to demonstrate the progressive movement of human history towards a social order based in moral right. Positivists sometimes saw this movement reflected in the development of positivism itself, arguing that social order evolved out of despotisms based on theological and metaphysical systems towards liberal states organized around natural science. But positivism was more directly concerned with the progressive character of natural order itself. Positivism thus reflected the general tone of Victorian social optimism by presenting itself not just as a methodology, but as the means of observing or even furthering social regeneration. The philosopher Frederic Harrison declared that the extension of science to the study of man's harmonious relationship with nature had made possible a new "religious" order: science reveals "a Force towards which we can feel the highest sense of Sympathy, to whose service we can devote ourselves, whose mighty Power over us we cannot gainsay."[13] In Comte, and in his most persistent Victorian advocates – Mill, Spencer, Harrison, Lewes, the utilitarian thinker John Morley, and others – positivism became something like a religion of science, or what Comte himself called the "Religion of Humanity" – a highly developed set of beliefs that promised to substitute humanity for God as an object of worship. The principal moral opposition in positivism was that of egoism to altruism, and its principal moral goal the demonstration that altruism conformed more properly to natural order.

Although some Victorian novelists subscribed fully to the positivist faith, the novelists usually explored the philosophical difficulties that came along with positivism. For example, in its insistence on the correspondence of psychological and social truth with observable natural order, positivism was often thought to have left little room for human agency, or for personal evolution. Positivism could seem excessively deterministic, subordinating human reason to the inevitability of natural law. Darwinian theory helped further expunge the belief that human will is a force for change, especially in its repudiation of Lamarckian "intentionalist" evolution – in which organisms were said to grope towards beneficial changes and to pass on their incremental progress genetically. Moreover, despite the pieties of scientists themselves, positivism tended to leave art and the imaginative faculties in a secondary relation to truth. The strict Comtean positivist saw the goal of art as the faithful representation of a natural order verifiable only through scientific method. This problem is illustrated quite clearly in Mill's essays on Jeremy Bentham and Samuel Coleridge: as much as Mill may have sympathized with Coleridge's pursuit of meaning or under-standing through art, he allied himself finally with Bentham's scientific pursuit of objective truth. These problems became more and more intransi-gent over the course of the century, and in the last two decades of the nineteenth century, we find both philosophers and novelists emphasizing the divergence of science and aesthetic imagination – a divergence later consolidated by modernist culture's emphasis on the autonomy of the artistic symbol.

An early sign of this divergence is Dickens's defiant opposition of fact to fancy in *Hard Times* (1854), and his blistering caricature of positivist thinking in the figure of Thomas Gradgrind. Unfortunately, *Hard Times*'s famous satire has often been taken to be the primary view of mid-Victorian novelists on the relationship between science and artistic imagination. But over much of the nineteenth century, novelists were more likely to try to reconcile the optimistic social vision of positivism with human will or imagination. They were not alone in this project, since later Victorian naturalism also attempted to find a synthetic relationship between human agency or creativity and natural law. The most powerful intellectual tradition rendered in the Victorian novel, in fact, is that concerned with adjusting the relationship between human creativity and scientific naturalism, in the pursuit of a social vision that might include active moral reform.

Nowhere is this struggle illustrated more clearly than in the works of George Eliot, which moved over the course of her career from an unqualified allegiance to positivist science to a kind of romanticized scientific naturalism.[14] Eliot's work, throughout her career, dwelt on the breakdown of traditional moral values, and on the quest for an alternative personal and social order – an order that she idealized as perfecting the interdependence of individual and community. Her early novel *Adam Bede* (1859) is essentially a positivist allegory, in that Eliot portrays Dinah Morris as the pure embodiment of nature's altruistic moral order – so pure that she can serve as a reference point for the moral development of Adam himself. And through Adam, Eliot makes it clear that the sexual instinct itself is the originator of altruistic human love, as Adam's moral development depends on his growth beyond his desire for the narcissistic Hetty Sorrel and toward his love for Dinah. In these ways, the novel contends not only that social order depends on altruism, but also that the germ of altruism lies in human nature itself, and particularly in the sexual instinct – that is to say, in biology. In her next novel, *The Mill on the Floss*, Eliot repeats this theme, showing how Maggie Tulliver's instinctive desires for sexual love put her outside the degraded, commercialized society of St. Ogg's, and ultimately make her a martyr for moral progress. Maggie's progressive development through several kinds and stages of love charts out the evolution of her desire into a kind of altruism that finally – if tragically – unites her with her brother Tom and restores to her the sense of wholeness she had known with him in childhood.

But in *Middlemarch*, Eliot seems to pose once again the question – what is the relationship between biological life and moral reform? – only to answer it by satirizing her positivist figures, Lydgate and Casaubon, and their attempts to establish such a relationship in the areas of biological science and cultural anthropology, respectively. Both Lydgate's search for the "primitive tissue" and Casaubon's quest for the "key to all mythologies" attempt to find primitive ordering principles from which social perfection might be derived. Their goals are essentially congruent with Comte's: to find a fundamental natural structure that has an archetypal relationship to reformed social order. But *Middlemarch* frustrates these goals, and Eliot suggests in this novel – as she does throughout her later work – that there is no interpretation of natural order that lends itself to a single system of moral values. Instead, she suggests both that all experience is filtered through symbolic systems of various kinds, and that human attempts to project moral order onto a degraded social world depend in some fundamental way on a power of desire intrinsic to human nature, and representable in all its instabilities and uncertainties only through art. It is one of the great ironies of *Middlemarch* that while neither of its exemplary positivists discovers an original structure, the banner of political reform is carried at the end of the novel by an artist, Will Ladislaw. In her middle and late work, Eliot begins to turn to the prophetic imagination of her central characters for her faith in social regeneration.

This emphasis on imaginative yearning in Eliot's work is not so much a breach with positivism, as an attempt to reintegrate it with aesthetics. Both Eliot and George Henry Lewes (her lifetime partner and intellectual collaborator) sought, in their later work, a comprehensive study of the role of symbolization in human thought. Lewes argued that organizing structures are a property of knowing rather than being. He claimed that cognition imposes a form on sensation, but that cognition itself remains rooted in biology – that is, he sought to develop a kind of physiology of the mind. This led him to shift notions of verifiability away from external correspondences, and to locate them instead in the emotional affects of art. His *Principles of Success in Literature* opposes science to art by stressing the role of symbols in the creation of moral order, yet he resisted seeing the symbolic imagination as autonomous, arguing instead that its goal is to organize affective responses around socially-coherent principles of moral good. Lewes thus attempted to solve one of the problems of positivism – how to explain the evolution of human behavior or social order – by attributing moral agency to human will. And in her later work, Eliot herself seems preoccupied with the shaping power of human will (even giving the political reformer in *Middlemarch* the name Will). That is to say, she retains her faith in an essential and natural good, but she locates it in the imaginative as much as in the rational character of the mind. In doing so, Eliot hoped, like Lydgate, to reinforce the *rapprochement* between litera-ture and science, to effect "the most perfect interchange between science and art; offering the most direct alliance between intellectual conquest and the social good."[15] Eliot's optimism about the reconciliation of art and science through imagination was shared by a number of other novelists, most notably by George Meredith. Seconding Eliot's endorsement of spiritual aspiration, rather than analysis of the order of external nature, Meredith has a character in *The Egoist* (1879) proclaim: "We know not yet if nature be a fact or an effort to master one."[16]

Eliot herself expresses skepticism about the fulfillment of such imagina-tive yearnings in *Middlemarch* – a skepticism that will be sustained by many novelists later in the century. After all, Will Ladislaw pursues his political reforms in "those times when reforms were begun with a young hopefulness of immediate good which has been much checked in our days" (*Middlemarch*, 894). Yet in Eliot's work, this note of irony often stresses the efficacy of the human will in the historical process, even in the absence of that process's completion. Eliot may not be interested in discovering an ideal mental structure on which to base social order, but she tries to apprehend human desire for such order, and to affirm that desire through art. Dorothea Brooke's prophetic role is to defend "desiring what is perfectly good, even when we do not quite know what it is" (427). And in *Daniel Deronda* (1876), Eliot concerns herself with the role personal vision has in the moral transformation of others. Through Mordecai's transforma-tion of Daniel, and Daniel's transformation of Gwendolyn, Eliot stresses the profound moral function of the prophetic seeker, rather than trying to define an ideal moral order. Eliot thus begins to modify positivism in ways similar to those of William James's pragmatism, which, growing out of positivism as it did, nevertheless placed its faith in a bedrock humanism that, however intuitive, might guide scientific inquiry. What Eliot gives us, in effect, is a kind of demystified romanticism, in which, while fully aware of the gap between human desire and possibilities for its fulfillment, we are aware also of the natural spirituality of human desire: in her specifically scientific diction, the "inward light which is the last refinement of Energy, capable of bathing even the ethereal atoms in its ideally illuminated space" (*Middlemarch*, 194). The very title of *Middlemarch* suggests that this spiritual aspiration is an ongoing process.

Among scientists, difficulties with the adjustment of imagination to empirical science eventually caused a split between logical positivists (uninterested in the moral implications of science) and pragmatists, who, like Eliot or Meredith, came to see scientific method not as the pursuit of truth or reality, but as an instrument in service of deeper human intuitions of moral good. In the second half of the century, there were powerful if relatively isolated protests raised against the narrowness of scientific naturalism, or what the psychologist Frederic W. H. Myers referred to as the "new orthodoxy of materialistic science," which he saw as "too narrow to contain [human] feelings and aspirations."[17] Henry Sidgwick, James Ward, Alfred Russel Wallace, James Martineau and other moral and scientific philosophers disputed naturalism's claim that all human experiences and values could be referred to scientific laws and categories. The legacy of these thinkers on twentieth-century science – which has revolted against positivism on purely scientific grounds – has been negligible, but among late-century novelists, the increasing sense of a divergence between scientific and humanistic world views led in two opposite directions, which we can see latent in two very different sides of Eliot – her modified naturalistic meliorism, on the one hand; and her skeptical ironies about the possible reconciliation of human needs and worldly order, on the other.

The increasing prevalence of philosophical pessimism in the last two decades of the century, however, sustained the more tragic moods of Eliot's fiction. Two principal problems facing any optimistic account of social progress from a naturalistic point of view were the apparent cruelty of natural selection and the randomness of variation through mutation. Henry Sidgwick, in 1876, proclaimed that it was simply not possible to derive a moral consciousness harmonious with history from the principle of natural selection.[18] Similarly, Darwin himself confessed that "I cannot persuade myself that a beneficent and omnipotent God would have designedly created Ichneumonidae with the express intention of their feeding within the living bodies of caterpillars, or that a cat would play with mice."[19] Philosophers of science like Arthur Schoepenhauer and Eduard von Hartman began to develop a scientific basis for such pessimism. They argued that the innate cruelty of natural selection, together with the randomness of evolutionary variation, undermined notions of historical progress and opened the door to theories of evolutionary degeneration, as well as to visions of the insignificance of man in cosmic processes. Advances in biology, genetics, heat theory (particularly the second law of thermodynamics), atomic theory, and astronomy all reinforced this sense of man's insignificance. Darwin himself exclaimed, in *Origin of Species* (1859): "How fleeting are the wishes and efforts of man! how short his time! and consequently how poor will his products be, compared with those accumulated by nature during whole geological periods."[20]

Hardy's work dramatizes this scientific pessimism, and demonstrates how the loss of faith in a humane providence could be caused directly by scientific discoveries – despite scientific naturalism's hopefulness about the compatibility of natural and moral order. Hardy's pessimism was rooted, above all, in his conviction of man's insignificance in natural processes. This conviction arises as early as *A Pair of Blue Eyes* (1873), in a famous scene in which Charles Knight, while exploring theories of air currents at the edge of a cliff, slips and ends up hanging precariously over the edge. While suspended, Knight finds himself staring into the eyes of a fossilized trilobite exposed in the surface of the rock, and in this moment of imminent death he contemplates the meaninglessness of evolutionary time and racial development in the face of universal extinction. St. Cleeve, the scientist hero of *Two on a Tower* (1882), echoes Knight's thoughts when he proclaims: "Until a person has thought out the stars and their interspaces, he has hardly learnt that there are things much more terrible than monsters of shape, namely, monsters of magnitude without known shape. Such monsters are the voids and waste places of the sky."[21] Hardy's novels continually feature protagonists whose will to live is sapped by the knowledge of human insignificance, from Knight through Boldwood in *Far From the Madding Crowd* (1874) through Jude Fawley in *Jude the Obscure* (1895).

Just as late-Victorian scientists bemoaned the randomness of evolution, Hardy's work illustrates the prominence of chance in shaping human destiny, and the consequent dimming of faith in progress: "In the ill-judged execution of the well-judged plan of things the call seldom produces the comer, the man to love rarely coincides with the hour for loving . . . [S]uch completeness is not to be prophesied, or even conceived as possible."[22] Hardy's stress on the immutability of character – the hereditary flaws of Jude and Sue Bridehead – or on incestuous love relations in many of his late novels, underline the non-progressiveness of human life, and contribute to the pervasive atmosphere of decay and degeneration in his novels. One of Hardy's most devastating breaks with naturalistic optimism, however, was his conviction of the illusoriness of altruistic love. Hardy's novels consistently reduce love to physical desire, despite the moral fantasies of his characters. In the process, Hardy demonstrates the fundamental incompatibility between natural desire and social order – an insight that Hardy's work shares in a general way with much late-Victorian psychology, and, in particular, with Sigmund Freud. In this sense, the progressive, symbol-making potential of man, which Eliot saw as a means of reconciling imagination and science, is considered by Hardy to be delusory, and productive only of misery. Hardy's late novels are preoccupied with the tragic victory of civilization over sexual nature – most dramatically, in the misery endured by Jude and Sue because of their free union: "We went about loving each other too much," Sue laments.

> We said – do you remember? – that we would make a virtue of joy. I said it was Nature's intention, Nature's law and *raison d'etre* that we should be joyful in what instincts she afforded us – instincts which civilization had taken upon itself to thwart . . . And now Fate has given us this stab in the back for being such fools as to take Nature at her word![23]

Worse, Jude and Sue's love for each other is demystified as each discovers that the idealized object of their desire is simply a projected counterpart of their own narcissistic ego – a theme that dominates Hardy's allegorical final novel, *The Well-Beloved* (1897), and that forms one of the crucial insights of Freudian psychoanalysis as well. Hardy's novels ultimately undermine naturalistic faith, by showing that moral and religious belief are not so much statements about the world as they are the illusions by which culture seeks relief from the burden of instinctual nature. In this way, Hardy parallels Freud's ironic completion of the positivist project, in that he identifies man with nature only to discover the imperfectibility and the amorality of both.

Hardy was certainly not the only Victorian novelist to explore a scientifically-inflected pessimism, although he did ground it more completely in philosophical thought than did other writers. The adventure novels of H. Rider Haggard, for instance, are conditioned by the melancholy awareness of vanished civilizations, extinct races, and the meaninglessness of individual death. Similarly, Stevenson's adventure stories explore the animal-like, instinctual evil lurking beneath human naiveté and moral rectitude. Kinglsey's *Water Babies* (1863) is also, in some sense, a parable of human degeneration. Other late Victorian novelists did follow Eliot and Meredith, in seeing nature, as revealed by Victorian science, to be commensurate with human ideals. Samuel Butler, author of *Erewhon* (1872) and *The Way of all Flesh* (1903), was perhaps the most notable. But much late-century fiction, including the novels of George Gissing and Olive Schriener, shares Hardy's pessimism about the congruence of human desire with natural and social order. This pessimism is perhaps the most powerful philosophical legacy of Victorianism to the modern period, and it contributes to the widening division between art and science in the twentieth century.

Finally, the impact of science on the novel – in particular its quest to find or impose secular order – can be seen in fictional representations of professionalism. The professionalization of intellectual life increased dramatically over the course of the nineteenth century – particularly in medicine and law, but in other fields as well. Early in the century, intellectuals tended to see themselves as amateurs; but intellectual life grew increasingly specialized as the natural sciences were turned into a discipline, as the reformed universities incorporated scientific training and research, and as professional organizations and credentialing institutions came to regulate standards of professional competence. Novelists participated in this development (the Society of Authors, the first literary professional organization, was founded in 1884, for example), but in highly ambivalent ways. In the second half of the century, marketplace changes enabled writers to see themselves as self-sufficient producers of their work. The rise of a unified mass market, the growth of a middle-class reading public, and technological innovations in publishing that reduced prices – all contributed to the professional autonomy of the novelist. Moreover, novelists took from scientists an ideology of professional exactitude – not just exactitude as a formal method, but as a complex code of ethics, decorum, and business practices that helped define the difference between the novelistic artist and the hack. Moreover, for novelists as well as for scientists, professionalism signified the achievement of a kind of intellectual order and authority formerly represented by the Church. But novelists could never be entirely comfortable regarding themselves in a professional light. Among other things, the truth-telling claims of science and the truth-telling claims of realism came increasingly to clash – the more so late in the century, as the scientific outlook became less humanistic, less congenial to concerns with human agency and morality; and as novelists sought to recover the romantic faith in imagination that had lapsed through the mid-Victorian years. Social resistance to extending the label "professional" to novelists was also difficult to overcome, and in both compensation and prestige writers found themselves lagging behind scientific professionals. Increasing philosophical pessimism about scientific discoveries further weakened the novelist's desire to emulate the professional – even though professionalism had come to seem the primary route to intellectual authority after mid-century. Given novelists' ambivalence about professionalism, the convergence of epistemological or formal principles that I presented earlier eventually became more of a grounds of competition for intellectual authority between scientists and novelists than of comfortable co-existence.

The strongest sign of this competition lies in the contested figure of the professional intellectual as a character in Victorian novels – beginning in the 1860s, and continuing through the end of the century. The rivalry between scientific or professional intellectuals and non-scientific intellectuals, as guardians of truth, surfaces clearly, for example, in Wilkie Collins's pitting of these two groups against one another. Collins consistently offers us pretentious scientific professionals who are outwitted in their detective-like search for truth by what we might call "cultural intellectuals" – artists, writers, dilettantes, proto-bohemians – who occupy the margins of intellectual life, and who combine the methods of scientific deduction with creative imagination. In *The Woman in White* (1860), doctors and lawyers are played for fools by the villainous trickster Count Fosco, who combines a wide range of scientific knowledge with artistic and imaginative brilliance. But Fosco himself, who is a negative image of the (upper-class) artist as charlatan, is in turn overcome by the supremely earnest Walter Hartright. A humble draughtsman, journalist, and explorer (i.e., a non-specialist), Hartright, like Fosco, combines rationality and creativity. But he does so with the respectable – and not necessarily professional – middle-class goal of "present[ing] the truth always in its most direct and most intelligible aspect."[24] In *The Moonstone* (1868), a dreamy dilettante and erstwhile student of philosophy, Franklin Blake, proves to be more than a match in investigative acumen for the novel's assortment of bumbling private detectives, lawyers, and medical professionals. And in *Armadale* (1866), the bohemian Ozias Midwinter outdoes a psychologist in his interpretation of the dreams of Allan Armadale – dreams that warn of impending disaster. In these novels, the intellectual power of the aesthete is proved in very scientific terms – through the aesthete's ability to solve mysteries and produce truth – at the expense of the various scientific professionals who fail in the same quest.

Yet Collins's heroes always seek legitimation in the same professional arenas that they disdain. Playing on a conventional Victorian linkage of literature and the law, Hartright conceives his narrative as a series of depositions, "as the story of an offense against the laws is told in Court by more than one witness – with the same object, in both cases."[25] Collins's heroes want not so much to displace professional intellectuals as to earn their respect. Similar kinds of ambivalence haunt most representations of professionals in Victorian fiction. In Dickens, "helping" professionals – doctors, in particular, who are often represented as relatively autonomous, tender-hearted, and spontaneous – are good, and sometimes play the role of redeemer for other good characters. But lawyers, seen as bureaucratic functionaries for a cruel and inhuman society, are bad. In Hardy, the figure of the pedagogue is often seen as both inspiring and misleading. Jude's mentor, Mr. Phillotson, plants in Jude a dangerous desire for intellectual and quasi-religious fulfillment through a university education, but later proves to be only a figure of moral degeneration himself. Angel Clare's anti-religious, progressive education leaves him strikingly unprepared to confront the dilemmas of female sexuality and social convention, and in some ways makes him more intellectually brittle, and less empathetic, than his evangelical parents.

If the professional intellectual is on trial in late-Victorian fiction, it is not just as a nemesis of the novelist. The professional, as the quintessential symbol of intellectual order, embodies the ambiguities of Victorian intellectual life itself, and often merges them with the discourse of intra-class struggle. That is to say, many of the very same questions that were raised in the scientific debates I have outlined – questions about human agency and determinism, about the role of imagination in knowledge, about the prospects for moral regeneration through secular knowledge, about egoism and altruism, and about the inhospitality of the universe – were transformed in Victorian fiction into questions raised about the power and authority of the professional intellectual class itself. Secondary professional characters (for the professional is rarely a central character) regularly generate these questions by their actions. Such characters often provoke Victorian protagonists to ask themselves whether they have the will-power and the resources to survive crises on their own, or whether they must resign themselves to the cold prognoses of doctors and lawyers. Collins's protagonists often do find such resources in themselves; Hardy's characters do not. Professionals sometimes force protagonists to determine whether their imaginative and creative powers can prove more fruitful than the rational calculations of the professional himself. Eliot's heroines often exemplify this triumph, but even Brontë's Jane Eyre has spiritual visions that seem more compelling than the world-view of the cold and calculating professional clergyman, St. John Rivers. Professionals sometimes compel protagonists to wonder whether the ordered world of professional knowledge is an enabling or a repressive one. Jaggers in *Great Expectations* presents Pip with a chilling vision of all the children in the world being "so much spawn, to develop into the fish that were to come to his net – to be prosecuted, defended, forsworn, made orphans, bedeviled somehow," but then lionizes himself by describing Estella, whom he spares, as "one pretty little child out of the heap who could be saved" – a rescue with highly problematic consequences for both Estella and Pip.[26] Professionals make protagonists try to determine which social group owns a disinterested and morally redemptive intellectual vision – the professional intellectual, or his half-brother, the cultural intellectual. This test is enacted throughout Victorian fiction, from *Middlemarch* through *Hard Times* to the novels of Hardy and Collins. Finally, professionals like Tulkinghorn in *Bleak House* or Dr. Downward in *Armadale* seem to embody the harsh and unforgiving, sadistically rational social world – much like Hardy's nature – that stands in the way of the protagonists' human desires.

Such competition over prophetic authority makes it clear that the professional is not just a spokesperson for disinterested intellectual dogma in late-Victorian novels. In the latter part of the century, Victorian novels reveal that he (professionals are almost always male) is also an interested player in the scramble for social authority, whose intellectual views are inextricable from class competition of the most vulgar kind. The novel's ambivalent cultural status – both an intellectual exercise and a marginalized social practice – makes this recognition of the relationship between ideas and social power seem inevitable. But the ambiguities of such recognition are applied to the figure of the professional with unusual ferocity, as that figure is used to merge questions about intellectual ordering systems with questions about the disordering effects of social power.

The most dramatic instance of the inextricability of ideas and power in Victorian fiction is its representation of conflicts between professionals and women. Women were systematically excluded from most aspects of Victorian professional life. Though they did begin to make inroads as professional educators late in the century, they were absolutely excluded from most other professions – certainly from careers in religion or science. As a result, Victorian fiction is littered with frustrated intellectual women, especially in the novels of Eliot, but also in those of Charlotte Brontë, Collins, Gaskell, and others.[27] Reade's *A Woman-Hater* (1877) is a particularly strong indictment of the medical profession for refusing to admit talented women. As Mary Poovey has argued, the relation between professionalism and women was a charged one because professional work bore such crucial resemblances to the domestic work of middle-class women. Such work was not considered wage-labor; it depended on assumptions of disinterest; and, in the case of doctors and lawyers, it entered into deeply private matters. Above all, both forms of work were regarded as unalienated labor, free of the taints of the capitalist market-place, and they took a certain amount of dignity from this distantiation. But the male professional in Victorian culture also strove to disavow the association of his work with feminine labor, and to stress its competitive public value instead. Poovey demonstrates how David Copperfield's growth into a professional writer depends on a basic contradiction: on his identification with the supposed "effortlessness" of women's labor, and on his rigid distinction between the competitive successes of his own work and the indifference to success or recognition of his angelic wife, Agnes.[28] The virulence of professional antipathy to intellectual women, then, had deeply ideological sources.

Many Victorian novels champion women in this conflict, dwelling on the injustices of professional power over women. The most popular novel of the century, Ellen (Mrs. Henry) Wood's *East Lynne* (1861), contrasts the social rise of the middle-class male lawyer with the fall of his formerly aristocratic wife, who ends up – however implausibly – as the governess to her own children. Sarah Grand's late-century blockbuster *The Heavenly Twins* (1893) ends with a chilling description of a doctor's ability to overpower his wife by diagnosing her as a hysteric. Many of these novels assert, in turn, the power of women's non-professional creative intelligence. From this point of view, even Eliot's struggles with questions of reason and emotion can be seen as attempts to reaffirm the proper place of women (whom Eliot identified perhaps too rigidly with emotion) in intellectual life.

It was not simply those excluded from professional life who saw professional intellectuals as problematic social figures. The Victorian middle class had generally ambivalent attitudes towards professionals and their increasing grasp on social power. On the one hand, the professional had come to replace the clergyman as a source of moral counsel and disinterested advice. On the other hand, though, the professional was regarded as something of a servant. Moreover, the professional secularization of knowledge sometimes made professional authority seem irreverent or even fraudulent. Professionals were thus regarded both as powerful figures of authority and as dangerous usurpers. As a representative of the kind of authority – grounded in moral values and in foundational knowledge about the world – that used to be claimed by religion, the professional intellectual absorbs all the reverence and hope, as well as the fear of repression and fraud, that accompanied Victorian attitudes toward the triumph of science. In the hands of late-Victorian novelists, this ambivalence often figures the general undermining of intellectuals' moral authority as a class struggle internal to the upper-middle class.

Hope in and dependence on the intellectual as a kind of surrogate clergyman could also slide into disillusionment, and late-Victorian doubt about the professional's claims to disinterested authority prepares the way for increasingly cynical visions of the intellectual as an entrepreneur – which are rampant in twentieth-century culture. Exposure of the intellectual as a class-bound figure, in novels from the 1860s onwards, together with the destabilizing of scientific certainties towards the end of the century – through the strange discoveries of late-century astronomy, and, eventually, through quantum physics – helped shatter the Victorians' faith in the self-evidence of intellectual authority. These developments suggest one reason why intellectual paradigms have not dominated fiction in the twentieth century as they once did in the Victorian period, when novelists mixed morality, science, and social relations in an exhilarating and provocative compound centrally related to the deepest anxieties of the age.

They also suggest one cause of the breakdown of Victorian distinctions between "disinterested" public life and the various interests of the domestic sphere, distinctions that were circumvented in a number of ways by the sometimes sublimated but always powerful intellectual roots of Victorian fiction.

NOTES

1 See Nancy Armstrong, "The Rise of Feminine Authority in the Novel," *Novel* 15 (1982),127–45
2 George Eliot, "The Influence of Rationalism," *Fortnightly Review* 1 (1865), 55
3 John Stuart Mill, "Theism," *The Collected Works of John Stuart Mill*, ed. J. M. Robson, 33 vols. (Toronto: University of Toronto Press, 1963–75), X: 429.
4 Beatrice Webb, *My Apprenticeship* (London: Longmans, Green & Co, 1926), 126–27.
5 See Robin Gilmour's excellent discussion of the moral basis for Victorian doubt in *The Victorian Period: The Intellectual and Cultural Context of English Literature, 1830–1890* (London: Longman, 1993), 85–94.
6 *Ibid.*, 89.
7 Terry Eagleton, "The Rise of English," *Literary Theory: An Introduction* (Minneapolis: University of Minnesota Press, 1983), 17–53.
8 John Tyndall, "Matter and Force," *Fragments of Science: A Series of Detached Essays, Addresses, and Reviews* 2 vols. (New York: D Appleton & Co., 1889), II: 56.
9 See Gillian Beer, *Darwin's Plots: Evolutionary Narrative in Darwin, George Eliot, and Nineteenth-Century Fiction* (London: Routledge & Kegan Paul, 1983) and *Open Fields: Science in Cultural Encounter* (Oxford: Clarendon Press, 1996); George Levine, *The Realistic Imagination: English Fiction from Frankenstein to Lady Chatterley* (Chicago: University of Chicago Press, 1981), and "One Culture: Science and Literature," in George Levine, ed., *One Culture: Essays in Science and Literature* (Madison: University of Wisconsin Press, 1987), 3–32.
10 Georg Lukács, *Studies in European Realism* (New York: Grosset & Dunlap, 1964) See esp. 11, 83–84.
11 Thomas Hardy, "The Science of Fiction,"in *Life and Art* (New York: Greenberg, 1925), 87.
12 John Tyndall, "Scientific Use of the Imagination," *Fragments of Science*, II: 453.
13 Frederic Harrison, *The Philosophy of Common Sense* (New York: Macmillan, 1907), 414.
14 I am deeply indebted, for my reading of Eliot's development – as well as for my general perspectives on Meredith and Hardy – to Peter Allan Dale, *In Pursuit of a Scientific Culture: Science, Art, and Society in the Victorian Age* (Madison: University of Wisconsin Press, 1989)
15 George Eliot, *Middlemarch* (1872; Harmondsworth: Penguin, 1965), 174.
16 George Meredith, *The Egoist* (1879), in *The Works of George Meredith*, Memorial Edition, 29 vols. (New York: Scribner's, 1909–12), XIV: 262.

17 F W. H. Myers, Introduction, E. Gurney, F. W. H. Myers, and F. Podmore, *Phantasms of the Living*, 2 vols. (London: Trubner & Co., 1886), I: liv–lv.

18 Henry Sidgwick, "Theory of Evolution in Its Application to Practice," *Mind* 1 (1876), 65–66.

19 *The Life and Letters of Charles Darwin*, ed Francis Darwin 2 vols. (New York: D. Appleton & Co., 1896), I: 554–55.

20 Charles Darwin, *Origin of Species*, ed John Burrow (Harmondsworth: Penguin, 1968), 133.

21 Thomas Hardy, *Two on a Tower*, The New Wessex Edition (1882; London: Macmillan, 1975), 56.

22 Thomas Hardy, *Tess of the d'Urbervilles*, The New Wessex Edition (1891; London: Macmillan, 1975), 67.

23 Thomas Hardy, *Jude the Obscure*, The New Wessex Edition (1895; London: Macmillan, 1975), 348.

24 Wilkie Collins, *The Woman in White* (1860; New York: Oxford, 1973), 1.

25 *Ibid.* See also George Eliot, *Adam Bede* (Harmondsworth: Penguin, 1980), 177: "my strongest effort is . . . to give a faithful account of men and things as they have mirrored themselves in my mind . . . I feel as much bound to tell you as precisely as I can what that reflection is, as if I were in the witness-box, narrating my experience on oath."

26 Charles Dickens, *Great Expectations* (1861; Harmondsworth: Penguin, 1965), 425.

27 See Deirdre David, *Intellectual Women and Victorian Patriarchy: Harriet Martineau, Elizabeth Barrett Browning, George Eliot* (Ithaca, NY: Cornell University Press, 1987)

28 Mary Poovey, *Uneven Developments: The Ideological Work of Gender in Mid-Victorian England* (Chicago: University of Chicago Press, 1988), esp Ch. 4, "The Man-of-Letters Hero: *David Copperfield* and the Professional Writer," 89–125.

II

ROBERT WEISBUCH

Dickens, Melville, and a tale of two countries

Herman Melville, a subscriber to *Harper's Monthly Magazine* in 1852, would have found there the serialization of Charles Dickens's *Bleak House*. Melville had just completed *Moby Dick* and was busily composing *Pierre, or The Ambiguities*. *Bleak House* might well have startled this alert, despairing American mind. Dickens, the best-known, best-selling Victorian author on the New York newsstands, could have been seen by Melville as writing a novel unmistakably indebted to the works of Nathaniel Hawthorne, the mentor-author whom Melville had nominated as the American equivalent of Shakespeare. If one considers Melville's "Bartleby the Scrivener: A Tale of Wall Street" (first published anonymously in *Putnam's Magazine* in 1853) it seems he fired back across the Atlantic a rejoinder to Dickens's apparent appropriation of Hawthorne. This textual encounter moves us quickly to the literary relations between British Victorian novelists and their American contemporaries, and it suggests how American writers in the mid-nineteenth century enacted a second war of independence in their major writings.

The very title of *Bleak House* would not have been sufficient to make Melville think of another House, Hawthorne's Seven Gables, but after one or two installments, Melville might well have suspected that Hawthorne's explicit moral issue in his novel – "the truth, namely, that the wrong-doing of one generation lives into the successive ones"[1] – was getting illustrated anew in Dickens's Chancery suit of Jarndyce and Jarndyce. Further, the ruinous obsession with the suit on the part of Dickens's young Richard Carstone, an obsession shared by many of the novel's characters as a kind of disease, recalls the delusion on the part of Hawthorne's Pynchons, whose "impalpable claim" to a vast Western territory "resulted in nothing more solid than to cherish, from generation to generation, an absurd delusion of family importance." Hawthorne avers that, by the writing of a will, "A dead man sits on all our judgement seats" (*House of the Seven Gables*, 19) and Dickens's Chancery makes that notion of judgment into a literal, contemptible court. Finally, in each work inheritance becomes the passing down from generation to generation of a consciousness of original sin.

Literary similarity, however, is not always a sign of influence, but the disclosure in *Bleak House* of the curse of the seventeenth-century Restoration sympathizer Lady Dedlock upon the Dedlock progeny certainly suggests Hawthorne's presence in Dickens's literary imagination. As the Dedlocks' loyal housekeeper, Mrs. Rouncewell, recounts, Lady Dedlock is supposed to have said, "I will walk here, until the pride of this house is humbled. And when calamity, or when disgrace is coming to it, let the Dedlocks listen for my step!"[2] In *The House of the Seven Gables* (1851), "old Matthew Maule, it is to be feared, trode downward from his own age to a far later one, planting a heavy footstep, all the way, on the conscience of a Pynchon" (*House of the Seven Gables*, 20). In *Bleak House*, kindly Mr. Jarndyce mournfully tells Esther Summerson, "we can't get out of the suit on any terms for we are made parties to it, and *must* be parties to it, whether we like it or not" (*Bleak House*, 73); in Hawthorne's novel, Maule's curse and Judge Pynchon's power hang over Hawthorne's characters like a foreordination. It is notable, too, that in both works this sense of inescapable inheritance of responsibility for an original sin is ameliorated by the eventual establishment of pastoral serenity. Hawthorne's lovers "transfigure the earth, and make it second Eden again" (*House of the Seven Gables*, 307); and in the grounds of the second Bleak House, replete with "the shadows of the apple-trees" (*Bleak House*, 648), a widowed Ada sees the realization of her wish that her infant son might grow up to think of his father, the Chancery-doomed Richard, as "ruined by a fatal inheritance, and restored through me" (624).

The most telling echoes of Hawthorne's *House* tend to occur more specifically in that half of *Bleak House* that is told by a grimly satiric narrator confronting the public sphere of Chancery. In the sections of the novel devoted to the domestic sphere, Esther Summerson's autobiography, they appear more generally. Yet as the serialization continued in *Harper's*, there are aspects of Esther's story that could have led Melville to a second discovery, and to thoughts of another nineteenth-century American novel. Esther's very existence is revealed to be the result of a clandestine love affair between a Captain Hawdon and the woman who came to be the current Lady Dedlock. That is to say, in *Bleak House*, an illegitimate child is born of a passionate romance to a woman who must keep the guilty secret of the child's paternity – which echoes the situation in Hawthorne's *The Scarlet Letter* (1850) where Hester Prynne cannot reveal the paternity of her daughter. Furthermore, Esther is hounded by an elderly man, "black" in appearance, dim-eyed but acutely perceptive, cold, formal, and inscrutable: the lawyer Tulkinghorn, who is remarkably similar to Hawthorne's Chillingworth.[3]

Dickens's readers have long noted the psychological complexity of Esther Summerson; Dickens's assessment of Hawthorne's skill in character-ization may well be one reason for this complexity. He termed "the psychological part" of *The Scarlet Letter* "very much overdone, and not truly done"[4] and it is possible that as an instructive example of psycho-logical characterization, he endowed Esther Summerson with the troubled psyche imperfectly realized in Hawthorne's characters. However, he simul-taneously seems to underplay this element of Esther. In the first instance, much of Esther's altruism is the result of her wrathful godmother's sense of inherited sin: "Your mother . . . is your disgrace as you were hers" (*Bleak House*, 180). This, one could argue, is what makes Esther dutiful – that word that she repeats as a mantra – to the point of agreeing to a marriage proposal from Jarndyce that is asexual and possesses incestuous implica-tions. But Dickens frequently undercuts Esther's psychological reality by the sentimental tributes of other characters: "You're a pattern, you know, that's what you are," exclaims the otherwise reserved Inspector Bucket (606). And elsewhere, as Esther coyly reports the compliments of others towards herself, she can seem embarrassing in her desire to accrue the esteem of all around her. It is possible that Dickens's low opinion of Hawthorne's success at psychological characterization propels him into a more complex form of conveying individual character than is previously apparent from his novels; yet at the same time, he seems to undercut his own attempts as he falls into sentimental stereotyping of the sweet Victorian heroine.

In general, however, the influence of Hawthorne is mostly suggestive of a competitive admiration. Interestingly, Hawthorne himself betrays the influ-ence of Dickens upon his work, as one sees in *The House of the Seven Gables*, his most British-seeming novel. Hawthorne never writes elsewhere as he does, for instance, as he describes the motionless body of Judge Pynchon: "Rise up, thou subtile, worldly, selfish, iron-hearted hypocrite, and make thy choice, whether still to be subtile, worldly, selfish, iron-hearted, and hypocritical, or to tear these sins out of thy nature, though they bring the life-blood with them" (*House of the Seven Gables*, 283). Consider this passage from *Bleak House*:

> Call the death by any name Your Highness will, attribute it to whom you will, or say it might have been prevented how you will, it is the same death eternally – inborn, inbred, engendered in the corrupted humours of the vicious body itself, and that only – Spontaneous Combustion, and none other of all the deaths that can be died. (346)

And, to return to the literary exchanges between Melville, Hawthorne, and Dickens, consider the events in *Bleak House* that preface the extraordinary spontaneous combustion of Mr. Krook.

In *Bleak House*, Krook's imminent demise is anticipated by a noxious odor that is detected by Mr. Swills, "a comic vocalist, professionally engaged by Mr. J. G. Bogsby" (347). Mr. Bogsby then mentions the odor to one Miss M. Melvilleson, "a lady of some pretensions to musical ability, likewise engaged by Mr. J. G. Bogsby" (347). Earlier, Miss M. Melvilleson is described by a gossip as "married a year and a half, though announced as Miss M. Melvilleson, the noted siren," and we are informed that her baby "is clandestinely conveyed to the Sol's Arms every night to receive its natural nourishments during the entertainments" (337). Melville's mother's name was Maria and as read by Melville this set of coincidences suggests Dickens might seem to insult Melville by gendering him female with a covert child, or by presenting him as a lower-class comic vocalist. This minor, comic coincidence makes one wonder how Melville might have felt while reading a novel probably understood by him as strongly influenced by Hawthorne. In creative response, Bogsby becomes Bartleby; the Sol's Arms is darkened to the sunless Wall Street; the utterance of Mr. Swills that the noxious fumes emanating from Krook's room make him feel "like a post office, for he hadn't a single note in him" (374) is transformed into the rumor that Bartleby had worked in the Dead Letter Office. Indeed, Melville's narrator, himself a Chancery lawyer, exclaims, with a look back not only at Bartleby but also at Krook, "Dead Letters! Does it not sound like dead men?"[5]

In short, Melville may be said to have taken on Dickens, and it is this sense of competitive jousting that characterizes much of the relationship between transatlantic literary cultures during the Victorian period. Dickens represented the dominant, established, inherited literary world and Melville the still-subordinate, still-struggling one. I shall return to the competition between Dickens and Melville at the end of this chapter; for the moment I wish to explore the important contemporary debate about the place of literature in nineteenth-century American society, and in particular, the novel.

What should the novel become in a democratic United States? This question, or its larger version that asks how an American literature might be created, dominates the pages of the cultural periodicals in the first half of the nineteenth century. The question – and Melville's probable retort to Dickens as an attempt to answer it – is informed by a distinctly post-colonial set of attitudes. A spirit of hostile assertion, its vehemence in each case a function of cultural insecurities, prevails on both sides of the Atlantic. I want briefly to document the stormy climate for British and American novelists in order to understand why competitive mockery was the keynote of the relations and why national loyalties undercut personal friendships and various forms of individual admiration. Then I wish to look at two effects of the transatlantic battle for control of the novel: first at the shaping of individual careers, and then at the ways in which these contestations shape the entire project of writing fiction in the United States, with the British novelists handing to the Americans the key to creating a New World advantage.

In a verse written in 1788, the American poet Philip Freneau asks with frustration, "Can we never be thought to have learning or grace / Unless it be brought from that damnable place / Where tyranny reigns with her impudent face?" The damnable place is England, the colonial power from which the new states had freed themselves politically but to which they were still bound culturally. The cultural domination is unabated, Freneau implies, and it stifles native thought. It would seem that the domination is felt well into the nineteenth century, as one learns from the remarks of Orestes Brownson about a minor novel, "none but an American could have written it; for none but an American could have shown us the same evident effort to write like an Englishman . . ." In the middle of the century, Margaret Fuller observed that most American books were, simply, "English books," and in 1847 Walt Whitman wrote in the *Brooklyn Eagle* that "as long as we copy with a servile imitation, the very cast-off literary fashions of London" American cultural destiny will be doomed to imitation and impoverishment.[6]

Of course, during this very period many of the novels and poems that now rank as American classics came to be written. Even the degree to which a distinctively American literature did not recognize itself as such is another symptom of the influence of British culture. Sydney Smith's 1820 query, "In the four quarters of the globe, who reads an American book?," is the best-known example among hundreds. They stretch from an announcement in *The Quarterly* in 1809, "No work of distinguished merit in any branch has yet been produced among them," to *The Universal Review* declaring in 1860: "For almost every work of note which has been produced there, the mother nation can show a better counterpart." These failures of cultural achievement were assessed by the British as inevitable, as one sees in the observation by the anonymous critic in an 1818 number of *The British Critic*: Americans possess "neither history, nor romance, nor poetry, nor legends, on which to exercise their genius, and kindle their imagination." Again, in 1825, in *The Literary Gazette*: "Unlike other nations . . . she [has] no religion, no manners, and, above all, no language, essentially her own. Peopled chiefly by the fanatic, the adventurer, and the criminal." In general, from this perspective, America lacked an authentic language, a powerful history, and inspiring heroes: how could she have poets?[7] No wonder, then, that with such goading, New York became the center of "Young America" clubs trying to force a national literature into being.

Two qualifications do not change the main lines of this narrative of literary competition, but they deserve notation. First, in America, a party of literary loyalists had some strength; for example, a character from Long-fellow's *Kavanagh* (1849) observes that because Americans "are, in fact English under a different sky, – I do not see how our literature can be very different from theirs."[8] And, second, the British were not uniformly scornful. George Eliot called Hawthorne "a great favourite of mine," reread *The Scarlet Letter* with Lewes seven months before beginning to write *Adam Bede*, and openly allowed Hawthorne's Hester to inspire her characterization of Hetty (given name, Hester) Sorrel.[9] More generally, in the last two decades of the nineteenth century no fewer than ninety editions of Hawthorne's works were brought out by British publishers – as well as thirty-five editions of Poe, sixty of Irving, fifty of Cooper, and sixty of Twain. Clarence Ghodes, chalking up the score, notes that "the English people read more books by American authors than by all the writers of the European continent combined."[10]

Even so, the British were more insulting than otherwise, and in America insult was a spur to the literary imagination. Those who believed the new nation must fashion a new literature held sway, and for at least five reasons that combined to shape the debate, which was not merely whether someone in the United States might write a good novel, but what a distinctly American novel might be. The first encouragement to the shaping of a national novel was the rise of nationalism itself, especially the romantic folk nationalism that took root in eighteenth-century Germany and found its most effective advocate in Mme. De Stael. The notion that the universal must spring from the intensely local spurred Americans to find, or at least invent, a national past. Second, the achievement of political independence made cultural subordination to Britain unacceptable. Like their seventeenth-century forebears, the original settlers, American rebels had to justify independence on the basis of being exceptional, of possessing a special destiny, while simultaneously reaffirming European roots as a defense against charges of "going savage." An American literature was required either way, as a proof of superior difference or as evidence of civilized equality.

The democratic nature of America's independence constituted a third pressure. Democracy became a distasteful concept for those British who lamented the loss of their colony, and even the most liberal Victorian could become less so when confronted by a lost America. A critic in *The Atheneum* wrote in 1829 that not only did America lack a literature but that "we do not believe it can have one till its institutions are fundamentally changed." Certainly, Americans would agree to a connection between political system and literary culture, and Emerson's famous plaint, "We have listened too long to the courtly muses of Europe" makes that link, as does Orestes Brownson's sally that, despite some excellences, English literature "is not exactly the literature for young republicans."[11] Americans worried about the effects of democratic leveling but they also could be inspired to imagine what it might mean to make the democratic a literary principle: what might be realized, for instance, in a radical rearrangement of established hierarchies as found in Whitman's *Song of Myself*. Given that the novel is in itself an essentially democratic form that affords importance to the lives of ordinary people, it would seem to be tailor-made for an America that had trumpeted such principles in its federal documents.

Two additional causes for the special pressure for Americans not merely to write but to write as Americans are of a different sort. The European myth of the West, which has classical and early Christian origins, the notion that God's plan would be fulfilled where the sun sets, is powerfully revivified in myths of the American continent. Christopher Columbus wrote, "God made me the messenger of the new heaven and the new earth of which he spoke in the Apocalypse"; Harriet Beecher Stowe found in Cotton Mather's *Magnolia* her conviction of "the glorious future of the United States of America . . . commissioned to bear the light of liberty and religion through all the earth and to bring in the great millennial day"; and Thoreau would ask, if America is not "the Great Western pioneer whom the nations follow," then "to what extent does the world go on, and why was America discovered?"[12] Anxiety increases in proportion to the claim that the failure of an American literature and its culture will doom the entire world, whose destiny is now America's. Indeed, there had long existed in English culture a negative version of the West as representing, in Richard Slotkin's description, a horrifying regression to savagery, a land of "the sunset, death, darkness, passion, and dreams," the latter mostly all for the worse.[13] It is the place of de-creation, the swampy, New Eden of Dickens's *Martin Chuzzlewit* (1844).

Finally, the Puritan custom of considering one member of the community as the microcosmic representative of the entire community, and of believing the community to be the community of God, contributes to the idea of the individual author becoming "The American Author," and of "The American Author" as the embodiment of Spirit itself. Hence a young Emerson's complaint when he met the great English writers Landor, Coleridge, Carlyle, and Wordsworth: he found them disappointingly "sensible, well-read, earnest men, not more."[14] The author as prophet, as actualized Spirit, is part of the New England tradition that the nineteenth century half inherits, half rediscovers. It is a demanding role, scripted with unreasonable expectations, that led to the outsized but oddly sincere public personalities of writers such as Thoreau and Whitman most obviously, who deliberately confuse their literary and actual personae. Emily Dickinson and Henry James are more subtle examples of this same fusion, and later writers from Twain, Hemingway, Fitzgerald, and Gertrude Stein to Henry Miller and Norman Mailer are more blatant ones. From the giddy perch of an impossibly unreasonable demand to be both lofty prophet and public personality, this requirement to actualize the literary vision in daily life allows the American to look down upon the British nineteenth-century writer as uninteresting and conventional. And it enables Americans to transport their habit of nominating a few individuals as above and beyond the ordinary realm of literary production to the creation of "The British Writer": Matthew Arnold but not Francis Newman, Tennyson over Browning, Dickens but not George Eliot.

For these same reasons that writers in America were encouraged or even pressured to consider themselves "American Writers," Anglo-American literary influence was generally perceived as more than personal or individual. It was felt as a defining force on the emerging national literature that must be contested. The contesting inclined to the historically selective, and contemporaries seemed to matter more than eighteenth-century British authors. James Fenimore Cooper argued that pre-Revolutionary authors were common Anglo-American property, and most Americans agreed. Alexander Pope and his contemporaries became ignored figures in the early nineteenth century and the Romantic poets emerged as the chief opponents in the American fight for transatlantic cultural supremacy. American responses to the Romantic poets are profound, a complex mix of acceptance, extension, and completion on the one hand, and of subtle misreadings, cunning transformations, and troubled refusals on the other. At the beginning of the Victorian period, the battle begins to heat up: as British writers begin to push American literature off the bookstand shelves in Manhattan, angry refutations, destructive parodies, deliberately wild misreadings, and undisguised competition becomes the norm. And the novel becomes the chief genre at stake.

In this battle, the careers of American novelists tend to be directed by the worry of American difference, a struggle to define national originality. Edgar Allan Poe's relationship to Dickens is particularly instructive in this regard. Poe began by accusing Dickens of plagiarizing from Joseph Neal, the Philadelphia journalist and humorist whose *Charcoal Sketches; or, Scenes in a Metropolis* (1838) was reprinted in Britain; he then took a warm personal note to him from Dickens that recounted how Parke Godwin, a political journalist, had reversed the usual process of composition by writing a story from end to beginning, and claimed the information about Godwin was his own, not that of Dickens. Next Poe claimed that backward composition was his own invention. And, finally, Poe was convinced that Dickens had written an anonymous review asserting that Poe's poems were plagiarisms of Tennyson's. Dickens had not written the review and the review itself made no accusation of plagiarism, which eventually forced Poe to concede that while this may have been the case, a lot of Americans *had* plagiarized Tennyson.[15]

Poe is unique among his contemporaries, but there is no one utterly apart from him either, not even Cooper, to think of an author considered more psychologically balanced than Poe. Before he became known as the American Walter Scott, Cooper attempted to become the American Jane Austen. He began his career by responding to Austen's last novel *Persuasion* (1818) with the remark, "I could write a better book myself." This better book, as unfortunate as its strange title, was *Precaution* (1820), an irritatingly awkward treatment of English country life. By the next year, Cooper had taken Scott as his model. He grew eventually to despise this comparison with Scott, and despite a strong personal friendship between the two men, often wrote harshly of him. And yet he chose, in *The Spy* (1821), to dramatize an historically important conflict (the Revolution) between opposing members of a single race as mirrored in a family conflict; in other words, he adopted the conventions of plot as practiced by Scott. In the same year he wrote *The Pilot*, in his words "a sort of provocation to dispute the seamanship of 'The Pirate,'" a work by Scott. As for the Leatherstocking tales, a series of five novels depicting the life of the early American frontier, Scott himself, in his introduction to *Rob Roy* (1817), had compared the conflict between Augustan England and wild Scotland to the American conflict between European settlers and indigenous Indians. The Rob Roy narrative was a formula ready-made for an American writer, and Cooper did not hesitate to use it.[16]

In recognizing the resistance to British influence displayed by Poe and Cooper, it is important to remember also that each of these writers succeeded in creating a distinctively American literature. Poe responded to the demand that the visionary be made material by creating tales that uniquely combined emotional terror and spiritual ecstasy. Cooper increasingly and importantly replaced Scott's social contexts with the image of an individual man's self-discovery in the wilderness, a replacement that drew upon Puritan captivity narratives and other frontier materials. As the Leatherstocking tales continued, he more greatly emphasized Indian mythology and more finely described a distinctly American landscape. In one sense, he had an advantage over Scott in terms of working within a frame of geographical or social divisions; his frontier-divided civilizations were far more different than those Scott depicted; his American geographical expanse was continental as Scott's was not, and the temporal expanse created by the conflict of Native American and Euro-American groups was far more dramatic as well. Cooper deployed this difference with increasing self-awareness and as his career advanced, he became less bound by European culture and more inspired by America's brief history. Moreover, Poe and Cooper were able to stake claims for originality on grounds that are specifically determined by the Anglo-American conflict. It is these grounds that we need next to consider.

American writers attacked the Victorians by creating four specific areas for American advantage: scope, originality, profundity, and earnestness. To many British novelists who were engaged in this literary battle, such qualities signified their own particular strengths and the obvious shortcomings of the Americans. In addition, Victorian novels in particular, in criticizing various aspects of contemporary English society, actually aided the American side by highlighting weaknesses on the British side of the Atlantic.

The British, with page upon page of recorded history were in an apparently perfect position to create encyclopedic novels: prose fiction with the comprehensive nation-building proportions of epic. Consequently, British writers and critics reminded New World authors that they lacked the authority to provide truly great fiction since they lacked a sufficiently full history. From this perspective, the absence of history produced feeble literature: there was little to commemorate and there was an insufficient passage of time to allow for the mythic enlargements of event on which epic largely depends; there was no authentic national identity and thus coherent national morality; and there was no established class system that provided the novel, as a genre, with so much of its conflict and characterization.

Americans took up this litany of absence and appropriated it for their own ends. In Cooper, it becomes a claim for American moral fitness: "There are no annals for the historian; no follies (beyond the most vulgar and commonplace) for the satirist; no manners for the dramatist; no obscure fictions for the writer of romance; no gross and hardy offences against decorum for the moralist; nor any of the rich artificial auxiliaries of poetry." Half a century later, Henry James embellishes this appropriation of absence for American cultural superiority. In his book on Hawthorne, with gristly insistence he lists "the absent things in American life" which an "English or French imagination" would find "appalling," an "indictment . . . shedding an almost lurid light." James's list is satirically comprehensive: "No state, in the European sense of the word, and indeed barely a specific national name. No sovereign, no court, no personal loyalty, no aristocracy, no church, no army, no diplomatic service, no country gentlemen, no palaces, no castles, nor manors, nor old country houses, nor parsonages" – and on it goes, to end with "no sporting class – no Epsom or Ascot!" James wraps it all up by saying that while the Old World writer would believe "if these things are left out everything is left out . . . The American knows that a good deal remains; what it is that remains – that is his secret, his joke, as one may say."[17]

Every itemized "missing thing" can, of course, be made into a virtue. This is the American's secret, his joke – that what remains when all of the social institutions on which the Victorian novel depends are removed is, in fact, something authentically vibrant, something American. If the British critic asks how can you possibly hope to write without a rich social and political history, then the American responds, how can you possibly hope to write with so much clutter in the way. How, the American question goes, can you possibly hope to see through to woman, and man, and God, and law, with all this cant clouding your vision? The American novelist substitutes what we might call epistemological epic, a work that creates an encyclopedia of ways of knowing (Melville's *Moby Dick* comes immediately to mind) for the British novel's focus on a vast array of types and experience; this epistemological American novel may be said to attempt to subsume unto itself everything that characterizes the British Victorian novel, and in that subsuming to reveal the British novel as narrow in its concerns.

The claims and counter claims for appropriate scope overlap with the claims for originality, and the American novelist begins to portray his or her counterpart as limited in vision because dull and blinded by habit. As an instance, consider Emerson's ambiguous praise of Dickens: "Dickens, with preternatural apprehension of the language of manners and the varieties of street life, with pathos and laughter, with patriotic and still enlarging personality, writes London tracts. He is a painter of English details, like Hogarth; local and temporary in his tints and style, and local in his aims." For Emerson, in general, the British Victorian novelist is the very type of the "good Englishman" who "shuts himself out of three-fourths of his mind, and confines it to one-fourth." And what is true for the ordinary, decent Englishman is also true for their best thinkers: they are guilty of suppressing the imagination, of lacking "the highest aims."[18]

There is one way in which the British Victorian novelist may be said to have provided a weapon for the Americans in this battle for literary supremacy. In a preoccupation with cultural maturity and degenerating social systems, the Victorian novel often opened the door for charges of depicting cultural senility. The London of *Bleak House* is a senseless garbage heap of cultural accumulation, of overgrown systems gone wild, of institutions such as Chancery so aware of their age, their tradition, their custom, that they have become dismissive of human need. And to turn to Emily Brontë's *Wuthering Heights* (1847) and George Eliot's *Middlemarch* (1872) as specific examples of how the British Victorian novelist might have unwittingly aided his or her American counterpart in mounting charges of cultural senility, one sees that in the case of Brontë, cultural time seems clogged, and that in the case of Eliot, it seems slowed to the point of virtual stasis.

In *Wuthering Heights* the deadening atmosphere of Thrushcross Grange seems to defeat the hero's ungovernable vitality and to rob the heroine of her very breath. Brontë's tale is told by the novel's most repressed, over-civilized, and attenuated character, Lockwood. He recounts the stories of Nelly Dean, with whom he shares an interest in well-mannered custom and order, and the novel's interweaving of fallible narrations serves as a further indication of separation from the vital source of things embodied in Heathcliff's albeit savage vitality and Catherine's narcissistic drives. The narrative travels backward from its present-tense beginning and establishes a pattern of impeded progress: Heathcliff comes to imitate his victimizers, and his son by Isabella Linton is a living replication of the values of Thrushcross Grange and its over-civilized and fatigued defeat of natural energies. The relation between the younger generation, Catherine and Linton, parodies by exaggerated repetition of events the conflict of the first, Catherine and Edgar. Clogged time in *Wuthering Heights* leads to a sense of entropy, despite the ending that establishes a calm union between the younger Catherine and Hareton. The second half of the novel attempts to isolate and combine the positive aspects of both the early and the late, the savagely natural and the ennervated civilized – or, perhaps, to argue for the persistence of nature in a scene of predominating civilization. As the younger Catherine and Hareton begin to conspire to create the purified combining of Heights and Grange values, the tale catches up to the time of the narrative's beginnings – the year 1801, the dawn of a new century. The couple will marry on New Year's Day and the narrative is freed for a slow movement forward.

Similarly in *Middlemarch*, George Eliot begins by invoking the struggles of St. Theresa to dramatize by contrast the feeling of temporal and historical disjunction felt by "later-born Theresas [who] were helped by no coherent social faith and order." This disjunction is experienced by modern idealists such as Dorothea Brooke and Tertius Lydgate and it leads them to "dim lights," "tangled circumstances," and an inability to join thought and action in "noble agreement." Eliot teaches us that failings we might otherwise impute to the individual may be traced, in part, to a temporal alteration that is objectively historical. Of Theresa (and Antigone) Eliot concludes, "the medium in which their ardent deeds took shape is for ever gone."[19]

The title of the final section of the novel, "Sunset and Sunrise," certainly implies a cyclic return to vitality; but this sun rises upon a reduced landscape of private virtues, good acts that can inform individual relationships but that do not issue in a larger political change. Throughout the novel, Eliot seems to alternate between a view that espouses the epic-heroic life and disdains the social mediocrity that prevents its full actualization, and a view that seeks out, even recommends, a reduced domestic vision of the heroism now historically not possible. This reduced heroism makes itself known in acts of comprehensive understanding, in a radical empathy, which is, of course, the dominant mode of the novel's narrative voice. However admirable such an empathy, it does not seem enough, and the ending of Eliot's novel does not gainsay a sense of sadness, of irretrievable loss.

The temporal disjunction, the historical stasis, and cultural entropy that may be found in some British Victorian novels furnished American novelists with the means to turn the tables; for the Americans, the absence of a wealth of historical time could be interpreted as natural vitality, and its presence in British culture as decrepitude rather than maturity. Thoreau's *Walden* (1854) can serve as an example of the uses to which an American writer took the Victorian novelist's preoccupation with temporal disjunction.

Thoreau's narrative celebrates "first" things and denigrates the aged on every page. Its self-chronicling author writes in the first person for "it is after all, always the first person that is speaking." He hears no other voices, least of all those of elders, for age "has not profited so much as it has lost." He writes for "poor students" who must rely on their own experience and he celebrates a Walden spun out of the self's morning: "when I am awake there is dawn in me." Walden is a place "to front only the essential facts of life," "already in existence" perhaps "on that spring morning when Adam and Eve were driven out of Eden." In this booming American "earliness"

(Thoreau moved to Walden on a July 4), it is time before time, and scope beyond all space. England, contrarily, is "an old gentleman who is travelling with a great deal of baggage, trumpery which has accumulated from long housekeeping, which he has not the courage to burn." In the face of such claims, no wonder Oscar Wilde could later observe, "The youth of America is their oldest tradition. It has been going on now for three hundred years."[20] Thoreau's imagery of the dawn, the spring, and beginnings, suggests that originality in literature may be tied to living near the origins of life, and that kind of living gives an advantage to the New World.

While some American writers would provide the very history that the British claimed did not exist, others tended to disparage the historical and cultural past as a means of understanding the present. Hawthorne, for example, in the opening chapter of *The House of the Seven Gables* elaborates historical time so thoroughly that the seventeenth century seems closer to the very beginning of time than to the 1840s, and Cooper creates a kind of archetypal time in his Leatherstocking Tales where the Indian-European American conflict becomes a conflict between the primitive and the civilized, a conflict between members of each "race" who embody the ideals of the whole. The young Emerson termed history "a vanishing allegory" that "repeats itself to tediousness, a thousand a million times;" and later, in the essay "History" becomes "a shallow village tale." For Emerson, history can do nothing but express what we already know, especially in terms of our own thoughts and feelings: "We are always coming up with the emphatic facts of history in our private experience and verifying them here. All history becomes subjective; in other words, there is no history, only biography." If, as Emerson claims, "all the facts of history preexist in the mind as laws," it is logical, he argues, that anyone "can live history in his own person." Morever, in accordance with this view, Thoreau, in *A Week on the Concord and Merrimack Rivers* (1849) sees entire past cultures recapitulated in one or another of our momentary moods: "the history which we read is only a fainter memory of events which have happened in our own experience."[21]

In American literary culture of the nineteenth century, the alternative to history as authoritative and objective record of human behavior is present in images of visionary quests. "Forever – is composed of Now's – " Emily Dickinson argues; or in another place, "The Only News I know / Is Bulletins all Day / From Immortality." Walt Whitman, "looking a long while for the history of the past," finds it "in the present – it is this earth today . . ."[22] However, the traditional linear form of novelistic narrative would seem to indicate an alignment of fiction writing with the writing of history. In American nineteenth-century novels, this narrative pattern tends to prevail but there are moments of deviation from it; Richard Brodhead observes about *The Scarlet Letter*, for instance, that "at critical moments . . . the story stands still and we are left staring at the scarlet letter itself, at a mute symbol that seems to reabsorb into itself and communicate instantly the 'tale of human frailty and sorrow.'"[23] Brodhead goes on to characterize the commitment of American writers to the novel form as tense and equivocal to a breaking point: so ambivalent at certain points that British Victorian realism appears tame and ordinary. There is an overall edginess to American nineteenth-century fiction, then, a sense of heuristic experimentation, that also capitalizes on the problematical identity involved in being an American in the nineteenth century: "Who are we? Where are we?" cries Thoreau, as he climbs Katahdin – "Contact! Contact!" he begs. And Whitman in "As I Ebb'd" confesses to a monumental sense of visionary failure: "O I perceive I have not understood anything – not a single object – and that no man ever can."[24]

Sometimes, though, this ontological insecurity borders on boasts of profundity: "I unsettle all things," Emerson cries in his essay "Circles" and Dickinson proclaims, "The Soul should always stand ajar." In the novel, too, a scarlet letter or a house of seven gables or a whale becomes a central mystery that encourages multiple forms of attempting to know it, and the emphasis upon epistemology that is shared both by poetry and fiction in American nineteenth-century literature seems to imply that British writers have not thought deeply enough, have not understood that the answers set forth in the British Victorian novel to questions of how man might live in society are only the *beginning* questions.

What I have been summarizing here are the various arguments of a spate of critical studies published between, roughly, 1950 and 1980; these studies sought to define enduring qualities in American fiction. Inevitably, if sometimes unconsciously, they tended to invoke the norm of the British nineteenth-century novel as the comparative term. I have been arguing that however we define American fiction in the nineteenth century – by its Adamic heroes and Edenic hopes, or in opposite fashion, by its Apocalyptic tendencies to think of ourselves in spiritual terms, by its interest in taboo relations or by its rebellion against inherited novelistic conventions – it is, at root, a deliberate, calculated attempt to separate itself from the British Victorian novel. The British Victorian novel dominated the marketplace in America, and this returns us to the instructive case of the rivalry between Melville and Dickens.

Melville's perspective on American literary nationalism, as on everything, imitates the eyesight of the whale: it is double-visioned. "Let us away with the leaven of literary flunkeyism toward England," Melville proclaims in his essay on Hawthorne. "If either must play the flunkey in the thing, let England do it, not us." And, again, "no American should write like an Englishman or a Frenchman; let him write like a man, for then he will write like an American." Yet this spirited literary nationalism is sometimes offset by a ridicule of its potential foolishness, as we shall see now in a return to consideration of "Bartleby."[25] "Bartleby" offers a critique of Adamic/ Edenic myths, and at the same time it is primary piece of textual ammunition, I believe, in Melville's literary fight with Dickens.

"Bartleby"'s negotiation of the tension between deflation of American Edenic myths and its own status as textual rejoinder to Dickens may be seen, first, in the characterization of its storyteller, the Lawyer. So self-consigned to his occupation that his identity deserves no proper name, the Lawyer represents three different figures. For an initial moment, he is Melville. He announces as a topic of general interest law-copyists, and the drudge work of mindless copying may be seen to evoke the chief anxiety felt by American writers: that the influence of British literature is so powerful and pervasive there will be nothing original for them to say. The narrator then notes that nothing "that I know of" has been written of such law-copyists. Coming from a man who identifies himself as a Master in Chancery in the State of New York and coming in a tale published in *Putnam's* one month after *Scribner's* has concluded its serialization of *Bleak House*, and considering the fact that Chancery is a court that judges inheritance, and that literary influence is a form of inheritance, the suit of Melville vs. Dickens seems to be well begun.

By this same reference to Chancery, though, the Lawyer sheds his identity with Melville to become a compendium of Dickens's mean-spirited lawyers. The view of his Wall Street office, "deficient in what landscape painters call 'life'" ("Bartleby," 17) recalls the ghoulish lawyer Vholes and his "remarkable . . . lifeless manner" (*Bleak House*, 404). Melville's Lawyer boasts of a "snug business among rich men's bonds, and mortgages, and title-deeds" ("Bartleby," 16), just as Dickens's Tulkinghorn is "reputed to have made good thrift out of aristocratic marriage settlements and aristocratic wills" (*Bleak House*, 8). When Bartleby's unblinking presence bothers the Lawyer, his solution is to build yet another wall on Wall Street, a partition whereby he can order Bartleby without seeing him. Like Tulkinghorn, "watchful behind a blind" (*Bleak House*, 287), the Lawyer investigates Bartleby as Tulkinghorn pries into the hidden life of Lady Dedlock. And finally the Lawyer embodies the entire Chancery system. He is a mechanism within a mechanism to the extent that Bartleby's private utterance "I would prefer not to" constitutes a public resistance to this view. Preference and the individuality it implies are outlawed by this Wall Street.

In all of this, Melville seconds Dickens in indicting an absurdly abstracted system that attempts to replace an organic, vital society. Melville sees New York as Dickens sees London. Furthermore, Melville both acknowledges his shared moral indictment of society with Dickens, and at the same time asserts his own artistic ability to *do* Dickens, as one discovers in narrative tone and in characters who resemble minor Dickensian figures. As early as 1856, a contemporary reviewer noted that "Melville's 'Bartleby' is equal to anything from the pen of Dickens, whose writing it closely resembles, both as to the character of the sketch and the peculiarity of the style."[26] In some ways, too, the Lawyer's relentlessly self-satisfied tone recalls the voice of Esther Summerson at her most self-satisfied moral moments, just as the omniscient narrative voice that is heard in the other parts of *Bleak House* seems to be taken as an object of parody. Dickensian outrage becomes pompous, as one hears in the final words of Melville's tale, "Ah Bartleby! Ah Humanity."

Melville's Lawyer also seems sometimes to refuse responsibility for the scrivener whom he has turned away. Bartleby becomes, in Kingsley Widmer's phrase, "an image of self-pity in a social tract" in the Lawyer's "last moralizing and rationalizing gesture . . ."[27] But these moralizing gestures also show how Dickensian sympathy can become a cowardly substitute for a more challenging position: one, say, that would not relegate Bartleby's ills to the woes of universal humanity without acknowledging one's part in causing those ills. Instead, the Lawyer fulfills his promise to tell a tale "at which good-natured gentlemen might smile, and sentimental souls might weep" ("Bartleby," 16). If, then, the actions of the Lawyer indicate his meaning as one of Dickens's cold-blooded, self-advancing villains and his narrative voice is evocative of the omniscient narrator in *Bleak House*, then Dickens's familiar and oft-discussed retreats from social malaise into domestic harmony become part of the very problem that is the subject of both Melville's and Dickens's texts.

But the Lawyer has yet another identity: as Bartleby's key-word "prefer" creeps into the Lawyer's lexicon, he is shown to contain within himself a latent Bartleby. For this reason, he is both unable to shed Bartleby and is frantic to do so. And as Bartleby becomes the Lawyer's potential *doppelgänger*, the Lawyer stops sounding like Charles Dickens and seems to speak like a character out of Edgar Allan Poe: "nevertheless I felt something superstitious knocking at my heart, and forbidding me to carry out my purpose, and denouncing me for a villain if I dared to breathe one bitter word against this forlornest of mankind" ("Bartleby," 36). The "superstitious knocking" superficially recalls the knockings of the ancestral Lady Dedlock but the voice and language here suggest more powerfully the cadences of Poe. At this moment, at least, the Lawyer abides by Melville's injunction to "write like a man, for then he will write like an American."

When the Lawyer writes like Dickens, then, imitation becomes contempt; Bartleby's "I would prefer not to" works in the same way since it suggests Jo's "I don't know nothink" in *Bleak House*. Bartleby and Jo are respective scourges of an uncaring society, with the crucial difference, of course, that Bartleby possesses an agency entirely absent from the miserable existence of Jo. Bartleby's famous refusal recalls perhaps even more strongly the words of a character in another Dickens novel, Sam Weller in *The Pickwick Papers* (1837), who follows his master into debtors' prison and touchingly continues to behave as a subordinate, repeating "I'd rayther not, sir" when Mr. Pickwick asks him to sit down. Sam's class deference sentimentally validates the social system, and Melville wants none of this. His Bartleby's negative is polite but not deferential, and in a reversal of the Fleet Prison scene where Sam Weller and Mr. Pickwick are together, the Lawyer visits Bartleby, who refuses to acknowledge this gesture of tardy and false commitment. By such allusions-with-a-difference, the Lawyer's own toadyism towards the rich and condescension to the low and strange also suggests a criticism of Dickens. Melville seems to make Dickens's reformist indignation appear trivial as he discloses what he sees as an endorsement of the class system he believes Dickens opposes.

In addition, and most obviously, Bartleby recalls Dickens's Nemo from *Bleak House*. He is a scrivener with an obscure background whose identity has been nullified, and who embodies a terminal despair. Upon the Lawyer's final visit to the Tombs, Bartleby appears to be asleep, just as Nemo appears asleep but is soon discovered to be dead upon Tulkinghorn's only visit to his room above Krook's shop. The New York City prison, whose light-refusing walls Melville emphasizes, is an extension of the Lawyer's Wall Street office; both wall in the natural world as an expression of an American society stifling human nature as it dedicates itself to material gain. Bartleby lodges with the Lawyer, sleeping in his office for a time, just as Nemo lodges with Krook, who is a parodic Lord Chancellor, his evil disarray recalling the Chancery court system. In addition to these similarities, it is important to note a crucial difference, one that suggests perhaps more fully Melville's critique and replacement of Dickens's *Bleak House*. The brevity and concentrated meaning of Melville's tale mocks the length and dispersed meaning of Dickens's serialized novel. Dickens writes epic fiction through the exhaustive (and for some American writers, exhausting) portrayal of society at all levels and in all its myriad connections. Melville tells not the story of all things, but of all the ways of thinking a story. Bartleby is multigeneric: everything from allegorical victim to transcendent principle; the Lawyer's speculations about him range from the common-sensical to the biblical to the occult; and the everyday and the emblematic mingle. In some ways, then, "Bartleby," although formally utterly different in its scope and length from *Bleak House*, is magically larger.

Bleak House is, of course, more brilliant and complex than the parodic elements of "Bartleby" would suggest. Moreover, the very nature of the parody and echoing indicates on another level Melville's admiration for Dickens and also the seeming inescapableness for an American author of the British Victorian writer whose domination of the literary marketplace (although he was not getting paid for it) seemed unshakeable. It is in Melville's deployment of the imagery of the dead letter that we find his most devastating commentary on this domination.

The imagery of dead letters enables Melville to deliver a telling blow to British influence. Aside from the minor Bogsby post-office joke, to which I referred earlier in this chapter, in *The Pickwick Papers*, Dickens has the uncle of one of his characters dream of a yard full of worn-out mail coaches. What might they carry? Why, the character quips, the dead letters of course. And then there is the damaging letter from the dead in *Bleak House*, the letter written by Captain Hawdon (Nemo) that Tulking-horn discovers and uses to destroy Lady Dedlock. But Melville diminishes the private importance of this seemingly serious dead letter in Dickens by showing the far greater public significance of a rumor about Bartleby: that in a dead-letter office in Washington, the nation's capital, he would have been made aware of all the national failures of communication, of all the dashed hopes of letter-writers, of all the metaphorical instances, in sum, of American failed communications and on a cosmic scale of all failures of the human condition. Melville offers an American literature of unsettling discomfort, in contrast to the ultimately reassuring fictions of Dickens.

If the British claimed in the nineteenth century that America lacked a history and thus could claim no literature of any note, then "Bartleby" affirms sadly that America now has its sufficiency of classes and alienating systems. It rivals England in a negative way in terms of impediments to natural expressions of vitality. So even in this negative sense, "Bartleby" shows Melville asserting American supremacy. This kind of contestation, which I have tried both to describe generally and then to show in action in a particular case, leads to an American acknowledgment of British victory, albeit of a dispiriting sort. Sarcastically and ironically, Melville signals in "Bartleby" that for his generation of American writers, the dead letters from the British Victorian novel have finally been delivered. They are the letters of stifling and cruel social conventions that are read and adopted by the Lawyer and, for Melville, by too many Americans. Melville makes of Bartleby exactly what the Lawyer calls him, "a wreck in the mid Atlantic" ("Bartleby," 39), and he may be read, finally, as a symbolic victim of Old World social corruption, all too successfully transported to America. But if Melville mourns an America gone British, he can forge a new literature for a new nation in opposing the dead but potent letter of a representative Victorian novelist.

NOTES

1 Nathaniel Hawthorne, *The House of the Seven Gables* (1851), in William Charvat et al., eds., *The Centenary Edition of the Works*, 12 vols. (Columbus: Ohio State University Press, 1962), II:2. Subsequent references are to this edition.

2 Charles Dickens, *Bleak House* (1853; Boston: Houghton, Mifflin, 1956), 69. Subsequent references are to this edition.

3 For an interesting discussion of this relationship, see E. Stokes, "*Bleak House* and *The Scarlet Letter*," *AULMA Journal* 32 (1969), 177–89. See also Ghulam Ali Chaudhry, "Dickens and Hawthorne," *Essex Institute Historical Collection* 100 (1964), 256–73.

4 *The Letters of Charles Dickens*, ed. Walter Dexter, 3 vols. (London: Nonesuch Press, 1938), II:335.

5 Herman Melville, "Bartleby The Scrivener" (1856) in *Piazza Tales*, ed. Egbert S. Oliver (New York: Hendricks House, 1962), p. 54. Subsequent references are to this edition.

6 "Literary Importation," in Fred Lewis Pattee, ed., *The Poems of Philip Freneau*, 3 vols. (New York: Russell and Russell, 1963), II:303–04; Orestes Brownson, unattributed, 1864, in Richard Ruland, ed., *The Native Muse: Theories of American Literature* (1972; rprt. in soft cover, New York: E. P. Dutton, 1976), 406; Margaret Fuller, *Papers on Literature and Art* (New York: Wiley and Putnam, 1946), II:126–27; Walt Whitman quoted by Perry Miller, *The Raven and the Whale* (New York: Harcourt Brace, 1956), 187.

7 All quoted material in this paragraph is taken from essays reprinted in part or in full in Ruland, ed., *The Native Muse*, 167, 70, 392, 155, 185.

8 Henry Wadsworth Longfellow, *Kavanagh*, ed. Jean Downey (New Haven: College and University Press, 1965), 86.

9 See Allan Casson, "*The Scarlet Letter* and *Adam Bede*," *Victorian Newsletter* 20 (1961), 18–19.

10 Clarence Ghodes, *American Literature in Nineteenth-Century England* (Carbondale, IL: Southern Illinois University Press, 1944), 45–6.

11 "America and American Writers," *The Atheneum* (1829), 639; Ralph Waldo Emerson, *Nature, Addresses and Lectures*, ed. Robert F. Spiller and Alfred R. Ferguson, in Alfred R. Ferguson, ed., *Collected Works* (Cambridge: Harvard University Press, 1971), II:69; Brownson, "Specimens of Foreign Literature" (see Ruland, ed. *The Native Muse*, 272).

12 Columbus's *Book of Prophecies*, quoted in Charles L. Sanford, *The Quest for Paradise* (Urbana, IL: University of Illinois Press, 1961), 10; Harriet Beecher Stowe, quoted in Edmund Wilson, *Patriotic Gore: Studies in the Literature of the American Civil War* (New York: Oxford University Press, 1962), 84–85; Henry David Thoreau, "Walking," *Atlantic Monthly*, 9, 56 (1862), 662.

13 Richard Slotkin, *Regeneration Through Violence: The Mythology of the American Frontier, 1600–1860* (Middletown, CT: Wesleyan University Press, 1973), 27, 117.

14 Ralph Waldo Emerson, *Journals and Miscellaneous Notebooks*, ed. William H. Gilman et al., 16 vols. (Cambridge, MA: Harvard University Press, 1960–82), IV:78–79.

15 I am telescoping here Gerald Grubb's impressive, three-part essay, "The Personal and Literary Relations of Poe and Dickens," *Nineteenth-Century Fiction* 5 (1950), 5.1:1–22; 5.2:101–20; 5.3:209–21.

16 See James Fenimore Cooper's "Preface" to *The Pilot* for an instance of his criticism of Scott. See also George Dekker's *James Fenimore Cooper the Novelist* (London: Routledge & Kegan Paul, 1967), 20–32, for an account of the relation of the two authors.

17 Cooper in Ruland, ed., *The Native Muse*, 224; Henry James, *Hawthorne* (New York: Harper and Brothers, 1880), 42–43.

18 Ralph Waldo Emerson, *Complete Works*, Centenary Edition, 12 vols. (Boston: Houghton Mifflin, 1903), V:246, 252, 255.

19 George Eliot, *Middlemarch*, ed. Gordon S. Haight (1872; Boston: Houghton Mifflin 1956), 3–4, 615.

20 Henry David Thoreau, *Walden*, ed. J. Lyndon Shanley, vol. II in Walter Harding, ed., *The Writings* (Princeton, NJ: Princeton University Press, 1971), 3, 9, 4, 90, 179. Oscar Wilde, *A Man of No Importance*, in *Complete Works*, ed. Robert Ross, 10 vols. (Boston: Wyman-Fogg, 1909), VII:20.

21 Emerson, *Journals and Miscellaneous Notebooks* II:83; Emerson, *Collected Works* II:22, 6; Henry David Thoreau, *A Week on the Concord and Merrimack Rivers* (Boston: Houghton Mifflin, 1961), 310.

22 Emily Dickinson, *Poems*, ed. Thomas H. Johnson and Theordora Ward (Boston: Little Brown, 1960), poems 624, 827; Walt Whitman, "Chants Democratic," no. 19, in *Leaves of Grass, 1860*, Facsimile Edition, ed. Roy Harvey Pearce (1961; rpt. Ithaca, NY: Cornell University Press, 1969), 192.

23 Richard Brodhead, *Hawthorne, Melville and the Novel* (Chicago: University of Chicago Press, 1976), 11.

24 Henry David Thoreau, *The Maine Woods* (Boston: Ticknor and Fields, 1864), 71; Whitman, *Leaves of Grass*, section VI.

25 Herman Melville, "Hawthorne and his Mosses" (Part two), *Literary World* 7 (1850), 145–46.

26 Rpt. from the Boston *Daily Herald Traveler*, in M. Thomas Inge, ed., *Bartleby, the Inscrutable* (Hamden, CT: Archon, 1979), 39.

27 Kingsley Widmer, "The Negative Affirmation: Melville's 'Bartleby,'" *Modern Fiction Studies* 8 (1962), 276–86.

Guide to further reading

Altick, Richard D. *The English Common Reader: A Social History of the Mass Reading Public 1800–1900*. Chicago: University of Chicago Press, 1957.

Anderson, Amanda. *Tainted Souls and Painted Faces: The Rhetoric of Fallenness in Victorian Culture*. Ithaca, NY: Cornell University Press, 1993.

Arac, Jonathan. *Commissioned Spirits: The Shaping of Social Motion in Dickens, Carlyle, Melville, and Hawthorne*. New Brunswick: Rutgers University Press, 1979.

Ardis, Ann L. *New Women, New Novels: Feminism and Early Modernism*. New Brunswick, NJ: Rutgers University Press, 1990.

Armstrong, Nancy. *Desire and Domestic Fiction: A Political History of the Novel*. New York: Oxford University Press, 1987.

Bakhtin, M. M. *The Dialogic Imagination*. Ed. Michael Holquist. Trans. Caryl Emerson and Michael Holquist. Austin: University of Texas Press, 1981.

Baldick, Chris. *In Frankenstein's Shadow: Myth, Monstrosity and Nineteenth-Century Writing*. Oxford: Clarendon, 1987.

Banton, Michael. *Racial Theories*. Cambridge: Cambridge University Press, 1987.

Barnes, James J. *Free Trade in Books*. Oxford: Clarendon, 1964.

Beer, Gillian. *Darwin's Plots: Evolutionary Narrative in Darwin, George Eliot, and Nineteenth-Century Fiction*. London: Routledge & Kegan Paul, 1983.

Belsey, Catherine. *Critical Practice*. New York: Routledge, 1980.

Bersani, Leo. *A Future for Astyanax: Character and Desire in Literature*. Boston: Little Brown, 1976.

Blackburn, Robin. *The Overthrow of Colonial Slavery, 1776–1848*. London: Verso, 1988.

Bolt, Christine. *Victorian Attitudes to Race*. London: Routledge & Kegan Paul, 1971.

Brantlinger, Patrick. *The Reading Lesson: The Threat of Mass Literacy in Nineteenth-Century British Fiction*. Bloomington: Indiana University Press, 1998.

　Rule of Darkness: British Literature and Imperialism, 1830–1914. Ithaca: Cornell University Press, 1988.

　"What is 'sensational' about the sensation novel?" *Nineteenth-Century Fiction* 37 (1982): 1–28.

Briggs, Asa. *The Age of Improvement, 1783–1867*. London: Longman, 1959.

　Victorian People: A Reassessment of Persons and Themes 1851–67. Chicago: University of Chicago Press, 1955.

Bristow, Joseph. *Empire Boys: Adventures in a Man's World*. London: Harper-Collins, 1991.

Byron, Glennis, ed. *Dracula: A New Casebook*. London: Macmillan, 1999.

Butler, Lance St. John. *Victorian Doubt: Literary and Cultural Discourses*. New York: Harvester Wheatsheaf, 1990.

Carey, John. *The Intellectuals and the Masses: Pride and Prejudice among the Literary Intelligentsia, 1880–1939*. London: Faber, 1992.

Carlyle, Thomas. *Past and Present*. 1843. London: Chapman & Hall, 1886.

Cawelti, John G. *Adventure, Mystery, and Romance: Formula Stories as Art and Popular Culture*. Chicago: University of Chicago Press, 1976.

Chadwick, Edwin. *Report on the Sanitary Condition of the Labouring Population of Great Britain 1842*. Ed. M. W. Flinn. Facsimile Reprint. Edinburgh: Edinburgh University Press, 1965.

Cheyette, Brian. *Constructions of "the Jew" in English Literature and Society: Racial Representations, 1875–1945*. Cambridge: Cambridge University Press, 1993.

Childers, Joseph W. *Novel Possibilities: Fiction and the Formation of Early Victorian Culture*. Philadelphia: University of Pennsylvania Press, 1995.

Cohan, Stephen. *Violation and Repair in the English Novel*. Detroit: Wayne State University Press, 1986.

Cohen, William A. *Sex Scandal: The Private Parts of Victorian Fiction*. Durham, NC: Duke University Press, 1996.

Collins, Philip. *Dickens and Crime*. Bloomington: Indiana University Press, 1968.

Conrad, Peter. *Imagining America*. New York: Oxford University Press, 1980.

Coslett, Tess. *The "Scientific Movement" and Victorian Literature*. New York: St. Martin's, 1982.

Cross, Nigel. *The Common Writer: Life in Nineteenth-Century Grub Street*. Cambridge: Cambridge University Press, 1985.

Cvetkovich, Ann. *Mixed Feelings: Feminism, Mass Culture, and Victorian Sensationalism*. New Brunswick, NJ: Rutgers University Press, 1992.

Dale, Peter Allan. *In Pursuit of a Scientific Culture: Science, Art, and Society in the Victorian Age*. Madison: University of Wisconsin Press, 1989.

Dalziel, Margaret. *Popular Fiction 100 Years Ago: An Unexplored Tract of Literary History*. London: Cohen and West, 1957.

David, Deirdre. *Fictions of Resolution in Three Victorian Novels: North and South, Our Mutual Friend, Daniel Deronda*. New York: Columbia University Press, 1981.

Intellectual Women and Victorian Patriarchy: Harriet Martineau, Elizabeth Barrett Browning, George Eliot. Ithaca, NY: Cornell University Press, 1987.

Rule Britannia: Women, Empire, and Victorian Writing. Ithaca, NY: Cornell University Press, 1995.

Davidoff, Leonore and Catherine Hall. *Family Fortunes: Men and Women of the English Middle Class 1780–1850*. London: Hutchinson, 1987.

DeLamotte, Eugenia. *Perils of the Night: A Feminist Study of Nineteenth-Century Gothic*. Oxford: Oxford University Press, 1990.

Dooley, Allan C. *Author and Printer in Victorian England*. Charlottesville: University of Virginia Press, 1992.

Dunae, Patrick A. "Penny Dreadfuls: Late Nineteenth-Century Boys' Literature and Crime." *Victorian Studies* 22 (1979): 133–50.

Dyos, H. J. and M. Wolff, eds. *The Victorian City*. 2 vols. London: Routledge & Kegan Paul, 1973.

Eigner, Edwin. *The Metaphysical Novel in England and America: Dickens, Bulwer, Melville and Hawthorne*. Berkeley: University of California Press, 1978.

Eigner, Edwin M. and George J. Worth, eds. *Victorian Criticism of the Novel*. Cambridge: Cambridge University Press, 1985.

Eliot, Simon. *Some Patterns and Trends in British Publishing 1800–1919*. London: The Bibliographic Society, 1994.

Ermarth, Elizabeth Deeds. *The English Novel in History 1840–1895*. London: Routledge, 1997.

  Realism and Consensus in the English Novel. Princeton: Princeton University Press, 1983.

Feather, John. *A History of British Publishing*. London: Routledge, 1988.

Feltes, Norman. *Literary Capital and the Late Victorian Novel*. Madison: University of Wisconsin Press, 1993.

  Modes of Production of Victorian Novels. Chicago: University of Chicago Press, 1986.

Flint, Kate. *The Woman Reader 1837–1914*. Oxford: Oxford University Press, 1993.

Friedman, Alan. *The Turn of the Novel*. New York: Oxford University Press, 1966.

Foucault, Michel. *Discipline and Punish: The Birth of the Prison*. Trans. Alan Sheridan. New York: Vintage Books, 1979.

Ghodes, Clarence. *American Literature in Nineteenth-Century England*. Carbondale, IL: Southern Illinois University Press, 1944.

Gilmour, Robin. *The Novel in the Victorian Age: A Modern Introduction*. London: Edward Arnold, 1986.

  The Victorian Period: The Intellectual and Cultural Context of English Literature, 1830–1890. London: Longman, 1993.

Green, Martin. *Dreams of Adventure, Deeds of Empire*. London: Routledge and Kegan Paul, 1980.

Greenwood, Thomas. *Public Libraries: A History of the Movement and a Manual for the Organization, and Management of Rate-Supported Libraries*. London: Cassell, 1891.

Griest, Guinevere. *Mudie's Circulating Library and the Victorian Novel*. Bloomington: Indiana University Press, 1970.

Hepburn, James. *The Author's Empty Purse*. London: Oxford University Press, 1968.

Hill, Frederic. *Crime: Its Amount, Causes, and Remedies*. London: John Murray, 1853.

Hitchens, Christopher. *Blood, Class and Nostalgia: Anglo-American Ironies*. New York: Farrar, 1990.

Hobsbawm, E. J. *The Age of Capital, 1848–1875*. New York: Scribner, 1975.

Hollingsworth, Keith. *The Newgate Novel 1830–1847: Bulwer, Ainsworth, Dickens & Thackeray*. Detroit: Wayne State University Press, 1963.

Hughes, Winifred. *The Maniac in the Cellar: The Sensation Novel of the 1860s*. Princeton: Princeton University Press, 1980.

James, Louis. *Fiction for the Working Man, 1830–1850*. London: Oxford University Press, 1963.

Jann, Rosemary. *The Adventures of Sherlock Holmes: Detecting Social Order.* New York: Twayne Publishers, 1992.

Jordan, John O. and Robert L. Patten, eds. *Literature in the Marketplace. Nineteenth-Century British Publishing and Reading Practices.* Cambridge: Cambridge University Press, 1995.

Kayman, Martin. *From Bow Street to Baker Street: Mystery, Detection, and Narrative.* New York: St. Martin's Press, 1992.

Keating, Peter. *The Haunted Study: A Social History of the English Novel 1875–1914.* London: Secker and Warburg, 1989.

Kelly, Thomas. *History of Public Libraries in Great Britain 1845–1975.* London: The Library Association, 1977.

Kiernan, V. G. *The Lords of Human Kind: Black Men, Yellow Men, and White Men in an Age of Empire.* New York: Columbia University Press, 1986.

Knight, Stephen. *Form and Ideology in Crime Fiction.* Bloomington: Indiana University Press, 1980.

Knoepflmacher, U. C. *Laughter and Despair: Readings in Ten Novels of the Victorian Period.* Berkeley: University of California Press, 1971.
Wuthering Heights. Cambridge: Cambridge University Press, 1989.

Kucich, John. *Repression in Victorian Fiction: Charlotte Brontë, George Eliot, and Charles Dickens.* Berkeley: University of California Press, 1987.

Lane, Christopher. *The Ruling Passion: British Colonial Allegory and the Paradox of Homosexual Desire.* Durham, NC: Duke University Press, 1995.

Lease, Benjamin. *Anglo-American Encounters: England and the Rise of American Literature.* New York: Cambridge University Press, 1981.

Ledger, Sally. *The New Woman: Fiction and Feminism at the* Fin de Siècle. Manchester: Manchester University Press, 1997.

Lee, Alan J. *The Origins of the Popular Press in England, 1855–1914.* London: Croom Helm, 1976.

Leps, Marie-Christine. *Apprehending the Criminal: The Production of Deviance in Nineteenth-Century Discourse.* Durham, NC: Duke University Press, 1992.

Levine, George. *The Realistic Imagination: English Fiction from Frankenstein to Lady Chatterly.* Chicago: University of Chicago Press, 1981.

Loesberg, Jonathan. "The Ideology of Narrative Form in Sensation Fiction." *Representations* 13 (1986): 115–38.

Lorimer, Douglas A. *Colour, Class and the Victorians.* Leicester: Leicester University Press, 1978.

MacDougall, H. *Racial Myth in English History: Trojans, Teutons, and Anglo-Saxons.* Montreal: Harvest Home, 1982.

Malchow, Howard. *Gothic Images of Race in Nineteenth-Century Britain.* Stanford, CA: Stanford University Press, 1996.

Marcus, Steven. *Engels, Manchester, and the Working Class.* New York: Random House, 1974.
The Other Victorians: A Study of Sexuality and Pornography in Mid-Nineteenth-Century England. New York: Basic Books, 1966.

Masse, Michelle. *In the Name of Love: Women, Masochism and the Gothic.* Ithaca, NY: Cornell University Press, 1992.

Mayhew, Henry. *London Labour and the London Poor.* 1851–52. 2 vols. 1861–62. 4 vols. New York: Dover, 1968. 4 vols.

Maynard, John. *Victorian Discourses on Sexuality and Religion*. Cambridge: Cambridge University Press, 1993.

McLintock, Anne. *Imperial Leather: Race, Gender and Sexuality in the Colonial Context*. New York: Routledge, 1995.

Meyer, Susan. *Imperialism at Home: Race and Victorian Women's Fiction*. Ithaca, NY: Cornell University Press, 1996.

Miller, Andrew H. and James Eli Adams. *Sexualities in Victorian Britain*. Bloomington: Indiana University Press, 1996.

Miller, D. A. *The Novel and the Police*. Berkeley: University of California Press, 1988.

Miller, J. Hillis. *The Form of Victorian Fiction*. Notre Dame: University of Notre Dame Press, 1968.

Mitch, David F. *The Rise of Popular Literacy in Victorian England: The Influence of Private Choice and Public Policy*. Philadelphia: University of Pennsylvania Press, 1992.

Mitchell, Sally. *The Fallen Angel: Chastity, Class and Women's Reading, 1835–1880*. Bowling Green, OH: Bowling Green State University Press, 1981.

Moretti, Franco. *Signs Taken for Wonders: Essays on the Sociology of Literary Form*. Trans. Susan Fischer, David Forgacs, David Miller. London: Verso, 1983.

Mulvey, Christopher. *Transatlantic Manners: Social Patterns in Nineteenth-Century Anglo-American Travel Literature*. New York: Cambridge University Press, 1990.

Murch, A. E. *The Development of the Detective Novel*. New York: Philosophical Library, 1958.

O'Farrell, Mary Ann. *Telling Complexions: The Nineteenth-Century English Novel and the Blush*. Durham, NC: Duke University Press, 1997.

Ousby, Ian. *Bloodhounds of Heaven: The Detective in English Fiction from Godwin to Doyle*. Cambridge, MA: Harvard University Press, 1976.

Patten, Robert L. *Charles Dickens and His Publishers*. Oxford: Oxford University Press, 1978.

Perera, Suvendrini. *Reaches of Empire: The English Novel from Edgeworth to Dickens*. New York: Columbia University Press, 1991.

Pick, Daniel. *Faces of Degeneration: A European Disorder, c. 1848–c. 1918*. Cambridge: Cambridge University Press, 1989.

Poovey, Mary. *Making a Social Body: British Cultural Formation, 1830–1864*. Chicago: University of Chicago Press, 1995.

Uneven Developments: The Ideological Work of Gender in Mid-Victorian England. Chicago: University of Chicago Press, 1988.

Porter, Dennis. *The Pursuit of Crime: Art and Ideology in Detective Fiction*. New Haven: Yale University Press, 1981.

Punter, David. *The Literature of Terror: A History of Gothic Fictions from 1765 to the Present*. London: Longman, 1980. Revised two-volume edition, 1996.

Pykett, Lyn. *The Improper Feminine: The Women's Sensation Novel and the New Woman Writing*. London: Routledge, 1992.

The Sensation Novel from "The Woman in White" to "The Moonstone." Plymouth, UK: Northcote House, 1994.

Pykett, Lyn, ed. *Reading* Fin de Siècle *Fictions*. London: Longman, 1996.

Wilkie Collins: A New Casebook. London: Macmillan, 1998.

Qualls, Barry. *The Secular Pilgrims of Victorian Fiction*. Cambridge: Cambridge University Press, 1982.

Ragussis, Michael. *Figures of Conversion: "The Jewish Question" and English National Identity*. Durham, NC: Duke University Press, 1995.

Richards, Jeffrey, ed. *Imperialism and Juvenile Literature*. Manchester: Manchester University Press, 1989.

Rothfield, Lawrence. *Vital Signs: Medical Realism in Nineteeth-Century Fiction*. Princeton: Princeton University Press, 1992.

Ruland, Richard, ed. *The Native Muse: Theories of American Literature*. 1972. New York: E. P. Dutton, 1976.

Said, Edward. *Culture and Imperialism*. New York: Knopf, 1993.

Orientalism. New York: Random House, 1978.

Sedgwick, Eve Kosofsky. *Between Men: English Literature and Male Homosocial Desire*. New York: Columbia University Press, 1985.

Epistemology of the Closet. Berkeley: University of California Press, 1990.

Senf, Carol. *The Vampire in Nineteenth-Century English Literature*. Bowling Green, OH: Bowling Green State University Press, 1988.

Shillingsburg, Peter L. *Pegasus in Harness: Victorian Publishing and W. M. Thackeray*. Charlottesville: University of Virginia Press, 1992.

Skilton, David, ed. *The Early and Mid-Victorian Novel*. New York: Routledge, 1993.

The English Novel: Defoe to the Victorians. New York: Barnes and Noble, 1977.

Slinn, E. Warwick. *The Discourse of Self in Victorian Poetry*. Charlottesville: University of Virginia Press, 1991.

Solomon, Pearl Chester. *Dickens and Melville in Their Time*. New York: Columbia University Press, 1975.

Spencer, Benjamin T. *The Quest for Nationality: An American Literary Campaign*. Syracuse, NY: Syracuse University Press, 1957.

Spender, Stephen. *Love–Hate Relations: English and American Sensibilities*. New York: Random House, 1974.

Stepan, Nancy. *The Idea of Race in Science: Great Britain, 1800–1960*. Hamden, CT: Archon Books, 1982.

Stewart, Garrett. *Dear Reader: The Conscripted Audience in Nineteenth-Century Fiction*. Baltimore: Johns Hopkins University Press, 1996.

Stocking, George. *Victorian Anthropology*. New York: Free Press, 1987.

Stockton, Kathryn Bond. *God Between Their Lips: Desire Between Women in Irigiray, Brontë, and Eliot*. Stanford, CA: Stanford University Press, 1994.

Stowe, William W. *Going Abroad: European Travel in Nineteenth-Century American Culture*. Princeton: Princeton University Press, 1994.

Suleri, Sara. *The Rhetoric of English India*. Chicago: University of Chicago Press, 1992.

Sutherland, John A. *Victorian Fiction: Writers, Publishers, Readers*. London: Macmillan, 1995.

Victorian Novelists and Publishers. Chicago: University of Chicago Press, 1976.

Thomas, Deborah. *Thackeray and Slavery*. Athens: Ohio University Press, 1993.

Thomas, Ronald. *Detective Fiction and the Rise of Forensic Science*. Cambridge: Cambridge University Press, 1999.

Thompson, Dorothy. *The Chartists*. London: Temple Smith, 1984.

Thompson, E. P. *The Making of the English Working Class*. New York: Vintage, 1966.

Thorwald, Jürgen. *The Century of the Detective*. Trans. Richard and Clara Winston. New York: Harcourt, Brace and World, 1965.

Turner, Frank Miller. *Between Science and Religion: The Reaction to Scientific Naturalism in Late Victorian England*. New Haven: Yale University Press, 1974.

Vincent, David. *Literacy and Popular Culture: England 1750–1914*. Cambridge: Cambridge University Press, 1989.

Weisbuch, Robert. *Atlantic Double-Cross: American Literature and British Influence in the Age of Emerson*. Chicago: University of Chicago Press, 1986.

Welsh, Alexander. *Reflections on the Hero as Quixote*. Princeton: Princeton University Press, 1957.

West, Shearer, ed. *The Victorians and Race*. Aldershot: Scolar Press, 1996.

Williams, Raymond. *Culture and Society, 1780–1950*. New York: Harper and Row, 1966.

Wilson, Charles. *First with the News: The History of W. H. Smith, 1792–1972*. London: Jonathan Cape, 1985.

Wolff, Robert Lee. *Gains and Losses: Novels of Faith and Doubt in Victorian England*. New York: Garland, 1977.

Young, Robert. *Colonial Desire: Hybridity in Theory, Culture and Race*. London: Routledge, 1995.

Index

Adorno, Theodor, 211n
Allen, Grant, *The Woman Who Did*,
   94–95
Altick, Richard, 60n
American Puritan tradition, 240–41
American West, and European myths, 240
American response to Romantic poets,
   241
Anglo-American literary conflict, 237–48
Armstrong, Nancy, 148n, 232n
Arnold, Matthew, on popular fiction, 22;
   Culture and Anarchy, 91, 149
Austen, Jane, *Emma*, 97; *Northanger
   Abbey*, 117; *Pride and Prejudice*, 66,
   97

Baker, Samuel, *Cast Up by the Sea*, 157
Bakhtin, M. M., 67–68
Ballantyne, Robert M., *The Coral Island*,
   161–62
Banton, Michael, 166n
Barker, Pat, 5
Beer, Gillian, 217; *Darwin's Plots:
   Evolutionary Narrative in Darwin, George
   Eliot, and Nineteenth-Century Fiction*,
   122n, 232n; *Open Fields: Science in
   Cultural Encounter*, 232n
Belsey, Catherine, 210n
Bentham, Jeremy, *Rationale of Judicial
   Evidence*, 182
Bertilllon, Alphonse, and criminal
   detection, 185
Besant, Walter, success of *All Sorts and
   Conditions of Men*, 49, 58
Bodenheimer, Rosemarie, 96n
Booth, Charles, *Life and Labour of the
   People in London*, 93
Bourdieu, Pierre, 31

Braddon, Mary Elizabeth, *Aurora Floyd*,
   54; *The Doctor's Wife*, 20; *Lady
   Audley's Secret*, 181, 203
Brantlinger, Patrick, 27, 95n, 209
Breuer, Josef, and female hysteria, 109
Briggs, Asa, 15n
Bristow, Joseph, 167n
Broadsheets, nineteenth-century, 42
Brodhead, Richard, 248
Brontë sisters, and African stories, 159;
   and female gothic, 199–200
Brontë, Charlotte, *Jane Eyre*, 9, 111–12,
   and female homosexuality, 133–38,
   159–60, 199; *Villette*, 9, 24, 111, 199
Brontë, Emily, *Wuthering Heights*, 61,
   64–67, 103, 160, 161, 199, 245
Brontë, Anne, *Agnes Grey*, 40; *The Tenant
   of Wildfell Hall*, 127–31, 199
Broughton, Rhoda, *Second Thoughts*, 40
Brown, William Wells, 17
Bulwer-Lytton, Edward, *Eugene Aram*,
   174; *The Coming Race*, 165–66,
   Harold, The Last of the Saxon Kings,
   150
Burnett, John, David Vincent, and David
   Mayall, eds. *The Autobiography of the
   Working Class: an Annotated Critical
   Bibliography*, 36n
Burney, Fanny, *Camilla*, 37
Burroughs, Edgar Rice, 162
Butler, Samuel, and Victorian science,
   Erewhon, 226

Carey, John, 35 n.
Carleton, William, *The Black Prophet, a Tale
   of the Irish Famine*, 160; *Traits and
   Stories of the Irish Peasantry*, 160
Carlyle, Thomas, *Chartism*, 78, "An

Occasional Discourse on the Nigger
Question," 155; *Past and Present*, 78
Carroll, Lewis, *Alice's Adventures in
Wonderland*, 112, 116–17
Cazamian, Louis, *The Social Novel in
England*, 95n
Chadwick, Edwin, *Report on the Sanitary
Conditions of the Labouring Population of
Great Britain*, 78
Chapbooks, nineteenth-century, 42
Chartism, 5, 83–84, 151; and Newgate
novels, 173
Childers, Joseph W., 95n
Children's Employment Commission, 1842,
85
Cholomondeley, Mary, *Red Pottage*, 31
Cohen, William, 147n
Collins, Wilkie, *Armadale*, 228; *The
Moonstone*, 164, 183–84, 228; *The
Woman in White*, 169, 181, 228
Comte, Auguste, philosophical
"positivism," 219–23
Conrad, Joseph, *Heart of Darkness*, 62,
157, 162–63; *Lord Jim*, 61–64; *The
Nigger of the Narcissus*, 8, 62;
Nostromo, 7–10; *The Secret Agent*, 63
Cooper, James Fennimore, and Jane Austen,
242; and Walter Scott, 242–43
Cox, Michael, 198
Cunningham, Michael, *The Hours*, 5

Dale, Peter Allan, 232n
Darwin, Charles, and philosophical
pessimism, 224; and Victorian
anthropology, 109; *The Descent of Man,
and Selection in Relation to Sex*, 101–02,
150; *Origin of Species*, 5, 101, 150, 224
David, Deirdre, 167n, 168n, 233n
Davidoff, Leonore, 104; *The Best Circles:
Society, Etiquette and the Season*, 122n
Dekker, George, 154n
Dickens, Charles, and American slavery,
154–55; and education, 86–89; and
ghost stories, 197, and Jewish
characters, 151–52; and Niger
Expedition, 155; and serialization, 44;
as originator of detective story in Victorian
literature, 172; *All the Year Round*,
23; *American Notes*, 154; *Barnaby
Rudge*, 174; *Bleak House*, 172, as first
English detective novel, 176–78; *A
Christmas Carol*, 197; *David
Copperfield*, 65; *Dombey and Son*, 4,
25, 44, 45, 89–90, 103–04, 155; *Great
Expectations* 2, 25, 44, 229; *Hard
Times*, 5, 44, 86–89; *The Haunted
Man*, 197; *Household Words*, 23;
Little Dorrit, 3, 90; *Martin
Chuzzlewit*, 154, 155, 178; *The Mystery
of Edwin Drood*, 164; *Nicholas
Nickleby*, 31; *The Old Curiosity Shop*,
44; "On Strike," 89; *Oliver Twist*,
7–10, 44, 175; *Our Mutual Friend*, 31,
142–47; *Pickwick Papers*, 7, 252; *A
Tale of Two Cities*, 44
Dickinson, Emily, and visionary quests,
247
Disraeli, Benjamin, *Lothair*, 149; *Sybil, or
the Two Nations*, 84–85, 151;
Tancred, 149, 152
Dixon, Ella Hepworth, *The Story of a
Modern Woman*, 25
Dolan, Tim, 168n
Dooley, Allan C., 60n
Doyle, Sir Arthur Conan, and British
imperialism, 187; and medical
diagnosis, 188–89; popularity of
Sherlock Holmes stories, 185–88; "The
Adventures of the Naval Treaty," 186;
"The Final Problem," 190; *The Hound
of the Baskervilles*, 186; "The Norwood
Builder," 186; *The Sign of Four*, 187;
A Study in Scarlet, 186

Eagleton, Terry, 61, 216; *Heathcliff and
the Great Hunger*, 160
Eigner, M., and George J. Worth, 15n
Eliot, T. S., and detective fiction, 179
Eliot, George, and anti-Semitism, 152; and
Nathaniel Hawthorne, 213; and
philosophical "positivism," 221–24; and
rural nostalgia, 91; *Adam Bede*, 2,
138–42, 221; "Address to Working Men,
by Felix Holt," 92; *Daniel Deronda*, 4,
9, 29, 46, 70, 72–74, 152, 223; *Felix
Holt, the Radical*, 29, 91–93; "The
Lifted Veil," 193; *Middlemarch*, 3, 26,
45, 71–72, 106–7, 218, 221–23, 246; *The
Mill on the Floss*, 23, 65, 66, 221; *Silas
Marner*, 106; "Silly Novels by Lady
Novelists," 25
Ellis, Havelock, *The Criminal*, 187
Emerson, Ralph Waldo, on Charles
Dickens, 244–45
Engels, Friedrich, female sexual desire,
109; Irish immigrants, 99

Fielding, Henry, *Tom Jones,* 37
Fin-de-siècle, fantastic fiction, 205–09; fears of racial degeneration, 115–18, 209; racism, 161
Foucault, Michel, panopticism, 176, 188; *History of Sexuality,* 128–29
Freneau, Philip, 238
Freud, Sigmund, 109; *das Unheimlich,* 200–01; *Totem and Taboo,* 198
Froude, J. A., and Frank Newman, *The Nemesis of Faith,* 214
Fuller, Margaret, 228

Gallagher, Catherine, 71
Galton, Sir Francis, *Finger Prints,* 186
Garrett, Peter, 68
Gaskell, Elizabeth, *Mary Barton,* 5, 81–82, 178; *North and South,* 28, 70–71
Gaultier, Jules de, *Bovarysm,* 124n
Gilbert, Sandra M., and Susan Gubar, *The Madwoman in the Attic: The Woman Writer and the Nineteenth-Century Literary Imagination,* 123n
Gilmour, Robin, 15n, 215, 232n
Gissing, George, *Demos,* 93; *The Nether World,* 93; *New Grub Street,* 50; *The Odd Women* 1, 26; *Thyrza,* 20; *Workers in the Dawn,* 93
Gobineau, Count, *Essay on the Inequality of Human Races,* 149
Gosse, Edmund, *Father and Son,* 18
Grand, Sarah, *The Beth Book,* 26; *The Heavenly Twins,* 231
Grant, James, *First Love and Last Love: A Tale of the Indian Mutiny,* 164
Great Exhibition of 1851, 6, 95
Greenwell, Dora, "Home," 69–70
Gunn, Simon, 122–23n

Haggard, H. Rider, scientific pessimism, 226; *King Solomon's Mines,* 157; *She,* 157–8
Hall, Catherine, 104; *Family Fortunes: Men and Women of the English Middle Class,* 122n
Hardy, Thomas, Freudian psychoanalysis, 126; philosophical pessimism, 224–25; sexual desire, 225–26; *A Pair of Blue Eyes,* 225; *Desperate Remedies,* 193; *Far from the Madding Crowd,* 106; *Jude the Obscure,* 24; *Tess of the d'Urbervilles,* 4, 74–75, 126; *Two on a Tower,* 225

Hawthorne, Nathaniel, *House of Seven Gables,* 234–36; *The Scarlet Letter,* 235
Heller, Tamara, 210n
Hennell, Charles, *An Inquiry Concerning the Origin of Christianity,* 213–14
Henty, G.A., *By Sheer Pluck, A Tale of the Ashanti War,* 162
Hirschman, Albert O., *The Passions and the Interests: Political Arguments for Capitalism Before its Triumph,* 133
Hobsbawm, E. J., 148n, 190n
Hogg, James, *The Private Memoirs and True Confessions of a Justified Sinner,* 206
Hollingsworth, Keith, 190n
Houghton, Walter, 5
Hurley, Kelly, 201
Huxley, Thomas, "On the Physical Basis of Life," 5

Ingham, Patricia, 71

James, Henry, on Mary Elizabeth Braddon, 191n; on Wilkie Collins, 184; on Conrad's style, 20; criticism of Victorian novels, 2–3, 67; on sensation novels, 202; satire of English society, 244
Jordan, John O. and Robert Patten, *Literature in the Marketplace: Nineteenth-Century British Publishing and Reading Practices,* 36n

Kingsley, Charles, *Alton Locke, Tailor and Poet,* 82–83; *Hereward the Wake,* 150; *Water Babies,* 226
Kipling, Rudyard, 9, 150; *Kim,* 164
Knoepflmacher, U. C., 76n
Knox, Robert, *The Races of Man,* 149–50

Le Fanu, Sheridan, *In a Glass Darkly,* 196; *Uncle Silas,* 202
Lefebvre, Henri, 148n
Lennox, Charlotte, *The Female Quixote,* 117
Levine, George, 217, 232n
Levine, Philippa, 124n
Levy, Amy, *Reuben Sachs,* 152
Lewes, G. H., as Eliot's literary agent, 46; on *Pickwick Papers,* 22; *Principles of Success in Literature,* 222
Literacy, nineteenth-century, 42–44
Livingstone, David, 156

Index

Locard, Edmond, and forensic medicine, 185
Locke, John, "Essay on Paternal Authority," 98
Longfellow, Henry Wadsworth, *Kavanagh*, 239
Lukács, Georg, 113–14, 148n; on novel form, 171; on realism, 218

Machen, Arthur, *The Great God Pan*, 207–08
Malchow, Howard, 167n
Malthus, Thomas, *Essay on the Principle of Population*, 97–100
Marcuse, Herbert, 148n
Marryat, Captain Frederick, 9; *Mr. Midshipman Easy*, 158–59; *Newton Foster*, 159; *Peter Simple*, 159
Martineau, Harriet, *The Hour and the Man*, 156; *Illustrations of Political Economy*, 85; *Poor Laws and Paupers, Illustrated*, 85
Marx, Karl, 102, 130; "The Commodity Fetish and its Secret," 105
Maurier, George du, *Trilby*, 32
Mayhew, Henry, and working-class women, 109–10; *London Labour and the London Poor*, 93
McCabe, Colin, 210n
Melville, Herman, on British literature, 248–49; relation of "Bartleby the Scrivener" to *Bleak House*, 234–37, 249–52
Meredith, George, *The Egoist*, 223
Meyer, Susan, 159
Mill, John Stuart, Victorian religion and science, 213
Miller, J. Hillis, 3
Mitchell, Sally, 15n
Moers, Ellen, 198
Moore, George, *Literature at Nurse, or Circulating Morals*, 41; *A Mummer's Wife*, 22, 41
Moretti, Franco, 147n
Morris, William, *News from Nowhere*, 93
Mudie, Charles Edward, 21; library system, 39–41
Myers, Frederic W. H., 224

New Woman fiction, 25, 94–95
Newgate novels, 172–76
Newspapers, nineteenth-century cost, 46–48

Nordau, Max, 205; *Degeneration*, 116
Nunokawa, Jeff, 147n

Oliphant, Margaret, on literary detectives, 169; *Miss Marjoribanks*, 29
"Ouida" (Marie Louise de la Ramée), and sensation fiction, 202

Paperback novels, nineteenth-century, 51–52
Peel, Sir Robert, reform of justice system, 175–76
Periodicals, nineteenth-century cost, 46–48
Pick, Daniel, 168n
Platt–Simonds U.S. Copyright Act, 52
Poe, Edgar Allen, relationship with Dickens, 242; "Murders in the Rue Morgue," 172
Poor Law, 1834, 6
Poovey, Mary, 230
Population, growth in Victorian period, 5
Prince Albert, 6
Printing, nineteenth-century technology, 51–52, 54–55
Public Libraries Act, 1850, 59

Radway, Janice, 29
Reader, W.J., 124n
Reform Bill, 1867, 5
Reform Bill 1832, 5
Richardson, Samuel, *Clarissa*, 37
Ruland, Richard, 252n
Rushdie, Salman, 5
Ruskin, John, "Sesame and Lilies," 26

Said, Edward, 3, 152, 171
Schreiner, Olive, 9; *The Story of an African Farm*, 33, 121
Scott, Sir Walter, nineteenth-century popularity, 37–38; *Ivanhoe*, 150–51
Sedgwick, Eve Kosofsky, 145
Shelley, Mary, *Frankenstein*, 114, 160
Shires, Linda M., 76n
Sidgwick, Henry, philosophical pessimism, 224
Simmel, Georg, 148n
Slotkin, Richard, 254n
Smith, W.H. and Son, circulating library, 21
Smith, Sydney, 228
Social Darwinism, 165
Spivak, Gayatri Chakravorty, 123n

Stanley, Henry Morton, *How I Found Livingstone*, 156; *In Darkest Africa*, 156; *My Kalulu: Prince, King and Slave*, 156; *Through the Dark Continent*, 156
Steel, Flora Annie, *On the Face of the Waters*, 164
Stepan, Nancy, 166n
Stephen, Leslie, criticism of Victorian values, 1
Sterne, Lawrence, *Tristram Shandy*, 37
Stevenson, Robert Louis, 9, 30, 34; *Dr. Jekyll and Mr. Hyde*, 161, 206–8
Stocking George, 123n, 166n
Stoker, Bram, *Dracula*, 95, 114–15, 119–20, 161, 200, 208–9
Stoler, Laura Ann, 123n
Stoneman, Patsy, 35n
Stowe, Harriet Beecher, popularity of *Uncle Tom's Cabin* in Victorian Britain, 31, 33, 58, 156
Strachey, Lytton, *Eminent Victorians*, 15
Sutherland, John, 31, 60n

Taylor, Edward Burnett, *Primitive Culture*, 150
Taylor, Jenny Bourne, 210n
Taylor, Philip Meadows, *Confessions of a Thug*, 163; *Seeta*, 163
Thackeray, William, attack on Newgate novels, 175; Irish characters, 160–61; racial stereotyping, 153–54; *Barry Lyndon*, 161; *Catherine*, 175; *The History of Pendennis*, 45; *The Newcomes*, 45, 153–54; *Philip*, 154; *Vanity Fair*, 3, 9, 45, 65, 131–33, 153; *The Virginians*, 45
Thomas, Deborah, 154
Thomson, Joseph, *Ulu: An African Romance*, 157
Thoreau, Henry David, *Walden*, 246–47; *A Week on the Concord and Merrimack Rivers*, 247, 248
Todorov, Tzvetan, 192, 194, 200
Trollope, Anthony, criticism of detective fiction, 180; on George Eliot's prose, 33; Jewish characters, 152–3; *Autobiography*, 19, 49; *Can You Forgive Her?*, 45; *The Duke's Children*, 54; *The Eustace Diamonds*, 107–08, 117, 152–53; *He Knew He Was Right*, 45; *The Landleaguers*, 161; *The Last Chronicle of Barset*, 45, *Orley Farm*, 45; *Phineas Redux*, 153; *The Way We Live Now*, 45, 153
Trollope, Frances, *Michael Armstrong, the Factory Boy*, 79–80

Uglow, Jenny, 36n

Victorian abolitionist movement, 154
Victorian autobiography, 33
Victorian fiction, aesthetic of realism, 65–66, 113, 192–94, 218–19; anti-Semitism, 151; cannibalism, 161; centrality of detective narrative, 170; circulating libraries, 21; contemporary cost, 20, 38–40; contemporary criticism, 29; embodiment of intellectual debates, 213; fallen women, 75; female gothic, 198–200; femaleness and femininity, 110–13; femininity, 100–08; ghost stories, 196–97; gothic tradition, 192–93, 195–96; Hollywood adaptations, 2; imperialism, 9; India, 163–64; intellectual heroines, 120; Irish characters, 160–61; masculinity, 101–08; moral instruction, 29–30; omniscient narrators, 216; portraits of evangelicals, 214–15; price differentials, 53; intellectual characters, 227–32; Dissenters, 18; intellectuals as readers 20; religious rhetoric, 215–16; "railway novels," 51; rise of psychological realism, 189; Romantic individualism, 66; Romanticism, 61; relation to scientific writing, 217; scientific pessimism, 224–26; sensation sub-genre and female sexuality, 204–5; sensation novels, 113,179–84; serialization, 23; three-volume publication, 39–41, 49–50; comparison to Victorian poetry, 68–70; volume publication, 23; women characters as stereotypes, 27, as physical bodies, 99–100, as intellectuals, 230–31; working-class readership, 32
Victorian literacy, 19
Victorian novelists, income, 55–57; minor and publication, 44–45; as professionals, 227
Wallace, Edgar, *Sanders of the River*, 62
Wallis, Sarah Lee, *The African Wanderers*, 156
Webb, Beatrice, and Victorian science, 213

Wells, H. G., 1; *The Island of Dr. Moreau*, 208; *The Time Machine*, 116, 165–66; *The War of the Worlds*, 210; *When the Sleeper Wakes*, 93–94

Whitman, Walt, 238, 247, 248

Wigmore, John, *Principles of Judicial Proof*, 182

Wilde, Oscar, and America, 247; *The Picture of Dorian Gray*, 117–118, 126, 207

Williams, Raymond, 30

Wills, Gary, 15–16n

Wilson, Edmund, 254n

Wilt, Judith, 210

Wood, Ellen (Mrs. Henry), *East Lynne*, 111, 181, 231

Working-class, nineteenth-century reading, 42

Young, Robert, 166n

Young, G.M. Young, 16 n.

Zangwill, Israel, *Children of the Ghetto*, 152